Your Choice

Unravel Life's Secrets

John H. Leckie

Your Choice

John H. Leckie

All rights reserved. No part of this publication may be reproduced, stored in a retrieval system or transmitted in any form or by any means electronic, mechanical, audio, visual or otherwise, without prior permission of the copyright owner. Nor can it be circulated in any form of binding or cover other than that in which it is published and without similar conditions including this condition being imposed on the subsequent purchaser.

ISBN: 978-0-9575676-0-3

This book is published by Future Reality Limited (www.yourfr.com) in conjunction with **WRITERSWORLD**, and is produced entirely in the UK. It is available to order from most bookshops in the United Kingdom, and is also globally available via UK based Internet book retailers.

Copyright © 2013 John H. Leckie

Copy edited by Professor Gus John & Sue Croft
Cover design by Jag Lall
Cover photographs courtesy of dreamstime.com

WRITERSWORLD
2 Bear Close Flats, Bear Close,
Woodstock, Oxfordshire,
OX20 1JX, England
☏ 01993 812500
☏ +44 1993 812500

www.writersworld.co.uk

The text pages of this book are produced via an independent certification process that ensures the trees from which the paper is produced come from well-managed sources that exclude the risk of using illegally logged timber while leaving options to use post-consumer recycled paper as well.

The author, John H Leckie, has made his best effort to provide a high quality, informative book. He makes no representation or warranties of any kind with regard to the completeness or accuracy of the contents of the book. He accepts no liability of any kind for any damages or losses caused, or allegedly caused, directly or indirectly, from using the information contained in the book. The information provided is intended to complement, not replace, the advice of your own medical doctor, health care professional or therapist, whom you should always consult about your individual needs and any symptoms that may require diagnosis, medical attention, or therapy, and before starting or stopping any medication or any course of treatment, exercise or diet. Do not practise any of the techniques when driving.

Contents

Foreword

Acknowledgements

Introduction — 1

Chapter 1 — 15

Energy – the Secret Behind Everything

Opening that 'Virtual Box' of Thinking to Achieve Success	18
We are Energy Beings – is this Important?	18
A 17th Century Revolution in Thinking – is it a Deception?	20
20th Century Revolution in Thinking - Unravelling the Deception!	21
Entering the Quantum World - the World of Energy	23
The Force	24
In the Quantum World we are all Energy Beings	26
The Quantum World's Basic Building Blocks	26
Energy Strings	27
String Theory	29
The Quantum World Connects Everything to Everything	29
Zero Point Field of Energy – The Foundation of all Creation?	30
Particles have a Life of their Own!	31
The Copenhagen Interpretation	32
A Particle Knows it is being Measured	34
Conclusion 1:	34
You Affect what You are Looking At or Thinking About.	35
Conclusion 2:	36
Into the Spooky Stuff	36
Bell's Inequality - Quantum Entanglement – Non Locality	36
Conclusion 3:	38
Can a Bar Magnet Float on a Block of Lead?	38
Your Chance to Think Outside the Box . . . what is Energy?	39
What Quantum Physics is Suggesting to Us	39
Changing our Thinking Changes our Reality	40

Improving a Positive Feeling of Inner Wellbeing	41
Thinking Out of the Virtual Box is the Way to Go	41
Change Limiting Beliefs and Achieve Success	42
Faith (Unconditional Belief) is the Path to Achieving Success	42
You Do Make a Difference	42
Comparing the Dimensions of the Reality of the Fabricated-self and Authentic-self	44
Dimensions of the Reality of the Fabricated-self	45
Dimension of the Reality of the Authentic-self	45
The Truth about Spiritual and Personal Development	47
Personal Development	49

Chapter 2 — 53

Empower your Destiny through the Fifth Dimension

The Most Powerful Energy Tool we have – a Thought!	54
Where is the Mind Located?	57
Structure of the Mind	58
Conscious Mind - the Thinking Operations Centre	58
Unconscious Mind – Multiple Programs Running 24/7	61
Intuition (Hunches) and Intuitive Intelligence	63
Higher Conscious Mind	67
Multi-dimensional Communication	69
To Achieve Greatness it's Time to Change	71
The Human Brain: a Dynamic, Neuroplastic, Regenerating Structure	72
Frontal Lobe (Pre-frontal Cortex)	75
Parietal Lobe	76
Occipital Lobe	76
Temporal Lobe	76
Amygdala	77
Brain Stem	77
Cerebellum	77
Cingulate System	77
Basal Ganglia System	78
Deep Limbic System	78

Hypothalamus	79
Two Other Remarkable Brains: the Heart and the Gut	79
Heart Brain	79
Gut Brain	80
Thoughts Empower your Destiny	81
Passage to a More Fulfilling Life - the Best Has Yet to Come!	82
A Gift to you - Get into a Peak Performance State and the Zone	84
Getting More Out your Brain with Less Effort	90
Creating a more Desirable Destiny	91

Chapter 3 — 95

Understanding Consciousness: the Quantum Self

The Human Quantum Bio-magnetic Field	100
As Human Beings – We are made up of Layers of Energy	102
There are Seven Subtle Energy Body (SEB) Fields of Consciousness	103
Understanding Consciousness and its Purpose	104
First SEB: Etheric or Base (physical)Template Body	104
Second SEB: Emotional Template Body	105
Third SEB: Intellect Template Body	106
Fourth SEB: Causal (heart) or Astral Template Body	107
Fifth SEB: Etheric (blueprint)Template and Higher Intellect Body	108
Sixth SEB: Connection to Cosmos – Celestial Template Body	108
Seventh SEB: Ketheric Template Body	108
Polarity – Discover your Complex Quantum Bio-magnetic Properties	109
Vortex Energy Centres (VECs) – Connecting to the SEBs	112
Energy and Information Highways Driven by Consciousness	114
How each VEC Spins	116
Inner Happiness Properties of each VEC	117
First VEC: Base of Spine	119
Second VEC: the Sacral	121
Third VEC: Solar Plexus	123
Fourth VEC: The Heart	126
Fifth Vortex Energy Centre: Throat	129

Sixth Vortex Energy Centre: Brow	131
Seventh Vortex Energy Centre: Crown	133
Change in Consciousness as each VEC Connects with an SEB	134
Emotional Nested VECs connecting with Seven SEBs: 2.1 to 2.7	135
Heart Nested VECs Connecting with Seven SEBs: 4.1 to 4.7	136
Be your own Great Explorer	138

Chapter 4 — 141

Turn Your Life Around – Take Control, Let Go and Fly

Time to Change?

Who am I and what is the Purpose of my Being Here?	144

BELIEFS:

It is to your Advantage to Review what you Believe	146

DOUBT:

Curtailing Doubt - a Destroyer of Happiness	149

The TRIAD: ANXIETY, FEAR, WORRY

Move Out of Your Stress Zone – Be Happy!	151
Levels of Stress	154
De-stressing Your-self: Breathing to Reduce Stress	155
The De-stress 6-3-6-3 Exercise	156
Diet and Stress	157

AUTOMATIC NEGATIVE THOUGHTS - ANTs

Where Do ANTs Come from?	158
Recognising the Level of ANT Infestation	158
Recognising the Damage Caused by ANTs: Depression	160
To Remove those ANTs - Cut Off their Food Supply	162
To Get to a Life – Stop those ANTs!	163
Eradicate those ANTs and Get a Grip on Depression	170

SELF-ESTEEM

Victim-consciousness: an Infiltrator Causing Low Self-esteem	176
How Self-esteem is Conditioned Within Us	177
What Low Self-esteem does to us	179

Sins of the Father Begot the Son – Including Self-esteem	180
Attributes of Self-esteem	184
Balancing your Self-esteem	186
Identifying Outer Indicators that Reveal Low Self-esteem	186
Identifying Inner Causes of Low Self-esteem	187
Preparing to Deal with Low Self-esteem	187
Getting into the Process of Changing Low Self-esteem	189
Time for a Shock – are you Sitting Comfortably?	195

LAW of ATTRACTION

Change your Luck: Change your Attractor Energy Field	197
Understanding the Attraction (Attractor) Factor	198
Attraction Factor Blocks	199
Working on the Attraction Field	200
Law of Attraction and Relationships?	202
What's Happening in your Relationships?	203
Parents Effect on their Children's Future Well-being	205

POWER OF EXPECTATIONS

A Miracle that Empowers Success – Expectations	206
Expectations: It's all About the Integrity of Communication	207
Applying the 'Power of Expectations' Process to Succeed	209
Fathers/ Mothers/ Corporate Managers Please Note	211
Expectations Create the Outcome	212
Time to Take Off and Fly	214

Chapter 5   219

Understanding Relationships and Self-empowerment

Ask your-self – Who am I?	222
Attraction Energy in a Relationship	224
Who's Pulling Your Strings?	226
Recognising Personalities	227
Inner Child Personality	228
Innocent Child	231

Hurt Child	231
Playful Child	232
Imaginative Child	233
Parent Personality:	233
Protector	234
Controller	235
Nurturer	235
Driver Personality	236
Pleaser Personality	237
Critic Personality	239
What Masks are YOU Wearing Today?	240
Houston: We have a Shadow!	241
At Birth Shadows are in Balance	243
Shadow Hunting – They're in Season!	245
Boosting your Relationships	248
Personal Relationships	249
Attracting a Rewarding Personal Relationship	250
Invisible Relationship Challenges	252
Getting on with Each Other	253
Whoever you Partner with – You are Right for Each other!	255
After the Honeymoon	256
Guess what Lasting Relationships Need?	256
Can you Sense your Partner's Feelings?	257
Tuning into your Partner's Feelings	259
The Truth about Relationships!	260
Family Relationships	264
Addictions Start from within the Family	268
Cutting the Ties that Bind	273
Relationships in a Work Environment	274
Relationship Needs in a Work Environment	277
How do you Create a Successful Work Relationship?	279
A Company's Culture is a Key Part of 'Life's Stage'	280
Values	281
Activity	283

Company Structure and Behaviour	284
Recognition	285
Communication and Culture Communication	286
Veritable Priests	287
Undercover Agents	287
Influencers	287
Gossips	288
Legend Makers	288
Storytellers	288
Back Office	289
Relationships with Land and Buildings (Work and Home)	289
Balancing a Land and Buildings Energy State	292
Energy Empowerment	294

Chapter 6   297

Life-leadership: Personal Responsibility and Inspiring Others

Emotional Intelligence (EQ) - A Key to Successful Leadership	299
Surprise for Parents: Your Baby's EQ Starts from Conception	303
Identifying your EQ	305
Basic External Human Needs	308
Basic Inner Human Needs	312
Getting More Out of Your Brain with Less Effort	315
Dare Yourself - Use Your Right-brain Hemisphere	318
What is Your Communication Preference?	319
How to Identify Similar Communication Preferences	321
Visual	321
Auditory	322
Kinaesthetic	323
Using Your Communication Preference Power to Bond	323
External Attributes	324
Body Language	324
Tone of Voice	324

Language & Words Used	324
Breathing	325
Experience	325
Internal Attributes	326
Authentic-self	326
Beliefs and Values	326
Thought	327
Emotion	328
Expectation	328
Use the Power of Expectations to Achieve Success	328
Goal Setting: An Integral Step to Achieving Success	329
Confidence - Optimism: A Required State in Life Leadership	334

Chapter 7 — 337

Life's Journey: Re-awakening to Create an Inspiring Story

You are the Change	339
Can our Authentic-self help us to Change?	341
Sorting out what Need's to Change	343
Outer and Inner Potential	348
Inner Power	349
Idiosyncrasies of a 'Being of Energy'	350
Why Life can get Difficult – the Ego Trap!	352
Do You Trust?	353
Is Life Just?	355
Dealing with a Loss – How can Life be Just?	356
Abundance and Manifestation - Some Truth	359
Living in the Now (the Present)	360
Negative Abundance and Manifestation Stoppers	363
Automatic Negative Thoughts (ANTs)	363
Low Self Esteem	364
The Triad:	365
Fear	365
Worry	366

Anxiety	367
Triad Supporters:	368
Doubt	368
Stress:	369
being fearful	370
lack of trust	370
guilt	370
Abundance and Manifestation Success Drivers	373
The Power of Intent	373
Focus (attention)	374
Expectations	375
Creating a Flow of Abundance	375
Abundance Flow Process	377
Abundance Manifestation Technique	379
Abundance in Health – is it Possible?	383
Abundance of Wealth	388
Abundance of Relationships :	391
Driver 1: Know your-self	392
Driver 2: Relationships: - a Teaching Platform	393
Driver 3: Relationship Harmoniser - Emotional Response	394
Driver 4: Being of Energy - Attractor Factor Field	396
Driver 5: Mirroring - Recognising Ourselves in Others	398
Boost your Abundance of Relationships	399
Navigating Through Life	401
Abundance Flow and Understanding your Life's Work	403
Writing an Inspiring Life Story	409
Epilogue	415
Bibliography	416
Appendix 1. List of Emotions	420
Appendix 2. Organisations of Psychology & Therapy	421
Specific Therapies	422

Foreword

Consciousness is an act of creation. All life is conscious and all life is made of energy. Energy is the building block of creation, takes many forms and flows in all directions. You are energy and consciousness combined - the perfect expression of creation. Do not seek to understand everything for it will only take you further from your truth. Seek to understand your-self, for in that journey of discovery everything can be revealed.

Allow your-self the privilege of knowing all you are, all your wonder and majesty. Energy and consciousness work together as perfect partners, spinning the web of existence on behalf of creation. Do not see your-self trapped in this web for you are not. Instead see your-self as we, in the world of spirit, see you - one of the many beautiful strands it is made of. Understanding your-self allows you to see the web and flow with the force of creation. Once you step into knowing, you can step into balance.

Our friend John has written a path to know your-self, a path to being you - in balance and harmony with the web of all things. This journey is full of twists and turns, not because you are going wrong but because you are an intricate being full of details and knowledge, experiences and emotions. Following this path will help you see your-self and your pattern. Seeing the *great* pattern is then only a step away.

Read this book with love in your heart, not for what it holds but for who you are.

                                                          Master Chou
                                                          Circa 360 BC
                                                          Channelled by Sarah Tyler-Walters

Acknowledgements

A defining moment in my life happened during my teens, when my parents migrated south from a village called Dunoon in Scotland to the town of Eastbourne in East Sussex. I was undoubtedly fortunate to meet a wonderful set of young people of my own age group there. Importantly, my friends had a major positive effect on my life's path by adding what I call an extension to my social and emotional intelligence. These warm and generous souls contributed to civilising a traditional tribal Scotsman by introducing me to a quite different culture and society structure. In fact, I owe a great deal to them for their close friendship, which equipped me to successfully venture forth onto the international and challenging path that my professional career was to follow. They really were like a 'band of brothers' - and sisters - showing me the way forward. Heartfelt thanks to Keith and Rosemary, Graham, Hugh, Keith and Gilda, Sarah, Richard, Chris and Penny, Prilly, Paul, Jack and Di, Antony, Frank, Roger, Joan, John and my late parents for all their support, and above all, friendship.

Master Chou (a cover name) through Sarah Tyler Walters (ask@voicesofspirit.co.uk) while in trance, was my tutor and spiritual teacher throughout the writing of the book. He is a remarkable higher conscious being who enabled me to clarify many concepts, from quantum mechanics to psychology to spiritual dynamics. My sister Sylvia has been a constant supporter, enthusiastic promoter and independent reviewer of the book. To dear Amanda, (www.pure-creation.co.uk) who made creative suggestions, including the book title, and also offered advice on the energy aspects of life. An amazing woman, who actually sees and is able to interpret the meaning of energy structures. I thank Georgina, a dear friend, for her enthusiastic support and comments while writing the book, which encouraged me to keep going. Eudes, Penny, Sheila and Sabine - your support also helped enormously and I thank you all. To my son Leonardo, an inspirational thinker who offered an artist's view, softening the impact of the concepts used.

Heartfelt thanks to my editor Professor Gus John for his support and goodwill. Nothing escaped his keen eye, and his sharp mind significantly improved the book's flow. Finally, to my copy editor Sue Croft for her patience and diligence in ensuring that the final draft was of the highest standard.

Introduction

'The only thing that is constant in life is change.'

John H. Leckie

This book is the ultimate guide to help the reader successfully navigate through life's most challenging times. I would never have guessed that getting to know my-self in depth would have caused a transformation in my life. Moreover, it created a power shift which enhanced my awareness and perception of what life is about for the better. Is it possible for everybody to experience this? I respond to the question in the book by 'unravelling life's secrets'. Acting as a guide, the book explores looking at life from many different angles. Instructions are given to support you on your life's journey. In fact, the book can be described as a series of mini action plans to make your journey through life much more interesting and fulfilling. Each of the book's seven chapters reveals a part of the action plans. Getting to know your-self is a main theme. As you get to know your-self you empower your inner authentic-self (we all have one) to take the lead. In this state, manifesting what you desire will happen automatically.

Fulfilling a desire to boost relationships, health and happiness, and to experience the flow of abundance of all kinds, is an age-old pursuit. Taking into consideration that we are 'beings of energy', I show how these tasks can be accomplished, and more. Exploring the causes of what may be stopping this from happening, and what to do about it, is a key focus. Many of life's secrets began to unfold as I investigated the causes. Befitting this 21st century, my approach in writing the book is to bring together the latest understanding of the hidden processes working behind the scenes in each of our lives. I make use of some physics (quantum mechanics), psychology, philosophy and what I refer to as spiritual dynamics, to explain life's hidden processes. The book represents my findings and my own truth.

If you are curious, a seeker of meaning and the unknown, and want to make beneficial changes to your life, then this book is for you. It is worth investing time to read the book through and keep it handy to refer to, should you find that life's challenges become too demanding.

I am naturally inquisitive and an explorer at heart. As a physicist, my curiosity about life was stimulated through developing an understanding of matter and energy. Later, my curiosity about us as human beings was enhanced by working in a profession which enabled me to explore how the world operates politically, financially and economically. Finding out how I fitted into the scheme of things was my quest. The paths I followed provided a platform to get to know my-self in depth. A question remained: when my life is both challenging and difficult is it possible for me to maintain a balance of acceptable attitudes and behaviour, plus an inner feeling of happiness? The answer to this question is 'yes'. That is, once I discovered the reasons behind certain situations that arose, and why different people came into my life.

In my twenties, I began to realise that I had taken on a few interesting challenges in this life that could either work for me or against me. For example, being slightly dyslexic from birth is actually a gift that has provided me with many of the difficult challenges that I faced academically and in the work environment. This was counter-balanced by a natural inner positive enthusiasm which increased my self-motivation. Fortunately, I have achieved most of what I chose to do in life. There were times though, as I journeyed through life, that I followed a path which did not lead to the type of outcome I expected. A point of considerable importance here is that it is the experiences gained, as I followed different paths, which enabled me to make, slowly but surely, better choices and decisions along the way.

As I look back along my life's path, the conclusion I have come to is that firstly, it is the journey and the essence of the experiences I engage in, and that remain with me, that matter most, and secondly, the outcome. If I am observant, each step I take tells me something about my-self.

This book is written, in part, to provide you with a framework of how to look at your-self. It also provides a map of life, taken from different vantage points. These are the vantage points that I reached along my own journey. In providing you with this 'mirror' to look at your-self, I address such subjects as relationships, personal responsibility, abundance, self-awareness, self-esteem, success, beliefs, doubt, acceptance, forgiveness, life's journey and love, amongst others. The book is also written to help engender a greater understanding of the purpose and meaning behind life. Its content is designed to enhance your awareness, question what is generally accepted as being true and query the perception behind why things happen to you in life. My goal is to offer you an opportunity to move towards a more illuminating and fulfilling course of action. Such a course has the potential to empower you to achieve your hopes and dreams.

It took me an inordinate amount of time to realise and accept what you may consider to be a rather unbelievable concept, namely, that, in general, *we are all 100 percent responsible for what happens to us in our lives*. Of course, that is usually after we finally leave home and start work. Imagine, for example, the riches we obtain, or lack of; the good people, or not so good people we attract into our lives; the good times and what may be viewed as the bad times we experience; and the love, or lack of love that comes into our lives. The full 100 percent of it is due to us!

People can become stunned by this prospect and some get angry at the thought. How can this be so? What about those who are born into great wealth or high positions in society? I answer these questions and provide sufficient information and direction for you to deal with the concept. This will give you an opportunity to steer your way through life on a course that will be to your best advantage. As we venture forward on our life's journey, we achieve success in whatever we are doing when we have a special moment of understanding (a revelation) and 'get it', whatever 'it' may be. I elaborate on what 'it' is throughout the book.

During the years 1998 through 2008, I discovered some remarkable information that enabled me to put a few more key pieces into what can be described as a jigsaw puzzle of my '*map of life*' and action plan. These pieces were to affect my belief system (how I was conditioned to see and understand the way things are) and perception (the lens through which I view the world and myself) of what happens in life and why. My understanding of how to create different types of abundance, interact with people, create a warm supportive relationship, maintain an inner feeling of positive wellbeing and happiness and so on, all changed for the better. My old way of thinking did not answer, in a satisfactory way, such questions as:

- why, at times, did I face what I regarded as problems in my life?
- were the problems I faced not really problems at all but opportunities to solve my own internal issues (life lessons)?
- was I responsible for manifesting everything in my life?
- why did I attract particular types of relationships into my life?
- why was a long-term partner not available to me for quite some considerable time?
- was there really a human bio-magnetic energy field of attraction which operates outside the laws that we understand at a material (form-based) and physical level?

I began to slowly but surely recognise, over a twenty-five year period, the limitations of my thinking and perception of the reality of life. And during the spring of 2005, a particular major piece of my map of life was put in place. It was an empowering 'eureka' moment. The actual missing piece was connecting quantum mechanics (what is happening in the sub-atomic world) with the human bio-magnetic energy field that we all have. I translate this connection in the book into an understanding of what it means to us on a day to day basis, and also spiritually. Knowing how to alter your bio-magnetic field can lead to a spectacular change in your life for the better. You will gain an appreciation of why your life is as it is. Happiness needs be a dream no longer, it can become a reality.

Introduction

Venturing along my life's path, I discovered that most of us are unknowingly trapped within what can be described as a 'virtual box' of thinking caused by our belief system. This 'virtual box' limits our perception and prevents us from really understanding what is going on around us, and why it is happening. It took me some considerable time to substantially open my own 'virtual box' of thinking. In fact, the virtual box only began to slowly open from my 34th year onwards when I left Italy, where I was working in the United Nations in Rome, to travel to America to work with the World Bank in Washington DC. How did this come about? As I look back along my life's path, this and many more of the revelations I had as my 'virtual box' opened up wider and wider, usually came about through meeting some truly enlightened people. This happened more noticeably in the United States.

Recently, I met two enlightened people who have no problem operating outside of their 'virtual box' of thinking. Both are women. I was researching a particular type of communication ability called trance-mediumship when I met the first woman. Through trance, Sarah (see Acknowledgements) is able to tune into higher levels of consciousness, communicating through an advanced being called (amongst other names) Master Chou. He exists in the world of spirit and has had about 2,000 lives so far! He was able to answer a range of questions on just about anything, including quantum mechanics, philosophy, psychology, spirituality, the purpose of life and so on. I used Master Chou as a tutor and assistant editor for my book and I am grateful for the wise guidance and counsel he has given me. Without his guidance, many of the concepts explored here would have been incomplete.

The second woman, Amanda, is quite extraordinary and able to sense and see the surrounding energy fields that affect what is happening to an individual in their life. One of her natural strengths is visual energy geomancy associated with land, building structures and also people. She is able to locate energy blockages and remove them to allow the natural energy to flow through. What effect does this have? It makes habitable, land and buildings which were previously virtually uninhabitable. It also induces inner feelings of positive wellbeing in those who occupy the land and buildings. This has a knock-on effect on efficiency, creativity and productivity, resulting in a healthier bottom line in businesses. The concept of a 'sick' building is still very unfamiliar to a great number of people, but they certainly feel and know the difference once these energy blockages have been removed. Amanda's energy healing ability is exceptional. She brought to my attention the seldom recognised power of 'mirroring' ourselves in a relationship and what that means. No one taught her, she already knew within herself energetically, what the psychology of mirroring is really about.

Introduction

Because of ongoing world changes, I felt the need to produce a book that makes a strong contribution to our understanding of the causes of what is happening in our world. When you read the first three chapters you will appreciate the reasons for this. I found it breathtaking, for example, when I discovered that today's thinking is still being strongly influenced by concepts advanced by great philosophers who existed over two thousand years ago. In ancient Greece, the work of philosophers like Aristotle, Plato, Socrates and so on created a change in thinking that still has a major influence on our present way of thinking and perception of how things are today. They put forward ideas of solid matter, a mechanistic thinking approach and linear time, which affect how we understand life's processes. A brief review of the work of some of the Greek philosophers provided ample clues as to why our way of thinking seems to be trapped in a tight 'virtual box'. These amazing men, and others like them, were responsible for setting us onto a path which was enhanced, during the seventeenth century, by other notable giants of their time such as René Descartes and Sir Isaac Newton. Of course there are many more great men of that period, such as Francis Bacon, Gottfried Leibniz, Baruch Spinoza, amongst others, but I prefer to use Descartes and Newton as my examples. My point here is that to meet the changes and challenges of the 21st century, it is necessary to upgrade our thinking. Old ways need to be superseded by new.

Our virtual box of thinking received a boost at the beginning of the 20th century when great scientists and mathematicians like Niels Bohr, Albert Einstein, Erwin Schrodinger, and so on were practising. The effect of this thinking was uplifted again as we entered the 21st century. This was due to some young scientists linking the world of quantum mechanics to their particular scientific discipline, for example in biology, botany, anatomy, neuroscience and so forth. There are two major points to be made here. The first is that they could do this because there has been little interference arising from the ruling elite, religious bodies, and cultural norms of our time. This is quite different in comparison with 17th century times for the likes of Newton and Descartes. They were constrained to follow the path of a matter- (form-) based, mechanistic and linear-time-biased approach to life because of the ruling elite (church and state). If they did not a painful death could have been their reward.

The second point is that science and mathematics have advanced a great deal in helping us to understand what is happening at a sub-atomic level (the quantum world). Physicists have entered deeply into the world of quantum mechanics and particle physics. This gives us access to a greater understanding about our inner authentic-self and soul, if we dare to explore. Why is this important? It is important because the laws which operate at a sub-atomic level are Universal Laws, quite different in comparison with physical laws that we deal with on a day to day basis. As we enter the world of energy, we have a chance to understand many mysteries which have been closed to us. These range from the cause of illnesses, how abundance truly works, what is going on in relationships, miracles, and so much more. I elaborate on these in the book.

The various routes I followed along my life's path have provided me with many changes and challenges which encouraged me to look over the horizon and open my virtual box of thinking. I was most fortunate to have been brought up with the River Clyde in front of my home which was surrounded by a forest with rolling Scottish hills behind, close to a small town called Dunoon. I had an older sister who was always studying and I lacked a playmate to share this huge potential playground with me. To amuse myself I had to stretch my imagination to the full. Such was my rather lonely but most fortunate and colourful life during my pre-teens. Boredom is a word that was not in my vocabulary, only opportunities to create a new experience out of very little. This was to stand me in good stead in later life and helped me to push open the lid of my virtual box of thinking further. Luckily for my future, my parents migrated south to England to a town called Eastbourne, in Sussex, when I was seventeen. I left Scotland with only the minimum of qualifications.

Fate was kind to me in Eastbourne and I had the good fortune, after much searching, to find an opening as an electronics apprentice in a newly formed, close circuit television company. I was able to satisfy a passion I had for electronics. I even joined the ranks of the local Royal Auxiliary Air Force as an ac2 specialising in ground radar. This, together with my apprenticeship in a hi-tech electronic business, was what kick-started me back onto the ladder of learning. Why? To my uneducated and inexperienced mind, the senior men seemed to be doing very little in comparison with my busy day - and they had University degrees. It was one of those epiphany moments for me. I believed that I had suddenly 'got it'. I felt I recognised what I needed to do to get to the top, and that was to get a degree! This filled me full of enthusiasm to move ahead in life.

Journeying along my early life's path, the strategy I adopted was to study hard, get qualifications, titles, and perhaps find a hi-tech job, as well as to make lots of money. I managed to conquer the dyslexic disability I had by recognising that I needed to read through academic works three times with a concentrated focus, to absorb and remember the information. This got me back onto the learning ladder. Filled with a new-found passion, I gained a special physics degree, majoring in nuclear physics, and later a master's degree in computer science and business studies, thanks to some compassionate and understanding professors and tutors en route. By then I actually believed that I really had 'got it', although the lure of a hi-tech career had gradually faded as my inner gut feeling by that time was to move into the business world and I was being driven by a strong new passion that was propelling me to explore this world.

Now what does the 'it' in the term 'to get it' truly mean? Understanding how to stimulate our creative abilities is certainly an 'it'. Understanding the steps to take in life for us to successfully achieve our goals can be another, as can understanding how to attract a warm, supportive, loving relationship. The list can be endless, but understanding how to 'get it' comes about through raising our awareness and by gaining an appreciation of life's real purpose. And the 'it' usually changes as we grow, because of the different life experiences acquired on our journey. An understanding of 'it' also changes rapidly as soon as we begin to think outside of that 'virtual box'. I provide some techniques later to help in this regard.

What I also learned in the process of achieving success in my studies and continuing to learn throughout my career, was the importance of keeping an open mind. This helped me enormously, together with discovering how to stimulate my natural creative abilities. Adding these two attributes to my curious nature, my career took me into international consulting, the United Nations, and finally into the world of finance within the International Bank of Reconstruction and Development (the World Bank) in the United States, the City of London in Merchant Banking and the Gulf Co-operation Countries' premier investment bank Gulf Investment Corporation. This path demanded that I keep an open mind. Keeping an open mind eventually created a major shift in my awareness, allowing me to eventually 'get it' over a broad range of the challenges that we all face in life. I also discovered that by working *without* 'getting it', life became quite stagnant, uninteresting, dull and sometimes overly turbulent. Such is the awesome power of 'getting it' that I felt I needed to share the process with you.

In putting this book together, I wanted to ensure that you have a reference guide which includes different techniques and processes to help you achieve the life you desire. Removing what is blocking you is important here. I combine both how to achieve success with how to remove what is blocking it. I offer contributions to improving your life's action plans - only you can tailor-make them to suit. The book is also designed to open doors in your awareness so as to empower you to 'get it', as you journey along your life's path. It is about:

- giving you alternative paths to achieve your desires
- demonstrating that you have more choices than you think, as you journey
- showing you how to boost your relationships
- recognising that there really is infinite abundance out there, and that you can learn how to attract it
- adding to your awareness and perceptions about life to help you deal with 21st century changes and challenges

- recognising that you are more than just a physical body with a mind; that you have a purpose, and that what happens to you in life is not just a series of random occurrences
- recognising that you can heal your-self and in the process appreciate that you are also healing those around you.

All of the above involves expanding those conscious and unconscious ideas you may have that influence your perceptions and beliefs of what life is about and how it works. This should empower you to get the best out of your life, no matter what your circumstances are. The book will also provide you with an insight as to why you have relationships with the different people who enter your life. Understanding your partner, for example, should take on a different dimension with respect to what you think a relationship is about, or what you were brought up to believe it is about. It is more than just sex, love, procreation, money, or camaraderie.

Increasing numbers of people are beginning to recognise the fact that they live a very limited and unfulfilling life in this busy 24/7 society. This is because so many simply bury themselves in their work and in activities which in effect have become addictions. Many people, I feel, are not prepared to recognise this, although of course financial commitments are a major driving force. The main point here is that too many people are just too busy 'doing'. My parents worked very hard all their life and I too followed suit until I began to 'get it'. With today's fast pace of life it is in our best interest to work *smarter* and not longer. Is it possible to become more efficient and produce more in less time? Getting into the other 90 percent of your brain/mind system can help here and I show how to do it.

My journey has shown me that there is a need to appreciate the power of emotions and feelings. Together they contain such an important key to understanding why things happen to us, both good and what may be wrongly perceived as bad. Emotions and feelings should not be ignored as they have the power both to lift us to the highest sense of wellbeing, or drive us into a state of depression and dis-ease, if we ignore them. Emotions and feelings, therefore, have an important effect on our level of productivity at work.

Through the many and varied experiences gained, as I travelled, I increasingly questioned what life is about. At best, I had a limited understanding of the mechanics behind human sensitivities, attitudes and behaviour during interactions with my family, at work with colleagues and also with friends. My focus in life was mainly directed towards building a career path, wealth creation, and acquiring material goods. In those early days, it would have been most helpful to have been directed towards books or courses on personal development. I had no idea about what personal development really meant. It would have helped me to recognise that the real challenges in life are in relation to inner growth and not material gratification. It would also have helped me to understand specific life-challenging situations, such as being made redundant or going through a divorce. Without such guidance I had to develop my own ways of coping and coming to terms with difficult and stressful situations.

As I participated in personal development activities, especially over the last ten years, I could not help but notice that an upgrade or 'make over' in the approach is necessary. In this 21st century, full of the most amazing technology and potential instant gratification opportunities to satisfy our wants, there is a need to incorporate some spiritual dynamics (back to our roots) to clarify what life is really about and why we face different changes and challenges: to 'close the circle' so to speak, to ensure the obvious becomes obvious without much difficulty. And how do I do that? By putting forward for your consideration the conclusions of my research, as I travelled the world, into what life is truly about and why we are here in a physical body. By recognising and encouraging the use of some of the most amazing inner abilities that we all have. In addition, appreciating that by 'being busy and always doing', we are like a ship without a rudder, leaving us exposed to the stormy seas of life. We are without any real ability to change course to steer ourselves comfortably through the challenging situations we may find ourselves subjected to. In this type of situation, we are in a position of simply failing to 'get it'!

Changing the way we think in terms of our limiting beliefs, negative attitudes, behaviour, or the way we do things, and so on, can be a tricky proposition. Tricky in the sense that we all tend to label people (and ourselves) and put them into boxes which reflect who we think they are (or in some instances who we think we are or should be!) and how they will perform, react and behave in different situations. If a person should break out of the mould of their box, then they are usually put into yet another box. Should they be going through a period of change, this can cause great discomfort to the observer who may want them to behave or perform in their usual way. I have heard many times from couples, where only one of them has gone on a personal development course, how unhappy they were after their partner had changed. Even though the change was for the better, they were now not so predictable. It is a human trait to prefer predictability! In reading this book you will become less predictable to the observer. But your life will become more predictable to your-self, and at the same time much more interesting and fulfilling. To that end, everybody will benefit in one way or another, including your-self. So be prepared to make that change in direction and, of course, to 'get it'.

The education establishment focuses mainly upon the intellect (gaining information, knowledge and applying logic and reason) and its development, as it has done over past centuries. Our society is built around this premise. What about creative thinking and bringing out creative abilities? 'I beg your pardon', would be a response from some academic circles, 'you cannot teach that.' 'Oh yes you can,' would be my reply. Change is slowly happening in the educational arena as a greater understanding of the development of the right-brain hemisphere (the home of creative talents) gains momentum. Blending the intellect (the preserve of the left-brain hemisphere) and any natural creative abilities (the preserve of the right-brain hemisphere) is certainly the way to go.

There are techniques in the following chapters that disclose the process of blending the use of both brain hemispheres, bringing them together. Some of the techniques will help to bring out your creative talents. We all have an amazing inner creative-self that is just waiting to show itself! However, what about emotions and feelings and how do they fit into the overall scheme of things today? There is a quick answer here and that is they usually do not. Towards the end of the 20th century, a new subject called 'emotional intelligence' began to gain acceptance. Why did it not do so before? As neuroscience and psychology began to break free of its Newtonian/Cartesian limitations, so the power of emotions and feelings as a multi-dimensional energy force that can have a major impact on our lives and those around us began to gain more recognition. Emotions take us into feelings which lead us into the new psychology called emotional intelligence.

Emotional intelligence can be understood from a mechanistic viewpoint (left brain - intellect). But it is also regarded as a right brain or subjective force and, therefore, is usually not readily accepted by some academics. Emotional intelligence involves how we react to and work with the emotional climate that surrounds us. But anything that is subjective or involves intuition (hunch or gut feeling) tends to get a bad press. One of the greatest intuitive attributes we all have is that of the 'hunch'. Hunches transcend time and space and are a prized attribute of those at the top of their profession. The mechanisms behind intuition are part of the structure of our inner or authentic-self. Understanding and practising emotional intelligence is a major step forward towards improving relationships.

In writing this book one of my goals is to empower you to take a step forward to a more fulfilling life, whatever you may be involved in. In doing so, the chance of setting a better course for more satisfying and happier life experiences increases as you journey. You put your-self into a position of being free - free to do what you want, and that should result in a strong inner feeling of positive wellbeing and self-confidence. Being happy in what you are doing is no longer a dream. It is a reality. This book suggests action that will help *create your own reality* the way you want it.

I have always found a creative solution to the challenges that have been put before me since I started practising the techniques outlined in the book. The techniques are deceptively easy and straightforward, and should contribute to strengthening your self-esteem, self-worth and self-image amongst others. I must warn you now, though, that you are the captain of the ship that is your own life and destiny. You are captain of your own reality, something that many people do not recognise. This means that you have the ability to set your own course and effectively steer your-self towards the destination of your choice. Sometimes you might do this consciously and other times unconsciously. The key is to know that you are doing it. As you begin to recognise that you alone are responsible for your achievements or lack of, it can be a bit frightening.

As you 'get it', you will begin to recognise that there are no failures or losers in life: lessons learned, most certainly, failures - certainly not! How come? Quite simply, we are here on this planet to learn from the situations/experiences we attract and from the choices/decisions we make. This allows our inner authentic-self (and spiritual-self) to grow. We learn to make choices/decisions that are supportive to our life goal direction. Understanding this is a most important part of 21st century personal development. I elaborate in the book on how I found out what the purpose of being here in a physical body is and what it means. By knowing this we are presented with an opportunity to increase our prospects of having a happier and more contented life. You, too, can find an inner security and lead a life of fulfilment.

We are living through a most amazing period of time, especially in Western countries. Technology increasingly makes our lives so much easier, following the rapid development of science throughout the last 50 years. We have huge supermarkets, leisure centres, home entertainment and much more than our parents could ever have dreamt about. Information on just about anything is available on the internet. I still find this quite amazing, even though I like to think of myself as someone who thinks 'out of the box'. That is probably because I was born in a period of time that did not offer such gifts. As I share my enthusiasm about the great scientific achievements of our time with many people around me, I usually get a blank expression and a negative feeling of their sense of 'status quo'. I try, pointlessly, to engage them in a conversation that might involve how quantum physics has irreversibly changed our lives by providing us with new ideas for cancer treatment or some amazing electronics. History too, and our seeming inability to learn from the past, also produces a lack of interest. It seems that both science and history are taboo subjects . . . a complete turn off!

History has shown that most people are usually more interested in what is happening close to home. Looking back at the days of ancient Rome (or even further back), conversations focused upon famous gladiators, other celebrities and gossip about the neighbours. Graffiti on ancient Roman ruins certainly confirms this fact. Little seems to have changed! In the West, we still seem to be living in a world where control is exercised through the power of 'bread and circuses' or in modern terms 'the economy and entertainment'. Yet both science and history contain not only the clues but the very essence of what it takes to bring about achievement and success in major parts of our lives, if we only knew where to look. I extract some of these essences in the book, and provide an opportunity to consider using them in your life's action plan.

From a quantum mechanics' perspective in physics, '*all is not as it seems*' within the very material or substance of life that we think we know. And from a historical perspective it is clear that '*history influences the present and programs the future*'. Understanding these two statements immediately puts us into an arena where we become more able to 'get it'. All begins to become much clearer. Life can and does have miraculous and magical properties. We are also faced with an interesting concept that '*what we do in life echoes in eternity*'. What do I mean by this statement? As time and space are effectively coexistent in the sub-atomic world, what we do in the 'now' (the present) affects and changes not only what has happened along our ancestral chain but also what will happen to future generations. This may take some time for you to assimilate. Moreover, when you heal your-self in the 'now' you also heal the same issue for your ancestors and future generations. This is a form of programming that is transferred through our energy structure and genes. Our multi-dimensional existence within the time/space continuum we live in makes this so. Quantum mechanics provides us with some clues as evidence of this, if we know where to look. Such is the power of the sub-atomic world's Universal Laws. All of this is a part of 'getting it'.

In writing this book I particularly want to bring to your attention some facts and concepts that you may not have been taught at home, school, college or university. They can make it easier for you to open that 'virtual box' of thinking. The book also provides you with some techniques and processes to direct you towards a happier, more abundant and satisfying life, if you are at a stage on your journey where you have that need. I emphasize in the book that we are all built like quantum biological magnets, attracting to us, or being attracted to, particular people, activities, events, situations and challenges in our life, including our business life. This enables us to learn from subsequent experiences and to make better choices/decisions. It's also important to understand that most of the time we mirror ourselves in those whom we meet. Effectively, the issues that you may perceive within those you meet are most probably a reflection of the issues and life lessons running in your unconscious mind. This may be a bit frightening to accept at first and from my own experience I have found it to be true. Let me also say that it does not happen all of the time (although perhaps most of the time).

We all face unknowns in life and my goal is to unravel some of the unknowns. The book aims to bring to your attention the awareness that we all have issues and life lessons to work through. One of my goals here is for you to gain a broader perception of some of the major issues/life lessons that you may be facing and/or working through. There are some questions here that are worth considering such as:

1) are you happy with your life and if not how can you improve it beyond all recognition?

If you *are* happy with your life, the next question is:

2) do you know what is your purpose for being here in this lifetime? Are you a soul having a physical experience or just a physical being with a persona?

I can assure you that once you 'get it' you are on your way to achieving what you are here to do in this lifetime.

Finally, the contents of this book represent an evolution of my own truth, one which has changed greatly since I began to think outside of my virtual box. This has added much value to my life and I am sure that the book will add value to yours. Journeying along life's path, we write our own story and have an opportunity to make it a good one. Do you appreciate that the story you write about your-self not only influences your wellbeing, but also the wellbeing of those around you and beyond? This is an awesome responsibility for each of us. As empowered individuals we make a significant difference to ourselves and to what is happening in the greater scheme of things. We have more choices than we think with respect to the paths we select on our life's journey, and recognising that we have the ability to choose different paths is an important skill to learn. I wish you good health, great abundance, hope, harmony and love in your life.

Chapter 1

Energy – the Secret Behind Everything

The opposite of a correct statement is a false statement. But the opposite of a profound truth may well be another profound truth.

Neils Bohr: Danish Physicist 1885 -1962

Energy - the Secret Behind Everything

When I asked some friends *"Do you realise that we are all beings of energy?"*, some replied "of course", some "tell me more", some "rubbish", some were not interested and the rest replied "so what!" Those who replied "of course" just knew it intuitively. The "tell me more" genuinely wanted to know what I meant. The "rubbish" and "so what" friends were just not interested. In writing this chapter, I have crafted the subject of energy in a way I hope will be of interest to all readers. I touch upon what is happening at a sub-atomic level from a quantum mechanics perspective, in an easy to understand way. I also look at today's increasingly expansive thinking and how old scientific concepts from the past kept my awareness about life unknowingly boxed in.

As we are beings of energy, I take you along a path that leads to a broad understanding of what I call 'the Force' – the secret behind energy. Appreciating the power of the Force has the potential to expand your perception of what life is really about, as it did for me. The conclusions I was able to draw from quantum mechanics and the experiments described below, were equally as important. These conclusions have enabled me to improve and increase the choices and decisions I make in life. They have encouraged me to take action and move onto a more rewarding path. I conclude by taking you into the different dimensions that support beings of energy at a sub-atomic level and what they mean. At this level we enter the realm of spiritual dynamics (back to our roots) where we are all eternal beings.

Before launching into energy from a basic scientific perspective, I will briefly look at energy for what it means to us in everyday life. For example, in terms of human energy, the emotions we harbour within the physical body represent a powerful force that can have life-changing effects upon us. In fact, emotions can be likened to an energy antibiotic with constructive or destructive effects. This energy is at the very core of our existence, yet we really know very little about it. How we feel and how much we are able to do in a day depends upon the quantity and quality of the energy we have. Now, do you feel that you are getting the best out of your life? Do you feel full of energy? Are you happy? Do you see a bright future? If you do not then I offer you a challenge, and that is for you to raise your awareness so that you can achieve what you desire. How can you do this?

For a start, it requires you to open a door in your consciousness and take a step into your imagination and into the fifth dimension, which is energy. It also requires you to recognise that you live in two realities. Each one of these realities operates within a different paradigm or model. The first reality is associated with the outer-self which includes the physical body – the part you see. I call this our 'fabricated-self'. The second reality is associated with the inner-self (and includes the soul) which is composed of pure energy – the part you do not see. I call this our 'authentic-self'. Yes, believe it or not, we do live in two realities! The authentic-self (sometimes called your energy-self), as you will discover in the next two chapters, is a set of subtle energy bodies. I discuss this more fully in later chapters. Part of this chapter is about creating an appreciation of the two realities we live in through the fifth dimension. I conclude by explaining the dimensions of the reality of both our fabricated-self and our authentic-self and what it means to us. To maximise an inner feeling of positive wellbeing and happiness, it is important to have an understanding of the two different realities, their paradigms, dimensions and how to operate within them. My life has gone from strength to strength since I recognised, ventured into and worked with the second paradigm of reality.

Most people are aware of the four dimensions of physical reality that they live in. These dimensions belong to the fabricated-self and are length, breadth, depth and time. From the perspective of the fabricated-self, stepping into its fifth dimension (energy) will enable a strengthening of our capacity to sense and feel what is really happening to and around us. By stepping into and working within the fifth dimension it automatically strengthens our natural manifesting capability. Nonetheless, to gain maximum benefit here, there is another step we can take which can have a beneficial effect on our long-term positive feeling of happiness and wellbeing. This step involves recognising that although we live in a five-dimensional physical reality, there is also an additional five-dimensional reality within our energy-self (the authentic-self). When we work with the second set of dimensions of the authentic-self, we are accessing the sub-atomic or quantum world. Is this important? Yes it is, because it offers an opportunity to strongly empower our capability for manifesting that which we desire.

Both the fabricated-self and authentic-self are really one energy reality. They are not separate at birth but grow apart due to our conditioning after birth. Nevertheless it is advantageous for us to be aware of the powerful effect both of them have on our day to day existence. The home, or location of our authentic-self, is within our subtle energy body structure. This is beginning to be recognised more and more as our energy structure is understood. Most of the answers to major questions we face in life can be obtained when we learn how to communicate with our authentic-self. The authentic-self communicates with us through that silent voice that speaks to us in our conscious mind, from time to time, if we care to listen. Just one small step to ensure that your fabricated-self and the authentic-self are in full contact can change your life forever. Finding your passion is also made a lot easier when we communicate directly with your authentic-self.

At the beginning of the 20th century, the way that scientists theoretically modelled different natural processes to investigate what is happening in physical reality, changed dramatically.

This created a new paradigm that non-scientists are only recently becoming more aware of. Slowly but surely, over the last 100 years, the new paradigm shift has affected traditional Western thinking. What was the old paradigm? Three hundred years ago and even to date, the traditional way of thinking was dominated by several 17th century masters including Sir Isaac Newton and René Descartes. Throughout the book I call the traditional way of thinking a metaphorical *virtual box.* The new way of thinking we engage in today encapsulates a different way of looking at not only the physical reality that we perceive but also the Universe itself. This produces a much bigger virtual box of thinking that includes the sub-atomic world as defined by scientists. New insights present us with an appreciation that the sub-atomic world provides an interface to understand the authentic-self (including the soul) and beyond. That is if we care to expand our awareness and explore.

To the poets, we are made of Eros and dust. In the real world, we are constructed of human cells: bone, blood, skin, heart, stomach cells and so on - which are made up of molecules which are made up of atoms which finally break down into what are called energy strings. The sub-atomic world (the world of quantum mechanics) deals with atoms and all things smaller. And the laws that govern the sub-atomic world (these are Universal Laws) are quite different in comparison with the laws that govern the physical world, the world we actually perceive. The important point here is that we live in both these worlds, which are governed by two sets of different laws.

The second set of laws, derived from quantum mechanics, are Universal Laws which most of us are unaware of. They contain secrets that enable us to make unimaginable changes to our life. One hundred years after the birth of quantum mechanics the Universal Laws have influenced technological growth beyond belief. They have broadened the understanding of the processes involved in sciences such as biology, botany, and medicine. These new laws also present a different insight into psychology, or engineering, or even concepts involved in finance and the financial markets. They have truly taken us into the fifth dimension of energy. This book attempts to raise awareness of the infinite power behind energy. The following simple, down to earth statement holds a key to alter how we are consciously and unconsciously writing our continuing life story so as to create a better one:

'energy follows thought and thought changes beliefs'

A belief is what we accept as being true. In fact, the above statement is so deceptively powerful that I will bring it to your attention several times. Why? This is because understanding energy is a major key for all who want to create the life that they are meant to have. All that we create, the employment we engage in, the sport we engage in, relationships, abundance, prosperity, health and so on starts with a thought, and that thought is in itself energy.

Opening that 'Virtual Box' of Thinking to Achieve Success

Studying for a degree in physics did not induce any creative spark within me or push me to think out of my virtual box. Perhaps this was due to my being slightly dyslexic. Most certainly my degree course expanded my intellect and gave me much knowledge. The course also introduced me to a new way of thinking called quantum mechanics, now popularly called quantum physics. Many years later, after a career in project/business development and international finance, I felt an urge to go back to review quantum physics to see if it could produce answers to some age-old questions. These questions were: *What is the purpose of me being here?*; *Why do certain things keep happening to me?*; *Why can life be so difficult and emotionally distressing at times?* I found answers to these questions and I share my findings with you in the chapters that follow.

Because of the career path I followed, I have been most fortunate to travel around the world, and to live in four different continents and countries. This enhanced my perception (how I see the world and what is happening around me) of what life is about. Observing and learning from different cultures and beliefs in the countries I lived and worked in was essential for me to be accepted locally. I began to notice that the way I looked at and interpreted local customs and behaviour, needed updating. It was necessary for me to broaden my Western concepts of how things are done and how to make things happen, to be more effective in what I was doing. I began to look at life, slowly but surely, through the eyes of the people in the countries in which I was working. I was also drawn, through the synchronicity and experiences of life, to some workshops in the United States and Britain that questioned the perception of how we see things in life. I was introduced indirectly to the concept of myself as a being of energy. The techniques presented in the workshops affected the way I view reality. My awareness expanded to enable me to understand the unlimited potential we have locked inside us. My task now is to unlock this potential in you by sharing how to do it.

We are Energy Beings - is this Important?

As I continued my research into us as energy beings, nothing prepared me for what I was to find out about the amazing properties that all human beings have. What are these properties? The properties are related to a series of subtle body energy fields that surround the physical body. I totally lacked appreciation and understanding of the importance of the different types of subtle body energy fields. My education was bereft of any reference to this. Let me begin by asking you to imagine your-self as a walking, talking energy generator - a biological one that supplies the energy you need to support your life. Your body, brain and mind have a complex energy structure that requires not only a daily energy input but also regular maintenance to make it run smoothly. To promote a greater understanding of this energy structure and how it affects our lives, I have divided a human being into three integrated parts. These (parts) are:

- what I call the physical or external aspect of the expression of the fabricated-self that is involved in day to day activities. This part is really the mechanical part of us, like the parts of a machine. It is driven by the unconscious mind and thoughts generated within the conscious mind that are translated into a recognisable form within the brain. We express ourselves externally through conscious/unconscious thoughts. Walking, running, swimming, skiing, eating and so on are end-products of the mechanical part of our-self. As physical effort is one form of external expression, so body language and verbal communication are another. These all require the use of energy, and some forms such as physical effort require more energy than others. This physical part of us eats, drinks and sleeps to generate energy and rebalances the energy structures on entering into a sleep state.

- the second part is our inner physical life which generates how we feel and supplies what is necessary to keep our brain and body functioning. It represents what is happening inside of us. It is affected by our emotions and runs 24 hours a day, 7 days a week, 365 days a year. Our muscles, organs such as the heart, liver, and kidneys, the endocrine system, immune system and so on, as well as their functioning are all a part of our inner physical life. Most of what is going on within the physical body is driven by internal systems of which we are not consciously aware. Conscious and unconscious thoughts can operate like control mechanisms to the brain and body to provide external and internal direction to keep us going both physically and emotionally. If our life is handled badly in the way we look at, or deal with the issues/life lessons that confront us, then this part of us can get out of balance energetically and can lead to a state of dis-ease, with dire consequences.

- last but not least, the third part of us is a set of external subtle energy bodies. I elaborate on subtle energy bodies later. Subtle energy bodies are part of the structure of our inner authentic-self. Thanks to NASA's American and the Soviet Union's space programs there are devices that can now measure some of these energy bodies. The subtle energy bodies contain such components as an energy blueprint of the human physical form, the conscious and unconscious minds, emotions, intellect and much more. Subtle energy bodies are affected by what happens to us both externally and internally. This is a two-way process and the subtle energy bodies affect the intellect, thinking process, emotions and physical body. Each subtle energy body is connected through a series of vortex energy centres (I explain these in the next chapter) and also connects to the physical body through a set of organs associated with the endocrine system. The subtle energy bodies also connect down to the cellular level of the physical body.

The above three parts run together in parallel and require the use of energy generated mostly within ourselves through ingesting food and liquids. Energy is also generated through thoughts and through internal chemical changes that are brought about by what happens during day to day activities such as in the office, at home, or while travelling. Some of our energy requirements are absorbed externally from the earth's magnetic field. Scientists have discovered that the earth's magnetic field and its frequency (it vibrates at about 7.83 cycles per second) is an important ingredient in sustaining human life. Increasingly, it is also being recognised by some scientists that the frequency of the earth's magnetic field affects our thinking process and beliefs. This is of particular importance because the frequency is changing at present and magnetic poles are shifting. Our energy balance can also be affected by planetary influences, especially moon cycles, sun spots and solar winds.

Each of the above three parts consumes different levels of energy and we should note that usage of each part comes with a price attached. Most of us are so busy 'doing' that we give little time to considering the effect it is having upon us as we use up our energy. The price comes in two forms. Some of the energy generated can be beneficial (positive in nature), contributing to an inner feeling of positive wellbeing, and some detrimental (negative in nature), such as stress, which contributes to us feeling unwell. In other words, how energy is managed and expended can either strengthen or weaken us. Ultimately, we are responsible for the energy generated within us and the requirement to keep it in balance. A feeling of happiness and an overall feeling of positive wellbeing depends on the state of our energy. So is it important to understand that we are beings of energy? Absolutely! As I investigated the human energy structure, a question kept recurring in my head: *How come this knowledge is not yet mainstream?* Perhaps the answer is shaped by our past?

A 17th Century Revolution in Thinking - is it a Deception?

I wanted to get to the roots of why it took me so long to recognise that my own thinking was quite blinkered. Furthermore, as I tried to explain to others the human energy structure and its importance, I got glazed looks! Was the concept too way out or new? There are certain historical time periods where, with reflection, it can be seen that the seeds of a new way of thinking had been sown. This thinking can be described as revolutionary as it provided the basis for further development in education, especially in science and engineering. The new thinking also worked its way into how business developed, the structures that support business and commerce, including finance, and the structures and management of organisations. Such a revolutionary time period was the 17th century. A new dawn had begun. The men responsible for this can be described as giants of their time. These giants recognised that to reach their level of excellence they were standing upon the shoulders of previous giants. René Descartes and Sir Isaac Newton as mentioned above were two such leviathans. Their work (amongst others) laid the foundations for improving education standards which continues to affect us today.

Most of us have been educated to understand the natural laws pertaining to nature that operate at a physical, material level of life. Some of them include Newton's law of universal gravitation and his use of linear time in the laws of motion. What may not be realised here is that these laws only operate at a physical material level. Nor is the significance of this understood. All of Newton's laws have been easily validated through laboratory experiments. Although obeying these laws got us to the moon and back, they trap our minds in what I have described above as a 'virtual box' of thinking. This puts limits on the perception of how things are and why things happen. I call this type of thinking 'mechanistic'. Such thinking is strongly influenced by the accepted reductionist approach to science.

We are taught to see things as objects, or some type of material. This creates a form-based dimension that leads to what I call form-based thinking. A deception arises here that most of us seem to be oblivious of. We are trained to look at life and the processes of life's development in a mechanistic, form-based way. Scientists in particular are taught to take things apart and drill down to an ever finer level. Education develops the intellect and the ability to remember facts at the expense of the imagination and creative self. All of this works its way through to the belief system, where we are unknowingly blinkered in relation to what we accept to be real. We are, in general, unknowingly driven further and further away from understanding what it means to be human. How could this possibly be so? I would suggest that it is because we have become too narrow in the way we think, especially in a world that is constantly measuring time and space, and forever using material things to judge success. Clearly, this type of thinking is now past its sell-by date, although that fact is not yet commonly accepted. Nonetheless, a series of scientific developments came to fruition at the beginning of the 20th century which helped to change everything. Once again, a new dawn had begun and, for some, the virtual box of thinking was being prised open.

20th century Revolutionary Thinking - Unravelling the Deception!

What I am about to tell you probably falls outside conventional thinking but is now becoming an increasing ingredient of the sciences such as physics, biology, biochemistry, botany, medicine and even psychology. It is at the cutting edge of broadening an understanding of what life is really about. It is very much post-Descartes, Newton, Darwin and neo-Darwinian thinking. New seeds were sown at the turn of the twentieth century which have the power to open our 'virtual box' of thinking. Who was responsible for planting these new seeds?

In the first decade of the 20th century an amazing group of physicists and mathematicians were studying what was happening at a sub-atomic level (the level of atoms and all things smaller). These physicists and mathematicians, Neils Bohr, Max Planck, Werner Heisenberg, Erwin Schrödinger, Wolfgang Pauli, amongst others, developed a new science called quantum mechanics or quantum physics. They put forward new laws to show what happens at a sub-atomic level. These laws turned out to be Universal Laws which operate throughout the Universe.

Universal Laws that operate in the quantum world are quite different in comparison with the laws that operate at a physical/material level. Scientists have proven that Newton's laws do not operate at a sub-atomic level. As time passed, some of the Universal Laws have been validated through experiment in laboratories, while others were reformulated in the light of experimental results. Gaining an understanding of what happens in the quantum world has the potential to upgrade our belief system and perception of how things really function in the physical world and the universe. An outcome of this understanding will be the recognition that:

'as an individual you can and do make a difference'

in the world you inhabit. As we explore the world of energy, you will discover that you have the power to write your continuing life story for the better and with a greater ease. That is, of course, once you recognise and work with the new Universal Laws. To be truly educated means travelling with a different view.

The difference between classical physics and quantum mechanics is enormous, the equivalent of darkness and light. Quantum physicists really do think outside of that 'virtual box'. They have to use their all-powerful imaginations to help them deal with concepts and mathematics that modern classical scientists would not consider. To those of you who are uninitiated in the concepts of quantum physics, this chapter will open a door in your awareness that has the potential to blow the lid off your 'virtual box' and beliefs. To others it may just add some further momentum to help you understand what life is about and why things happen as they do. My ultimate goal here is to continue to apply this new thinking so as to: upgrade the concepts used in the field of personal development as a power shift strategist; to understand life's challenges; to create techniques to empower you to achieve success in what you are doing; and to increase your inner feeling of positive wellbeing (including happiness).

Some threads that use the concept of energy are woven into the personal development suggestions in the following chapters. This is designed to help you to set a new course, to enable you to get where you are going in life with a greater ease. *You* will truly begin to be captain of your own ship and no one else! But you may be thinking *How can this possibly add to my understanding of how to secure the type and quality of life that I want?* Recognising that we are a being of energy is a first step. Why? Because the consequence of this increases awareness of how things work in life, and why they happen. It also offers an opportunity to change direction to actually improve the quality of our life. This is possible by removing some energy blocks in our system that may be causing life to be less than satisfactory. We all develop blocks in our energy system at different times in life. The blocks are caused by energy frequencies getting out of alignment. Changing how we think is the first important step to correct this as it contains a major clue about how to change our energy frequencies. I elaborate on all of this in the following chapters.

I realise that most people only want a watch to be able to tell the time and are not interested in the intricate details of how the watch works. If you want to know the basic details of what energy is and how it can work for or against you, then read on. I elaborate below upon some of the quantum physics experiments that can have a significant effect on your thinking. If you just want a watch to tell the time, go now to the *Conclusions* which are towards the end of this chapter starting from page 34.

Entering the Quantum World - the World of Energy

All is not as it seems in this quantum world!

A house and its content, a car, boat, caravan and so on are all energy. Oil, gas, electricity, magnetism, light, and gravity are energy. Human beings, animals, birds, fish, insects and plants are energy. Money is energy. Thoughts too are energy. All of these examples are energy vibrating at their own individual frequencies. Now most of us are familiar with such concepts as electrical energy, atomic energy, magnetic energy, but what is this energy? A dictionary definition of energy is:

> *'action, force, activity: the capacity of a physical system to perform work'*

The above definition did not do much for me, and I had to expand it so it could be useful in some of the concepts used in this book. I felt that I began to get to the heart of energy from the following definition:

> *'energy represents the interaction between geometric multi-dimensional sub atomic energy shapes made up of the Force and arranged within the Force'*

The above may also seem like a bit of gobbledygook but I will attempt to refine the definition through a quotation from the physicist Max Planck, and in a bit more detail below. Basic geometrical shapes such as triangles, through to more advanced ones like octahedrons and dodecahedrons and so on are, apparently, important building blocks in the formation of particles and matter.

Max Planck was one of those amazing physicists who was in tune with what energy is and had a natural feel about the meaning of life. He recognised that:

'energy cannot be created or destroyed'

My own breakthrough in understanding the secret of how we as human beings function and why we are here, began to develop many years after leaving the physics profession. It began by contemplating the meaning of some words written by Max Planck where he stated:

'all matter originates and exists by virtue of a Force'

He elaborated by focusing attention upon a most important assumption, stating:

'we must assume that behind this Force is the existence of a conscious and intelligent mind; this mind is the matrix of all matter'

I define matter as a form of substance and a matrix in two ways. The first, where the matrix is seen as the womb (the centre of creation and producer of life) and the second, a situation or surrounding substance within which something else originates, or is contained. Perhaps an elaboration of the concept of the Force may prove helpful in thinking about energy.

The Force

Energy is always vibrating at different frequencies. It is, therefore, always in motion and represents an expression of all that is. In trying to define energy we are attempting to define what can be called the Force, which is itself an energy form that flows between all things. Energy also flows through the Force which empowers itself through this energy. Just think of George Lucas and the films 'Star Wars' where the actors used the expression *May the Force be with you*, and you are getting close. This leads me to the conclusion that God, the source and the Creator is really the Force, for the Force is an intelligent consciousness. And energy can be transmuted into a form-based biological structure by an intelligent consciousness.

From a sub-atomic or quantum perspective, energy is a Force and the Force is the basic building block of everything. It has no gender; in the process of creation it is neither masculine nor feminine, it is both but it is also neither. The Force stems from the original source of creation and is infused into all matter, all substance, and all energy, be it light, dense or dark. The Force is able to:

- flow into everything that needs it
- flow out of everything that no longer needs it
- create for itself what it believes is needed

The Force has a conscious layer to it so that it can manifest into a complete conscious form. Or it can manifest as a simplified conscious form. The flow of the Force is to merely know of its existence. In conclusion, energy is the life-Force at a physical level and is the intrinsic life-

Force at a spiritual level. In the end, everything is energy and some energy has layers of consciousness.

For the above statements plus the second energy definition to make sense, it is true to say that:

'all matter originates and exists by virtue of the Force'

It may prove helpful if I now take you into the world of quantum physics. Why? because understanding what is happening in the quantum world provides an opportunity to enhance your perception of reality. My goal here is to bring to your attention the fact that you have the ability to do so much more in life than you believe you can. Changing false beliefs that have led you onto a lesser path of achievement begins by understanding the mechanics of why things happen to you. And understanding why things happen to you can be found in the world of energy (the sub-atomic world). All of this is part of the process of getting to 'know your-self'.

We all perceive that we live and operate in a three-dimensional world (length, breadth and depth) plus a fourth dimension which is the linear dimension of time. This conditions our consciousness to see things in a limited way. In reality, the world we live in also operates at a molecular, atomic and sub-atomic level in quite a different way to the physical reality of the four-dimensional world. A lack of understanding of this concept has the effect of limiting the perception we have about life and the processes that are involved, and because most of us have unknowingly a limited perception, the choices/decisions we are able to make in life are greatly reduced. This can hold us back from reaching our full potential. Expanding our awareness to understand what is happening in the sub-atomic or quantum world increases the range of choices/decisions we are able to make along life's path. It also empowers us to be able to question our belief system. Does our belief system need an upgrade to meet the challenges of the 21st century? Absolutely!

My research and that of many others has shown that the mechanistic, form-based and linear-time-biased way we are taught at home and at school limits the breadth of our thinking. We do not realise that we are trained to look at and to believe the reality of things around us (the status quo) from a limited perspective of four dimensions. In addition, present education develops mainly the analytical left-brain hemisphere plus the intellect and memory recall at the expense of the creative right-brain hemisphere. There is little, if any, understanding of the difference between knowledge and wisdom! We also are biased to understand evolution at a physical/material level from what can be considered a Darwinist, neo-Darwinist perspective. But there is much, much more to consider, and it can be found, in part, from within the quantum world which operates at a multi-dimensional level that is beyond the four-dimensional world we perceive we live in. Each of us is an integral part of this quantum world as are our planet, the Universe and the Multiverse (we have parallel Universes). But what is this quantum world?

In the Quantum World we are all Energy Beings
As human beings, we appear to be made of a solid biological/anatomical material. Whether you wish to believe this, or not, I can assure you that we are certainly not solid! We are, as I stated earlier, a form of pure energy (that is, compressed pure energy) that vibrates within a frequency range which makes us *appear* to be solid. When we touch each other we appear to be solid because we are all vibrating within a similar frequency range. The atoms that make up the body, and everything else on this planet, are just clusters of vibrating energy. This pure energy is made up, in its most elementary form, of what some quantum physicists call energy strings. They form the basic building blocks of elementary particles such as electrons, protons and neutrons that are the building blocks of atoms (see below). Everything is made up of atoms and these atoms form molecules which are the building blocks of water, oil, the body's cells, gold, diamonds, wood, tomatoes, ice cream and so on.

The Quantum World's Basic Building Blocks
Now what is an atom, what is it made of, and what does its structure look like? I use the model of a *nitrogen* atom as an example (diagram 1.1) to describe what an atom is made of, and its structure.

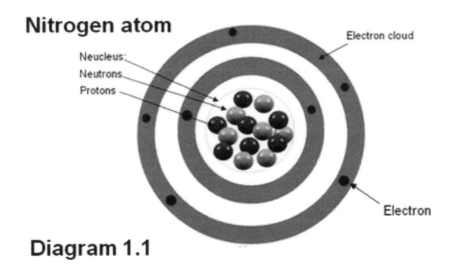

Diagram 1.1

A nitrogen atom is made up of electrons, protons and neutrons. The inner core, or nucleus, is composed of an equal number of protons and neutrons. In this atom there are 7. The two outer circles represent clouds of electrons in a waveform state. There are two electrons in the inner cloud and five in the outer. An electron is still considered in most physicist circles to be able to behave like a particle (think of a billiard ball) or as a wave (think of the sea). In the above diagram the electrons show themselves in a wave form (or fuzzy cloud around the nucleus), but I also include the solid dark particle shape of the electrons in each ring (this is for demonstration purposes only). There is either a particle or a wave at any moment of time, never both.

In the nucleus the protons and neutrons break down into smaller elementary particles. As an example, I use a proton which is a large elementary particle called a quark. I elaborate further on electrons, neutrons and quarks in diagram 1.2.

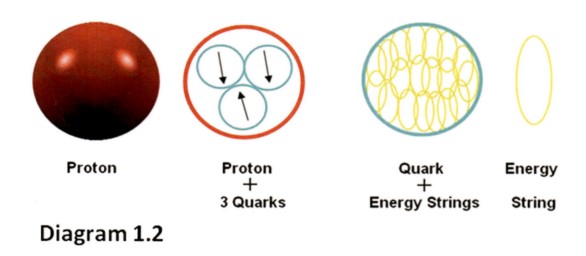

Diagram 1.2

Protons, as well as neutrons, are made up of quarks which are themselves made up of energy strings. What are these energy strings?

Energy Strings
Energy strings take us into the depths of the quantum world. Some theoretical quantum physicists and mathematicians consider that they are the building blocks of everything in the Universe (and Multiverse). There are two types of basic energy strings: a closed loop energy string and a single energy string as shown in

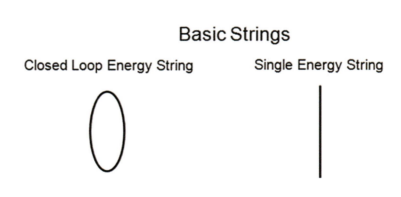

Diagram 1.3

diagram 1.3. They are two dimensional. Can you imagine, at a base level we are made up of a circle and a straight line; how cool is that! This closed loop energy string is actually full of energy. A closed loop energy string is an important form as it is self-contained and self-balancing. What do I mean by being self-contained? Human beings are like a closed loop energy system and we perform like a self-contained energy source. A closed loop provides feedback within itself and is affected by what is happening around it. Whatever happens, a closed loop has the ability to re-balance itself, provided its energy has not been totally dissipated. The single energy string cannot balance itself and takes on the characteristics (like the closed loop) of the energy environment surrounding it. Each of these energy strings can combine with a similar one to form different shapes. Single energy strings can form three-dimensional triangles and loops can form three-dimensional spheres. A closed loop can also combine with a single energy string.

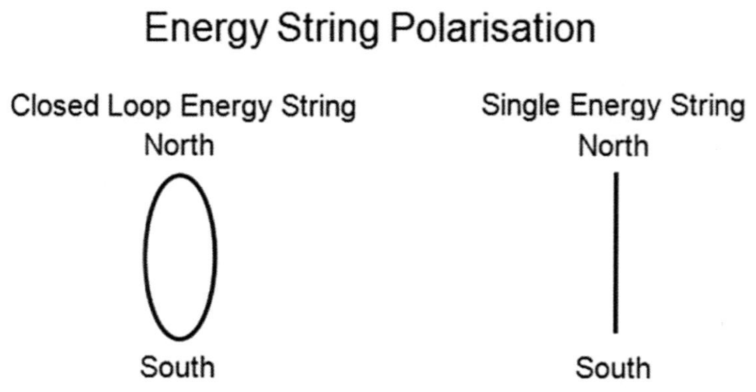

Energy String Polarisation

Closed Loop Energy String
North

○

South

Single Energy String
North

|

South

Diagram 1.4

Polarisation is important in energy forms as it indicates that the energy field has two opposite charges. With closed loop and single energy strings the energy flows within the loop from North to South (diagram 1.4). These strings are the smallest indivisible thing that not only makes up you and me, but also the planet, the Universe and the Multiverse.

To conclude this section on elementary particles and the atom, I explain a few more basic details of what a proton, neutron and electron in the nucleus of an atom are made of as we descend further into the quantum world.

Protons are made of quarks. There are two types of quarks: one with an upward polarisation (the direction of the quarks energy field flows upwards) and the other with a downward polarisation (the direction of the quarks energy field flows downwards). This is shown in diagram 1.2 above by the two arrows pointing downwards and the other pointing upwards. (shown as up and the other as down.)

Neutrons are also made up of quarks, but this time with two upwards polarised energies and one downward.

Electrons are a member of a family called leptons. Muons and Taus are the other family members. Some recent work by physicists has shown that an electron may be formed from clusters of vortexes of energy (like mini energy tornadoes).

String Theory

Scientists throughout time have been searching for a theory of everything (a theory that connects the universe and sub-atomic world with gravity). In doing this they hope to pull together, or unify, previously accepted concepts involving such questions as 'what are we and what are we made of?' Einstein was very much a big picture physicist studying the universe, gravity (the energy, or Force, that controls the motion and behaviour of galaxies, stars and planets) and he put forward his ideas in his theory of General Relativity. In comparison, quantum physicists look into the microscopic sub-atomic world. The Force of gravity is a difficult phenomenon for string theorists to integrate into quantum mechanics.

Some physicists currently show the force of gravity as a representation of an energy string's vibration (the charge/spin). String theorists show space and matter as being inseparable, that is you cannot have one without the other. In developing their mathematical equations, string theorists use up to 11 dimensions or more to make things work. What is this all about? It is about trying to unify Einstein's theory of General Relativity with quantum theory, as these are two different ways of looking at the world and the Universe. Each of these theories has its merits and faults. As we venture into the sub-atomic world and the Universe it can be described as a way of finding out how to join what is happening in a spiritual reality with what is happening in a physical reality, all of which can be described as an illusion.

The Quantum World *Connects* Everything to Everything

Truly, what happens at the sub-atomic level may take your breath away. Molecules, atoms and even particles have been found to have an awareness of each other. Some other weird (or spooky at a distance, as Einstein once said) things also happen at this level. I will start by looking at the big picture and focus upon what is happening within this picture. In the big picture the space surrounding galaxies and planets within the universe was once believed to be an empty vacuum. Scientists have shown this belief to be untrue (a false belief!). In fact, the vacuum is like a sea (or soup if you prefer) of vibrating energy composed of different types of particles. In addition, the world is constantly being bombarded by particles emitted from the sun and from elsewhere in the galaxy. Some of these particles pass through the atmosphere and then pass straight through the human body without any effect on us. How solid do you feel with that in mind? Scientists also discovered that the space within an atom's structure is not empty but is filled with vibrating energy. The atom was once thought to have 99.9 percent empty space.

Theoretical physicists working at a sub-atomic level in quantum mechanics discovered that, when they cancelled out different energy fields in the mathematical equations they had formulated, there was always one energy field left. Could this possibly be true on a practical level in a laboratory experiment? Some experiments have been, and are being carried out, to investigate the characteristics of this remaining energy field. It is often referred to as the zero point field.

Zero Point Field of Energy - the Foundation of all Creation?
Physicists carrying out quantum mechanics experiments sometimes conduct these experiments at very low temperatures. Why they do this is because at the very lowest of temperatures (close to what is called minus 273 degrees Kelvin) the vibrating energy of most substances shuts down. Unusual things also happen. At this temperature all energy should have stopped vibrating (and disappeared) but they discovered that one field of energy remained - the zero point field of energy as it is popularly called. Furthermore, they later discovered that the field itself was filled with vibrating energy – it was not empty! This zero point field of energy is approaching the energy field of what is called the Force (see above) which is the creative template from which everything on this planet, the Universe and beyond, is manifested. It is the field from which all creation stems. Although we are all connected to this field, knowing how to tune into it to make it work for us is another matter! I give you a method for doing this (that is, getting into the other 90 percent) later in the book.

Some people believe that the zero point field is the field that connects everything to everything. This statement is true but it is also a bit misleading, because it is not this particular field that connects us to everything. We are all connected through the different fields of energy that exist all around us. For example, the fields of energy connect you, me as well as sheep, cats, dolphins, the sea, water, rocks, trees, the desert and everything elsewhere in the Universe (and Multiverse) through what can be described as an invisible energy field (like a web or matrix of energy) which operates at the quantum level. This becomes more intriguing as the laws that operate at the quantum level are investigated.

To whet your appetite, understanding the Universal Laws that operate at a quantum level gives an insight to develop new forms of transport. For example, as everything is connected through the energy fields that exist around us, should I enter the quantum world and wish to travel, I just need to think about my destination and I will be there. There is no time delay as time and space are co-existent within the quantum world. And most importantly, energy follows thought. Such is the connective power of energy. The example I have just given you is real. During the Cold War the American military developed a psychic spy program called the Sun Streak. This was a very successful program and involved individuals projecting themselves in their mind (and some out of their body) to a target destination which they could then investigate. After gathering the required information the individuals returned and reported their findings. The Russians were also leaders in the field of what was called psychic warfare in the KGB's department F in Moscow (and elsewhere).

There are some intriguing examples of experiments that have been carried out to investigate what happens in the quantum world. The results are nothing short of mind blowing! For those of you who are not interested in the experimental aspects then go straight to the conclusions starting at page 34. These conclusions begin the process of changing false beliefs that, unknowingly, we have been conditioned to believe.

Particles have a Life of their Own!

It is fascinating to consider that a particle can act as a wave or as a discrete particle (imagine it as a very small sphere) and the particle seems to be aware of when to change its form! A simple but remarkable experiment was set up to investigate how particles behave under controlled conditions. Thomas Young, a physicist, originally set up this experiment at the beginning of the 19th century, and it is called the *double slit* experiment (diagram 1.5: source, Wikipedia).

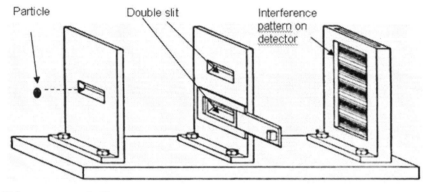

Diagram 1.5

He used a source of light to show the results. The experiment has been carried out many times throughout the twentieth century using particles such as photons (these are individual particles of light), and also electrons, protons, neutrons and even atoms. Each experiment produced a similar set of results. The purpose of these experiments was to interpret what was going on in quantum mechanics. It also allowed physicists to see if the laws that operate at a material level (the three/four dimensional world that obeys Newton's laws) also operate at the sub-atomic level. Experimental results show that they do not.

In the 1920s, three physicists/mathematicians were leading players (amongst others) in the development of quantum mechanics: Neils Bohr (a Danish physicist), Werner Heisenberg and Erwin Schrodinger. Their work was to change the way we look at ourselves, the world and the Universe forever. It was to take about a century for this new thinking to begin to make an imprint upon the false beliefs that had been accepted unquestioningly by scientists and non-scientists in the past. These false beliefs appeared to be true at the time. Powerful social, political and religious forces in that period exerted huge influence on the development of ideas and beliefs about the natural world. This is why some new scientific concepts and theories, even those that resulted from scientific research, were not developed until about the middle of the 19th century onwards.

The Copenhagen Interpretation

Neils Bohr and his associates took Thomas Young's experiment a step forward in the early 1920s. A special physics laboratory was built for Bohr outside Copenhagen called the Bohr Institute. Their findings and conclusions, as a result of the experiments carried out at the laboratory, led to the 'Copenhagen Interpretation' in 1927, which in simple terms stated that:

'Quantum mechanics cannot provide an objective description of reality at a sub-atomic (microscopic) level. It also shows that measurement affects what is happening.'

Bohr's team of physicists discovered a new world of energy quanta. In this world, the classical physics' approach to dealing with waves and particles did not work. Quantum physics moved thinking from an objective world to the subjective world (the world of probabilities). To classical physicists, this was tantamount to heresy, but it was exciting and life changing for Bohr and his team.

The term Quantum Superimposition arose from the double slit experiments which can be defined as:

'all particles exist not in one state but all possible states together'

I elaborate on a deceptively simple experiment, as it may help you to grasp the significance of the conclusions that arose from the Copenhagen Interpretation. In truth, the conclusions are quite mind-blowing, and they shatter so many of the false beliefs that we have all been brought up to accept. In the following experiment, the results are the same whether or not a stream of particles, or atoms, or a single particle or atom is used.

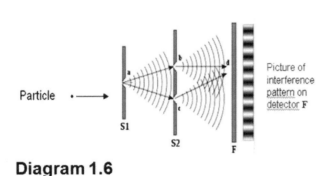

Diagram 1.6

If a single particle is projected onto the screen with a single slit at S1 (diagram 1.6: source, Wikipedia), the particle, has to be travelling in the form of a wave to pass through S1. On the way to S2 and the double slits (b & c,) the particle still has to be travelling as a wave. The particle travelling as a wave causes further waves to be emitted at each of the slits at S2, which then travel onto a detection screen F (a photographic plate or receiving device that can show what is happening via a computer screen). What is it that happens at F? An interference pattern and not just images of the slits occurs on the detection screen F. But an interference pattern can only be obtained from a series of interlocking waves that are recorded at F. A stream of particles (in particle form) would only produce blobs of light taking the shape of each of the two slits. How the interference pattern happens is where things get interesting.

Before summarising the unusual characteristics of this experiment, it is important to restate that a particle can exist in two forms. It can exist either as a wave or as a discrete particle. Whichever form it takes depends on what is happening. For example, when the particle hits screen S1 (diagram 1.6) it is in the form of a wave, otherwise it would just leave a blob of light somewhere on screen S1 and not pass through.

The particle seems to be aware of the experimental layout as it is able to find the slit (a) on S1, pass through it and make its way towards screen S2 once again as a wave. The particle is able to sense that there are two slits at S2 (b and c) and passes through them both as waves to cause the interference pattern (dark and light patches) at F. For there to be an interference pattern means that the waves at F must have collapsed back to a particle again at a particular point in space on the measuring device. The dark and light patches are caused by the waves coming together and collapsing, which creates both a constructive and destructive effect resulting in the dark and light bands on the interference pattern as shown on the right of diagram 1.7 (source, Wikipedia).

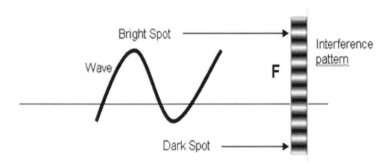

Diagram 1.7

To deal with the wave/particle duality, physicists describe a particle as a wave function, which is a mathematical representation used to calculate the probability (that is, the likelihood or possibility) of it being found in a location, or alternatively in a state of motion. It is a bit like 'we seek it here, we seek it there, we seek that particle everywhere'. Werner Heisenberg (a German theoretical physicist), while working with Neils Bohr, put forward a theory called 'Heisenberg's Principle of Uncertainty'. This is a work of sheer genius, like the rest of Bohr's team's work, and in simple terms shows mathematically that:

> *'when a particle's position has been located it limits how precisely its velocity can be determined vice versa'*

Another leading physicist, Wolfgang Pauli (an Austrian theoretical physicist), whose work was also sheer genius, won a Nobel Prize for what is called 'the exclusion principle or Pauli Principle'. His work showed that no two electrons could exist in the same quantum state. His work also introduced a new theory called *spin theory* which underpins the structure of matter and the whole of chemistry.

When you enter into the world of quantum physics, interesting concepts arise, such as that 'a particle has awareness'. As scientists get further into quantum physics experiments, what was deemed impossible yesterday is now possible today. For example, the ability to store the contents of the Encyclopaedia Britannica on an atom might seem an outrageous suggestion to some of you today, but is it? I would suggest to you that this is going to be possible. How can I make such a seemingly outrageous suggestion? Quite simply, because I believe it, and so do many practising physicists, which unleashes the infinite power of creative thinking. It is purely a matter of time – and money – before they do it!

A Particle Knows that it is being Measured

Unexpected things happen if a measuring device is now placed beside either of the slits on screen S2 on diagram 1.8:

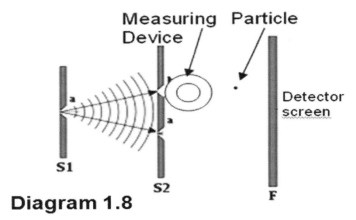

Diagram 1.8

The wave which was passing through the top slit on S2 meets the measuring device and immediately collapses to become a particle. The particle passes through the measuring device to form a blob of light on the detector F and not an interference pattern. In addition, nothing passes through the lower slit on S2. A blob of light is made on F each time a particle passes through the measuring device.

Conclusion ONE:

Three important conclusions can be drawn from the double slit experiment where a particle:

1. *knows when to change its form from a wave to a particle and back again.*
2. *creates its reality when observed. If measured, the particle instantly changes (collapses) its wave property to take up physical reality as a particle.*
3. *seems to know what is happening in the experiment.*

There is nothing in classical physics laws that can handle this type of phenomena or thinking. This leads us to consider that out in the real world, by a process of observation, we unknowingly affect what we think about. That includes our-self, other people, situations, material things, the Universe and beyond. I deal with the effects of thought energy in the next chapter.

Taking Heisenberg's Principle of Uncertainty a step further leads to another interesting conclusion and that is with respect to *faith,* which I define as unconditional belief. In the above experiment we know that a particle is somewhere, so we have *faith* that it is there even though it may be in the form of a wave. How come? Because there are interference patterns in the experiment carried out to prove it. Therefore, another conclusion can be derived from Heisenberg's Principle of Uncertainty, and that is:

    4. *faith is a prerequisite at the sub-atomic or quantum level*

We Affect what we are Looking At or Thinking About!
A more recent experiment set up by a physicist by accident in the 1990s introduced the effects of observation and thought on the results of the experiment.

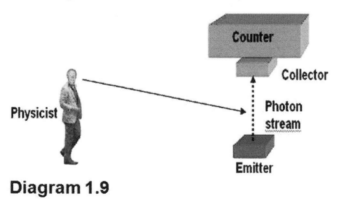

Diagram 1.9

In the experiment (diagram 1.9), a regular stream of photons (light particles) was passed from a cathode (or emitter) to a receiving anode (or collector) where each particle was counted by an electronic device (the Counter) as it arrived. When the physicist looked in the direction of the photon flow, he noticed that it affected the regular flow of the photons - the count changed. The stream returned to its steady state after he stopped looking at it. Intrigued by this result, he decided to think about the photon stream after moving to a different part of the building. The same effect was repeated again; he had interfered with the regular stream of photons. When he stopped thinking about the stream of photons, it returned to a steady state. All of this was quite outside what he had expected.

To further test this interesting result, he decided to think about the stream of photons at a set time while visiting another university. Once again, the effects were the same. When he went through the same procedure, during a visit to Australia, the same result was evident. Distance had no effect, nor was there a time lag, irrespective of how far from the location of the actual experiment he travelled. The non-effect of time was checked by making reference to the reading of an atomic clock (a very accurate time piece) to improve the accuracy of the results. What does this tell us? The energy transmitted by an observer through their thoughts has a direct effect on the photon (energy) stream under investigation. Several interesting conclusions can be drawn from this experiment:

Conclusion TWO:
1. *energy follows thought*
2. *an individual's thoughts affect what they look at*
3. *an individual's thoughts affect what they think about in their conscious mind*
4. *distance is irrelevant to the outcome*
5. *there is no time delay with respect to distance*

What does the above mean to you and me? It means that each one of us affects reality. It means that:

6. *as an individual you do make a difference to what is happening around you, through your focus, intent and thinking.*

Most importantly, it also means that as an individual, through your thoughts:

7. *you make a difference to what is happening in the world and beyond.*

Into the 'spooky' stuff –

Bell's Inequality - Quantum Entanglement - Non Locality
Einstein never felt comfortable with quantum mechanics and disagreed with some of its theoretical mathematics and assumptions. For instance, in his Special Theory of Relativity (1905) he proved that nothing can travel faster than the speed of light. Theoretical quantum physicists have shown that this assumption is not strictly true. An Irish physicist John Stewart Bell put forward a mathematical/statistical theorem in the 1970s which basically proved that:

'all conceivable mathematical models of reality must incorporate an instant connection'

This is called Bell's Inequality Theorem. This theorem stands its ground in spite of the fact that the following three statements in the 1970s were upheld:

1. *relativity does not allow for instantaneous connections (because nothing can travel faster than the speed of light in any communication)*
2. *no such connections have ever been observed in any experiments (at that time).*
3. *quantum theory itself predicted no observable instant connections (at that time).*

Nevertheless, an instantaneous connection does exist and it is non-local (that is it allows for instantaneous effects to act over extremely long distances (for example: at the other end of the universe)). What does this all mean?

Bell's theorem provided a mathematical proof of the built-in connectedness of everything in the universe. But can this be proved practically? Yes, and physicists are now very close to proving the theorem in the laboratory. To prove it, they needed to enter the spooky nature of quantum reality once again. Experiments were conducted where a single photon was taken and split to make two separate photons. They were then separated by about 11 kilometres. One of the photons was rotated and the effect on the other was measured. The second photon instantly turned in the same direction. Two photons in this type of situation are said to be *entangled,* hence the term *'quantum entanglement'*.

Professor Alain Aspect (a French professor) carried out such an experiment in the 1980s and came extremely close to validating the theorem. Why only close? Because other physicists disputed the accuracy of Prof Alain's measuring devices. To provide evidence of 100 per cent proof of Bells Inequality Theorem, more advanced technology is required. It is just a matter of time before this happens and some physicists around the world are hot on the trail, although there are many sceptics in the physicist community due partly to the limitations of their virtual box thinking. Changing well-established classical thinking can be a slow process, as pointed out by physicist Max Planck. It seems that it is mostly new, younger physicists who adapt quickly to new concepts and theories whereas older ones do not!

Bell's Inequality Theorem shook most scientists to the core (and still does). Einstein had proven through his Special Theory of Relativity that a particle could not travel faster than the speed of light. This was set as a limitation on most things travelling or communicating in space. Physicists expected a delay to occur as the two parts of the photon in the above experiment were thought to be communicating with each other. It was expected that there would be a minute time lag before the opposite photon turned. Even though more advanced technology is required for final proof, there appears to be no such delay. Einstein's speed of light limitation is under threat. He may very soon be proven wrong. Theoretical physicists have already shown Einstein to be wrong. Therefore, we have a suggestion, yet to be proven conclusively, that it is possible to travel faster than the speed of light. Bell had theoretically proven that particles (the photons) can be *superluminal*. Summarising some conclusions from the above:

Conclusion THREE:

1. *distance is irrelevant to outcome.*
2. *there is no time delay communicating over a great distance*
3. *everything is connected through a matrix of energy*
4. *we are in a time period where experimental evidence is expected to show that it is possible to travel faster than the speed of light.*
5. *something happening at one point in our universe can have an instantaneous effect at the other end of our universe and at all points in between (not within the Multiverse because of a small change in energy frequencies between universes).*
6. *in the objective reality of the fabricated-self (see below) in the physical world, each of our perceptions can be different.*
7. *faith is a reality within the quantum world and our universe because although we cannot predict everything, we know that something is going to happen.*

Can a Bar Magnet Float on a Block of Lead?

Many experiments have been conducted at temperatures close to -273 degrees Kelvin, using materials like lead, aluminium, chromium, to name a few, which are superconducting materials. These materials exhibit unexpected properties at very low temperatures. For example, they have no resistance. One such property is that a superconducting metal has an ability to repel a magnetic field when it is reduced to a very low temperature. An example of an unexpected property is where a bar magnet is placed on a block of lead (see photograph on the right). The lead block is then placed in a bath of liquid nitrogen. As soon as the lead cools to close to -273 degrees Kelvin, the magnet lifts off the lead and floats on its own magnetic field. This is called the Meissen effect, after the physicist who discovered it in 1933. A practical application of this phenomenon can be shown where superconducting magnets are used in transportation. A railway train floats on a bed of superconducting magnets to reduce friction, thereby improving its efficiency. It is also used in electrical power distribution, electric motors and so on.

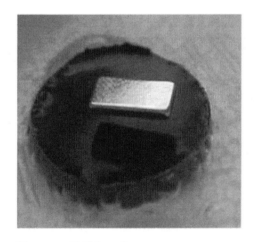

Picture: Wikipedia

Leonardo da Vinci would be impressed!

Your Chance to Think Outside the Box . . . What is Energy?

We might be able to sense it, but we cannot see it, we cannot touch it, we cannot taste it and yet it is there. It is the building block of ourselves, the planet, the Universe and the Multiverse. It can be transmuted and transformed into different types of power. Energy can be found in a compressed solid, liquid and gaseous form. An example of energy that produces more energy is coal, oil and gas. These can all be ignited to create heat-steam-electricity. Compressed solids and liquids such as oil come from a living form (trees). Importantly, as human beings we too are basically compressed energy as we are made up of strings of energy at a sub-atomic level. We are an exquisitely constructed biological human form crafted from atoms, molecules and cells, which all started as energy. Even our thoughts are a form of energy. Yet, to craft a human being required a conscious and intelligent mind!

What is it that drives the physical part of us (the fabricated-self)? As human beings we are driven by several different energy forms. As we shall explore in later chapters, these energy forms are, for example, the soul (or inner-self), free will, ego, personality and supporting sub-personalities, masks, beliefs, subtle energy bodies and an interconnecting energy structure. Imagine all these energy forms interacting with your consciousness! I like to call the inner-self (or soul), which affects the way we think, a mini energy fuel cell. Do not forget that the inner-self drives the authentic-self. Without the inner-self driving part of consciousness, the human body would just be a biological machine with no purpose. Although the human body runs automatically (breathing, pumping blood, walking, keeping temperature in balance and so on), most of the time, it cannot truly function without the soul. I say 'most of the time' as there can be occasions where an individual may need to be put on an artificial life support system during an operation. Even when the soul leaves the physical body and an electroencephalogram (EEG) shows no brainwaves, a human body can be kept going with an artificial life support system. Reducing everything to a common denominator of energy means that it is now possible to figure out just what is happening in life both internally and externally.

What Quantum Physics Experiments are Suggesting to Us

Some of my most intense working experiences have been in the United Nations and in investment banking. At such times, working in a team, I noticed that a vital attribute that we are all born with was missing. That missing attribute was *imagination.* Great scientists, mathematicians, artists, teachers, engineers, chefs, those who work in the creative fields, all have exceptional imagination. We are all born with an imagination yet it is sparingly promoted in education. An American Scientist, Richard Feynman, whom I admire greatly, is reputed to have said that 'science is imagination in a straightjacket'. Perhaps he meant classic science? I would suggest that some of today's amazing scientists and theoretical mathematicians succeed by thinking outside of the constraints of their 'virtual box'. They wear no straightjacket and have flexible beliefs in what is possible.

Lacking an imagination is a key to disaster. Take, for example, Senator Tom Keene in the United States who reviewed the reports as to why 9/11 occurred. His leading opening statement made it quite clear that:

> *'the one thing which stood out was the lack of imagination shown in the senior ranks of the intelligence services, plus the FBI, to determine what was going on from the facts that were gathered prior to the event'*

But surely, I suggest again, that it was also due to that mechanistic, form-based, linear-time-biased upbringing to which we are all subjected. Doing everything by numbers, combined with the politics and the massive egos within these agencies that are themselves driven by the conditioning of a numbers/information-based society certainly displaces the imagination at the best of times, let alone when faced with an unfolding major crisis such as 9/11.

To interpret the results arising from the simple quantum physics experiments described above requires us to think outside of our virtual box. This demands the use of the imagination and the raising of self-awareness to include the fifth dimension. There is now sufficient scientific evidence and facts to facilitate an understanding of the fifth dimension and what it means on a day to day basis. So, I have asked myself, in terms of self-development, what do the above quantum physics experiments suggest? The following are a series of my personal understandings derived from those experiments. I have found that they provide useful inputs when I prepare my action plans as I journey, especially when I need to make important choices/decisions.

- ❖ **Changing our Thinking Changes our Reality**
  Keeping an open, positive and when possible neutral mind is important as we go through life. Why? Because if we do not do this, it greatly reduces the chance of understanding what is really happening to us and around us. Education trains us to be mainly analytically and intellectually driven with an eye for detail. This is a strength as well as a weakness. We have been taught to believe that the physical world we see is reality. Such a reality can be described as an objective view. But an objective view of the world is certainly not a true reality. We do not realise that a great part of reality is created through the power of the subjective world (the world of the mind, the imagination, intent and attention). Beliefs are the filters through which reality is constructed. Beliefs affect how things are seen. In the quantum world, the reality of what

is happening is affected by thoughts. The quantum world is also the home of subjective reality which links us with the spiritual dynamics of life as well as with intuition (hunches) and intuitive intelligence. And we are all part of the quantum world. Progressive, positive thinking with the support of the imagination is a powerful route to follow in life. Try holding a positive thought supported by a positive emotion for some time (say for five minutes) in the conscious mind. This generates strength within the thought's energy form as it passes through to the unconscious mind. Let the thought and emotion go when you feel that the time is right. Your thinking ultimately creates your reality, so think well!

- **Improving a Positive Feeling of Inner Wellbeing**

  Particles, atoms, molecules and brain/body cells all have an awareness of one another at a sub-atomic level. Neuroscientists have discovered that the human mind is an energy field that surrounds the physical body. This field communicates not only with the brain but also with the body and its cells, which are aware of the thought energy at a sub-atomic level. An outcome of the effect of this field is that we affect our own wellbeing, the wellbeing of those around us, and of others at greater distances. As everything is connected at an energy level, it means that everything on the planet and beyond, which we focus upon, is affected to some degree by our thoughts. To an overwhelming degree we are influenced and affected by our thoughts and patterns of thinking. Positive thoughts are not only a main contributor to inner wellbeing but also to happiness. A word of caution here; it is important for a positive thought to be in balance and not over-intense. As with life in general, keeping everything in balance and doing everything with moderation reinforces self awareness and induces wellbeing.

- **Thinking Outside the Virtual Box is the Way to Go**

  It is in everybody's interest to be able to think outside of the virtual box of thinking to which we are conditioned, for it does not always serve us well. We are unknowingly chained inside this box, and as the psychologist Eric Berne nobly wrote, *'we love our chains'*. They form part of our comfort zone. An important point that I discovered along my journey is that life begins outside of my comfort zone! Raising our awareness into the fifth dimension of energy enables us to begin to see, hear and feel reality for what it is. Recognising that energy and the sub-atomic world are one takes us into a different dimensional reality than that which we are used to. The dimensions of this new reality are explained below. Removing the chains of our thinking is greatly enhanced by cultivating the imagination, which is *a gateway to the creative self.* By accessing the world of energy, manifesting our desires becomes more of a certainty rather than a possibility.

- **Change Limiting Beliefs and Achieve Success**
In this 21st century, it is important to recognise that the belief system we have been conditioned to accept and which is accepted as being true, has limitations. Each person's belief system is programmed through parents, family relations, school, college, friends, the media, authority figures and so forth. The belief system has powerful foundations that actually trap us into a limited, mechanistic, form-based, linear-time-biased understanding of what life is about. As a door is opened in our consciousness to the quantum world (the world of energy), there is a golden opportunity presented to step back and look at our belief structure.

Let me give you a rather dated, but nonetheless relevant example of changing limited beliefs. Roger Bannister, who broke a record by running the first four-minute mile (1956) believed that he could do so. He managed to get into a state of mind while he was running where he was not aware of his running. He had connected with an energy field within which athletes call *the Zone,* which gave him super-human stamina and agility. Those athletes during the same time period who believed that it was not possible, could not beat the four-minute mile. Nevertheless, with the four-minute barrier broken, other runners replicated the result and have improved on it ever since. They all broke an old false belief! Actions like creating a miracle, or the reality of manifesting great abundance cannot possibly be understood, or practised successfully, within a conventional belief structure and its limited perception of how things really are. Once again, using the imagination is a key to success. It encourages thinking outside of that virtual box!

- **Faith (Unconditional Belief) is the Path to Achieving Success**
Quantum physics experiments have shown that predicting and controlling events with a high degree of accuracy is not possible. What they also show is the necessity for faith that everything will line up the way it is meant to. This is especially so in life itself. Faith is an inherent characteristic of quantum physics. If someone says that they have no faith, then it follows that they have faith in having no faith. Hence, they have faith which is of course unconditional belief. In quantum physics *'what you believe, is'* can be taken to an infinite high. Such a statement has a controlling influence in the quest for abundance in all its forms. Having faith that we are abundant makes the outcome of abundance a greater certainty. Assuming, of course, that alongside our faith we have no doubts! (The effects of Doubt are covered later in the book.)

- **You Do Make a Difference**
In the fifth dimension you are aware that, because you are made of energy, you too are part of the quantum world. Two important ideas (amongst others) arise from the above quantum physics experiments. The first is that we are all connected through energy. The

second is that by understanding quantum entanglement we know that we instantaneously affect everything that we focus upon, wherever it is located. In simple terms, this means that we as individuals are all-powerful. We have an effect on everything we focus our attention upon. We also know from experiments that we make a difference on the planet and beyond. This all happens through our thinking, intent, belief structure and the information/energy flow from us into the quantum environment to which we are connected. You have, therefore, a responsibility for your life's story and how it turns out. Knowing this enables you to take the opportunity to write a better life story as you journey to achieve your desires and fulfil your dreams. This book will hopefully help you on your way to creating the life that you are meant to experience.

It is in the interests of each of us to recognise and to open our 'virtual box' of thinking, especially since health, wealth, an inner feeling of positive wellbeing and happiness depend upon it. Such a change is long overdue and it is a change that we can induce. To make the change requires looking further into that inner power house we all have, called the unconscious mind, the seat of the imagination. The brain and body have energy fields and these hold important clues about the effects of a feeling of positive wellbeing within the body, mind, emotions and spirit. A major part of life evolves from within and not from outside of us. This includes a feeling of happiness, a sense of security and the ability to generate abundance and prosperity. There are techniques and processes within the book that will enable you to change your energy field to your benefit. This should enable you to attract to you what you are meant to experience by using the effects of attention and intention on the energy field that you radiate.

Each of us has some remarkable properties and capabilities. One such property is that as a being of energy we are like what I call a quantum bio-magnet. The bio-magnetic field has special properties which can be influenced when you learn how to change it and I will show you in later chapters how to do this. Most self help and personal development books will have to be re-written over the next ten years or so, because they have not fully taken into account what is happening at an energy level. As we are physical and energy beings, our psychological (mind and emotions) and physiological (physical body and feelings) state depends upon what is going on within both. To really get to the root of how to manifest what you want in life it is essential to:

1. recognise both your fabricated-self and authentic-self
2. understand the dimensions involved within the physical reality you live in plus the dimensions of the energy reality associated with your authentic-self which are, in general, neglected.

A consequence of not following through on both of the above is that we are in a situation where we are like a metaphorical ship without a rudder; with or without the help of a supporting tidal flow and fair wind we may just get to where we think we are going, but it will be mostly by accident.

So, just what are the dimensions that operate at the level of our outer (fabricated) self and inner (authentic) self?

Comparing Dimensions of the Reality of the Fabricated-self and Authentic-Self
I place a lot of emphasis upon thinking in the fifth dimension, for the purpose of putting an anchor down within the conscious and unconscious minds to raise self-awareness of why our lives play out the way they do. It is useful to note that your mind may need some time to assimilate what follows. In this 21st century, experiencing feelings of positive wellbeing, happiness, success and security is dependent upon making changes to our awareness of reality. And as emphasised, we all have an authentic-self which has different dimensions in comparison with those of our fabricated-self. Nevertheless, the two dimensional systems are mutually inclusive, and understanding how to operate within them contributes substantially to our personal and inner (spiritual) growth, as we journey along life's path.

What is the difference between the reality dimensions of the outer, fabricated-self and those of the inner, authentic-self? The two columns in the table below show the five dimensions of both these realities which operate in the actual physical/ intellectual/ emotional/ spiritual/ energy environment that we occupy.

Dimensions Table

	First Paradigm Outer (Fabricated-self) Reality		Second Paradigm Inner (Authentic-self) Reality
Dimension 1	Length		Light
Dimension 2	Breadth		Shadow
Dimension 3	Depth		The soul
Dimension 4	Time		Time
Dimension 5	Energy		Energy

The fabricated-self reality dimensions are straightforward to recognise. Turning to the dimensions of the authentic-self's reality, a new paradigm (model) involving the sub-atomic world is entered. These dimensions incorporate the authentic-self's requirements (in energy terms) with respect to physical reality. To comprehend these dimensions, it is necessary to recognise certain characteristics of thinking with respect to our conscious mind and emotional self, plus what affects our attitude and behaviour. Appreciating the dimensions of the authentic-self is becoming a part of personal development and inner growth. I elaborate in detail on the authentic-self later. Knowledge of and working within these dimensions enhances our ability to improve the story that we write about ourselves, as we journey through life.

Dimensions of the Reality of the Fabricated-Self

The dimensions of the physical reality of the fabricated or outer-self are:

Dimensions 1/2/3 These are quite simply: *length, breadth and depth.* These dimensions are part of what is accepted as normal reality.

Dimension 4 *Time.* Linear time is an illusion that is in place to enable us to work through our life lessons. Linear time is created by the earth's twenty-four-hour regular rotation. Of course we can all tell the time and make measurements involving time, but this latter point is where we begin to lose it! How do we lose it? We lose it because time is measured and a value is put on it. The body's cells are programmed with observations and thoughts about linear time, causing us to enter an aging cycle which is accepted to be the norm. Other people are seen to be growing old and this is accepted to be the 'status quo' within our consciousness.

Dimension 5 *Energy.* Entering the fifth dimension of thinking involves activating the imagination. It involves seeing in the mind the connectedness and non-solidity of everything. Why, because in the fifth dimension everything is just energy. In this dimension we can take a step back and begin to feel the reality of what is happening around you. Everything is not as it seems!

Dimensions of the Reality of the Authentic-Self

I believe that it is true to say that most of us want the best for ourselves and for any children that we have. By raising our awareness of the two worlds (the physical and the sub-atomic world) that we live in, there is an opportunity to do this. To get into the second world requires recognising and working through each of the five dimensions listed on the above right-hand side of the dimensions table. Both these sets of dimensions are different parts of the reality of our total self as a human being. The fourth and fifth dimensions appear to be the same in both realities. Energy most certainly is, but time is not and I explain why below. To give you an explanation of the first three dimensions of the authentic-self, I need to relate them to the subtle energy bodies that surround the physical body. I explain in detail what our seven subtle energy bodies are in chapter 3. The dimensions are:

Dimension 1 *Light,* which is related to the third subtle energy body that deals with the Intellect (the thinking part of the mind). You have probably heard the expression that so and so are stuck in their head. Such people mainly describe what is going on in their life through their intellect. It also means that they often lack any capacity to express, or are only capable of a limited expression of their feelings and have difficulty in verbalising them. In this dimension, ownership is taken of our intellectual capabilities. The challenge is to recognise, understand and work with our intellectual capacity because importantly it has to be balanced against *feelings*, an attribute that also needs to be harnessed and kept in balance in our life (Dimension 3).

Dimension 2 *Shadow* or shade is associated with the first subtle energy body which has a direct (blueprint) connection with the physical body. In this dimension, ownership is taken of the physical self. The task here is to work on understanding the physical body and how to use it. Keeping the body in good shape is important as it can be described as the *'temple of the soul'*. Energies here are denser than in the previous 1st dimension.

When the 1st and 2nd dimensions have been understood and worked through, keeping them both in balance is important before moving on to working with the 3rd dimension.

Dimension 3 *The Soul* or inner-self has a close association with the second subtle energy body which is the emotional energy body. This is because the soul is here to experience different emotions. There is only one emotion in the spirit world and that is unconditional love. A main lesson for the soul being in a physical body is to deal with using the different emotions and feelings that arise during the experiences it attracts (Appendix 1, page 420 for list of emotions). This is a part of the soul's growth as we venture along life's path. In this dimension, ownership is taken of our emotions and our soul. Much emphasis is placed in this book on our emotions being a powerful energy force that we can use to our benefit. The challenge is to learn how to work with and to understand our emotions, and also the soul's purpose and needs.

Dimension 4 *Time.* In the sub-atomic, or quantum world, time is just energy. The importance of this fact is to get us out of the belief in linear time. Ownership needs to be taken of this dimension, recognising that it is just energy. This dimension promotes the concept of Divine timing. What do I mean? I mean that we always have enough time in life to complete what is in the soul's contract. Each soul has a contract containing the life lessons that are to be worked through. Let me emphasise here that this is not like a contract as we know it. It is fluid (or dynamic) and not a rigid set of life lessons. Think of the soul contract as a directive. No matter if we depart this life via an accident, or illness or some mishap, we will always have completed what we are here to experience, to learn and to grow from. We always have enough time. There is an exception here, where someone with an addiction takes their own life. We all have free will but addictions can override the soul's influence.

Dimension 5   *Energy.* This is an environment that encompasses all realities including, of course, the sub-atomic or quantum reality. The definition of energy stated above brings us into an understanding that energy and the Force just *'is'*. However, it is not only about knowing that we are energy, it is also about knowing that by the use of that energy we have the power to manifest what we desire.

In addition to the above, there are two other dimensions to consider - Dimension 6, which is the dimension of the spirit world, and Dimension 7, which is God consciousness. These dimensions are accessed through our 6th and 7th subtle energy bodies. I would suggest that given the state of humanity's energetic development to date, and this can be observed by looking at what is happening all around us and in the world at large, we have our hands full just trying to work through the first five dimensions.

The Truth about Spiritual and Personal Development
I did not know about the different dimensions of the authentic-self, nor had I realised the necessity of bringing them into balance, until the year 2010. This is equivalent to bringing the unseen part of our existence into what I call a singularity, by which I mean balancing and then merging each dimension and bringing them into our daily life. Before then, I had been too narrowly focused upon and too single-minded about my career direction through my fabricated-self. This meant that although I achieved what I wanted to do (eventually) I was usually oblivious to any synchronistic occurrences that might have taken me in what could have been a more desirable direction. I tended to ignore any inner promptings I was being given. Today, though, I appreciate the necessity of working towards integrating the five dimensions of the authentic-self (or soul) within my consciousness and I acknowledge the effect it has on my life's story. From my continued observations, many people are seeking to bring into balance the different dimensions of their authentic-self to create a singularity, without realising the importance of doing so.

There are four distinct steps to follow if one wishes to work with the dimensional reality of the authentic-self's domain. They incorporate personal development and include inner (spiritual) growth. The steps involve moving from the duality of two dimensions by understanding and working through both of them to create a singularity which is really a balanced state of being between the two. For example to work through:

Step 1: Dimension 1 (light); recognise that we have an intellect, take ownership of it, have a respect for it, understand its strengths, weaknesses, power, and work with it. Join with Dimension 2 (that is shade/shadow/physical body); take ownership of it. Develop a respect and understanding of the physical self and what it means to us. As we work through each of these dimensions, we are operating in a duality. Our task is to work towards bringing both into balance to create a singularity with no extremes of either.

In the material world of the West, many people are stuck in the 1st dimension or the 2nd dimension (or both) and do not know that it would be advantageous for their inner growth and personal development to balance both in their lifetime. There are those who are stuck in their head and are doing just about everything in their life using their intellect (1st dimension). And there are those who are stuck in the 2nd dimension – shade/dark/physical body. An example could be people who are obsessed with physical fitness and form. It is advisable to bring both these dimensions into balance before moving onto the third dimension.

Dimension 3 is the authentic-self's environment. It is possible to jump to any dimension you want to, but unless each dimension in sequence has been systematically balanced, worked through and integrated with the previous dimensions, then any work carried out will be incomplete and not totally effective.

Step 2: Moving onto the third dimension, the task here is to recognise that we have an authentic-self, plus a *soul*, and to take ownership of it. Developing a respect for our authentic-self and soul is most important. A major step forward in this regard is to understand that the authentic-self and soul is here to learn and to grow from the experiences that we attract to us. Once this has been accomplished, the previous two dimensions, which have already been integrated in a balanced state, and the 3rd dimension, can all be worked with and brought into balance to form a singularity. This latter step is in case one or more of the dimensions gets out of balance, due to an unexpected situation which might arise in our life.

Step 3: Here we accept that time is energy and that we too are also energy. This will enhance our ability to step out of the linear-time-biased constraint that we unknowingly experience in our thinking. We have a respect for and understand the purpose and power of time. The reality of Divine timing (we will always have enough time to complete what we are here to learn) opens up to us. Working with this concept so as to bring it into balance, we then bring in the previous three dimensions which are already integrated and in balance. We then take this newly-formed duality and bring it into balance to form a singularity.

Step 4: We finally move into energy, which is the Force that flows between all things and is the basic building block of everything. It is necessary to understand our subtle energy bodies (chapter 3) and how they function if we are to operate in this dimension. When we think within the fifth dimension, we have the power to influence the world and beyond to a greater extent than we could possibly imagine. To do this, it is advisable to ensure that our authentic-self is in balance. How do we do it? We take the newly-formed duality of energy which includes the previous integrated dimensions, work with them all and make another singularity. At this stage we will be (probably unknowingly) an expert at manifesting.

A lot of new age and spiritual gurus jump straight from the first dimension or even the 2nd dimension to the third or fifth without working through the previous two dimensions to bring them into a balance and form a singularity. These types of individuals are not truly *grounded* in what they are saying or doing. They are probably unknowingly misleading, in one way or another, many of those with whom they come into contact. This may be due to their own lack of understanding of what is happening within the world of energy and the soul.

From a dimensional perspective, if we grasp that we are light and shadow (1st and 2nd dimensions) and are in balance, then we are walking our path. If we then step into the concept that we have an authentic-self which is an energy form (the 3rd dimension) in a physical body, then we are growing towards enlightenment. This is a part of the development of our authentic-self, of our spiritual growth. At each stage of integrating the different dimensions we are bringing our energy state into balance. We have a choice to recognise and to upgrade which dimensions we care to work within. This book offers the potential to open some doors in your awareness and to redress any apparent imbalance which could lead you to being unknowingly stuck within the lower two dimensions.

Personal Development
Personal development is an expanding field covering a wide area as shown in diagram 1.10. It is much greater than simply the development of an individual as it also includes the development of other people involved with that individual. A good deal of research and practice goes into personal development and it has a dynamic structure. But, whether or not the development is personal, political, economic, organisational or whatever, a framework of reference is required to measure the changes that occur. Personal development presents an opportunity to increase awareness of what is happening to us and around us. It also offers

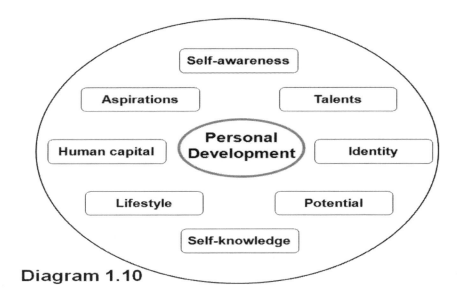

Diagram 1.10

an opportunity for us to broaden the decisions we make along our life's path. As I argued above, there is a strong bias in the development of the left-brain hemisphere in our educational curriculum (chapter 2). I would suggest that developing the right-brain hemisphere to a greater extent is a priority for survival in this 21st century.

By moving into the second paradigm (the sub-atomic or quantum world), and working through all of its five dimensions, integrating them within our consciousness, the framework of today's personal development training changes radically. In making these changes, we are moving into the world of the authentic-self and are more likely to find our true vocation in life. Ego is no longer the driver here, as the ego tends to be while operating within the first and second dimensions. These dimensions are part of the fabricated-self. I elaborate on the effects of ego in later chapters.

Most certainly, today's personal development includes developing the mind, body, emotions, and spirit. Diagram 1.10 focuses upon the mind, body and emotions, but what about spirit and the soul aspect? For most of us, only by recognising, accessing and working from the dimensions of the second paradigm can we truly empower ourselves. Following this path substantially increases our awareness and changes our perception of life.

How does this happen? It happens because there is a clearer understanding of the raison d'être for being here in a physical body. And what is that? We have a soul that works through the subtle energy bodies with our physical body and through our conscious mind, guiding us along our path, if we allow it to do so. Furthermore, the framework of personal development changes in unexpected ways. As you are aware, in both paradigms energy is the fifth dimension. Purely by thinking about and within this dimension enables us to bridge the gap between the life our fabricated-self perceives, and the life our authentic-self perceives. Both of these lives are mutually inclusive. They become merged into one after we have completed the process of dimension merging and balancing.

Once I recognised that the physical body is simply compressed energy and is part of an energy structure operating in an energy environment, it changed my life for the better. The real secrets behind such Universal Laws as the law of attraction, the law of expectations and so forth, unfolded. Attracting successful relationships, abundance, health and happiness took on new dimensions. How to boost them became clear. This book is designed, in part, to expand your awareness and to empower you to attract the life you desire. A key to unlocking this gift is the work you do with your authentic-self. Learning to work through your authentic-self awakens some amazing abilities that we all have but which usually lie dormant.

Ultimately, everything begins with a thought, which is, of course, energy, and this leads on to the next chapter.

Chapter 2

Empower your Destiny through the Fifth Dimension

By far the best proof is experience.

Sir Francis Bacon: 1561-1626

Empower your Destiny through the Fifth Dimension

Sitting at the back of a long haul Boeing 747 on an overnight transatlantic flight about 25 years ago, I read a short article where the subject of time travel was the main theme. What caught my attention was a statement that Einstein was reputed to have made:

*'the significant problems we face cannot be solved
at the level of thinking that created them'*

Why did it catch my attention? It caught my attention because I had never really thought about my thinking, or my thoughts to any great extent. Sure I did my best to get rid of any negative thoughts, or wrong thinking that arose every now and then. But I did not sit back to review just what was happening inside my head (my mind and consciousness). Why should I? I was on a roll and my life was quite exciting. I was achieving what I set out to do. But that article unknowingly pressed a button within me and raised my curiosity about consciousness, how the mind works and what part the brain plays in all of this.

Right at the beginning of everything is a thought, and I began my exploration into this chapter's content by studying the brain. Doing this was a bit like putting the 'cart before the horse'. I learnt a lot of technical facts, and although I quickly recognised the mechanics of the brain, I felt that something was missing. In fact there were two missing parts. The first part is that really we have three brains – one in the head which most of us are aware of and the other two in the heart and gut respectively, which only a few are aware of. The second part was – where is the mind? It took me quite some time to discover that it is not in the brain! What I really needed to do was to stop drilling down further into what was happening within the neuro-cells and synapses of the brain located in the grey jello-like matter in my head. I had to take a deep breath, clear my mind, take a step back and make a connection between energy, the mind and the brain. Yes, as some of you will probably have realised, it is all to do with the way I was thinking.

Einstein was right, and I had to go through a lengthy process of reframing my questions about the mind and brain to get onto the right path.

My next task was to investigate why we think the way we do. This involved understanding the effects that logic and reason, church and state, authority figures (past and present), the media and the soul, amongst others, all have on the way we think. Very quickly, I began to understand the reason we think the way we do. This chapter takes you through some of my findings, where I link consciousness with the fifth dimension (energy). To conclude the chapter, I present a very basic description of some parts of the brain, including the heart and gut brains, which I hope you will find useful. Understanding consciousness and the mind may help you to appreciate what is going on within that lump of grey matter that sits beneath your cranium – the brain.

The Most Powerful Energy Tool We Have is a Thought!

Understanding what a thought is, and the power it wields, has the potential to transform our life. A part of 'getting it' in life, whatever 'it' is, is the challenge to recognise the transformative or destructive property behind a thought. Thoughts send electrical signals throughout the brain and body. Thoughts contribute to programming the body's energy fields which act like a magnetic force-field attracting to us their very essence in terms of the relationships, situations, abundance activities and the events that we encounter. Thoughts have an effect upon the brain's and body's cells. Thoughts are, therefore, key drivers that affect self-development (personal and spiritual), happiness and wellbeing. An important characteristic to remember about a thought is that it's a subtle energy form (which is exceedingly small). Thanks to the concept of quantum entanglement the instantaneous effect a thought has on the body's cells can be understood. Another characteristic to note is, once again, that *energy follows thought*. Although a thought is a subtle energy form, it can have enormous power within us, affecting how we feel physically, depending upon the emotion that is attached to it. I elaborate on this later. A significant point to note is that negative thoughts should be regarded as energy pollution. Yes, you can even get pollution within the world of energy. How about that?

What creates a thought? Looking at something creates a thought; listening to something, feeling something, sensing something, tasting something, sometimes even doing nothing, creates a thought. (diagram 2.1).

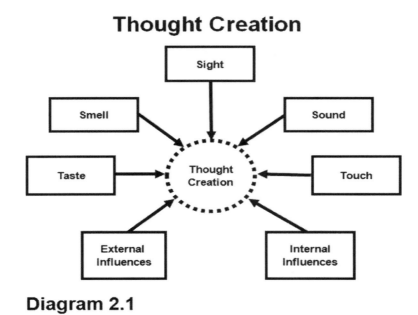

Diagram 2.1

Furthermore, a thought can be received from other external influences. For example, an individual can project a thought into your mind (telepathic transfer). When people look at television news this can create what can be called a mass mind thought (a collection of thoughts on a particular piece of news where each thought adds power, thus creating a thought cloud of energy which can affect other people's thought processes). Most importantly, the soul also creates thoughts which it imparts to us through the conscious mind, in the hope that we are listening.

There are times, when our thought processes can have a damaging effect on us both physically and emotionally, over the long-term. How does this happen? It happens because, as I said at the beginning of the chapter, thoughts are energy and energy follows thought. At a sub-atomic level where everything is connected, everybody can be affected at the same time. I say 'can' because there are ways to protect your-self from harmful mass mind negative thoughts. Scientists can measure thought generation from an individual's head by using what is called an electroencephalogram. Diagram 2.1 shows a basic selection of different sensory inputs (sight, sound, touch and so on) that provide a stimulus and information for the mind to create a thought.

Inner-self influences come from the authentic-self and are thoughts that are produced by the conscious, unconscious and higher conscious minds (see structure of the mind, diagram 2.4), the persona (through the unconscious mind) and the soul. External influences come from little discussed sources such as the effects of mass mind thoughts, discarnate thought forms, thought form fragments, discarnate souls, and so on. All thoughts flow through to the conscious mind and are translated by the brain into a form that we recognise. Consciousness and thoughts involve energy which operates outside of Newton's laws. They belong to the multi-dimensional, sub-atomic or quantum world that surrounds us. Entering the quantum world offers a pathway to begin to understand thoughts and the true nature of consciousness, plus what happens at different levels of consciousness.

A question arises first, though. What actually is a thought, and what does a thought do? A simple model of a thought will suffice to show its structure and the effects it has. Think of the dotted circle around the thought structure in diagram 2.2, as an energy bubble that has two energy components: information and an emotion/feeling that is attached to it. I define a feeling as the physical manifestation of an emotion within the body. A feeling stimulates action. For example, a feeling is the physical awareness you might experience in the solar plexus when something good or bad happens to you. An emotion is an inner sense of something (being happy or unhappy, content or discontent, comfortable or uncomfortable, love or hate, anxiety and fear, and so on).

Two key strong emotions that affect our life are love and hate. It is the emotion/feeling part of a thought that has the most potent energy content. Strong feelings have a powerful emotional and psychological effect or impact upon us. An ongoing correction that is slowly taking place within Western society is recognition of the need to pay attention to emotions/feelings as the major key to wellbeing, and I would suggest that rather than money being regarded as the cornerstone of society, which is probably what most people assume, emotions/feelings play a more important role. In the world of the fifth dimension (energy), whether we are looking at the physical or sub-atomic (quantum) world, emotions/feelings are all-powerful and need to flow. Most importantly, blockages in the flow of emotions/feelings cause dis-ease in many forms. I deal with this in more detail later.

Thought Structure and Effects

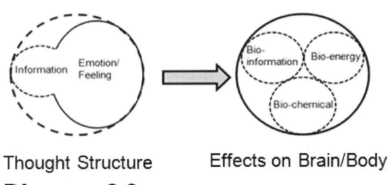

Thought Structure   Effects on Brain/Body

Diagram 2.2

As a thought is generated in the conscious mind, it affects the brain/mind system causing three measurable effects (diagram 2.2 on right-hand side). It creates a bio-information exchange in the brain/body system (right down to the body's cellular level) as well as a change in the brain/body's bio-chemistry and bio-energy. The last two, bio-chemistry and bio-energy, are more easily measured in today's hi-tech laboratories, but the first (bio-information) is hard to measure due to the difficulty in separating the information energy component and the emotional bio-energy component.

Thoughts can be categorised generally as positive, negative or neutral. Positive thoughts can have a constructive and healing effect on the brain/body system. Negative thoughts deplete the body's energy right down to the cell level. Moreover, negative thoughts can quickly build up to a level where they can cause damage to, and deplete, the human immune system, thus causing a state of dis-ease. I elaborate on the effect of thoughts on emotional and physical states later. If thoughts become repetitive, then the essence of the content of these thoughts get hardwired in the brain. For example, if you hate your job, or your partner, or have money difficulties and focus on this continually, then I can guarantee it will become hardwired in your brain. Each time you wake up in the morning a dominant thought in your mind will be about that awful job or, difficult partner or money problems! This can be dealt with in a satisfactory way, hopefully, without medication, and I provide you with some techniques to change this type of habit later. *Positive* thoughts that get hardwired, however, make a powerful contribution to your inner feeling of positive wellbeing and happiness. That is, provided they are not taken to an extreme.

There are three levels of intensity involved when thoughts arise in the conscious mind:

1. a primary level, where thoughts come and go without necessarily focusing on any of them for a period of time

2. a secondary level, where focus on a particular negative thought (unhappy about the job, or personal weight, or partner, or love life, or where life is taking you, or you have money worries and so on) can result in a negative train of thinking. At this level, therapy and the use of medication and/or complementary methods can be helpful for an individual to break the habit of focusing on those thoughts.

3. a third level of intensity called the tertiary level where focus on a negative thought, or a particular train of negative thoughts, occurs continuously. Strong drug therapy including complementary therapy is required here with psychological support to help return to normal.

Thoughts in the conscious mind come from different sources (diagram 2.1). We all have a conscious mind, but what is this mind and where is it located? Is it located in the brain? If not, where?

Where is the Mind Located?
Neuroscientists at the United States National Institute of Health (outside Washington DC) had by 1988 sufficient laboratory proof to suggest that the mind is a field which surrounds the body (diagram 2.3). They also had sufficient evidence which showed that the mind has an effect on the body right down to the level of the body's individual cells (the body has about 220 different types of cells). Previously, the old belief was that as a thought is generated, chemical messengers would be activated in the brain and travel through the bloodstream, triggering an appropriate change in the body's chemistry. This belief has changed. Similar to quantum physicists'

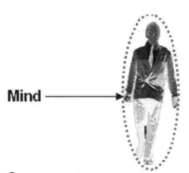

Diagram 2.3

discoveries about communication in the quantum world, neuroscientists discovered that there is an instantaneous awareness of an individual's emotions and thoughts at the cell level of the body.

I present below a detailed structure of the mind (conscious, unconscious and higher conscious mind) that I use for demonstration purposes. Most importantly, consciousness which forms our mind is located within a set of different subtle energy bodies surrounding the physical body and is not located in the brain. I elaborate on this in the next chapter. The mind's structure can be divided into three parts: the conscious mind, the unconscious mind and the higher conscious mind. The human brain is a bio-electrical/electronic device that detects thoughts from our consciousness after they go through a quantum collapse. A purpose of the brain is to translate the collapsed thought energy into a signal that we can understand. The brain is, therefore, the *mind processor.*

So what is the mind and how does it work? Is it possible to undo years of wrong or misguided thinking and false belief conditioning? And is it possible to change the brain's hard-wiring? Definitely, and I provide some techniques and processes on how to do the latter. One of the many challenges we face is to question what is happening to us and why it is happening, and it is only through this questioning that an enhanced perception can be developed. I hope this book will enhance your awareness and give you a more complete appreciation with respect to the events of your life. Consider the following wise words that Einstein is reputed to have said:

> *'the quality of the questions we ask determines the quality of the life we live'*

The choices we have and the decisions we make as we journey through life are indeed the greatest contributors to the quality of our life.

Structure of the Mind

To explore further the subject of the mind and consciousness, I believe that it may prove helpful to use the simple model I developed to demonstrate the mind's structure (diagram 2.4). This structure provides a framework to understand the mechanisms which are involved in our day to day life. In the above model the three individual parts are all components of our consciousness. Explaining each of the parts of consciousness may open a few more metaphorical doors in your awareness to help you on your journey.

Conscious Mind - the Thinking Operations Centre

The first mind I call the 'conscious mind'. This is where actual thought energy collapses into a recognisable form through the brain via the senses (diagram 2.1) including from both inner and external sources.

Model of the Body, Brain and Mind System

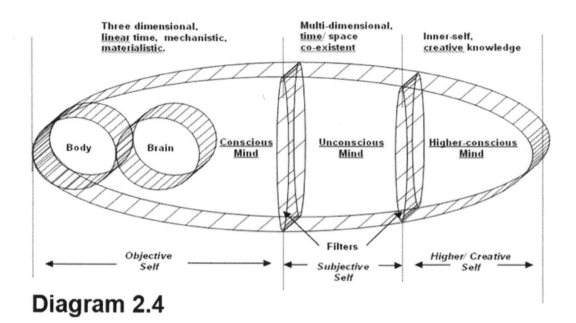

Diagram 2.4

The conscious mind is schooled into recognising the world as a mechanistic, form-based and linear-time-biased environment. These place an emphasis on developing the left-brain hemisphere (diagram 2.11, page 73). Nevertheless, the conscious mind can be looked at as the thinking operations centre where the ability to question what we are thinking about originates. There is an opportunity to reverse any negative thinking or negative tendencies within the conscious mind. Logic and reason are key drivers of the conscious mind and it can also be strongly influenced by emotions/feelings. The ego, free will and the persona communicate through to the conscious mind from the unconscious mind. The conscious mind's processing speed is far less than that of the unconscious mind. What I also found interesting from my research is that the soul communicates through the conscious mind by projecting words, or ideas, or intuitive thoughts, or dreams into it.

The conscious mind can also be regarded as the intelligence centre. But what is intelligence? It is the ability to compute (analyse) the various data inputs to the conscious mind and to make sense of them. These data inputs are gathered from the body's sensors, from academic learning, or experiencing and so forth. Intelligence has nothing to do with wisdom, which I define as the ability to extract the essence contained in a stream of data (information) under analysis. Those who continue to follow the path of gaining knowledge (absorbing and computing data) will discover that it is not possible to lay an original golden egg of knowledge. The conscious mind exists in layers of energy which thicken (become more dense) as more knowledge is absorbed. As the layers of conscious mind become denser, its working ability expands and in turn increases a framework of intelligence. The conscious mind operates within the linear time line of life.

The conscious mind is the home of the objective self, as shown in diagram 2.4. In reality, the conscious mind is made up of a part of each of the seven subtle energy bodies that surround the physical body. I describe each subtle energy body in detail in the next chapter. The term 'ego' is used to describe what I call the manager of the conscious mind operations centre. The rational self is expressed through the conscious mind. When we sleep, the conscious mind also rests.

Our authentic-self usually has difficulty communicating the soul's messages to us as we mature in age. Very early on in life, by about 7 years of age, the authentic-self begins to get pushed out of the thinking arena by the fabricated-self (see below). At this age the brain's prefrontal cortex begins to develop (our reasoning capability). By the time most individuals are in their teens, the authentic-self has been mostly cut off from communicating through to the conscious mind by the fabricated-self which takes over. Communication with the conscious mind can occur through dreams, but this can be unsatisfactory as interpreting dreams can be notoriously difficult. Western lifestyle does not promote a development of the authentic-self. Instead, as life progresses, the fabricated-self emerges more and more. Guess who is the main controller of the fabricated self? You probably guessed right – it is the ego! Now what is the difference between the fabricated-self and the authentic-self?

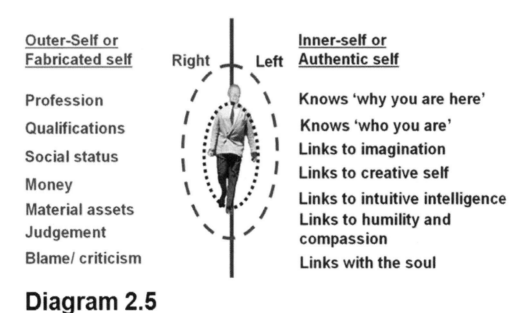

Diagram 2.5

Diagram 2.5 shows the main focus of both the fabricated and authentic selves by the time an individual has left education. To represent the outer/fabricated-self I use the large dash ellipse and for the inner/authentic-self, the dotted one. Ideally, both these ellipses should be merged together. The authentic-self is attenuated due to the influences (education, parents, media, authority figures and so forth) that have conditioned the individual. The ego-driven fabricated-self focuses upon professional development, qualifications, money, social status and so forth. A major life lesson for us all is to recognise these two selves and to merge them together. Once you question the world of the fabricated-self by asking *'is that all there is?'*, a door will open for the authentic-self to communicate with you more strongly.

Unconscious Mind – Multiple Programs Running 24/7

The second mind, the unconscious mind (it is also called the sub-conscious mind) never sleeps. It runs 24/7 and can be regarded as the subjective-self. The unconscious mind is separated from the conscious mind by what I envision to be energy filters, or gates. The filters or gates control the flow of thoughts between the two minds (unconscious and conscious). All thoughts and information from the conscious mind flow into the unconscious mind. They are, after being converted by the physical brain into the thought forms we recognise, stored in the brain. It is important to note that the thoughts are also stored, in their original form, in the subtle energy body structure.

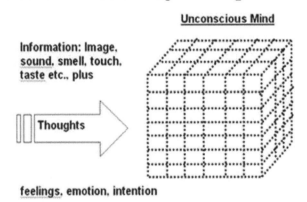

Diagram 2.6

As mentioned previously, thoughts flowing out from the unconscious mind to the conscious mind are managed by the ego, or free will, or the persona, or combinations of those. It is much easier to consider the information-retention capacity of the unconscious mind as a computer's solid state memory storage device, similar to a memory chip (diagram 2.6). The unconscious mind differs from the conscious mind in that it works in a multi-dimensional environment (more than four dimensions), which is a part of the subatomic world. It has no logic and reason and obeys all the instructions that pass through the conscious mind to it. The unconscious mind is very fast in comparison with the conscious mind.

Just imagine, all the thoughts you have had are stored within the unconscious mind (and the physical brain). Yes, including the good, the bad and the ugly! It is most important to realise that the intention behind a thought at an energy level is always followed through in some shape or form at a physical and emotional level. Raising awareness to the level of the fifth dimension, where infinite possibilities exist, there is a requirement to be even more aware of your thoughts. That is because you are now aware of the power that a thought has. This is good news because self-empowerment is possible which enables you to take control of your life, including your state of wellbeing, and your destiny. You can begin to write an actual life story that brings out your best attributes, and to live them. The challenging news is, though (and I initially found the following concept quite difficult to accept), that as we are operating in an energy environment we are 100 percent responsible for what happens to us individually. My fabricated-self rejects the concept because of ego, but my authentic-self accepts it.

In the unconscious mind there is no time or space because they are co-existent. Many things are happening, unknown to us, at higher dimensions (5 or more) due to the interaction of different thought forms. Thoughts are continually running within the unconscious mind in a loop and are never dormant. In diagram 2.2, an incoming thought has two components: a combination of information - energy in the form of an image, sound, smell, taste, touch or other sensory input, and an emotion/feeling. Intentions of future plans together with a supporting emotion/feeling begin in the conscious mind. These flow continuously into the unconscious mind until they are neutralised. It is important to realise that the brain only stores information which is a copy of the same information already stored in the third subtle energy body that is the centre of the intellect (next chapter). It requires the intellect and an emotion (the second subtle energy body), plus the information physically stored in the brain to work together so as to understand and relate to what is going on around us.

A thought has direct access to an associated emotion/feeling. At the quantum level the connection between information and emotions/feelings is instantaneous. For example, if you observe some large spiders or snakes, which make you fearful, this information would be transmitted from the conscious mind to the unconscious mind to form a reference library of spiders and snakes. Information is recorded within the brain and the third subtle energy body. The emotions/feelings associated with each thought would also be stored in its own reference library (second subtle energy body) and linked to the information part of the thought. Emotions/feelings energy also get physically stored in different parts of the physical body. Hence, if you spotted a spider or snake (or even thought about them), it may produce a very strong negative emotion which results in a strong physical feeling within, say, the solar plexus. That may get translated instantaneously into sweating. This would originate from the emotions/feelings reference library (see below). It would also cause a change within the adrenal glands, perhaps triggering a fright and flight response. The memory storage of the unconscious mind functions as a direct access information matrix device and there is no delay in retrieving any information.

To promote a greater understanding of the storage of information and emotions at a sub-atomic level, the following may prove to be of interest. Since the early 1980s, Russian scientists (at St Petersburg University and elsewhere) have had some success in studying the likelihood of matrices of information being stored on elementary particles that enter the earth's atmosphere on a regular basis. These scientists were exploring the correlation between periods of enlightenment on the planet and the showers of these particles. It is considered that the great creative geniuses (scientists, artists, engineers and so forth), going back through history, unknowingly had an ability to tune into the wave of particles which contained information matrices that were flowing through at the time. These particles, plus their associated information, are purely and simply packages of vibrating energy. Now quantum physicists today are working towards storing information on a molecule. The question arises, how long before they are able to do it? And how long before a level of technology that will store information on an atom is in place? Does this seem to lack credibility? It is certainly not impossible, as we observed in the earlier discussion about 'imagination' (chapter 1). It is all a matter of technology, which is driven by a scientist's imagination and his or her creative ability, plus, of course, time and money.

To summarise, from birth (and sometimes earlier) up to the present, thoughts are generated and stored for future reference in the physical brain and third subtle energy body. Emotions are stored in the second subtle energy body and in the physical body. Hypnotherapists can extract the finest details of these thoughts and emotions. They do this by taking the patient into their unconscious mind to extract appropriate information that was recorded while they were in their mother's womb, right through to the present time. What is really spooky here is that regression hypnotherapists can also induce an individual to travel further back in time within their unconscious mind, in order to identify an important issue/situation that has been carried over from a previous lifetime and is causing them a problem in this lifetime. Once located, it is possible to deal with the issue/situation by applying a healing protocol. This is achieved by accessing information/emotions stored within the appropriate unconscious mind parts of the subtle energy bodies and also the brain and physical body. Once accessed, the information part can be re-scripted and the emotion brought into balance or removed and replaced by a positive one. What is important here is to understand that time and space are *co-existent* in the unconscious mind. There is only 'now'.

Intuition (Hunches) and Intuitive Intelligence

Diagram 2.7 shows a representation the body's different senses that are part of the human sensor network. It is an expansion of diagram 2.1 at the beginning of the chapter. The senses around the inner circle are the classic ones that we are taught at school and include sight, sound, touch, taste and smell. There are five additional senses that should be considered. These are shown within the outer circle and are:

Body's Sensory mechanisms

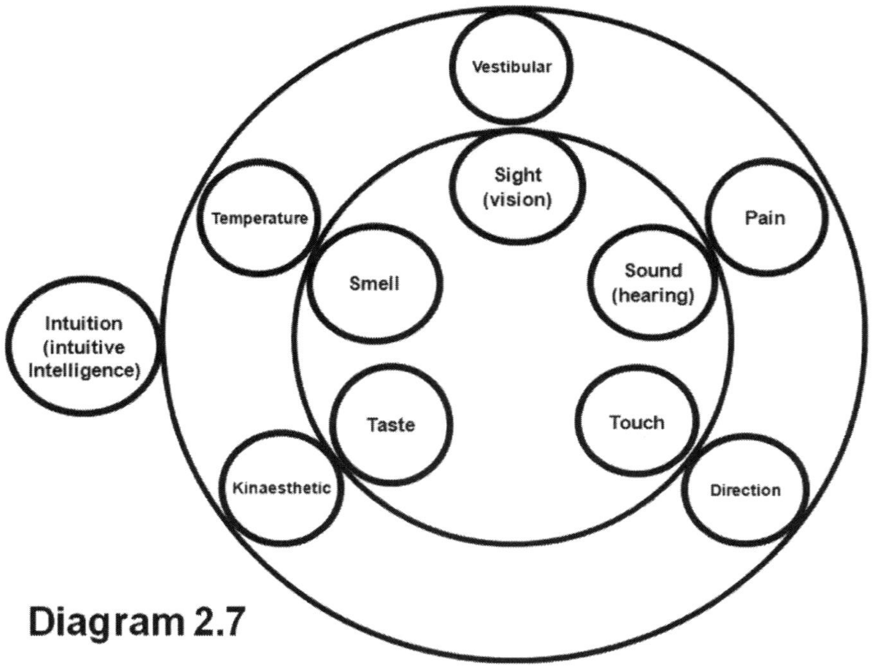

Diagram 2.7

vestibular – balance and acceleration

pain – warning of potential problem (nociception)

direction – directional awareness (magnetoception)

kinaesthetic – sense of relative positioning of body parts (proprioception)

temperature – sense of heat and cold internally/externally (thermoception)

We also have what is popularly called a sixth sense, 'intuition', that is mostly given a bad press, especially from academics. They find intuition difficult to quantify and, therefore, tend to reject it. Yet top scientists, business people and others value intuition greatly. It is an important key to achieving success. In this 21st century, to have a powerful intuition is a must if we are to successfully meet the upcoming challenges in life. Each of us has a 'sixth sense' which links with intuition (hunch capability) that operates out of the second and fifth subtle energy bodies (Chapter 3). As these bodies operate at a sub-atomic level it means that there is only now – no past or present, because time and space are co-existent. Hence, someone with a psychic ability can sense, or even see, something in the future which has a probability of happening.

It is possible to practise your psychic ability by entering into and travelling within the unconscious mind. I call this 'multi-dimensional communication' (see below), which is a natural human attribute. Someone who can see a potential future event happening, say for an individual, is clairvoyant, and can actually see the event in their mind. However, the reality of the vision they see has a probability attached to it as to whether or not it will actually manifest. If the probability of the vision manifesting is small it will most likely not happen. The higher the probability the more likely the vision will actually manifest. The probability is dependent on the choices/decisions the individual makes and what is happening in their life. Each of us has free will and may make a choice, or take a decision that can change the course we take in life and which in turn changes events and activities in the future. Where there is a high probability of something happening, no matter what changes an individual makes, it is going to happen.

Diagram 2.8 shows a CEO of a company who is on his way to a board meeting where three important decisions need to be made that will affect the future of his company.

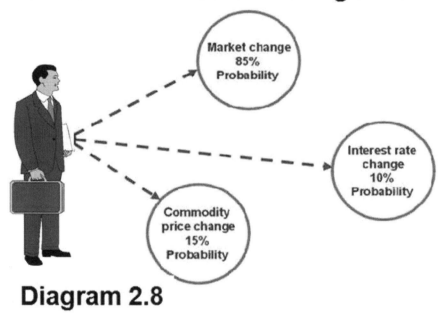

Diagram 2.8

He spent the weekend reading through the company's business plan, which provided convincing data and conclusions that there would be no change in the sales market the following year; interest rates were forecast to increase by mid-year and there was only a small chance of a price increase in the commodities the company uses. His gut feel (intuition) was telling him that he sensed a consumer market change in their favour (an 85 percent chance). In addition, he did not feel that interest rates would increase (quite the opposite to what the experts were saying!). He felt that there was only a 10 percent chance (very small) of them increasing. And his gut feel was that the commodities market would remain flat for a least another year (only a 15 percent chance of an increase). He

65

voted against the board and persuaded the marketing and sales team to make a substantial increase in sales. He also instructed the finance director to make an appropriate increase in the company's working capital and lines of credit. His intuition proved correct and the company had a bumper year. The CEO also enhanced his intuitive intelligence by looking at different charts/graphs to get a feel for patterns of market and consumer behaviour. This helped him to get a feel for whether or not banks would raise their interest rates and whether or not commodity prices would increase, and by how much.

Free will and intuition are always interesting subjects to explore, but doing so can be difficult at times. A close American friend once told me a story. He has some friends who are Jewish and former Polish nationals. Their parents left Poland in 1932 and travelled to the United States where they did very well in business. In 1938, they returned to Poland with sufficient money to bring their relations back to America with them. A few who lived in the country and in Warsaw refused to leave Poland even though it would not have cost them anything. The ones who used their intuition and went to the United States prospered and the ones who remained behind died in concentration camps in 1942. Some of those who remained in Poland did try to escape later but were captured. It seems, therefore, that certain things cannot be changed even if we want to change them. These events are what I call 'pre-destined', that is there is a high probability (of, say, above 80 percent) that they would occur.

Whenever I bring up the subject of intuition at business meetings, some executives react very negatively. It makes them feel quite uncomfortable. The concept becomes more acceptable when I inform those involved that I am really talking about 'gut feelings' and 'hunches'. However, intuition alone can be a dangerous tool unless it is backed up by what I call intuitive intelligence. Later in this book, I show how to reconnect with intuition/intuitive intelligence, especially for those who are disconnected.

The notion of intuitive intelligence certainly makes sense, taking into consideration that everything experienced is stored in the mental (Intellect) and emotional subtle energy body fields and in the brain. A rich storehouse of experience is created which is enhanced over time. If an intuitive thought arises, then the emotion that is associated with this thought is drawn from the emotional subtle body energy field. In other words, if an intuitive thought feels good or bad it is because it is accompanied by an appropriate positive or negative emotion/feeling. Just to use intuition alone, in some circumstances, could be disastrous. Common sense plays its part when an intuitive thought cuts in. For example, if you are a pilot of a passenger aircraft, sitting at the end of a runway in a snow storm and your intuition is telling you to go, common sense (part of your intuitive intelligence) would take precedence. What does the flight manual say? If it says 'stand down', then for the safety of the passengers and your own safety, it would be advisable to abort take off.

In summary, decisions can be influenced by intuitive intelligence operating from the brain as past experiences are stored there. Moreover, the authentic-self operating through the soul will have a feel for the future. This is because the soul is operating from the sub-atomic world where, once again, time and space are co-existent. Nothing is absolutely certain in the future and there is a probability from 0 percent to 99 percent of something happening. This will provide a gut feeling which can affect the decision to be made. Some techniques such as hypnotherapy time-lining (a method of entering the unconscious mind to view what is happening) can be a way to verify an individual's intuitive accuracy. Hypnotic regression can also be used to accurately look into the past, drilling down to the finest level of detail. Forecasting the future can be a bit tricky though, as each of us is capable of changing the future to a degree purely and simply by a change of thinking and intention. Such an influence can affect the choice/decision that will be made. It will also have an effect upon what we attract or are attracted to.

Higher Conscious Mind
There is no computing activity in higher consciousness. The goal of higher consciousness is to exist within all the data/information that has been gathered and received throughout eternity without any judgement and without the need to carry out any computation. The mission of our higher consciousness is to simply filter the data/information and to be within it. Should you move up from your conscious mind into the realm of higher consciousness and just observe the streams of data/information there, you will automatically know the answer without having to carry out any computation. This is the equivalent of being a savant who never needs to ask anything but knows the answer. Everything exists at the level of higher consciousness – all time, space, knowledge, information and so forth. Therefore, the higher self knows all and waits for the authentic-self to strengthen its connection with it, or reconnect if the connection has been broken.

Not everyone is expected to connect with their higher self during their lifetime, especially new souls experiencing their early incarnations. An individual may have an epiphany during their lifetime - such an experience occurs momentarily when they unknowingly travel up into their higher consciousness and return with a full understanding of something that they need to know in their lifetime. This is one of those moments where they have 'seen the light', in metaphorical terms.

During the first year of birth, each of us is at an original or authentic state (diagram 2.9). In this state, we are about to begin interacting with family, relations, friends, teachers, authority figures and so forth. The authentic-self, as shown by the solid blue ellipse on the left in this diagram, has a basic ego (solid red inner shape) and a persona brought in with it, plus a contribution transferred genetically and energetically from the parents. The authentic-self is

Intuition and Intuitive Intelligence

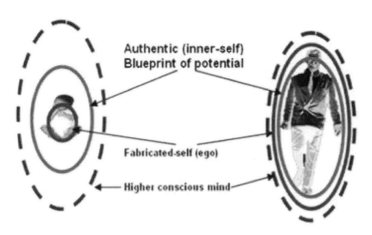

Diagram 2.9

not a clean slate at birth as is commonly thought, it comes part programmed (ego, free will and persona). Further programming that occurs after birth will also affect the ego and persona. Think of the ego as a suit of clothes that expands or contracts according to our size (where we are in terms of personal growth). And the persona, plus the personality masks that develop as we journey through life, will be affected to ensure that we attract the most appropriate experiences because of our quantum bio-magnetic attraction field (chapter 3). The right-hand shape in diagram 2.9 represents a typical adult who is run by their fabricated self. The authentic-self is subservient here to the fabricated self.

A child is only able to observe, feel, listen to and imitate what the surrounding giants (family, relations, authority figures, teachers and so on) are doing and saying. The child's conscious mind still manages to maintain a direct connection with the authentic-self, its soul and with the higher-self or higher conscious mind (see the outer broken ellipse in both shapes in diagram 2.9). As pointed out above, the higher-self knows all and is connected through to different levels of higher knowledge and expression. The higher self is, in my understanding, our spirit, and knows the soul's purpose. The soul is like a fragment of the spirit, like a piece of a hologram that communicates through the authentic-self. We all have a purpose, which is contained in what can be loosely called a contract or directive. The higher conscious mind is separated from the unconscious mind by an energy filter or gate (diagram 2.4).

For many people, the connection through to their higher conscious mind quickly gets isolated from the authentic-self, as their path in life may not require that channel to remain fully open. Those who seek enlightenment, or embark on creative endeavours during their life, usually re-connect with (if it has been disconnected) and strengthen the communication flow associated with this channel. Some schools and universities have only recently begun to recognise and teach methods that enable students to access their individual, unique, creative potential. Relaxation techniques to quieten the conscious mind and techniques to contact their creative higher consciousness (right-brain hemisphere linking through to higher consciousness) are used as a basis to successfully achieve such potential.

Rudolf Steiner, a gifted and far-sighted Austrian, set up special schools called Waldorf schools, during the early 1900s, to ensure that children did not lose the connection to their inner creative abilities. Rudolf Steiner schools are still open and teach children to develop mentally, emotionally and physically with an open belief system. Steiner was particularly concerned with the rapid development of sciences in a materialistic direction from the end of the 19th century. He established a scientific model that highlighted a need for homeopathic methods in medicine, organic methods in agriculture, an artistic approach to architecture, a compassionate approach to government and an inspired approach to education.

Today in public education, the main focus is on attainment and on gaining recognition within the professions, an approach that is highly dependent upon development of the intellect and recall of information. Achievement, in terms of the holistic development of individuals through the integration of the right and left hemispheres of the brain and a focus on emotional intelligence and insight remains an elusive concept. Still, many at the top of their profession have got there by knowing when to rely on their intuition and intuitive intelligence in comparison with what analysis is showing or their intellect is telling them. It is all about recognising the power of multi-dimensional communication.

Multi-dimensional Communication
What, then, is multi-dimensional communication? Creative scientists, artists, engineers, clairvoyants, clairaudients, clairsentients, gurus, savants, shamans, dowsers and so on, all have an ability to naturally tune into their unconscious mind and some into their higher-self and beyond. The conscious mind usually works sequentially through the tasks presented to it, operating and communicating within the present. However, the unconscious mind offers an interface to tuning into some amazing talents that may be lying dormant within you. We should remember that the imagination, that all-powerful bridge to the creative self, intuition and intuitive intelligence, operates within the unconscious mind, just waiting for you to tune in. Opening a door to the unconscious mind presents an opportunity to join the ranks of the world's great creative thinkers.

As stated earlier in this chapter, the unconscious and higher conscious minds have some quite extraordinary properties. In diagram 2.10, the unconscious mind is represented by the horizontal axis. This axis represents the subjective-self which operates within the unconscious mind and has the ability to look into the probability of something happening in the future and to connect with what has happened on the timeline of the past. People with precognitive abilities and those involved with divination tune into their unconscious mind which allows them to go backwards or forwards in time, depending on the questions asked. Those who wish to tune into their natural creative abilities do so through accessing the unconscious mind. I will provide you with a technique to do this. The vertical axis represents a communication channel to the higher-self and higher consciousness which has a capability to tap into different levels of higher consciousness, knowledge and expression. This level represents the source of infinite knowledge. Mediums who contact departed souls are able to communicate within specific levels of what is called the astral plain. It is a bit like having a bio-telephone link with the world of spirit. Higher creative understanding and thinking is accessed above the astral plane.

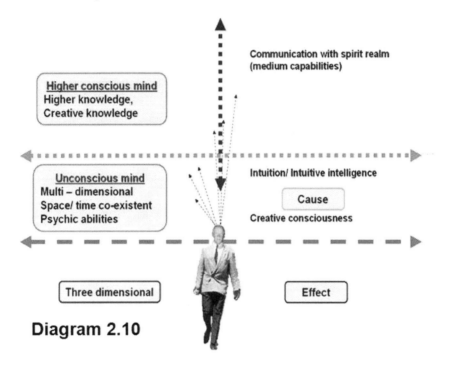

Diagram 2.10

An example of someone using multi-dimensional communication may clarify how it works. Leonardo de Vinci, amongst others, had a natural capability to tap into his individual level of higher creative expression. I must emphasise here that it was part of his soul's contract to do so. He also had the practical skills, which were developed at a lower creative level, to complete his work. He was, therefore, able to translate his creative thoughts and to express them through his conscious mind into a material form. His paintings, sculptural works and inventions are truly 'out of this world'! In comparison, a Bedouin tribesman may be able to visualise and sense Einstein's theory of relativity, but if he does not have the basic creative skill set at the lower level to understand and translate it in his conscious mind to give a meaningful explanation, then it may turn out to be just gobbledygook to him. On the other hand, he may impress his fellow Bedouin tribesmen around the camp fire with his philosophical views on time and space! It is all about the individual's different levels of creative expression that they bring with them into their life.

A more recent example is where the development of television unfolded over time with many people contributing to the final outcome. At the beginning, the development of television moved in two directions. One direction was by using an electro/mechanical device to scan a picture. This was invented by a famous Scottish inventor John Logie Baird as well as by a German inventor called Paul Nikov in 1895. Baird studied at a Scottish technical college while developing his device, which he completed in 1926. The mechanical transmission and receiver device was a rotating solid wheel with lots of holes in it which broke the image being observed down into packets of light which were received on a photoelectric cell and decoded through electronic circuitry to a cathode ray tube. He was able to visualise the system working in his imagination from where he went about manifesting it into physical reality.

Another inventor of television, who developed an electronic scanning device, was a poor mid-West farmer's son called Philo Taylor Farmsworth. He dreamt about electronic circuitry when he was asleep and could also visualise and see this circuitry in his imagination when he was awake. He had no training in this field. Creative thoughts came to him while he was mowing wheat using a horse-driven harvester in a straight line along his father's fields. Farmsworth realised that an electron beam could scan a picture horizontally and that this could be reformed and looked at on a dissector tube (a type of cathode ray tube) that he invented. He formed his own company later but was badly treated by leading television development companies of the time who needed his invention, not having been able to develop it successfully themselves.

To Achieve Greatness, it's Time to Change
Because Western education influences the mind and brain in a particular direction, the connection or channel through to the imagination, intuition, creative self and higher self is usually cut off or attenuated to a great degree. For some this can be temporary. People in Western societies are unknowingly being held back to a great degree by the way the education system works. What does this do to them? Although achievement in intellectual pursuits and the recall of facts is a principal measurement of success in Western Society, there are four disadvantages that arise from this. These are that:

1. by focusing on the development of the intellect and retention of information (gaining knowledge), the left-brain hemisphere is developed to the detriment of the right-brain hemisphere (the centre of creative thinking, intuition and so on). We are, unknowingly, out of balance.

2. feelings and emotions (an important sensory ability that everybody has) are given little, if any, attention. This greatly affects the development of emotional intelligence capabilities I explore this in more detail later.

3. the development of our belief system (what is accepted as true) is compromised. This teaches us to think within a limited virtual box that is controlled by the intellect.

4. Our ability to grow in perceptiveness (how we see ourselves and the world around us) is also compromised.

This book attempts to undo these disadvantages. Some important keys to unlocking the doors to our true capabilities can be obtained from understanding how the brain is structured and how the mind and energy bodies link with the brain and physical body. A synopsis of some important parts of the brain and what they do is given below. Details of the structure of consciousness are presented in the next chapter.

The Human Brain – a Dynamic, Neuroplastic, Regenerating Structure
Mainstream brain research experts worldwide still believe that the mind is part of the brain, even though there is growing evidence that points to this not being the case. How is it possible to change this thinking? Getting out of the limited virtual box of thinking by raising awareness to the fifth dimension of both physical and quantum realities is a first step forward to breaking the mould of limited thinking. It is all about recognising the strengths and weaknesses of solely using the intellect in research, as against using the intellect with a strong intuitive intelligence. In the old days, brain scientists believed that an adult brain was mainly unalterable, hardwired and rigid in its functions. They also believed that when people reached adulthood they were stuck with what they had. How untrue! Old beliefs (and these were, unknowingly at the time, false beliefs) die hard. The same is true about understanding intuition and intuitive intelligence. There were no suitable experiments in a laboratory to prove the power of intuition so it was effectively rejected and binned.

Most of the great scientists use their intuition (hunch capability) at the right time. It is that which makes them great. Certainly, as commented upon above, top successful business people rely on their intuition and intuitive intelligence in their decision making. My own basic research and experience has enabled me to substantiate that the brain is like a very sophisticated, dynamic, self-repairing, biological (electrical/chemical) machine which is, of course, an integral part of the physical body. Furthermore, describing the brain as a bio-electrical/electronic device that translates external information from the senses, internal information from the physical body, and information from the subtle energy bodies plus their interconnected energy circuits, is closer to reality. Neuroscientists have been able to show in the laboratory the dynamic nature of the brain, thanks to quantum physics-based measuring devices like the functional Magnet Resonance Imaging (fMRI) scanners. They call this dynamic nature of the brain 'neuroplasticity'.

During the Vietnam war, there were cases where young soldiers had a considerable amount of their brain shot away. These soldiers managed, with training, to lead a near normal life after rehabilitation. It is now scientifically recognised that because of the neuroplastic nature of the brain you can retrain the brain, even after a severe stroke or deep depression, to return to a near normal life. This retraining means that as someone grows older their brain does not need to decay – it can be trained to grow more neuro-connections: a touch of the 'if you don't use it, you'll lose it'. Or, if you feel that you have lost some neuro-connections, then you can grow some more. What does this mean?

It means that for each of us our future wellbeing rests in our own hands. We all have a continuing opportunity to retrain our brain and mental faculties throughout our life. People who have had a stroke can now receive a treatment called constraint-induced movement therapy. If they have lost the use of, say, their right arm, this therapy enables them to train a part of their brain which is close to the motor cortex (the part of the brain that controls the arm movement) to take over the task of moving the right arm. They effectively rewire that part of their brain to do the job of moving the right arm by changing its structure and function. Most importantly, they do this using their thinking processes! It is a sort of 'mind sculpting'.

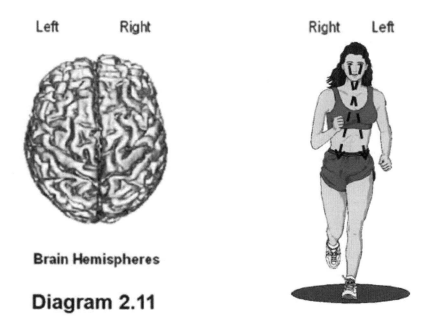

Brain Hemispheres

Diagram 2.11

The brain has an amazing dynamic structure which has the ability to do just about anything you want it to do - provided you know how to access it and make it work for you. The brain, or cerebrum, as shown in diagram 2.11, is divided into two parts: the left-brain hemisphere and the right-brain hemisphere. The brain's left hemisphere controls the right-hand side of the body and the right-brain hemisphere controls the left-hand side of the body. Both hemispheres are joined together in the middle through what is called the corpus collosum, and they work together. What is it that each brain hemisphere does? First, it is best to look at the brain as an information-processing organ integrating the various sensory inputs (amongst other functions) as indicated in diagrams 2.1 and 2.7. Second, to look at what the left and right hemispheres do. Each brain hemisphere is responsible for processing different elements of consciousness and activities, for example:

Left-brain hemisphere responsible for:	**Right-brain hemisphere responsible for:**
Logic, reasoning, writing, language, music	imagination, intuition, creative, art, arithmetic creative, ideas, visualisation, holistic expression
Analysing details	Putting together the big picture Spatial – judging position in space
Understanding and memory for spoken and written messages	Understanding and memory for things we do and see
Capacity to conceptualise and understand actual details	Provides instantaneous access to large parts of knowledge
Builds on information already there	Provides instantaneous access to large parts of knowledge
Wants structure, predictability and orderly instructions	Likes to be open ended, surprises and to go with the flow
Home of fabricated self/ego	Negative emotions
Processes positive emotions	Processes negative emotions
Social emotions (happiness)	Primary emotion such as fear
Intellect – IQ	**Emotional Intelligence - EQ**

The brain hemisphere comparison above is self-explanatory and provides a basic understanding about what each hemisphere does. Both hemispheres participate in analyzing sensory data. They perform memory functions and facilitate the learning of new information. In addition, they are also involved in the formation of thoughts (downloaded from the mind) and participate in decision making. Thought energy, from the subtle body energy fields (Chapter 3) goes through a quantum collapse and is received by appropriate parts of the brain. It is then translated into a thought form that we understand.

Both brain hemispheres are divided into a number of different functional parts. I shall describe a few of them so that we can understand how they affect us. Neuroscientists are discovering that each of the different parts of the brain is much more multi-purpose than was previously thought. As a range of activities and thinking tasks are conducted, different parts of the brain can become activated instantaneously depending on the complexity of the task. This is viewed on fMRI scanner's monitoring devices to investigate which parts of the brain are being utilised.

Taking a side view of the brain, as shown in diagram 2.12, there are six areas or parts that I want to explore with you. These parts are called the Frontal Lobe, Parietal Lobe, Occipital Lobe, Temporal Lobe, Cerebellum, and Brain Stem. They are located on both the left- and right-brain hemispheres. As I describe these different parts I will also indicate which ones are affected and are illuminated on an fMRI brain scan monitor when we feel happy, or depressed, or meditate, or pray, or practise psychic techniques like channelling or precognition.

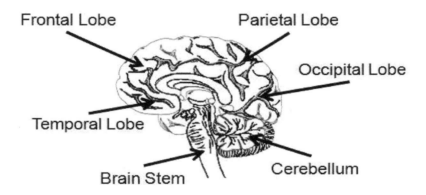

Diagram 2.12

Frontal Lobe (Prefrontal Cortex)
Neuroscientists consider this part to be responsible for consciousness. It influences the ability to concentrate and to elaborate on any thinking. The ability to engage in critical thinking, or forward thinking, or problem solving, or to make judgements, is all a part of the functions of the Frontal Lobe. If there is any short attention span, or lack of perseverance, or disorganised behaviour, or procrastination, then these are caused by a problem within the Frontal Lobe. It is a centre of emotional attributes, empathy, beliefs, intentions and desires. When people are happy, or feeling positive the left pre-frontal lobe is very active. In comparison, should they feel depressed, this increases the right pre-frontal lobe activity. The Frontal Lobe controls emotional responses and is responsible for personality mannerisms. It controls how people express themselves in terms of language and words used. Recurring negative thoughts (that is, automatic negative thoughts, or ANTs) are associated with the

right-hand side of this lobe. During deep relaxation (or meditation) the left Frontal Lobe becomes active. Seasoned monks can cause an overflow of positive energy, resulting from a compassionate mediation, to transfer into the right frontal lobe when they meditate. Lots of the problems associated with the Frontal Lobe can be solved through retraining the brain.

Parietal Lobe

The Parietal Lobe processes input from the body's senses (touch, feeling of physical pressure, temperature, pain and so on) and allows us to discriminate between them. It allows for the integration of different senses to enable understanding of a concept. It deals with eye/hand co-ordination and body orientation. It is a centre for visual attention and touch perception, and contributes to arithmetic and spelling abilities. At the front of the Parietal lobe is the sensory cortex which contributes to the control of perception and how sensation and movement is interpreted.

Occipital Lobe

What we see (vision) and how we visually interpret things and identify colours is controlled by the Occipital Lobe. It can initiate hallucinations and visual illusions. It is important in word recognition, reading and writing. The Occipital Lobe interprets movement of objects and the ability to recognise drawn shapes.

Temporal Lobe

The left temporal lobe is the dominant one and has several functions such as the understanding and processing of language, visual and auditory processing of the retrieval of words, auditory memory, long-term memory, and so on. When an individual has violent thoughts, or shows aggressive behaviour, or is irritable, or emotionally unstable, then this indicates a problem within the left Temporal Lobe. The less dominant right Temporal Lobe is responsible for recognising facial expressions and body language, music ability, rhythm, visual learning and the decoding of vocal intonation. Problems within the right Temporal Lobe usually show themselves as fearfulness, or anger of some sort.

In summary, the Temporal Lobe processes what is heard, and is involved in the understanding of spoken words. It is involved in short or long-term memory, the identification and verbalisation of objects. It is involved in the increase or decrease in sexual behaviour. It has a controlling influence on how talkative people are and on their behaviour. A key feature of the Temporal Lobe is that it becomes activated through different experiences in life. Writing a more positive story as you journey along life's path will keep this Lobe healthy and supportive. These stories affect your quantum bio-magnetic field attraction properties (chapter 3). So learn to look for the good news in each experience you have. Try to keep recalling the good news experiences. Why? Because the human brain automatically has a preference to lock onto negative experiences and thoughts.

Your challenge is to keep a balance and drift toward the positive - not the negative.

Amygdala

Located within the Temporal Lobe, the Amygdala carries out some primary roles in forming and storing memories associated with emotional events. It sends impulses to the hypothalamus (see below) to activate the sympathetic nervous system as well as to other parts of the brain/body. The Amygdala is involved in the creation of fear responses.

Brain Stem

The brain stem controls breathing, heart rate, temperature, sweating, swallowing, digestion, reflexes (seeing and hearing) without having to think about it. It controls the ability to sleep, affects alertness, sense of balance, and also perception.

Cerebellum

The Cerebellum has the task of co-ordinating any voluntary movement, balance and equilibrium. It is connected to different parts of the brain. It is responsible for contributing to the speed with which limbs move (motor function). It is also responsible for how quickly the mind works (mental function).

There are four other parts of the brain which are of interest as they affect our life experience negatively when out of balance. The problem here is if they are negatively affected over a period of time, say a few days or more, the cause of the negativity (automatic negative thoughts) can get hardwired into our personality behaviour. If this happens, the persona needs to be brought back into balance. Thanks to the brain's neuroplastic nature, it is possible to do this though special exercises. Stress has a powerful effect on the brain/mind/body system and it is wise to take care to bring any stress down whenever it is detected. I suggest how you can do this later. The other four parts of the brain I want to emphasise are the:

1. Cingulate System

The Cingulate system or Cingulate Gyrus links from deep within through to the Frontal Lobes of the brain. It affects the following:

- ability to see options open to you in life
- feelings of safety and security
- ability to manage change
- level of co-operation with others
- ability to accept new ideas
- ability to go with the flow in life

- o tendency towards compulsive behaviour
- o tendency to have repetitive negative thoughts
- o being very upset if things are not done a certain way
- o tendency to say no without thinking about the question
- o tendency to predict negative outcomes
- o ability to shift attention from subject to subject
- o behaviour with respect to road rage

When the Cingulate System gets out of balance, due to a child or adult being stuck in a negative form of thinking or behaviour, logic and reason cannot be applied to sort out the situation. At best a statement can be made that will plant the seed for what you want them to do. This will allow their unconscious mind to process the statement. It may take some time before the child or adult involved responds. Sometimes, reverse psychology may have to be used by asking the opposite of what is wanted. Most important of all, rather than giving direct orders, it is best to try to make it look as if the change that is wanted is their idea. Ask for the person's input and get them to give you some feedback on the request or statement made.

2. Basal Ganglia System

The basal ganglia system is located towards the centre of the brain and is a set of large structures that surround the deep limbic system (see below). It is involved with integrating thoughts, feelings and movement. It is very sensitive and reacts to what we are involved in. When it is:

- o over active it is because of a state of anxiety, increased awareness, heightened fear or a high level of tension.
- o under active it can cause problems with spontaneity, motivation and energy level.

The basal ganglia system is very sensitive to thoughts, especially when one enters into a state of repetitive negative thinking.

3. Deep Limbic System

The deep limbic system is located close to the centre of the brain. It processes the sense of smell and has an involvement in emotions by enabling us to experience and express them. If we have a passion, or emotion, or a desire to make things happen in life, then the deep limbic system is involved. It does not store highly charged emotional memories. It is the receiving centre of the brain that communicates with the second subtle energy body (the Emotional body, chapter 3). It sets the emotional tone in events involving the individual, causing them to be in either a:

positive and hopeful state of mind when its activity is low, or a *negative state of mind when it is more active, letting emotions take over.*

Different situations and experiences that arise in life cause distinct emotions to be associated with them. There is a tagging of emotions to a particular thought, image, sound or smell that creates an action or avoidance response which can be critical for survival. The deep limbic system has an effect on the sleep patterns, moods, motivation, appetite cycles, bonding, social connectedness and sexuality. It provides a filter to interpret the experiences of day to day events.

4. Hypothalamus

The hypothalamus is divided into two parts and is located at the base of the brain. It is a part of the deep limbic system and is called the brain within the brain. It is very much the control centre within the brain, managing the flow of various neurochemicals to different parts of the brain and body (autonomic regulatory activities). Its main function is to maintain the body's status quo. It manages the brain-body connections and forms a link from the mind to the body. The hypothalamus controls many complex emotions, feelings, moods and motivational states. It controls the amount of pleasure experienced and has an effect on creative activities. The hypothalamus also controls levels of hunger, appetite and the amount of food we eat.

It would be remiss of me not to say a few words about another two brains that we have which are beginning to receive increased media attention. What are these brains?

Two Other Remarkable Brains: the Heart and the Gut

Who would have thought that the heart and gut would have a brain of their own? Of course, these two brains are in constant communication with the main brain in the head. What do they do?

Heart Brain

Throughout history the heart has been recognised as a centre that influences our emotions and decision-making capability. Neuroscientists have made some interesting discoveries which show that the heart is a more complex organ than was previously recognised. They discovered that the heart has its own independent nervous system with its own neurons similar to those found in the sub-cortical centres of the brain. Now the heart communicates with the brain in four different ways:

1. neurologically, through transmission of nerve impulses
2. biochemically, through hormones and neurotransmitters
3. biophysically, through pressure waves
4. energetically, through the bio-electromagnetic field interaction from the subtle energy bodies.

The heart emits a magnetic field some 5,000 times greater than that emitted by the brain. There is also scientific evidence which shows that the heart communicates with the brain through intuitive and emotional signals. This leads us to an interesting conclusion, which is that the heart could be an intelligent force behind the feelings and intuitive thoughts that we receive. It also raises the question: is the heart the primary centre of our emotions? From a physical and energy standpoint the answer to this question is 'no'. The Heart energy body, which is the fourth subtle energy body, communicates with the sacral or second subtle energy body, the home of our emotions (see chapter 3). As an energy centre it is a balancing (harmonising) force for the emotional body. The neurons in the physical heart are there purely and simply to service the functioning of the heart (autonomous function). Because of constant conscious programming that the heart is responsible for emotions, this has caused an increasing number of the heart's neurons to be used for *other purposes* when our energetic system gets out balance. It appears that not only the brain has neuroplastic characteristics - the heart brain has similar characteristics. Statements like 'you have broken my heart' and 'I have got heart ache', are examples that produce a knock-on effect on the use of the heart's neurons. Yes, the mind does affect different parts of our body. The heart brain is being diverted to service additional activities and in my view this could well be giving rise to an increase in the number of heart attacks that occur.

Gut Brain
Who would have thought that there was more to our gut than digestion? The gut brain, or enteric nervous system, strongly influences our mood and wellbeing. Scientists are calling this the second brain. They have shown that it has a major effect on our mental state and plays a key role in a number of diseases throughout the body, such as osteoporosis. It seems that the gut brain does not contribute to our thinking but it does play a mediating role in our immune response. When we feel butterflies in our stomach, this is a manifestation of an emotional response in anticipating something like public speaking or meeting the father-in-law for the first time and so forth. The brain under our cranium is mirroring the emotional response in the gut brain. The neurons in the gut are there purely and simply to service the digestive requirements of the gut. Once again, because we are conditioning ourselves to believe that our emotions are centred in the gut, the gut neurons available for the digestive system have been reduced. This has given rise to a large increase in the number of digestive problems and associated disorders experienced in the West.

In the next chapter I describe the different subtle energy bodies that we have. These include the emotional subtle energy body, the centre of all our emotions. Compassion is an example of an emotion that is being experienced in the gut due to an energetic roll-on effect when the emotional system gets out of balance. In reality, compassion should emote from the subtle energy emotional centre (chapter 3).

Thoughts Empower your Destiny

The brain is like a bio-electrical/electronic communications transmitter/receiver which is tuned to an individual's consciousness. A lot of activity to do with personal development starts firstly within this individual consciousness. Thought energy is received, decoded and acted upon by the brain, which is followed-up physically and emotionally by acting out the messages and emotions received. Being responsible means understanding the effect we actually have on ourselves and others. For example, each of us:

- affects our brain and body through the experiences we attract, decisions we make and how we handle them.

- may not wish to recognise that we actually have a choice in what happens to us, although we do.

- would have a less stressful life if we recognised that a substantial part of what occurs in our life is driven by the thoughts (programs) running in our unconscious mind. This, together with the conscious mind, programs the quantum bio-magnetic field affecting what and who is attracted into our life.

From all that has been said above, it is evident that our destiny is influenced by our own thoughts. Each of us is 100 percent responsible for our thoughts and this will become clearer after reading through the following chapters. Such a statement on responsibility may come as a shock, as most people have been brought up with a blame belief system – 'it's not me, it's them'. By the time you have finished reading this book, you will have a better understanding of why each person is, in general, 100 percent responsible for what happens to them! Appreciating the power of thought and thinking, and recognising the flexibility of the brain is important. Why? This is because we are dealing with subtle energies which are very small. And small energetic shifts can result in major changes in your life. It is possible to retrain your brain and aim for a life filled with the achievements and outcomes that you are meant to have, a life filled with a greater degree of happiness and an inner sense of positive wellbeing. It is all up to you! The steps involved are deceptively easy. How do you do it? As a being of energy consider:

- bringing together the singularities of the authentic-self's dimensions (chapter 1),

- focusing within that fifth dimension (energy), recognising how everything connects through energy at a sub-atomic level. Just thinking about this has a powerful effect within the unconscious mind and will improve the outcomes in your life.

- bringing in the imagination and intuition which will guarantee opening some doors in, and expanding your awareness!

Thomas Jefferson (1743 to 1826) the third President of the USA eloquently stated:

> *'Do you want to know who you are?*
> *Do not ask. Act!*
> *Action will delineate and define you.'*

I have found the above statement to be very true, as my actions are driven by what is running in both my unconscious and conscious minds. And it all started with a thought! A particular action you may wish to consider is how to get more mileage out of your mind and brain system with less effort. If you do, the following may interest you.

Passage to a More Fulfilling Life - the Best Is Yet to Come!
Einstein is reputed to have said that we use only a small proportion of the mind and brain system. In fact it would be true to say that we use much less than 10 percent of the mind and brain system. Diagram 2.13 is a theoretical representation of the conscious and unconscious minds split within the mind and brain system (chapter 3 details the mind system).

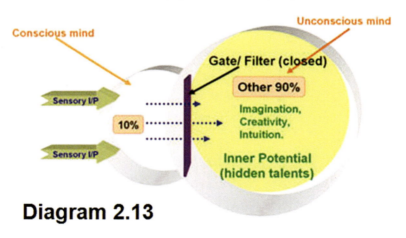

Diagram 2.13

The unconscious mind, which some scientists estimate operates some 500,000 times faster than the conscious mind, represents the other 90 percent. Can you imagine what you could do by using some of that other 90 percent on a regular basis? There are many examples of those who are able to do this, such as successful businessmen (like Richard Branson, Bill Gates, Andrew Carnegie...), artists (like Pablo Picasso, Paul Cezanne, John Cogan...), engineers (like Martin Cooper, Jack Kilby, Nikola Tesla...), scientists (like Albert Einstein, Ernest Rutherford, Max Plank...), chefs (like Jamie Oliver, Marcelo Zana, Michel Roux Jnr...), farmers (like John Chapman, Theodore Roosevelt, Thomas Jefferson...) and more. So how did they do it? They did it by naturally tuning in to their imagination, creative-self, intuition (hunches) and intuitive intelligence.

There is a deceptively easy and powerful step that will help you to increase your creative potential and intuition, as well as to engage in self-healing. What is this step? The step is to increase the level of alpha and theta brainwaves emitted by your brain. Before showing you how to do this, however, it may be helpful to know what is actually happening within the brain and what stops people from tuning into their inner powerhouse of potential (the other 90 percent).

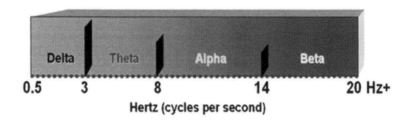

Diagram 2.14

Thinking generates an energy field around the head called brainwaves. These can be measured by a special device called an electroencephalogram (EEG). Diagram 2.14 shows the range of brainwaves that are generated by thinking.
These brainwaves are:

- beta waves, which are generated during day to day thinking and are in the range of 14 to about 20hz and even higher.

- alpha waves, which are in the range of about 8 to 14hz. Everybody has some alpha waves within their brainwave patterns. However, when these brainwaves increase, it opens a door for creative thinking and enhances the potential for using your intuitive ability by allowing direct access to the unconscious mind. It is usually possible to tune into any natural psychic ability which is dormant within you when your alpha brainwaves content is increased by about 10 percent plus. A process for increasing alpha and theta brainwaves is given below.

- theta waves provide an opportunity to engage in self-healing, and also to be open to healing from another person. Self-healing potential strengthens with an increase in theta brainwaves of about 5 percent or more. Having a busy and cluttered mind reduces the level of alpha and theta brainwaves that are generated. In a deep meditative state, theta brainwaves begin to increase substantially.

- delta waves, are in the range of 0.5 to 3hz. Delta waves occur while in a deep sleep or in a coma. If brainwaves are altogether at zero then it is more than likely that you have returned to your spirit and are dead. This has happened to some people after an accident, or during a medical operation for a short period where they have stopped breathing, but they returned to their body as they had not completed their soul contract, so started breathing again. Much has been written about these cases and there is a great deal of evidence available.

Now that you have a feel for the different types of brainwaves which we generate, how can you generate and use them to your advantage? To increase the level of alpha and theta brainwaves, I recommend that you consider trying the following process of getting into the other 90 percent (and the Zone). The steps involved appear easy but some of us have to persevere to gain full benefit from the process!

A Gift to you - Get into a Peak Performance State and the Zone
If Einstein recognised that he only used a small portion of his mind and brain system, what does that say about the rest of us? Because Einstein was able to naturally use his right-brain hemisphere with ease, his thinking was not trapped in a closed virtual box. He had found a natural way, through music, to open this box. If you accept that opening your own virtual box of thinking is a must for the 21st century, then you will be able to meet the challenges you face, and survive with a greater degree of ease. Balancing the use of both brain hemispheres is definitely the way to go. Why? This is because an individual's conscious awareness automatically begins to adapt more rapidly (energy follows thought) by using more of the right-brain hemisphere. Most importantly, the imagination works out of the right-brain hemisphere and this is a forgotten key to expanding conscious awareness. It is also a key to getting into the other 90 percent, a peak performance state and the Zone.

Our awareness automatically rises to a higher level, through recognising, accepting and thinking about new concepts which may appear to be outside of normal logic and reason. Breaking out of the rational mind, at times, is important. I have emphasised that attributes such as creative expression, hunches, and developing an understanding of what cannot be seen, work outside normal logic and reason. A few 'naturals', like Einstein and other people at the peak of their profession, seem to be able to tune into a whole new world of concepts with ease. How are they able to do it? They do it by connecting with their other 90 percent and then getting into a peak performance state and the Zone. This state and the Zone can be defined as:

'a part of the mind and brain system to which an individual connects that empowers them to achieve outstanding feats of physical and/or Intellectual performance, or a goal beyond what is possible by using the Intellect (conscious mind) alone.'

For brevity, I will call a peak performance state and the Zone simply the 'Zone' from now on. To enter the other 90 percent and the Zone, the logic and reason functioning part of the brain is required to be put on hold. Putting this part of the brain on hold enables entry to a part of consciousness that has been denied to most. An important point to emphasise is that if there are any false beliefs running within the unconscious mind they can stop a connection to the Zone being made. We all tend to have false beliefs running in our unconscious mind. In addition, if we do not consciously believe in the Zone or that we can connect with it, it would be advantageous to ask ourselves why not? Very successful people manage to do it, so why not the rest of us? Is it that we do not know of its existence? Or is it that we just do not believe it exists (in spite of the number of successful achievers who have spoken and written about it)? One thing beyond dispute is that if you want to increase your success and achievements in life leadership, then using both brain hemispheres and connecting with the other 90 percent and the Zone is 'the way to go'.

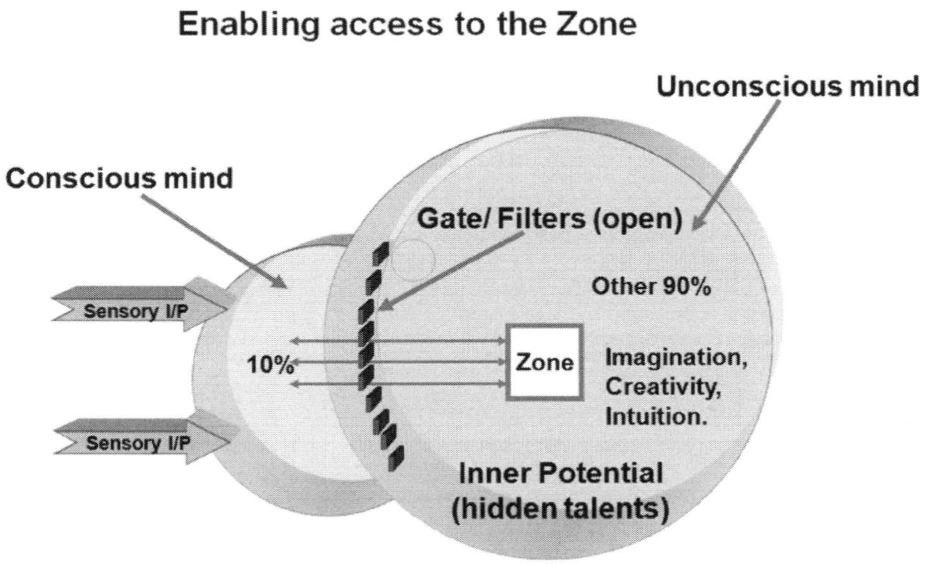

Enabling access to the Zone

Diagram 2.15

Diagram 2.15 represents a theoretical representation of the conscious and unconscious mind split in two, with the other 90 percent and the Zone on the right-hand side, and the conscious mind (the remaining 10 percent) on the left. Sensory input is, for example, through the eyes, ears, touch, taste, smell and sensory impulses pass through the mind and brain system into the conscious and unconscious minds.

The belief system, supported by the ego, dictates who we think we are or should be, the potential we think we have, and what we think we can do well, or not, as the case may be. Together with the appropriate personality(s), our belief system also dictates to us if we can do things with ease, or whether we have to work hard, or even very hard, to achieve our goals. The belief system is, as you are already aware, a filter process which controls how we see ourselves and the world around us. In diagram 2.15, the gate or filters are shown to be open, thus allowing the conscious mind to make contact with the Zone via the unconscious mind.

Due to much of the conditioning of the belief system that most people have been subjected to since conception, it is of little wonder that many may not be able to access their full potential. Not only has the right-brain hemisphere been blocked to a significant degree, so too, has any chance of getting into the other 90 percent. It is time for us all to claim our excellence by getting into the other 90 percent and the Zone. If you want to, of course!

To enter the other 90 percent and the Zone, practising the following process will generate valuable results.

Step 1: Breathing

In the West, we simply do not breathe properly. Yet breathing properly increases our IQ, according to psychologists, by about 10 percent, as more oxygen enters the blood, circulates around and stimulates brain cells. Proper breathing allows a major step to be taken towards entering the other 90 percent. The suggested breathing exercise can also stimulate an inner feeling of positive wellbeing. For this exercise to be successful it is most important to breathe through the diaphragm (solar plexus area) and not the upper lungs. This ensures that the whole lungs are filled and not just the upper part. Next, it is necessary to create a deep, regular breathing rhythm by breathing in to a slow count. A count of 6:3 has been chosen here as the rhythm is supportive to enter the Zone. To complete the rhythm:

1. Begin by breathing in for a slow count of six.
2. Hold your breath for a slow count of three.
3. Breathe out to a slow count of six.
4. Hold your breath for a slow count of three.

Continue with this rhythm for about 15 times and try to do it without thinking. This exercise increases the oxygen to the brain and blood stream and is also very beneficial to the heart.

Step 2: Muscle relaxation and sensing

Most of us seldom spend any time sensing the body's muscles unless something goes wrong. The muscles can be tense, yet there is a tendency not to be aware of the tension. For deep relaxation to be induced, the muscles must be relaxed. The technique here is to sit comfortably in a chair with feet firmly on the ground, keep the back straight in a comfortable position. Place your hands palm down on your thighs and when you start, begin with the feet muscles. Try the following exercise.

Pull the feet muscles tight and relax them. Do this three times.

1. Carry out the exercise for the calf muscles, thigh muscles, stomach muscles, chest muscles, shoulder muscles, arm muscles and forehead muscles.

2. When the muscle exercise has been completed, place your arms by your side and sense the weight of your left-hand. Concentrate on your left-hand and feel its weight increasing in your imagination. After a couple of minutes, focus on your left-hand returning to its normal weight.

3. Concentrate on your right-hand and, once again in your imagination, feel its temperature beginning to rise. After a couple of minutes allow the temperature of your right-hand to return to normal. Feel this change of temperature.

The above exercise will relax the muscles and sensing abilities will also be enhanced. If at first you do not feel the left-hand increasing in weight and/or the right-hand increasing in temperature, keep practising until you achieve some results. If you do not, then continue with step 3.

Step 3: Visualisation

In a relaxed state, with eyes closed, recall and try to see in your mind and imagination a favourite scene, which could be a forest surrounded by a morning mist, or a lake with trees around it and some islands on it, or sitting by the sea looking out at the expanse of the ocean, or on a tropical island with palm trees, a golden sandy beach and emerald green water, or on a snow covered mountain, or whatever. If you do not see any image then just sense it. If you have difficulty with both seeing and sensing the image, just think about it in your mind. If all of this proves to be difficult then find some actual favourite pictures. Keep looking at a picture, and if your mind wanders, focus on the detail and its structure. As you focus strongly on the image, recall any feelings you had. The exercise will help you to clear your conscious mind of any chatter and to reach a passive state of concentration where the image or feelings that you have recalled will be your only focus. Keep doing this until the chatter stops and you are able to hold the image without any interference. At this level of relaxation, more of the right-brain hemisphere is being exercised and used. You are also strongly linked into the imagination. The brain will also be generating a lot of neuro-chemicals that support an inner feeling of wellbeing. How does the brain do that? Because the brain cannot tell the difference between looking at a real scene with a positive emotional response and the one held in the mind with your eyes closed (or even open).

Step 4: Relaxation protocol

Having worked through the above three steps in the process there is a further relaxation-inducing process which will encourage an even deeper state of relaxation. To do this, take the following steps:

1. Count in your mind slowly down from 10 to 1. This will enable you to gain access to a deeper level of the other 90 percent (within the unconscious mind). At the end of the count you can move forward to empower your-self to enter the Zone.

2. Begin the process of entering the Zone, visualise your-self on a path in a forest, or on a tropical beach, or whatever, that leads to a cottage or hut which has a large wooden entrance door. Behind this imaginary door lies that all-powerful part of your mind and brain system called the Zone.

3. Open the door and enter the cottage or hut, but leave the door open (this keeps you connected to your conscious mind). You see before you a small room. Create in your imagination a comfortable chair in the middle of the room, and in front of this chair is a large flat (LCD or plasma type) colour television screen mounted on the cottage wall. On the same wall to the left of the TV is a clock and digital calendar showing the time, date and year. See your-self moving forward, sitting in the chair and making your-self comfortable.

4. The TV, clock and calendar are operated by your mind. To switch on the TV, just 'think' it on, and also think of today's date, year and time and the calendar and clock will immediately show it. When you have switched on the TV it will show you what you are thinking about (in technicolor) in real time simply by your instructing the TV to do so. If you want to go backwards, or forwards in time you can do so by instructing the calendar and clock to change. Should you do this, you can also instruct the TV to project the change of scene to that which you are thinking about at the new time period. You are now in a highly receptive state and in a position to make the Zone work for you.

Step 5: *Programming in the Zone for Successful Achievement*

When you have practised the above four protocols there is a useful technique which can be used that will empower you to recall the relaxed state with its supporting tranquil emotions that you have previously entered. With practice you can also use this technique to instantly enter the Zone without going through the different steps. The technique is a kinaesthetic one and is called an *anchor*. To construct and then to use an anchor, when you are in a relaxed state, or the Zone, bring the tip of your index finger, fore finger and thumb together, count your-self down slowly from 5 to 1 and then say to your-self silently within your mind:

"every time I bring my three fingers together, and say for example: 'I am relaxed' or 'Zone Entry', I will be instantly in this relaxed state (or in the Zone)"

These are passwords to enter the Zone and you can make up your own. When you have counted your-self down from 5 to 1, and brought your three fingers together, make your own statement (this is your password) silently within your mind that you wish to use to trigger entering a relaxed state, or the Zone. When you speak the password silently in your mind you will instantly induce the state that you wish to recall. You can use any combination of fingers you want that feel comfortable. The Zone is most important, as it is your operational area from which to power up what you want to do, or to hone up other physical and mental skills that you may wish to use. Successful sports persons, business leaders, artists, and scientists, amongst others, use the Zone either naturally or through training.

When you have completed the time you wish to spend within the relaxed state or the Zone, silently say within your mind:

> "as I release my fingers, I immediately return to a fully conscious state, and will be wide awake, feeling fine and in perfect health and feeling better than ever before and completely re-energised"

Increasing the use of your right-brain hemisphere and enabling access to the Zone opens up a world of infinite possibilities. You only have to practise to gain benefit from this process. These are deceptively easy but powerful techniques that you can use for your own development and in the leadership of others.

Going through the above process induces a level of relaxation that is similar to the state you experience before you fall asleep, or when you first wake up in the morning. It is a level where if you say some affirmations (short positive statements made in the present) to yourself, they are most effective as affirmations can affect a change in your quantum bio-magnetic field. Through this process, it is possible to improve what you are attracting into your life. Some examples of affirmations here are:

> I am following my true path in life.
>
> I have full control over my life and it is so.
>
> I am attracting great abundance into all areas of my life.
>
> I am only accepting suggestions that are for my greater good.
>
> I am always maintaining a perfectly healthy mind and body.
>
> My positive thoughts bring me the benefits and advantages I desire.
>
> I am automatically accessing my creative abilities whenever I need them.
>
> My intuition and intuitive intelligence is always strong.

Use your own personal affirmations here as well, but remember to keep them in the present tense, positive and short. If you use affirmations and nothing happens, then you will have an energy block, or blocks, that need to be identified, worked through and removed.

Getting More Out of your Brain with Less Effort

Ten years after leaving university I still thought that the way to get ahead in life was by absorbing knowledge, increasing my intellect (getting qualifications) and with very hard work. Little did I realise that I was using only a small part of my mind and brain system! I did not know about accessing a peak performance state. I also did not realise that because of the way the education system is structured, most people have to put a lot of effort into achieving educational and other goals. So, the question is, can we really do more by doing less? The answer to this is a resounding yes! Most certainly when we access our peak performance state. I keep emphasising that for most of us our thinking is unknowingly trapped within a virtual closed box. Once we become aware of this, it is advantageous to 'open the box' so as to quickly achieve our desires and create an inner feeling of wellbeing and happiness. Following this route, happiness will no longer be a distant dream, it will become a reality.

From time to time, I use the expression:

'history infiltrates the present and affects (or programs) the future'

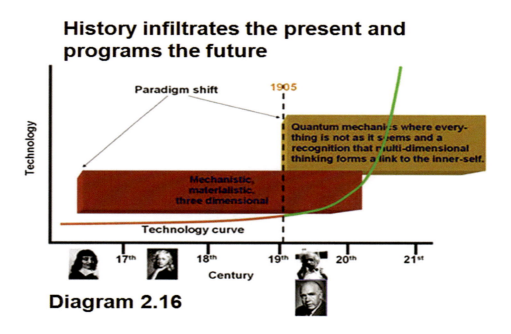

Diagram 2.16

The schematic diagram 2.16 shows two time periods where major changes in conscious awareness took place. There are some others over this historic period, but I have chosen these two for reference purposes. The two time periods are the 17th and 20th century.

Using these two time periods I focus upon two sets of famous names: Sir Isaac Newton and René Descartes, and Albert Einstein and Neils Bohr respectively. I do this for ease of understanding of what was going on with respect to raising humanity's conscious awareness. The two time periods represent a paradigm shift where scientific thinking, and the models created to understand what was going on in the Universe and the world, changed significantly. Both scientific thinking and technology changed rapidly from the beginning of the 20th century onwards as shown in diagram. Over the last three decades there have been major changes in thinking within the classical sciences (botany, biology, anatomy, chemistry, physics, medicine), chiefly through a greater awareness of what is going on at a sub-atomic level. This type of thinking also affects the fundamental understanding of other disciplines such as medicine, psychology and psychiatry. Thinking within the fifth dimension is now beginning to grow apace.

As Britain and Europe entered the industrial revolution (18th century), after a period of what was called 'Enlightenment' (13th to 17th century), the academic community's consciousness automatically rose to meet ongoing challenges. People's consciousness shifted mainly towards a mechanistic, material (form-based) and linear-time-biased approach. This affected and continues to affect scientific, industrial, political, economic and financial development. It still affects how we understand the functioning of an individual's body. Such are the effects of the reductionist scientific approach which accelerated from the 17th century onwards.

The subject of *emotional intelligence* had not then entered mainstream understanding, and most workers were viewed as a commodity to be used without any consideration for their wellbeing. There were enlightened families at that time, though (Cadbury, Peabody, Sainsbury to name a few), who, even as they were making their fortunes, felt compassion for their workers and for humanity as a whole, and they invested in their workforce by building proper housing, schools, recreational facilities and so on. The education system also changed its focus to support the industrial revolution and the current change in conscious awareness. Creativity was certainly enhanced during this time period but once again from a material (form-based) and four-dimensional perspective.

Creating a more Desirable Destiny
In the pre-industrial past, once-flourishing nations like ancient Greece believed that a balanced mind, body and spirit created a healthy, happy and content individual. The Greeks called the soul the spirit, as they may not have realised that the spirit is the host energy body of a soul. A soul is like an energy fragment of its spirit, something like a piece of a hologram. The Greeks did not bring emotions into their paradigm of ultimate contentment (happiness) although they may have included emotions as part of the mind. As pointed out, emotions are the real power drivers behind a thought. The type of emotion attached to an intention held in the conscious mind can accelerate the process of manifesting the desired outcome. Emotions are also a key to our state of health. Psychology has advanced to a level where the power of emotions and the effect they have upon an inner feeling of positive wellbeing and happiness, including our physical condition, is now more widely recognised.

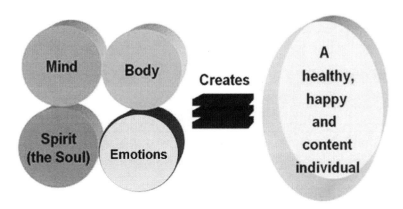

Diagram 2.17

Upgrading the ancient Greek paradigm to fit the 21st century, diagram 2.17 suggests that a balanced mind, body, emotions and spirit (the soul) create a healthy, happy and contented individual. Many influential sages in the past have stated that 'mind is the builder'. It has been so since the beginning of time. Today, it is clearly understood that not only is mind the architect and builder, but the emotions supporting thoughts within the mind have enormous power in the building process. An individual's emotions also have a major effect on their ability to manifest their desires and on their inner feeling of wellbeing and happiness. You may have noticed that money has not yet entered into the equation of happiness!

Is it possible to create the destiny we are meant to have, and for us to be happy and content without paying out shed loads of money? After all, we are all told by experts in the media that money is the cornerstone of society and that we live in a cash nexus society. I would suggest six steps to be happy and content and you do not have to spend a penny or cent or halala or whatever! The following steps will help to:

1. balance the use of the conscious mind and intellect with pursuits that engage your creative self and inner passion. Start regularly engaging the right-brain hemisphere. Find a deep relaxation, or equivalent meditation technique that involves diaphragmic breathing and positive visualisation such as the ones suggested in this book.

2. make sure that if you feel any negative emotions that you identify and clear them and replace them with positive ones. I suggest how to deal with negative emotions later.

3. attract to you what you are meant to have through your quantum bio-magnetic field. When you are thinking of something you want, you are setting up an intention. Think back to a special occasion such as a great holiday, or passing your exams, or meeting someone special. Pull in the emotion that you felt when you set up the intention. This can help to speed up attracting what you desire.

4. start working with the five dimensions associated with the authentic-self and systematically work through and integrate them at each stage (chapter 1, page 44). I cannot emphasise enough how important this exercise is for your future wellbeing and happiness. The exercise anchors your consciousness in the world of energy.

5. take a step back from those infinite wants that you may have and focus on your real needs. Create a list of your needs. Be honest and realistic as you make up the list, and try to recognise the influence of your ego.

6. take another step back from your-self and try to recognise patterns of behaviour and attitudes that have occurred and are occurring in your life that you dislike. You know that you have a quantum bio-magnetic energy field that attracts you to and also attracts to you everything that happens to you. It is programmed by the conscious mind (your objective self) and by the unconscious mind (your subjective self) - diagram 2.18.

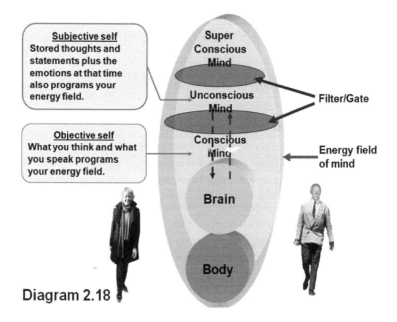

Diagram 2.18

7. try the different approaches to re-programming your bio-magnetic field so as to boost your relationships, abundance and so forth that are discussed in the following chapters. The objective is for you to attract the life that you are meant to experience.

8. consider dropping people who are predominantly negative, who drag you down and drain your energy. Give preference to those who are on your wavelength.

As you are working through 1 to 8 above, you are successfully dealing with mind and spirit (soul). But what about the physical body? There is a ninth step that you can add but this one may involve you spending some money. This step encourages you to:

9. appreciate your physical body and its needs. Balance your diet with fresh food, clean water, appropriate beverages and regular exercise. Avoid sitting continuously in front of your computer and television screen. Get up and go out - socialise, for everybody needs to feel wanted. Do your-self a favour and mix with positive-minded and inspiring people if you can.

In this chapter and the previous one, different aspects of the body, mind, emotions, soul and spirit have been brought into the discourse. Everything has been broken down to a sub-atomic level (the quantum world) and energy. In the next chapter I describe the seven subtle energy bodies that we have in addition to our physical body; the supporting seven vortex energy communication centres for each subtle energy body and what they mean on a day to day basis. They are all operate at a sub-atomic level and in the world of energy. They are also a crucial part of our self. The subtle energy bodies and vortex energy centres form part of our consciousness.

Chapter 3

Understanding Consciousness: the Quantum-Self

The Universe is change; our life is what our thoughts make it.

Marcus Aurelius Antonius: Roman Emperor AD161 - AD180

Understanding Consciousness: the Quantum-Self

In chaos theory, the example of a butterfly flapping its wings in Japan, which produces a hurricane off the West Coast of America, is intriguing. That a seemingly insignificant happening - a butterfly flapping its wings - should have such a catastrophic effect seems impossible. But is it? I would suggest not. Within our energy-self we are operating in an environment of subtle energies where small changes can cause major transformations in our life, both physically and emotionally. The secret is to know how to make the changes. Before explaining how to do this, it would help to understand the way in which consciousness and our energy-self function. I describe the energy-self as the physical body plus a series of seven subtle energy bodies and their supporting communication vortex energy centres (VECs). A major purpose of this chapter is to leave you with no doubt about the energy structure which makes up your whole being: body (including the brain), mind (or consciousness) and soul. In addition, I will elaborate on the 3rd dimension of the second paradigm which relates to our authentic-self. This will unfold as I describe the body's energy structure. The ability to gain access to the 3rd dimension is developed purely and simply by thinking about it. Not a difficult task, but one that may prove elusive for some. It all depends on your belief system (what you accept as being true).

Understanding the basic building blocks of our energy Self, which links with both the authentic-self and fabricated-self (part of which includes the physical body), enhances our ability to empower ourselves. It enables us to be in a much stronger position to utilise such capabilities as our self-healing ability, manifestation ability and intuitive (hunch) skills. An important point to make here is the need to merge the fabricated-self with the authentic-self. Why? For the simple reason that the fabricated-self usually grows over and away from the authentic-self, a process that begins at birth. A life lesson for us all is to try to merge both, to enable us to get the best out of our lives. Each individual's state of mind and personal conditioning dictates the degree of the separation.

It is also important to appreciate that seeing, or sensing, or just thinking about something in our imagination adds power to it and can have an effect on the eventual outcome. 'Seeing is believing' is an old cliché that still rings true in Western cultures. Does this mean that if we cannot see something we should disbelieve it? Not quite, and that for good reason. We cannot see a magnetic field, or x-rays, or radio and TV transmission waves, but they can be measured. These invisible fields can also be used to produce something, for example to generate electricity, or photograph a broken bone, or listen to the news on a radio and watch pictures on a TV screen. Therefore, it is credible to assume that we can believe in things that we cannot see, especially when we can see or hear an end-product of their existence, and/or even measure them. There is a paradox here, when the subject of recognising that the physical body has several subtle energy body (SEB) fields is raised, or even that we are really beings of energy. Western medicine is only just beginning to consider that we have an energy body and that energy medicine is real. Being able to detect SEB fields is important and there are people who can actually see them. How do they do that?

They do it, usually without thinking, by tuning the wavelength of the light their eyes can receive to higher energy frequencies within the fifth dimension, thereby accommodating the SEB frequencies. Why then has it taken so long for the subject of the physical body's different energy fields to be recognised and even discussed within the scientific community? A high proportion of Western scientists still maintain there is absolutely no scientific evidence to prove that the human body subtle energy fields exist. Why do they make such a statement which is clearly misleading, given the amount of evidence available?

There appear to be three reasons for the above paradox: one technical, one a conceptual block, and one that I call sociological. The first reason is because Western scientists had not, until recently, developed sufficiently sensitive measuring devices to detect the SEB energy fields so they simply did not believe in them. This last statement is not strictly true, as Russian scientists developed sufficiently sensitive devices to measure the SEB fields way back in about the 1920s (for example Professor Kirlian, through his special Kirlian photography). Other Russian scientists more recently - since the 1980s - have been able to measure the SEB fields (for example Professor Konstantin Korotkov of St Petersburg University) as a by-product of their country's space medicine program which has a focus on the SEB system. They are able to diagnose most medical problems an astronaut may suffer from by detecting them in the SEB field (see http://2012.korotkov.org). They are also able to treat medical problems by re-aligning and balancing the affected area of the SEB field system that is causing the problem, by using energy medicine. This in effect realigns the energy structure of the body's affected cells to create a homeostasis (balance). How this process takes place is better understood when it is realised that the physical body is the *visible part* of us. The physical body (brain, flesh and bones and so on) is made up of matter which is just compressed energy. There is also a series of seven inter-connecting SEBs which are the *invisible part* of us. They too are constructed of energy.

Within our operating energy structure, there is always a two-way communication between all the associated SEBs and the physical brain and body. The SEBs intermingle and communicate with each other through the vortex energy centres (VECs) – see page 102. I call the combination of the SEBs and VECs our *energy-self*. Anything that affects one VEC affects the others as they are all connected through an energy network. Quantum physics provides an avenue to enable us to come to terms with the physical body's associated SEBs and VECs which operate within a multi-dimensional environment. The SEBs and VECs have been known for over 2000 years by ancient cultures in Asia. VECs were called Chakras (wheels of energy spinning around a two-dimensional axis). My work attempts to update the reference work that is available on energy body structures.

The second reason for the paradox is complex, but forms a regular pattern for any subject that falls outside traditional thinking and beliefs. As I elaborated in chapters 1 and 2, belief systems in Western countries were and still are heavily conditioned in a mechanistic, form-based and linear-time-biased direction. We may be super analysers, but we can sometimes lose the plot by over-analysing (that is, we may not be able to see the wood for the trees!). An example of this can be seen in the steps that scientists have taken, over many centuries, to investigate how the human body works. This involved breaking down and analysing the body's different parts into ever increasing detail, in the quest to unravel all of its secrets. No one doubts that it is most important for us to understand the mechanics of how we function, but analysing from that specific direction provides only one aspect of the story. Although this may appear to be a major feature of the story, a substantial part still needs to be unveiled by exploring from the direction of the sub-atomic world and energy. A rethink outside of the traditional virtual box is required.

The third reason for the paradox is really to do with what I call our tribal sociological structure. In life, it is a human trait to feel a need to belong, to feel wanted and to be recognised. In most professional circles, if a traditional route of thinking and practice is followed, then it increases the chance of us being accepted by our peers and moving up the ladder of success. I am sure that most of us do not wish to be ridiculed and/or rejected at work by colleagues, or even by friends. I certainly am one of those who like to feel that I belong. If you have a radical idea that does not fit established thinking, then it is important to be working on an independently-funded project that encourages you to explore your ideas. That way you are less likely to be excommunicated from the fold! If you are not accepted, being rejected by your colleagues will be high on their agenda.

Why then did some scientists recognise, accept and develop technology to detect the SEB fields, yet most do not even accept their existence today? In answering this question it is important to recognise the type of conditioning we are all subjected to from birth. My own life's journey has shown me that I needed to question many of the things I was conditioned to believe. It took me some time before I recognised that in life:

'all is not as it seems'

My desire to explore this familiar though profound statement led me to look at the psychology and politics of scientific thinking. I wanted to find out why most scientists think the way they do, with all its strengths and sometimes with its limitations. Keeping in mind a wise old saying provided me with a major clue.

'history infiltrates the present and affects the future'

My conclusions about the reasons for the above paradox left me in a stunned state for a time. We are now into the second decade of the 21st century. It is a time of great change. It is a time when those who embrace an increase in their awareness outside of their virtual box of thinking will indeed achieve greatness. Increasing my own awareness to a level where I am comfortable with an understanding of my own purpose in life was not easy. At times, it was a bit de-motivating until I found like-minded souls who wanted answers to life's most challenging questions. I was helped by a good friend of mine in Kuwait, where I lived for five years, who said:

'do not let life discourage you for everybody who got where they are has to begin where they were'

The above statement sounds a bit convoluted, but it certainly rings true. Living in Arabia for many years isolated me from the outside world and gave me time to carry out my own research into investigating what life is about. I had time to explore such questions as *'what is the purpose of being here?'* and *'is there any synchronicity involved with respect to the people we meet, or is it just random?'* Another question that greatly interested me was *'is there a connection between the physical self and the concept of our being constructed of energy and having subtle energy bodies?'* I discovered through certain texts, some historic and some much more modern, produced by professionals like Anodea Judith, Dr Barbara A Brennan (at one time a NASA research scientist), Dr Deepak Chopra, Donna Eden, Choa Kok Sui, Ruth White and others that the body has indeed several different energy fields or SEBs. This led me to want to investigate them further.

It was during this investigation that a whole new dimension of understanding about life opened up. I was fortunate to have access to an ancient sage called Master Chou who was channelled through a Sarah Tyler Walters while in trance. Through Master Chou I was able to access further information on the different SEBs and VECs and how they function. Quite a unique and amazing research facility!

My research enabled me to take the essence of Darwin's great works (this is a form-based, mechanistic and linear-time-biased approach) to the next level of understanding within my own mind. Today's biology research scientists have taken Darwin's work well into the 21st century and I certainly am one of their supporters who felt it was time to raise Darwinian and Neo-Darwinian thinking to a level that befits 21st century thinking. Darwin's paradigm is being upgraded through a modern rigorous scientific approach. What is happening at the sub-atomic world of which we are a part is becoming a focus of attention. As the scientists' research enters into the fifth dimension – energy (chapter 1) - more answers to the mysteries of human evolution will be forthcoming.

Developing an understanding of the SEBs and their supporting energy infrastructure provided some missing parts of the jigsaw to answer such questions as *'have I a soul?'*, or *'has my soul a purpose?'*, or *'how does my consciousness work?'*, or *'are my relationships just random occurrences?'* Born naturally curious, just believing or sensing that I have a soul was for me not enough - I wanted to find some scientific proof. Investigating the purpose of the SEB fields, and what they do, provided me with a clearer understanding of:

1. what consciousness is about
2. how the soul actually communicates with the brain through the SEBs/ VECs to the conscious mind
3. the quantum collapse of a conscious thought within the physical brain

To strengthen my case, I gathered research on ways to prove we have a soul to satisfy some of the sceptics I came across. In summary, there are three ways we can prove that we have a soul, if you wish to do so. To carry out the research your-self, you may want to participate in the following:

1. enrol on an out of the body (OOB) projection course. These come in two types. The first is where you actually stay in the body but project where you want to go in the mind (your imagination in the unconscious mind). In this case it is possible to actually see where you have projected your-self too, while being conscious. You see what is happening on what I call the dream screen located in the pineal gland. This is where dreams are observed while asleep, except this time you are conscious.

    The second is where you actually project your-self out of the physical body. There are courses available that teach you to how to do this. After a process of relaxation you stimulate your fourth energy body (the Astral body) to travel. The Monroe Institute in the United States is a good place to start looking for such a course.

Both the Russians and Americans amongst others have used OOB techniques successfully for espionage purposes. This is so much cheaper than those expensive spy satellites! As stated above, it is the fourth SEB that is projected out of the body when someone wants to travel inter-dimensionally. As the energy structure of this SEB operates in the sub-atomic or quantum world, time and space are co-existent, enabling it to travel quite literally anywhere, and by anywhere I mean *anywhere*, on this planet or Universe or beyond. This is not for the light-hearted or amateur and should be carefully controlled. Moving on, another method for proving that you have a soul is to:

2. get together with a regression therapist and agree with some clients to ask them to travel between lives and have a dialogue with respect to what is happening to them

in spirit. Do the same for your-self if you are open to hypnotherapy techniques. Some people are not, as their minds are locked down.

During my research for this book, I investigated the Law of Attraction as it is a most popular workshop/seminar topic for people who may be in difficulty. Looking at the law of attraction from an energy perspective, that is from the fifth dimension, it began to make sense, especially when linked to the effect the conscious and unconscious minds have on the outcome of a manifestation exercise. This took me back into finding out what part, if any, the SEBs played in any attraction exercise. All of the SEBs and VECs contribute to what I call the quantum bio-magnetic field (diagram 3.1). This field attracts to us or attracts us to all of the situations we find ourselves in and is also the main contributor to any form of manifestation.

The Human Quantum Bio-magnetic Field
After researching the energy fields that surround all human beings, I began to recognise that we are like walking, talking, biological magnets, attracting to us and being attracted to everything that we experience as we journey along life's path. Diagram 3.1 shows an artist's impression of the outline of a typical quantum bio-magnetic field which is made up of *all* of our SEBs. I take you through the different SEBs that contribute to the quantum bio-magnetic field later in this chapter. The quantum bio-magnetic field radiates outwards

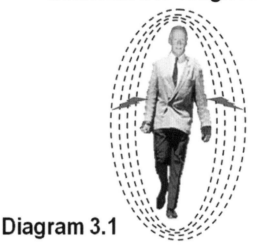
Diagram 3.1

and around the physical body. A key feature of the field is that we actually unknowingly programme it. How is it programmed? It is programmed through the conscious and unconscious minds. Both of these minds are also a part of the SEBs.

All generated thoughts are stored permanently in the unconscious mind where they run continuously. Let me remind you also that the information part of a thought is also stored in the physical brain. Strong emotions are stored in different parts of the physical body as well as in the second SEB. When asleep, the conscious mind shuts down but the unconscious mind keeps running. Whereas the conscious mind runs on logic and reason, the unconscious mind operates through the ego and free will. There is no logic and reason operating within the unconscious mind. The unconscious mind can be regarded as a bit of a free-for-all managed by our ego and free will. Our persona communicates through the unconscious mind to the conscious mind. The unconscious mind also continuously runs information passed to it from the conscious mind like a tape recorder. For example, everything that has been said to us, experiences in life, the belief system that we have accepted as the status quo since birth, everything that is running in the unconscious mind keeps repeating itself like a continuous tape until we make a change to the content (information and emotions). This can be done through conscious thoughts when we are awake, but is more effectively done when we are in a relaxed state. And, once again, the soul communicates with us through the conscious mind, if we are listening.

During my research I became more and more aware of two key fundamentals in life, which nonetheless took me some time to accept because of my conditioning. These were that I was totally responsible for myself and for my own wellbeing, and also for the programs that were running within my quantum bio-magnetic energy field.

As the pre-frontal cortex (the logic and reason thinking part of the brain) begins to develop, we are able, slowly but surely, to be in a position to reject what has been said to us and at times what we are experiencing. It is each adult's responsibility to question what is being said to them and to question what is happening around them. Does it feel right or wrong, positive or negative, good or bad, and so on? If a negative statement is made to us or a negative experience lies unchallenged in the conscious mind, then it passes through to the unconscious mind where it runs 24/7. From birth up to teen years the ability to question slowly but surely gains strength. It continues through the teenage years (and even after) to a degree. One of life's many lessons, as we journey, is to identify any false beliefs that may have been taken on. An approach to doing this is explained in the next chapter. Why would we want to explore false beliefs? I would suggest that it is necessary for us to do it as it will enable us to clean up our bio-magnetic field. And why would we want to do that? It will empower us to open a door to increase our ability to attract and manifest the type of life we are meant to have. Happiness and wellbeing is but a stone's throw away if we decide to open the door to clear out any false beliefs.

Most of us have read or come across articles on the Law of Attraction. Well, the attraction factor is real and is a powerful force that is in everybody's interest to master. The quantum bio-magnetic field is the driving energy force behind the law of attraction. I elaborate on how the attraction factor works in the following chapters. The quantum bio-magnetic energy field operates just like an ordinary magnet's field except that it is working at a sub-atomic level as well as in the physical material plane. In the quantum world, like attracts like. I use the concept of the quantum bio-magnetic field throughout the book as this field is the force that attracts us to, and attracts to us, all the experiences and challenges that we face throughout our life, without exception. Moving home, changing jobs, working abroad, being in relationship with someone, joining a club, making a choice of subjects to study, buying a house, or a boat, or a car and so on, are affected by the quantum bio-magnetic field. We can at times over-ride this field, but if we do it may not always be in our best interest. A major part of life's journey is to learn from the choices and decisions we make, which hopefully enables better choices and decisions to be made in the future.

As Human Beings We are made up of Layers of Energy

As human beings, we are indeed beings of energy with several associated SEB fields. I focus on seven of them below. The physical body is just compressed energy (the eighth body) and is the visible part of us (diagram 3.2) operating within the physical four-dimensional world. All of the SEB fields operate within a multi-dimensional environment outside of Newton's laws. They actually operate within the quantum or sub-atomic world, obeying Universal Laws. The SEBs communicate with one another through to the denser level of our brain and physical body. Several vortex energy centres (VECs) connect each SEB to

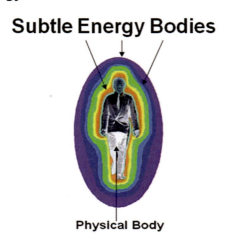

Diagram 3.2

the physical body. The physical body vibrates at a much lower frequency in comparison with each of the SEBs which all vibrate at higher frequencies. Each SEB frequency increases, moving from the 1st SEB to the 7th SEB. Therefore, in reality, human beings have a foot in both camps - the fourth-dimensional physical world and the multi-dimensional world of the fifth dimension (the sub-atomic world). This creates an ability to operate in the visible four-dimensional world that we see, and also within the invisible fifth-dimensional world that we do not see.

Most human beings only see the physical, four-dimension world. The invisible world of the SEB fields vibrates at frequencies in the upper ultraviolet spectrum, outside of a normal visual range. In diagram 3.2, the physical (visible) body is surrounded by seven (invisible) SEBs. Without these SEBs the physical body, and our consciousness could not exist. All of the SEBs represent part of our consciousness. Described below in detail are the different purposes of the seven SEBs. What do I mean by purpose? For a start, the simple model of consciousness that is described in chapter 2 is in reality much more complex. Each SEB, as well as their supporting VECs, contributes to our total consciousness. I will elaborate on this as I describe what each of the SEBs does. I define total consciousness as the conscious, unconscious and higher conscious minds (chapter 2). In an awakened state, we are only

Understanding Consciousness: the Quantum-Self

aware of what is going on in the conscious mind. Those who practise meditation techniques are more open to receive communications from their unconscious and higher conscious minds in comparison with those who do not. If our mind is still, just before we go to sleep and also first thing in the morning, then we are open to receive communications from our unconscious and higher conscious minds. These communications could be anything from a creative idea, an answer to a problem or issue that we are facing, through to feeling that it is time to move from our house or job and so on.

There are Seven Subtle Energy Body (SEB) Fields of Consciousness
So what are we? Are we just a brain, skin, bones, flesh and so on? How does consciousness really function? Is there more to us than the mechanistic, form-based and linear-time-biased understanding about how we function that we are led to believe? Does understanding energy (the fifth dimension) hold some clues to improving our life? Through investigating the SEB energy fields I discovered just how much more we really are. One of the challenges in writing this book is an attempt to raise the awareness and the perception we have about our-self. The ultimate goal is to empower you to bring the very best out of your-self on a regular basis, as well as for you to have a happier and more fulfilling life. Gaining a better understanding of what we are made of is a first step to enabling us to view life from a much broader perspective. It will help you become more aware of what is going on around you and what is happening to you. Each of us can benefit from knowledge of the complex series of seven SEBs that surround us. To explain the SEBs' purposes, I have separated them into three categories as shown in the exploded diagram 3.3.

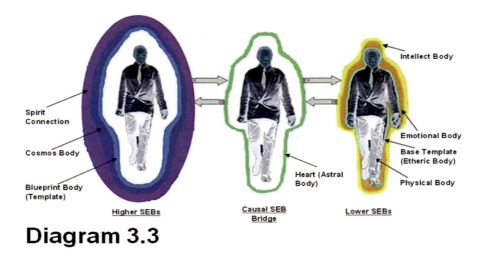

Diagram 3.3

As I noted above, we actually have more than seven SEBs, but gaining an understanding of these basic ones presents an easier platform to appreciate what is going on within our consciousness. To understand the SEBs and their link to the physical brain and body, it is important to recognise that we have a soul. This is because the soul influences what is happening within the consciousness of the SEBs. I use the term *spiritual dynamics,* defining it as how the soul and the authentic-self inter-relate, and how the inter-relationship affects the quantum bio-magnetic field through the SEBs.

A question that you may be interested in asking is *'where is the soul located?'* The soul's energy form resides in the lower three SEBs and mostly between the first and second SEB. It also operates at times with all the other four SEBs, plus the physical brain and body. Why the soul's home is located within the first three SEBs will unfold as you read through this chapter. The soul's communication with the physical brain and body is through the conscious mind. In diagram 3.3, the first three, or lower SEBs, are called the Base Template (Etheric) SEB, the Emotional SEB and the Intellectual (or Intellect) SEB. These are involved with physical life and with the issues (life lessons) that arise during a lifetime. The fourth SEB is called the Causal (or Heart) SEB which acts as an energy filter (or bridge) between the higher and lower SEBs. This is the balancing part of the total energy structure. It is all about giving and receiving on all levels. Finally, the top three or higher SEBs are called the Blueprint (Template) SEB, the Universal Understanding (Cosmos Connection) SEB and the Connection to Higher Realms (Spirit) SEB. These are all involved with higher consciousness and spiritual aspects of life. They influence our level of compassion, an understanding of why we are here, our purpose of being here, and so on. I am using my own words in naming the sixth and seventh SEB as it makes them more meaningful to me.

Understanding Consciousness and its Purpose
The seven SEBs contain important keys for us to understand consciousness and to appreciate why things happen in our lives and how we develop throughout life. Each SEB has a specific function, or purpose.

First SEB: Etheric or Base (physical) Template Body
Composition and Structure
The first or Etheric subtle energy body is located at ¼ inch to 2 inches from the physical body. It is an exact energy copy of the physical body, that is, skin, organs, brain, bones, blood vessels, blood, and so on. This energy copy is composed of lines of magnetic and light energy (it is made of photons) and takes the form of a web of pulsating light as shown in the diagram opposite. The photons vibrate at a frequency within the ultraviolet spectrum. The etheric body's photons in sensitive people, such as an artist, vibrate in a light-blue range in comparison with, for example, those of a sports person whose photons would vibrate in a greyish-blue range.

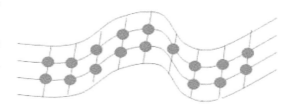

Purpose

The condition of the Etheric body is reflected in the state of health of the physical body. A problem within the physical body can usually be detected within the Etheric body before the physical body is actually affected. Alternatively, if the physical body is damaged, through radiation, or pollution, or alcohol, or drugs, or an accident, then this will affect the Etheric body, causing it to change to reflect the damage. The Etheric and physical body resonate in harmony with each other. Each part (brain, organ, blood veins, blood and so on) of the physical body is connected to its Etheric body counterpart by lines of energy which can be described as virtual energy fibre optic cables. The physical body cannot exist without the support of the first (Etheric) SEB and the other SEBs.

Conscious thoughts processed within the physical brain originate from the inter-connected different parts of the SEBs. The physical brain translates this activity which can be measured on an electro-encephalogram or fMRI scanner.

Second SEB: Emotional Template Body
Composition and Structure

The Emotional body is located 1 inch to 3 inches from the physical body. Every particle of the physical brain that processes emotions also has a corresponding particle in the Emotional SEB. Each of these particles is joined at irregular intervals through virtual energy connecting wires. They form an energy web. This body is quite different in comparison with the Etheric body in that it is composed of what can be described as clouds of different colours. The clouds are constantly changing their colour, which shows the type of emotions/feelings that are being stimulated by the thoughts processed through the Intellect body (3rd SEB) and brain. Each colour has a particular meaning, which can be quite complex given the different hues associated with an individual colour. Some brief general examples are as follows:

Black: hatred and malice; *red*: anger; *scarlet*: irritability; *brown/grey*: selfishness; *brown/red*: greed; *grey*: depression; *crimson*: selfish love; *rose*: unselfish love; *orange*: pride or ambition; *yellow*: Intellect; *green*: adaptability; blue: religious feeling; *pale blue/green*: sympathy/compassion, and so on.

As human emotions/feelings are usually mixed, so the coloured clouds are also mixed. The physical body is affected by energy from within the Emotional body.

Purpose

This SEB stores every feeling/emotion that we have ever had in life. The Emotional body energy field generates clouds of different photons of colour which are related to the thoughts that are being processed within our consciousness and brain. Thoughts stimulate an emotional response of some sort within the SEB. There are special cameras that can photograph this SEB, which gives us an excellent indication of the physical wellbeing and happiness state of the individual being photographed. Without the input of the emotions/feelings to the brain and physical body, we would all just be like a computer information retrieval device operating on the Intellect alone. In summary, the Emotional SEB has four functions:

1. to bring about feelings or sensations within the physical body
2. to operate as a link between the intellectual (Intellect) and physical body
3. to function as an independent channel between consciousness, awareness and action
4. to act as part of the human quantum bio-magnet energy field which attracts similar energies to us and causes us to be attracted to similar energies.

Third SEB: Intellect Template Body
Composition and Structure
The Intellect SEB extends 3 to 8 inches from the physical body. Every particle of the physical brain that processes thoughts started as a thinking particle in the Intellect SEB. These particles are only joined (within an energy web) at irregular intervals through what can be described as energy virtual light fibre optic connecting cables which form channels of communication. A simple schematic diagram of the connections between particles of the Intellect SEB (yellow) to particles of the emotional SEB (orange) connecting to particles of the brain (grey) is shown below.

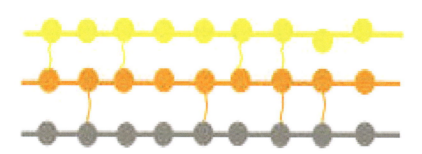

The Intellect SEB follows the shape of the physical body as a dense mist. It also surrounds the physical body at its outer extreme very close to an ellipse (or egg) shape of finer mist. Thoughts appear as blobs of yellow light within the Intellect SEB. The photons within the SEB vibrate in the yellow spectrum. The more intensely the mind is used, the brighter the Intellect SEB glows. This body permeates through and works with the emotional SEB and physical body.

Visualising the Intellect body as a matrix, or web-like structure, thoughts of a similar nature collect together forming their own storage area. This ensures an efficient functioning of thinking within the mind. Good thoughts have a finer vibration than bad thoughts (jealousy, hatred, greed, lust and so on) which are much denser due to their coarser vibration.

Purpose

The Intellect SEB (sometimes described as the lower mind) contains the thinking part of consciousness. It is the home of the intellect and rational mind. However, the being that causes the thinking (this is the soul/authentic-self) resides mainly in the first three SEBs. The information part of a thought is stored in the Intellect SEB. They appear as yellow clouds of thought forms.

When a thought form moves from the Intellect SEB, it experiences a quantum collapse of energy and has to find a channel (connection) to travel to the brain. It can only do so by finding a channel that vibrates with a similar resonance. These resonant energy channels are important as they determine if you are good at music, or literature, or science and so on. An engineer, for example, who cannot draw or may be a poor writer, lacks the requisite channels for him/her to do so. Nevertheless, it is possible to develop these channels provided that the individual has a passion to work at developing the appropriate talents. A thought can use a channel that is not of the same vibratory energy, but this would result in a lack of understanding or empathy when it is processed through the brain.

All that is stored in the brain is also stored in the Intellect SEB. And all that is stored in this SEB is also uploaded to the higher consciousness of the higher self. This is our spirit, which is host to our soul.

Fourth SEB: Causal (heart) or Astral Template Body
Composition and Structure

The fourth SEB (sometimes called the Astral or Heart body) extends some 6 inches to 12 inches from the surface of the physical body. This body is also made up of clouds of different colours but all are rather delicate and have a rose tint about them. The colours have the same meaning as those described in the Intellect body. The ego and persona reside in this body. This SEB is the central location of consciousness.

Purpose

The fourth SEB acts as a bridge between the three previous (lower) SEBs, which link to the physical world and to the soul's residence. It also acts as a bridge to the next three (higher) SEBs which are a link to where we came from (the world of spirit). This body filters a higher category of thoughts and ideas down from the higher SEBs through to the Intellectual body. It is the centre of abstract thoughts. Intuition flows through the Causal SEB. By practising relaxation techniques, we can make contact with our higher self through accessing this body. The higher self and soul can be invited to take up residence here during daily activities. The foundation of how we think and express our-selves during our life is a reflection of this body. The essence of powerful emotions and thoughts work their way up into the Causal body to become part of its fabric. Causal consciousness (the higher mind) deals with the essence of a thing while the Intellectual body, or the lower mind, deals with the details.

Fifth SEB: Etheric (Blueprint) Template and Higher Intellect Body
Composition and Structure
This SEB extends some 1½ to 2 feet from the physical body. It forms a complete energy blueprint or template of the physical brain and body. It provides the structure for the etheric body (the first SEB) and keeps it in place.

Purpose
Should disease occur within the physical body it is usually the result of an imbalance in the matrix energy structure of this energy body. It will be transmitted down to the lower etheric SEB and then into the physical body. Conversely, if any disease arises first within the physical body due to something like pollution or radiation, it will be transmitted to this SEB via the Etheric SEB. In these two cases, the frequency of the vibrational energy of the physical body, Etheric body and the etheric template have got out of phase. This will cause the equivalent etheric template structure that represents a particular part of the physical body to get out of balance and to become infected (just like a computer virus). Energy healing needs to be carried out on the etheric template to repair the damage. This healing will flow through to the Etheric body and in turn through to the physical body, provided nothing is blocking it. Sound has a particularly powerful effect on this body and can be used as part of a healing protocol when appropriate.

Sixth SEB: Connection to Cosmos – Celestial Template Body
Composition and Structure
The Celestial SEB is the body through which we connect with everything (for example the universe, infinite love and so on). It extends some 2 to 2 ½ feet from the physical body.

Purpose
This is where a higher level of consciousness exists that enables us to experience the *I am*. By the time we are able to raise our consciousness to this level we have understood that we have many layers of consciousness, each associated with the seven SEBs and more. We feel at one with the universe and can easily give unconditional love. We live at a level of acceptance, non-judgement, unconditional love, non-attachment and so forth. The very essence of our authentic-self.

Seventh SEB: Ketheric Template Body
Composition and Structure
The Ketheric Template SEB is an egg-shaped body, purple gravitating to gold in colour, that contains all the previous six SEBs. It extends about 2½ to 3½ feet from the physical body.

Purpose
Raising consciousness to the seventh level empowers us with a natural understanding that we are at one with the Creator.

All of the SEBs, including the physical body, require sustenance (and maintenance) of different sorts to remain in balance. For the physical body, this is easy as it is the food we eat, the beverages we drink, the air we breathe, absorption of sunlight, and exercises we take. But the physical body also requires another energy input to maintain a healthy state, namely, a magnetic energy. The body's cells require nourishment from the earth's magnet field. Without this we would simply die. Each of the SEBs receives sustenance from the earth's magnetic field.

As well as magnetic energy, there is yet another energy input required for us to survive, and this is received from what is popularly called the Universal Energy Field. The word 'Universal' is perhaps too narrow as it does not truly reflect the multi-dimensional nature of the Universe. In this multidimensional universe there are parallel universes and these have an effect upon one another. Astrophysicists and quantum physicists are aware of parallel universes. A more accurate word to use would be Multiverse (Universes running in parallel) and Multiversal rather than Universal. Each one of these parallel Universes feeds off the Multiversal energy field. Do we really need this Multiversal energy to survive?

Yes we do. This energy streams through us from the universe, plus the earth's energy that streams up from below and around us. Both are necessary to supply power to each of the SEBs. Power and information is supplied to each of the SEBs through a series of VECs, that I describe below. The power is generated by the Heart energy centre (it is like an energy power station). It transforms the two energies which flow down through the Crown VEC (top of head - positive polarity) and which flow up from the base VEC (negative polarity) into the power that is necessary for survival. In addition, the two energies form an input to each of the SEBs overall polarity. Yes, we do have a positive and negative charge within the SEBs and these contribute to our polarity.

Polarity – Discover your Complex Quantum Bio-magnetic Properties
What is polarity? It is the very force, or glue, that holds everything in and on this planet including our-self, the human body, its cells, molecules and atoms, and the universe, together. It is a reflection of each human being's duality. As beings of energy we have a polarity of which one pole represents the masculine side and the other the feminine side. A simple model to consider is a bar magnet which has a North and South Pole as shown in diagram 3.4. North is regarded as a positive charge and South a negative charge. Magnetic lines of force (or energy) flow from the North Pole to the South Pole. Within this field there is also an East and West component. The atoms and molecules of the metal that make up the magnet have a natural resonance (or vibration) creating the magnetic lines of force. When two magnets are put together, like poles repel each other, and unlike poles attract, as shown in the diagram.

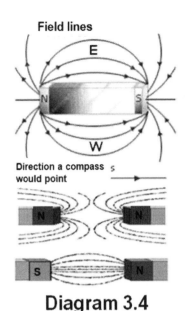

Diagram 3.4

Descending into the quantum or sub-atomic world, energy strings (chapter 1, page 27), are the building blocks of a fundamental particle that are the building blocks of an electron, neutron and proton, which together form atoms. Each energy string (diagram on the right), whether a closed loop or a single energy string can be considered as a magnetic dipole, that is, an extremely small packet of energy which behaves like a magnet vibrating at a specific frequency. So the glue or force that keeps us bound together is the magnetic attraction arising from the flow between the two poles. The cumulative effect of this is polarity.

Energy string

As human beings, it is the balance or imbalance of polarity that provides an indication of a state of happiness and physical wellbeing, or not. The physical body and each of the SEBs have a polarity. Thoughts affect the SEB's fields which in turn cause a change in the polarity of these fields. This should come as no surprise as we are beings of energy and all energy has a polarity. The first image on the left-hand side of diagram 3.5 is an artist's impression of the body's energy field showing its East (masculine +) and West (feminine -) component of polarity, which is in balance. Once again, the overall polarity is the sum total of the physical body's polarity plus the polarity of all the subtle energy bodies' energy fields. These energy fields in the diagram are evenly distributed across both sides of the body.

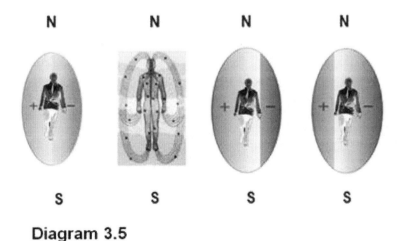

Diagram 3.5

The second image from the left provides a better schematic view of the flow of energy fields. What does having a balanced energy polarity mean? It means that the individual's consciousness has a clear access to work with all of the VECs and SEBs. There are no blockages. In the third image from the left, the individual has an excessively positive polarity which is skewed to their right-hand side, the masculine side. This indicates that their consciousness tends to be operating in a form-based, mechanistic, linear-time-biased world with little if any concept of spirituality. They have difficulty thinking out of their virtual box. They may lack compassion and humility and their integrity may be in doubt. Nonetheless, they probably have a very powerful intellect. Alternatively, in the fourth image, we see an individual's polarity in a highly negative state - the energy field is skewed to the left-hand side of their body, the feminine side, and they are probably swept away with spiritual concepts and pursuits. They are almost certainly not grounded and may be fearful about life, perhaps because of a trauma, and feel they would rather not have been born. They prefer to spend their thinking time in the realm of spiritual activities and perhaps some artistic pursuits. With an overly negative energy field, an individual may also feel trapped within their issues (life lessons). In the last two polarity examples the individual's consciousness is most probably unable to communicate with their Heart VEC (the balancer) and associated SEBs due to blockages probably in the lower VECs. How we feel physically, and what we perceive our state of happiness to be, are reflections of the status of the body's energy fields and of its polarity, which is an indication of what is going on in the conscious and unconscious minds. The following table provides some idea of the duality effects of polarity and how polarity can be affected.

Duality – The Happiness/Physical Wellbeing Effects of Polarity

	N-S East: Positive Energy
Acid/ alkaline body status (pH 7 neutral)	Acid if energy field is highly positive i.e. above pH 7 and can be over stimulated
Gender of Energy field	Masculine (Chinese symbol +Yang)
Perspective	Form-based/ mechanistic inclination
Musical connection	Fast rhythms
Colour connection	Colour red stimulates
Personality	Light side
	N-S West: Negative Energy
Acid/ alkaline body status (pH 7 neutral)	Alkaline if energy field is highly negative, i.e. below pH 7 and can feel tired.

Gender of Energy field	Feminine (Chinese symbol – Ying)
Perspective	Spiritual inclination
Musical connection	Slow rhythms
Colour connection	Colour blue sedates
Personality	Dark (Shadow) side

A classic example of the binding energy force of polarity is found in the structure of the water molecule (diagram 3.6). The North pole - the dark sphere which is called a South-seeking pole (the oxygen atom which has a dominant negative charge) - attracts two negative North-seeking poles (the hydrogen atoms which have a dominant positive charge) which represent the South pole. As unlike poles attract in the sub-atomic world, the positive North pole which is the South-seeking negative oxygen atom has attracted two positive North-seeking hydrogen atoms (the South Pole) to form a water molecule.

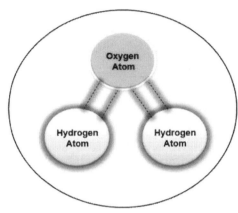

Diagram 3.6

Each of the 7 SEBS is grounded through what is called the Base VEC (see below). As human beings, most of our problems (emotional, psychological and physical) begin within an SEB which is not properly grounded. This is most probably due to a block within its supporting VEC structure. By grounding I mean connected through to the earth just like any electrical device. But what are these VECS?

Vortex Energy Centres (VECs) – Connecting to the SEBs

Diagram 3.7 is an artist's impression of a VEC. In reality, it resembles a spinning vortex of energy (like a spiral) acting like a valve which is either active (open) or inactive (closed). When it is active it allows a two-way flow of information and energy, into it or out of it. And when it is closed it only allows information and energy to flow out of it. Each VEC connects with the physical body along an energy line parallel to the body's spine (its root) and to each of the SEBs. The spin rate (or frequency) of the VECs increases, moving up from the base of the spine to the crown.

Diagram 3.7

Diagram 3.8 shows seven VECs starting at the Base of Spine which is associated with the physical side of life (for example pain, pleasure). This is followed by a second VEC called the Sacral which is associated with feelings and emotions. The third VEC is called the Solar Plexus and is associated with intellectual and analytical activities. The fourth VEC, called the Heart, is part of a bridge between the first three (lower) VECs and their associated SEBs. They are all linked with whatever is going on in an individual's physical life, their state of happiness and energy balance. In comparison, the upper (higher) VECs together with their SEBs are associated with an individual's spiritual life and with their state of happiness and energy balance. The fifth (Throat) VEC is associated with communication in general. It is also associated with different levels of creativity and the source of infinite knowledge. The sixth (the Forehead or Brow) is associated perception as it pulls together the information from the body's different sensors. Finally, the seventh (the Crown) is the link through to higher consciousness and the Creator.

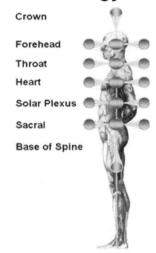

Diagram 3.8

From the second (Sacral) through to the sixth (Forehead), these five VECs connect with the back, front and also both sides of the body and each of the seven SEBs respectively (diagrams 3.8 and 3.9). There is only a single VEC connected to the Base of Spine (pointing downwards) and also only a single one connected to the Crown (pointing upwards). Nonetheless, both the Crown and Base VECs connect to all of the individual SEBs as do the other five. In other words, each SEB always has an appropriate set of VECs connecting it to the physical body along the spinal column. The front and back VECs also connect each of us to the future and the past respectively. These affect us by producing a tendency to become fixated, from time to time, with things that have happened to us in the past, or perhaps with what we think is going to happen to us in the future. Our conditioning to believe in linear time tends to intensify this tendency.

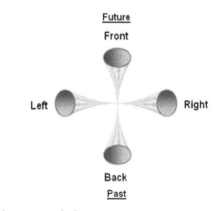

Diagram 3.9

There is not much written about the VECs located upon the left and right-hand side of the body as shown in diagrams 3.8 and 3.9. They are associated with duality (polarity) that is connecting the positive (right - physical world/masculine) energies with the negative (left -

spiritual/feminine) energies. They affect each of the SEB's polarity (diagram 3.5). As we become more aware of duality (polarity) through understanding the third dimension, in the second paradigm pertaining to the sub-atomic world (see chapter 1), today's personal development programmes will need to be rewritten to explain what this means to us.

Energy and Information Highways Driven by Consciousness

Each VEC is actually nested into the other and increases in diameter (diagram 3.10) as it moves out from its root position to join successive SEBs. The frequencies of each nested VEC also increase as each moves outwards, cutting through an SEB. Each VEC's surface is covered with what can be called an etheric web of energy. Importantly, the centre of a VEC now spins mainly in all directions (like a gyroscope) and acts, as explained above, like a gate, or valve, allowing energy and information to flow into or out of it. The VEC centre's average spin tendency can be either clockwise or anticlockwise depending on its location and what is happening. The direction of spin dictates whether or not it is in an active or passive state. When open or active it sends energy/information both in and out.

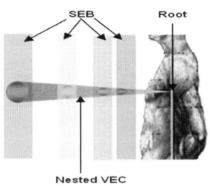

Diagram 3.10

When closed or inactive it allows energy/information to only flow out. Energy/information that matches its frequency (rate of spin) flows out (because the VEC is closed). It is the frequency of the spin of each VEC that determines the type of energy/information that flows into or out of it. Each of the nested VECs can be spinning in different directions at the junction of each of the SEBs, depending on what is happening within our consciousness. Because of human evolution over the last 2000 years, the VECs have changed how they spin and currently they spin on a three-dimensional axis. At times, a VEC's clockwise spin can be so powerful that energy/information is shot outwards and someone physically close may be able to tune into it like a radio receiver. The individual in this case may not be thinking of anyone in particular. It just happens that the individual receiving the energy/information burst was tuned into receiving it (probably unconsciously). Alternatively, if you are actually thinking of someone intensely with a lot of emotion then there is a strong possibility that they will pick up your thoughts in one way or another.

As the frequency of each VEC increases, moving vertically from its root to the crown, so the colour of the centre changes to match the frequency of the VEC. The VEC colours follow that of the spectrum of a rainbow. The logic behind the increasing light frequencies begins to make sense as they take into account the state of an individual's mind. Darker, cloudy colours, especially towards the greys and reds, tend to indicate an imbalance of some sort, either in the physical body, or mind, or both.

Each VEC has not only a particular colour associated with it, but also an endocrine gland which is located close to each centre's root. The location of these glands and colours are shown in diagram 3.11.

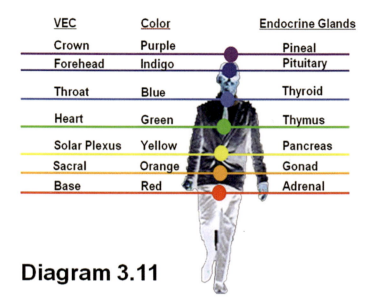

Diagram 3.11

Each VEC's colour and location is as follows:

- o base vortex energy centre, associated with the adrenal gland (colour – red)
- o sacral with the gonad (testes (m) or ovaries (f) (colour - orange))
- o solar plexus with the pancreas (colour – yellow)
- o heart (colour – green) with the thymus
- o throat with the thyroids (colour – sky blue)
- o brow with the pituitary gland (colour – indigo)
- o crown with the pineal gland (colour – purple)

The above colours indicate the energy frequency a VEC is sensitive to, allowing each to open within the hue range of that particular colour frequency. Although each VEC has a colour associated with it, because of the nesting and different spins (three-dimensional clockwise/anticlockwise) creating subtle changes of frequency, most of them are able to display several colours at once.

In summary, the function of each VEC is to:

1. ensure that the SEB fields are supplied with the appropriate energy/information within a defined frequency range and are kept healthy.
2. participate in the development of human consciousness. Each centre is associated with specific consciousness functions (see table below).

3. transmit energy/information, between each SEB and the physical body.
4. contribute to each of the SEB's polarity.
5. provide a channel to bring wisdom from the VECs at the rear (historic information) through to consciousness at the front centres to influence and to refine the choice/decision making, depending on what is happening in an individual's life.

All of the energy/information that forms consciousness within the SEBs and VECs is composed of photons of energy vibrating in a colour range above the visible spectrum that we observe. When SEB colours are actually seen, what is seen is a harmonic of those same colours that exist in the ultra violet spectrum. A harmonic is just a series of doubling (or halving) the frequency of the colour being viewed from its base frequency. The following table shows the range of colours associated with each VEC, its colour frequency (in nanometres: 700 nanometres = 7 millionth of a metre) and also the range of musical notes with its frequency in hertz.

Colour	**Red**	**Orange**	**Yellow**	**Green**	**Blue**	**Indigo**	**Violet**
Frequency+	700-630	630-590	590-560	560-490	490-440	440-420	420-400
Sound	G	A	A#	C	D	D#	E
Frequency*	392	440	466	523	587	622	659

+ nanometres   * hertz

Why do I show both light and sound together? Because they are both vibrational energy forms, which affect other energy forms including the physical body through its SEBs and VECs. Part of any healing process involves quite simply changing the vibrational frequency of diseased tissue back to its original healthy frequency by using other similar vibrational energy, just like two closely-positioned tuning forks coming into synchronicity and vibrating together at the same frequency. We are beings of energy and energy bodies respond to colours and sounds as well as to thought energy. The other part of a healing process is to investigate the psychology behind the disease and that means finding the cause of any imbalance.

How each VEC Spins

A lot of today's literature on VECs still describes them spinning in either a clockwise or anticlockwise direction (in two dimensions). Moreover, their description has not really changed since it was written over 2,000 years ago! As indicated above, the VECs were called chakras (or wheels) in those days as they are even today. I prefer the term VEC as humanity has evolved since then, and with the evolution that has occurred, structural changes have taken place within the human energy system that have affected the VECs and SEBs. Just like having an upgrade. Looking at today's nested VECs, the energy flow within them moves like a spiral which spins like a three-dimensional gyroscope, as described above. Certainly, the male Base of Spine VEC spins in an overall clockwise direction. In comparison, a female's Base of Spine VEC spins on average in an anticlockwise direction. Moving upwards (diagram 3.12) to the next vortex energy centre (the Sacral - orange) always spins in the opposite direction for both males and females. In other words, the centres are always contra-rotating as you move upwards from the Base of spine to the Crown.

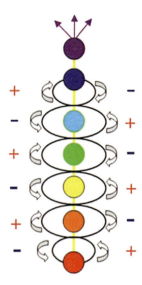

Diagram 3.12

Inner Happiness Properties of each VEC

An individual's feeling of inner positive wellbeing and happiness is influenced by the quality of the energy/information flow within each VEC and to the SEBs. The VECs are also responsible for maintaining the body's energy balance. From birth, as we mature, each vortex energy centre goes through a strengthening and development process. Should the energy flow within a centre get blocked for whatever reason, it will affect its performance, causing it to deteriorate. Its vibrational spin will become erratic, with the possibility of it being reversed in a direction contrary to how it should be spinning. If this happens, energy/information may flow in the opposite direction. Energy may be lost because too much is being vented (blown) out of a particular VEC. There will be a blockage here within the VEC system. But what causes a blockage? Before answering this question, we need to note that there are two forces at play within consciousness – thinking, and emotions/feelings.

During a child's earliest years, say up to about 7 years old, they are very vulnerable to emotional shocks caused by what can be perceived as a negative experience, and how those close by, such as family members, relations, friends, authority figures and so forth, communicate with them. Perhaps a family member dies and the child may show some emotion by bursting into tears at the loss. A parent or someone close might say 'stop crying, grown up people do not cry'. Now, that is really the problem of the person who makes the statement, as they may be suffering from suppressed emotions and have mirrored their problem in the child. This could shock the child to stop crying. It could also be responsible for causing an energy block (a trauma) within the child's sensitive energy structure. If the child goes through other similar experiences and does not allow their emotions to flow out, an internal unconscious pattern of behaviour would be set up. People may see the child, at a later age, as being a cold person who did not respond in a sympathetic way when confronted with something like bereavement or a difficult emotional situation. Another example could be where, at a young age, a child might want a hug as an expression of love and does not get one. If this happens regularly, or the child does not want to ask for a hug for fear of being rejected, then a blockage would most certainly occur.

Why is this important? It is important because we are all like a quantum bio-magnet with a surrounding vibrational energy and information field that is made up of what is happening within the VECs and SEBs, including our current thinking. We attract or are attracted to what happens to us, according to the energy and information field that we radiate. This includes people with similar energy blockages, that is, people with similar issues (life lessons) to our own. If we have issues of intimacy, or low self-image, or low self-motivation, or low self-esteem, or low self-acceptance and so forth, then we attract people and situations that mirror this back to us. As we mature, this continues. We attract or are attracted to people who act as a mirror for the different types of issues and life lessons that we have to learn from. Within the SEBs and VECs our issues and life lessons are represented by energy imbalances and blockages.

Mirroring is an essential part of our personal development. This is because issues and life lessons are reflected back to us to provide an opportunity for us to recognise, accept and work through them to bring them into balance. In the end, it is all about bringing emotions/feelings and their associated energy/information polarity into balance. There is a problem here, though, which is that many people are totally unaware of the mirroring energy/information exchanges that are going on around them at a sub-atomic level. Each of the VECs (and SEBs) is part of our consciousness and has an effect upon our feeling of inner positive wellbeing and happiness. Once a particular type of psychological problem has been identified (for example, depression, excess anger, addiction, abuse, low self-esteem and low self-worth, low self-acceptance and so forth) it is possible to rectify the imbalance by restoring homeostasis (balance) to the appropriate energy centres. I describe different ways of bringing VECs into balance below. Finally, each of the VECs also acts as a sensor for us to get a feel of the world around us.

Recognising that VECs play a major part in the makeup of an individual's consciousness is still outside most of today's psychiatrists', psychologists' and therapists' accepted thinking and practice. But there are those growing numbers of pioneers in the professions (C Maxwell Cade, Dr Barbara Ann Brennan, Dr Deepak Chopra, Dr Caroline Myss, and many more) who have opened that virtual box of thinking and studied the relationship between consciousness, the SEB fields, VECs and different types of psychological problems faced in Western society. Most of these pioneers appreciate that there is a need to look at the whole mind/emotions/body/spirit system. Most, directly, or indirectly, made this pioneering change recognising, consciously or unconsciously, that energy is a dimension which it is essential to take into account. Why? Mostly because approaching psychology, psychiatry and illness from an energy perspective enabled them to short-circuit many of the outdated approaches used in the traditional professions. Going directly to the cause of a problem is part of the course. To elaborate on the causes of common problems faced by people today, an outline of the states of consciousness associated with each VEC may prove to be helpful. These states of consciousness are:

FIRST VEC: BASE OF SPINE
Colour: **Red**   Endocrine Gland: **Adrenals**

Associated Inner Happiness State
The first VEC is located at the base of the spine. As beings of energy, there is a requirement for us to be linked energetically with the ground under our feet. This is because part of our feeling of wellbeing and happiness is affected by the magnetic energy that we take up through us from the planet via this centre and the Universal energy which passes down through us into the ground. Physical energy devices, not unlike electronic equipment, need to be earthed (or grounded) to operate properly. We too, as bio-electric beings, have to be grounded to function properly. All SEBs and VECs have to be energetically grounded down through the physical body to the base of the spine, and on down both legs and out of both feet into the ground, for us to be able to remain in a balanced energy state.

From time to time, you may hear people talk about someone using the phrase 'they are just not grounded'. What does this mean? It means that they may be scatter-brained, making no real sense, or that they never finish anything they start, or combinations of the two. They may behave in an unstable manner. They may be fearful with respect to their safety and financial wellbeing. These states of mind arise when an individual is not grounded. For this to happen, it means that there are blockages within the Base of Spine centre which is only allowing a small amount of energy/information to flow out of, or in through it. In extreme cases, such as trauma, a blockage may stop energy/information from flowing through it altogether. A lack of energy in this centre can give rise to an individual feeling physically tired. And should this continue over a long period of time it can lead to such symptoms as a conscious feeling of not wanting to live in a physical reality (they do not wish to be here). It can also lead to a state of depression. Some examples of the type of problems which can arise when a Base VEC is out of balance are as follows. An individual might:

- be afraid of any changes that may affect their life
- be overly cautious in their approach to life

- have a lack of passion for what they are involved in
- suffer from a lack of concentration
- not be able to take an idea through to its physical completion
- be lethargic, especially in situations where they are looking for employment, a condition which would make finding a job even more difficult
- fear becoming ill
- feel physically vulnerable
- feel unsupported by family, friends or colleagues around them
- be extremely anxious, and not wanting to get involved in the nitty gritty of life
- feel physically weak and require more rest than normal.
- suffer from lower back pain
- want to hide from reality by not going out socially and staying at home.
- have suicidal tendencies
- experience loss of financial abundance
- find money difficult to obtain.

What causes the base VEC to be weak? When this centre is weak it is not opening (becoming active) or shutting down (becoming inactive) properly. One or more of its nested VECs may be rotating in the opposite direction of its natural spin (energy is being pumped in the opposite direction, or there is no energy movement at all), thus causing it to lack sufficient energy to keep it in balance. The VEC's spin is affected by what is happening in an individual's day to day life. Any trauma arising from an activity or event such as an accident, getting the sack, experiencing a death in the family, being abandoned or dumped and so on, will cause a blockage within this VEC. The nested VEC centre's natural spin will be affected and may cause some to reverse. The energy flow to the other VECs above and below will also be affected.

What happens to us at birth and throughout the first seven years or so of existence, has a major effect on the stability of the base VEC. During this time period, the foundations are put in place that determine how strongly we will feel rooted (or grounded) in this lifetime. In other words, it affects how strongly we feel connected with physical reality. During those first few years, if we face issues such as abuse, a lack of security, lack of love, abandonment, fear and disruption, then the foundations of not being grounded in this life are formed. What does this mean? It means that this centre will be weak. An individual may expect symptoms of issues associated with this VEC to be reflected back to them from the situations they experience as they journey along their life's path.

Individuals who have a balanced Base VEC are very active, are strongly self-empowered and have a robust will to live. This can be positively infectious on those less fortunate. They are in touch with physical reality and enjoy their life. Their sexual energy should also be very loving.

Parts of the Body Influenced by the Base VEC:
adrenal glands, supply of energy to the spine, the kidneys, bladder, large intestine, prostate, blood circulation, teeth, legs, and feet.

Problems of Excess Energy in the Base VEC:
An individual may suffer from a high degree of perfectionism, greed, addiction to money and wealth, be overactive, aggressive, belligerent and have an urge to victimise people. They might also be aggressively over-sexed.

Problems of Lack of Energy in the Base VEC:
This causes an individual to be weak and have an inability to reach their goals; be unable to understand another's boundaries; show traits of being a victim; be easily confused, have suicidal tendencies and little or no interest in sex.

Physical Symptoms that Arise with Disturbances in the Base VEC:
obesity, insomnia, susceptibility to colds, haemorrhoids, varicose veins, lower back pain, bladder infection, constipation, body temperature fluctuations, leukaemia, and sciatica.

SECOND VEC: the SACRAL
Colour: **Orange**   Endocrine Gland: **Sexual Organs**

Associated Inner Happiness State
The Sacral VEC, sometimes called the spleen centre, is located close to the spleen, is the centre of emotions/feelings and also of procreation. It is a centre of giving and receiving. It is the emotions and feelings connection to all the SEBs. The emotions/feelings energy content of all relationships is retained in this centre and the information part of the relationship is linked with the third or Solar Plexus VEC. For example, the effects of being rejected by a parent; how we were nurtured; the amount of give and take within the family; how intimate we are and the vulnerability we are able to show and so on, are all stored in the Sacral VEC. We react according to the emotion stored here. A problem that might arise from this could be the establishment of 'wounded inner child' (chapter 5), during the early stages of upbringing. Should this occur, it is important that it is recognised, accepted, and worked with for us to bring about a balance with respect to our inner child. Most of us carry a wounded inner child of some sort within us. Some of the issues (life lessons) that may arise from having a disturbed family upbringing, can show up later in terms of poor parenting, abuse of all types, in relationships, and a lack of passion for life.

Sexual desire is a major energy which is associated with this centre. The front Sacral VEC is linked with how good a bond between two people feels, and the physical sexual expression arising from this. When this centre is functioning properly an individual should be able to enjoy a good sexual relationship, with their partner, reaching an orgasm if desired. In comparison, the back Sacral vortex energy centre is linked with how much sex an individual requires and how they sexually express themselves. If over active, then an individual may not be able to get enough sex to satisfy their urge. If under active, then the individual concerned may be frigid, impotent and have little if any desire for sexual activity. When both front and back centres are open, in balance, and spinning in an appropriate direction, then the desire to have a sexual relationship is strong. Should there be any blockages here (in the front or back) then it will lower an individual's sexual vitality. Having an orgasm is an important part of cleansing the body of energy blockages, releasing tension (stress) and helping in the clearance of toxic energies. Some examples of the type of problems that can arise when a Sacral VEC is out of balance are as follows. It can lead to symptoms where an individual might:

- be emotionally unresponsive
- show anti-social traits
- find it difficult to form boundaries
- have strong feelings of repression
- lack any originality of expression
- have symptoms of intellectual retardation
- be open to addictions
- in women, have menstrual pain and fertility problems
- show arrogant traits (be narcissistic)
- be selfish
- show victim-consciousness
- be lustful and over-sexed
- be overcome by other people's energy.

Parts of the Body Influenced by the Sacral VEC:
ovaries, testes, genitals, prostate, kidney area, urinary tract, gall bladder, spleen and the skin.

Problems of Excess Energy in the Sacral VEC:
An individual may be overly sensitive (take things to heart) and react through their emotions. They may want to be the centre of attention and have weak or no boundaries (cannot say no, or overstay their welcome). They may operate through their unconscious mind with a tendency to speak without thinking. Because they are so emotional they affect the emotional

climate around them. Such individuals tend to be over-needy and pleasure oriented - from sex to food, to partying and so on.

Problems of Lack of Energy in the Sacral VEC:
When this centre is under energised it can give rise to an individual experiencing limited sexual, emotional and physical movement. This may make them rigid and inflexible both physically and emotionally. Their breathing rate will most probably slow down, giving rise to a reduction in their metabolic rate. They may experience a fear of change and have a narrow and weak point of view on important issues. Avoidance of pleasure may dominate their lives and they will dislike those who participate in such pursuits. Such individuals may hide themselves behind an obsession with intellectual pursuits.

Physical Symptoms that Arise with Disturbances in the Sacral VEC:
drug abuse, alcoholism, gout, asthma, allergies, eating disorders, frigidity, sexual diseases, impotence, candida, depression, uterine problems and an imbalance in the body's polarity.

THIRD VEC: SOLAR PLEXUS
Colour: **Yellow**   Endocrine Gland: **Pancreas**

Associated Inner Happiness State
The Solar Plexus, or Intellect VEC is located at the solar plexus and is the centre of such human characteristics as the intellect, will-power, self-esteem, self-worth, self-respect, self-control, self-acceptance, self-confidence, personal empowerment, victim-consciousness, humility, awareness of the purpose and meaning of life and interpersonal relationship skills. It is also a centre of lower intuition (gut feel). To function in a balanced and healthy way, the Solar Plexus VEC centre is required to be in harmony with an individual's emotional life centred in the Sacral VEC. Western society's main focus is on the development of the intellect and the absorption of knowledge. It forms the basis of where we fit within the structures of institutions, companies and society as a whole. We have quite literally expanded this energy centre at the expense of the others and at what a cost! Emotional intelligence in Western society is only now being recognised as a problem area that requires attention. There is a requirement for governments, businesses and institutions to accelerate the trend to compensate for this imbalance. We are not simply commodities, or intellectual, fact-reproducing bio-machines; we are human beings with feelings and emotions that need to be recognised, worked with and not commoditised in some marketing/advertising campaign.

The conscious mind gains an understanding of the different emotions/feelings that arise in life, sorts them, and puts them into a framework that helps us to define reality. Different thoughts (information) have appropriate emotions/feelings attached to them. Emotions/feelings have a direct access through the second SEB (the emotional body) to the third SEB (the Intellect body) via the Sacral VEC and also from the Solar Plexus VEC. Should there be blockages here, this can give rise to a low self-image, low self-worth, lack of self-empowerment, lack of self-control and so on. If this energy centre is closed, then an individual will be devoid of feelings; because their consciousness does not recognise them, it has no reference point. There is no communication with the Sacral VEC and/or the Base VEC through the SEBs. Some examples of the type of problems that can arise when this centre is out of balance are as follows. An individual might:

- feel depressed
- have low self-esteem
- feel very shy and withdrawn in relationships
- be a people pleaser
- suffer from feelings of guilt and shame
- be fearful
- have a fear of failure
- lack self-discipline
- lack the strength to take responsibility for their life
- suffer from feeling a victim
- intellectually be unreliable
- be manipulative.

The Solar Plexus VEC is a very sensitive sensor with respect to the body and is likened to an energy receiver. We form here first impressions of people we meet, or of different situations at work, play, or at home. You will no doubt have heard the term 'gut feel' or 'gut reaction'. This is a response that arises from within the Solar Plexus centre. In reality, though, it is really intuition at work. When we interact with another person, intuition is used to determine if they can be trusted, or if they are telling the truth. Sometimes a silent voice within the conscious mind will give answers to questions posed, or we may get a positive or negative gut feeling (in the solar plexus). What is happening here is that there is an exchange of energy between two people. Intuition allows an interpretation of this energy to give an answer. Body language, tone of voice and the actual information spoken can also contribute to provide clues to answering any questions that are posed. One of the problems we face in a Western society is that we are educated out of using intuition. This is very much to our detriment as it limits the possibility of getting things right. Intuition, after all, is simply the unconscious recognition of patterns in life. Communications are received from our authentic-self through intuition.

The Solar Plexus VEC is also a strong powerhouse of energy, radiating or transmitting energy/information outwards. It has, therefore, an association with anything that involves power in life. The power may be related to an inner power structure and the way we react to power from external sources. If challenges are met from situations involving power, then there is potential for growth to come out of the experience. But if we retreat into ourselves, there will be no growth, and a blockage can be created that will have to be faced at a later time. It can be said that the purpose of the centre is also to transmute energy blockages caused by issues of power that have arisen. This enables the energy flow to continue upwards to the other VECs, thereby raising our awareness of the reality of a situation.

Parts of the Body Influenced by the Solar Plexus VEC:
pancreas, the nervous system, digestive system, the stomach, metabolic system, small intestines, liver and diaphragm.

Problems of Excess Energy in the Solar Plexus VEC:
An individual may always be very busy doing things all the time, round the clock, leaving no time at all to just be still and to contemplate where they are in their life. They can be very impatient and show a lack of compassion. Such individuals may also appear to have very strong will power but this is usually a cover as they most probably suffer from low self-esteem and have a weak ego. They will, however, be prone to always wanting to be in control of people, situations and themselves. Abuse of power is not uncommon on account of their dominating personality.

Problems of Lack of Energy in the Solar Plexus VEC:
This can lead to a lack of healthy boundaries with respect to people and situations. The individual concerned may have difficulty in saying no. They may be easily dumped upon. A lack of confidence will be predominant, together with high levels of fear. Having a weak will and being easily manipulated are other characteristics. They may avoid confrontation and any challenges at all costs. Playing it safe and letting other people lead is what they feel most comfortable with. From all this, it is easy to see that such an individual may suffer from low self-esteem, self-worth, self-acceptance and so on.

Physical Symptoms Arising with Solar Plexus VEC Disturbances:
blood sugar imbalance, diabetes, arthritis, hypoglycaemia, ulcers, hepatitis, nervousness, timidity, worms and parasites, liver problems, jaundice, toxicity, chronic fatigue, the flu, addictions to stimulants and poor memory.

*

Most people spend their lifetime coming to terms with, and working through, issues (life lessons) associated with the first three VECs and their associated SEBs. This is part of the purpose of being here and of living in a physical body. If you are reading this book, then you may already have felt that in a lot of what is going on in your own life, 'all is not as it seems'. If you have not given much consideration as to why you are here in a physical body or what the purpose of being here is, then this book has the potential to fill some gaps. It is written to provide you with some additional insight into what life is about and, hopefully, to make your life easier and happier. Key here is for you to be observant with respect to what is happening to you and in the world around you. You are aware that you are like a quantum bio-magnet attracting to you and being attracted to people, situations, places, towns, countries and so on, which provide you with experiences that contribute towards your growth. All of this, and more, gives you the opportunity to work through your life lessons, and it is vitally important to recognise that it is the questions you ask your-self and others, and the lessons you learn from the answers, which make an essential contribution to your inner growth and knowledge. Understanding this should hopefully lead you to the conclusion that there are:

'never any problems in life, only challenges'

If all that you can see in your life are problems, then I suggest you stop, reboot your mind (clear it of any negative thoughts and deep-rooted received 'wisdom') and look at life again from a different direction.

FOURTH VEC: The HEART
Colour: **Green**   Endocrine Gland: **Thymus**

Associated Inner Happiness State
The Heart or fourth VEC is located at the heart position and has a special position in the VECs and SEBs structures. It bridges the lower three VECs (these are about physical life) and the upper three VECs (these are about spiritual life - compassion, humility, and so on), including all of their associated SEBs. Its purpose is, in general, about giving and receiving with an emphasis on love. I am not talking about physical love here but of Universal and unconditional love. The back Heart VEC is the home of the ego, that pre-programmed energy structure which drives us to go after what we want. When ego is operating within the lower three centres, it tends to be self-centred (focuses on the physical aspects of life) and the challenge is to raise its awareness to include the upper VECs so that it can gain a perception of the 'big picture' of life.

Universal love and unconditional love are the core energy frequency of the Heart VEC. It focuses on relationships (with our-self and others) such as intimacy, compassion, and self-acceptance. One of its purposes is to bring about a balance in relationships and life in general. Unless a link is formed with this centre, we condemn ourselves to the narrow belief that the form-based, mechanistic and linear-time-biased world that we live in is what life is. In the case of sceptics, addicts, racists, worshippers of gurus, celebrities or other icons, consciousness is usually trapped within the lower three VECs. This is due to not recognising the blockages (the issues which are running) that need to be dealt with and cleared to enable consciousness to move up from the lower three VECs. A major part of life's purpose is to work through and balance the issues that are set up in our soul contract. These issues are our life lessons. In addition, as we progress through life, we may create other issues that also need to be worked with and brought into balance. This is all part of raising awareness and wisdom to a higher level, a key component of what life is about.

True love is always unconditional and has no co-dependency attached to it. A good measure of whether or not the Heart VEC is open is to listen to our-self, or our partner, when we or they express love. If there are any conditions attached, or if there are any co-dependency issues around, it will come out during a conversation. We will then know that this centre is not functioning properly and is probably closed (we have some blockages related to Heart centre issues). Most people find it difficult to understand and accept that non-attachment is also a key to true love. This is because if attachment is present, we are looking for someone to plug a gap within our-self so that we can feel whole and complete. Such a state of completeness can never occur through becoming attached to another person. It is one of the challenges in life to work towards growing into a complete and whole individual by clearing our issues, thus enabling us to become non-attached to anything. The main issue here for us all is to fully love ourselves. For if we do not love ourselves, it will not be possible for us to truly love others. If we are in this type of situation, there will be a blockage at the Heart centre. This is telling us that it is time to *identify, accept, work through and clear* the issues which are holding us back. The energy blocks causing the issues will be located within the lower three VECs. Only then will we be able to attract a truly fulfilling relationship and raise our awareness to a more enlightened and happier level.

A good test to see where we are in terms of self-love is to ask our-self the question 'on a scale of 0 to 10, (10 being the highest) how much do I love myself'? Should we place our score at 6 or less, we would be well advised to recognise that we have a lot of work to do on Heart centre issues with respect to the relationship we have with our-self. Each of us on this planet is the most important person in the Universe, and we are here to raise our awareness, to grow through the challenges we face, and to gain wisdom. We chose to incarnate so as to work through the challenges and issues that we agreed to in spirit for the soul to grow. Should we enter a relationship with low self-love we will most probably attract a partner who will mirror (reflect back to us) the issues that are there to contribute to our growth as we move forward. This might not be a pleasant experience.

So many times I have seen couples divorcing and remarrying only to discover they are, once more, getting more of the same from their new partner! And, of course, blame arises, as in their eyes it is always the other person's fault and has nothing to do with themselves. In true love, there is a natural, strong bonding which is unconditional, without co-dependency and without attachment. If we do not have these three elements in our relationships then it is advisable to work towards identifying the issues that are preventing us from achieving this state. When we do, we will be able to operate fully from within our Heart centre – the great balancer. The energies from the three lower VECs will be flowing freely, without blockages, upwards through the Heart centre into the upper VECs and vice versa.

Some examples of the type of problems that can arise when a Heart centre is out of balance are as follows. It can lead to symptoms where an individual might:

- have difficulty in giving and receiving
- be cold in their approach to relations
- be unable to form stable relationships
- feel very lonely
- be fearful of relationships
- show strong signs of jealousy in relationships
- have difficulty in being intimate due to fear
- have difficulty in setting boundaries in relationships
- be narcissistic through unconsciously feeling inferior
- be very needy and clinging in relationships
- lack forgiveness
- be overly critical of self and others
- be judgemental
- lack compassion.

Parts of the Body Influenced by the Heart VEC:
heart, lower lungs, bronchia, thymus gland, circulatory system, muscles, hands, arms, legs, immune system and lungs.

Problems of Excess Energy in the Heart VEC:
An individual may be very demanding in relationships, and/or in their expectations of what they want another person to do at work, at home, or socially. Perhaps one of the worst symptoms here is for an individual to be co-dependent in a relationship. Because of excess energy in the Heart centre, an individual may allow themselves to be taken advantage of and may not have recognised the need to set up sensible boundaries. They may have at best poor boundaries, leading them to expect too much from a relationship. Their judgement may also be poor.

Problems of Lack of Energy in the Heart VEC:
Individuals who lack energy in their Heart centre are usually the types who are waiting to be rescued from whatever situation they are in. Depression easily sets in and they will tend to isolate themselves, feeling very lonely as they do so. They may have a tendency to be critical and judgemental about others, and themselves. Should they be in a relationship they may experience problems in intimacy. As a cover, to hide from their shortcomings, they may

exhibit narcissistic tendencies. Lack of forgiveness may be quite common in their relationships and life in general. Self-love and self-esteem will be low.

Physical Symptoms that Arise with Disturbances in the Heart VEC:
heart problems, chest pains, high blood pressure, circulatory problems, immune system disorders, emphysema, muscle tension, upper back and shoulder problems, breathing difficulties, asthma, lethargy and passiveness.

*

As explained above, the lower VECs, and their related SEBs, deal with the physical material world and development from birth onwards. Moving from teens to adulthood, the upper VECs come into play, providing opportunities to increase spiritual development (compassion, understanding, helpfulness, trust, acceptance, non-judgement and so on). The upper VECs provide a direct link to the authentic-self and our spirit (our host) through the SEBs. Unresolved issues in the lower three centres affect what is going on in the fourth (Heart) and upper VECs because the issues cause blockages in the energy flow so that the fourth and other upper VECs do not function properly. Excess meditation and thinking/working on spiritual matters can lead an individual spending too much time away from the reality of why they are here. The issues and challenges faced in life are mostly associated with the lower VECs and related SEB systems so it is important to strike a balance between working on personal issues (life lessons) and spiritual or inner development. This requires, above all, the VECs, SEBs and physical body to be strongly grounded.

FIFTH VEC: THROAT
Colour: **Sky Blue**   Endocrine Gland: **Thyroid**

Associated Inner Happiness State
The Throat VEC is located at the throat. Once we are able to work regularly (rather than from time to time) within the Throat or fifth VEC, we will have reached a level of consciousness where we are in a position to tap into an infinite source of higher knowledge and different levels of creativity. To be able to do this means that any blocks in the lower three VECs and Heart centre have to be worked with and balanced. For those of you who wish to expand your creative talents, this is the energy centre to focus upon. If any creative expression is blocked, start by working on the lower energy centres first to determine the cause. Communication is also a main characteristic of this centre and it is about both listening and speaking.

The energy from this centre can act to push us to obtain what we want in life, or not, depending on its balance. When it is weak, a person will show signs of shyness, reclusiveness and introversion. A sudden emotional shock can affect this centre, such as that caused by the loss of a loved one, or loss of employment, or failing an examination.

Such a shock will impact an individual's energy state and most probably give rise to grief. Although the symptom appears in this centre, the cause will probably be located in the second or Sacral VEC. This is enough to cause a blockage within this VEC, which ultimately weakens it.

A blocked Throat centre can give rise to an individual being not only poor at communicating but also at listening. Such individuals may be prone to interrupt a person before they have finished their communication. In this type of situation they usually listen but do not hear. Some examples of the type of problems that can arise, when a Throat VEC is out of balance, are as follows. It can lead to symptoms where an individual might:

- be rather introverted and shy
- be uncomfortable speaking in public
- be prone to excessive gossiping
- have a loud dominating voice
- be prone to interrupt conversations
- have a lack of creativity
- lack of ability to express themselves
- show signs of being fearful about something
- have a powerful internal and external critic
- be unable to trust themselves and others
- be affected as a result of the need to keep a secret.

It is important to recognise that many of the above symptoms can also be due to a lack of grounding through the Base VEC (there will be a blockage there). This can give rise to the effect of an excess *or* a shortage of energy at the Throat centre. For example, an individual may give a brilliant presentation to some clients at work but may be unable to express their feelings with their partner in the evening in an intimate situation. A main task in life is to work towards balancing this centre and one of the best ways to do that is by learning to be a good listener and communicator. Anything which interferes with this task indicates that there are issues which have to be dealt with.

Parts of the Body Influenced by the Throat VEC:
thyroid gland, parathyroid, vocal chords, throat, tongue, neck, shoulders lungs, lymph glands and menstrual cycle. There is also an association with the large intestine.

Problems of Excess Energy in the Throat VEC:
An individual will attempt to control conversations and be the centre of attention. Although there may be much verbiage, perhaps about a situation in their life, in this energy state what

will usually be missing is an indication about how they actually *feel*. Feelings will be absent in an attempt to show that they are in control and exercising their power.

Problems of Lack of Energy in the Throat VEC:

When this centre is very weak an individual can show signs of paranoia. If someone is shy or very self-conscious, then this is a sure sign that the Throat centre is weak and lacking energy. Such an individual will also have problems speaking their truth with respect to their own inner feelings. Poor communication is inherent, especially in asking questions about difficult situations.

Physical Symptoms that Arise with Disturbances in the Throat VEC:

tonsillitis, gum difficulties, thyroid disorders, teeth problems, flu, fevers, respiratory tract infections, bronchitis, irritable bowel syndrome, herpes, itching, sores, blisters, swelling, infections, obsessive compulsive disorder.

SIXTH VEC: BROW

Colour: **Indigo**   Endocrine Gland: **Pituitary**

Associated Inner Happiness State

The Brow or sixth VEC located at the centre of your forehead is where information is pulled together from different sensors (sight, sound, touch, smell, taste, sixth sense) to form recognisable patterns of what is going on around us. It is, therefore, the major contributor to how we perceive the world. It is the centre where we are able to visualise, conceptualise, and invoke deductive reasoning and rational problem solving. It is the centre where the imagination lies, of higher intuition and where psychic abilities operate. It is the centre where inspiration is found. Given this centre's power of recognition with respect to the patterns experienced in life, especially recurring patterns, we have the ability to steer clear of situations that are not in our best interest, provided we are able to tune into the centre's attributes.

In the various relationships we enter into, recurring patterns can be identified which are not to the benefit of our inner growth and/or inner feeling of wellbeing. Intuition is a useful attribute that can be used here, as well as objective experience, to predict the outcome. Why go through, or prolong, a difficult emotional time when, through intuition, you already sense the outcome. Wisdom comes to those who recognise the patterns that keep recurring in their life, through their different experiences, and use this knowledge to make an appropriate change to their choice/decision. Travelling along life's path, this is the centre that helps us to grow through the experience, knowledge and wisdom gained. It helps us to see the big picture. Gaining true wisdom, though, requires keeping an open mind. Having fixed ideas and/or beliefs about anything traps us in an illusion of how things are, or should be. We effectively put blinkers on, trapping ourselves in a narrow focus where the benefit of seeing the big picture is easily missed. Recognising this illusion is a first step to breaking free. Those with whom we form relationships or partnerships with, or who simply live next door, or who work in the same place, are of course, as has been said, mirroring back to us the life lessons we need to learn. This is how we learn, grow and, hopefully, gain wisdom. The more ungrounded we are (blockages in the lower VECs), the more likely that we will be affected by illusions.

Some examples of the type of problems that can arise when a Brow VEC is out of balance, are as follows. It can lead to symptoms where an individual might:

- suffer from obsessions
- have poor concentration
- have little, if any, imagination
- be fearful of looking within to identify their authentic self
- be insensitive to what is going on around them and to other people
- suffer from an inferiority complex
- have great difficulty in getting any feel of what the future is about
- use their talents to destroy life forms
- have little or no self-realisation
- suffer from hallucinations.

Parts of the Body Influenced by the Brow VEC:
Besides supplying energy to the pineal gland, this VEC also supplies energy to: the eyes, sinuses, nose, ears, autonomic nervous system, cerebellum and forebrain.

Problems of Excess Energy in the Brow VEC:
Should there be blockages in the lower VECs this can lead to excess energy in the Brow centre. If this is the case, it will be very difficult for the individual concerned to discern between truth and fantasy. They may also have too much psychic energy and make outrageous statements with respect to what is happening in a situation, or to a person, or about their future. It does not mean that they are professionally psychically developed. There is clearly in this case a lack of grounding from the lower VECs. Individuals can also be very anxious and fearful about what is happening in their lives. Poor concentration is a common feature when there is excess energy in this centre.

Problems of Lack of Energy in the Brow VEC:
Individuals who lack intuition have an energy deficiency in the sixth vortex energy centre. They will tend to be driven by their intellect and judge everything through facts and figures. Such individuals can also be insensitive to other people's feelings, including their own and can have difficulty seeing another person's point of view. They may, at times, have a poor

memory. Imagination may be non-existent, so they are unlikely to offer creative suggestions. This type of individual will also tend to be very inflexible with respect to change.

Physical Symptoms that Arise from Disturbances in the Brow VEC:

headaches, migraines, eyesight problems, earache, disruptive sleep patterns such as insomnia and nightmares, fear, anxiety, manic depression, schizophrenia and paranoia, nervous breakdowns, blindness or deafness.

SEVENTH VEC: CROWN

Colour: **Violet**   Endocrine Gland: **Pineal**

Associated Inner Happiness State

The Crown, or seventh VEC, is located at the top of the head. It points upwards and connects with each of the body's seven SEBs. When in balance, it is associated with an individual's level of intelligence, their ability to analyse and assimilate information, and also the degree of wisdom they have reached. The ability to question is an attribute of this energy centre as well as how open-minded and aware an individual is, and their level of perception. The centre pulls together the different elements from other VECs that contribute to belief systems. This centre is also associated with an individual's ability to reach self-realisation, which means coming to terms with and understanding that we are a soul in a physical body having a spiritual experience in this lifetime.

A major function of this centre is to overcome the illusions in life, and the co-dependencies and attachments that have been formed. Having reached such a level of enlightenment, we are empowered to have a direct communication through to our higher self (our host spirit), to infinite higher knowledge and also to the Creator.

Some examples of the type of problems that can arise when the Crown vortex energy centre is out of balance, are as follows. It can lead to symptoms where an individual might:

- lack inspiration
- lack ethics
- be non-courageous
- lack compassion
- be living in their head and over-Intellectualising
- live in a state of confusion
- lack any faith whatsoever
- be excessively self-sacrificing
- lack the ability to see any opportunities to change
- be overly charismatic

- be fearful of any self development
- show signs of senility
- show signs of confusion with life, unable to see the big picture.

Parts of the Body Influenced by the Crown VEC:
Cerebrum, cerebral cortex, central nervous system, hair growth and muscles.

Problems of Excess Energy in the Crown VEC:
When the Crown centre is over energised, an individual, by and large will be insensitive to people's feelings, can tend to over-intellectualise and talk over the heads of people to the level where interest is lost and the individual becomes a bore. Unfortunately, being highly intellectual is a chronic but much prized condition in Western society. Excess energy in this centre can lead individuals to suffer from constant feelings of frustration, unrealised power, depression, confusion, or even psychosis. They may be addicted to spiritual matters and be overly dependent on gurus, or specific religious texts.

Problems of Lack of Energy in the Crown VEC:
An individual may have a closed mind, and have fixed ideas on certain aspects of spiritual and non-spiritual matters. They may be unable to consider any new knowledge, or take a broader perspective outside their educational, intellectual background on what life is about. They always want to be right, as they live in a delusion where they think that they know everything. They seldom, if ever, question their beliefs. Experiencing feelings of indecision, low vitality, post traumatic stress disorder, depression indulging in drug abuse, are signs of having low energy flow in this centre.

Physical Symptoms that Arise with Disturbances in the Crown VEC:
skin rashes, eczema, warts, problem with the lymphatic system, confusion, paralysis, senility, Intellectual illness, depression, multiple sclerosis, neuralgia, bone disorders and migraine headaches.

*

Change in Consciousness as each VEC Connects with an SEB
The above description of the seven Vortex Energy Centres provides a basic outline of their complexity and functions. It may prove helpful to follow through two examples of different nested VECs connecting with their associated Subtle Energy Bodies and what it means within the consciousness of each SEB. In diagram 3.13, the second VEC, (the Sacral or Emotional VEC – colour orange) and Heart VEC (colour green) are chosen as the two examples. Diagram 3.13 is a simple two-dimensional matrix, drawn for demonstration purposes, showing the different VECs (the vertical coloured lines) and the SEBs (the horizontal coloured lines). I have highlighted the Sacral and Heart VEC lines so that they stand out on the demonstration matrix.

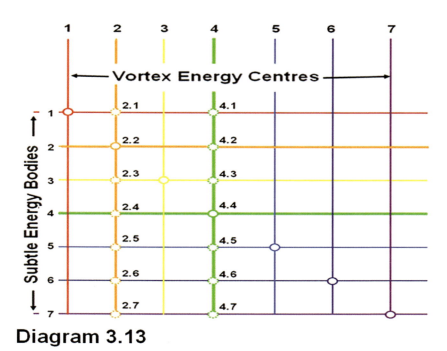

Diagram 3.13

Emotional Nested VECs connecting with Seven SEBs: 2.1 to 2.7

Starting from its root or base (an energy line that follows the spine) the Emotional/Sacral VEC (2.1 in the diagram) connects with the first SEB (its base template) and then follows through, connecting with each of the SEBs through to the last or seventh SEB (2.7), called the Ketheric Template. At each connection, an individual will experience different levels of thought and emotion within their consciousness. As this is all energy, a thought and emotion will transmute through to the brain and body to create thoughts and physical feelings that we experience. For example:

2.1 **Emotional VEC connecting with Base 1st Template "T" (Base) SEB**

From a physical day to day perspective the emotional VEC translates different emotional experiences from situations that are encountered into how they are felt within the physical body, for example those butterfly feelings in the stomach before opening an important letter, shedding tears in extreme circumstances, feelings of joy when laughing during an amusing incident.

2.2 **Emotional VEC connecting with the 2nd T (Emotional) SEB**

This is the home of the Emotional (Sacral) VEC and it is the seat of all genuine emotions (true emotions and not those an individual may fantasise about). It is where emotions are experienced energetically.

2.3 **Emotional VEC connecting with the 3rd T (Intellect) SEB**

Emotions are intellectualised here. For example, the intellectual body tells an individual whether their emotions are right or wrong. If they are furious, their Intellect (the thinking

SEB) may tell them that they are weak for being so. On the other hand the Intellect may blame someone else for making them furious. The Emotional body holds the anger but the Intellect body deflects it.

2.4 **Emotional VEC connecting with the 4th T (Heart) SEB**

An individual does not emote from the Heart. Rather, they feel from the Heart SEB. It is here that they show the ability to receive and to give love. They experience their emotions in a physical and spiritual way in the Heart SEB. They also work at how they express love and how they hold love in the Heart SEB.

2.5 **Emotional VEC connecting with the 5th T (Throat) SEB**

If an individual is angry and cannot express this anger, they have a block in the Throat VEC. The emotion in the Emotional VEC is unable to be expressed through the throat, and the energy will back up in the Heart SEB. They may hate themselves because they are angry and they are unable to tell the person responsible that they are angry.

2.6 **Emotional VEC connecting with the 6th T (Brow) SEB**

The spiritual dynamics of emotion come into play here. At this connection, the energy created by the VEC and the SEB impels the individual to get into harmony with their own emotions. This is where they develop the ability to see synchronicity occurring, the signs that direct them to their goal. Their consciousness at this emotional level asks such questions as: *Do I want to be loved? Do I want to attract someone to love me? Am I attracting a bully to me because I am a victim and the purpose is for me to grow?* All this is their intuition coming into play to attract them to or deflect them from what they are meant to experience.

2.7 **Emotional VEC connecting with the 7th T (Crown) SEB**

Great spiritual masters have achieved a level of consciousness that connects them with the Crown SEB, or enables them to connect with the Crown SEB and to spend time there. To be connected here is to be at one with the Universe and the Creator. At best, an individual may get a flash of ultimate knowing, or an epiphany which changes their life and puts them onto a spiritual path.

Heart Nested VECs connecting with seven SEBs: 4.1 to 4.7

4.1 **Heart VEC connecting with 1st Template "T" (Base) SEB**

At this level of the Heart VEC, an individual's consciousness translates what is happening to them down to a physical level. They can actually feel a pain in the heart after the loss of someone or something important to them. If they are in a relationship, then they may feel elated by the power of love in their heart.

4.2 Heart VEC connecting with 2nd T Sacral (Emotional) SEB

This is a most important connection for an individual's consciousness, for it is where they sense what love means to them. It is where they discover if they are able to receive and to give love.

4.3 Heart VEC connecting with the 3rd T (Intellectual) SEB

At this junction, an individual debates in their consciousness what life is about. For example, questions can arise in their consciousness such as: can they use love as a weapon or a tool to control someone? Can they commoditise love to bring them financial benefits?

4.4 Heart VEC connecting with the 4th T (Causal - Astral/ Heart) SEB

If the heart VEC is not blocked here (and it tends to be for a high proportion of individuals in Western society) then an individual's self-love flows freely and with great ease; they can give and receive love on an equal basis.

4.5 Heart VEC connecting with the 5th T (Etheric - Throat) SEB

An individual's consciousness begins to operate here in the upper, or spiritually-orientated SEBs. Thoughts focus on balancing the expression of both the physical and spiritual aspects of the love they feel. Their consciousness encourages them to practise what they preach, or quite simply to walk their talk.

4.6 Heart VEC connecting with the 6th T (Brow) SEB

Operating at this level, an individual is able to express unconditional love. They are able to connect with feelings of infinite love and have the capability to receive this love from others.

4.7 Heart VEC connecting with the 7th T (Celestial – Crown) SEB

Once an individual's consciousness has entered this realm, they are able to express their love unconditionally. Not only that, but their love will have expanded to a love including the planet and all that resides in and on it. In this case, from a polarity perspective, both their feminine and masculine energies will be in balance, which equates to a high level of self-acceptance.

The above two examples of nested VECs provide a basis to see additional logical connections between VECs and SEBs and what it means in terms of a particular state of mind, physical feelings, attitude and behaviour.

Everybody on this planet functions at a sub-atomic level. I pointed out in chapter 1 that it is advantageous t be conscious of the difference between the dimensional aspects of living in the world of the fabricated-self in comparison with the dimensional aspects of living in the world of the authentic-self (includes the soul) at a sub-atomic level. One of my own main quests in life is to seek out the truth wherever it lies. Most importantly, I realise that truth is not absolute. I seem to be eternally curious and therefore love exploring life's challenges. I try to do this with an open mind and with as minimal a bias as possible. Identifying my false beliefs has certainly helped me in this quest. During my 20s and 30s, it did not occur to me that I had false beliefs, nor the effect they were having on my perception about life and what was happening to and around me. During my study of nuclear physics I fell in love with another branch of physics called particle physics, and was similarly blown away with quantum mechanics. However, I did not relate these new insights to myself as a human being. I only related my newly-found knowledge to nuclear physics outcomes such as radioactive isotopes for hospitals, particle accelerators that study the collision of individual particles, and so on. My awareness had not yet expanded to include what it actually meant in terms of being human. I had an absolute blank there, it was as if my mind was 'out to lunch'! Much later in life when I began to explore the sub-atomic world and what it meant to me in a physical body, it seemed as if a veil covering my perception had been removed. Those blinkers just fell away. Reality began to unfold in much richer and more meaningful forms.

Be your Own Great Explorer
Just imagine - you too can be like Christopher Columbus, Captain R Scott of the Antarctic, Neil Armstrong or Ellen McCarthy, to name a few great explorers. They all had one thing in common and that was a passion to explore the unknown. They explored the unknown within themselves and the unknown surrounding them. You may wish to raise the question, 'how could I be like them?' You could be like them purely and simply by having a passion to explore the qualities of both your authentic-self and your fabricated-self. Your fabricated-self provides you with an opportunity to explore why life brings certain things to you at times and why it does not at other times. You may also wish to explore why you are attracted to certain types of people and why at times you are unable to attract the type of person you desire (this is explained in the following chapters). You may wish to explore why you are short of money at times and there never seems to be enough. You may wish to explore why being happy and content on a regular basis seems a distant memory. These apparent downsides in life are all driven by your fabricated-self. Your authentic-self knows why this happens and provides you with opportunities to discover and practise the upsides in life. My aim is to provide guidance that will empower you to change your downsides to upsides. The mechanism to begin this change is in your thinking.

You may be thinking, what is this authentic-self? Your authentic-self is the SEBs and their supporting VECs (your consciousness), plus your persona and your soul. Describing the SEBs and VECs as I have just done, will provide you with some idea as to what the function of your energy self is. And your energy self is most certainly real. Just by accepting the energy self's reality, thinking about its structure and what its purpose is, takes you into the 5th dimension (chapter 1). You enter the world of consciousness and energy.

Our fabricated-self is a structure and challenge that we all unknowingly build around the authentic-self. Ego is the master builder here. Ego does not want any interference from the authentic-self; it demands a free range to do what it wants. The fabricated-self has a much denser energy structure and we engage the physical world through it. Our task is to bring the authentic-self into play with all the advantages it brings with it. Each life is a personal journey and balancing the use of both the fabricated and authentic-self is a core objective and one of the principal reasons for being on this earth plane.

I feel sure that you, the reader, are interested in building a life that provides freedom, irrespective of what age you are. How do you do it? You can do it by strengthening the connection you have with your authentic-self. You can do it because you are the most important person in your Universe. This is not giving your ego free rein, for *you* are the most important person in your life. You have life lessons to learn and only you can do this. You have a reason for being here and one of your challenges is to find out what this is and to engage in it. Understanding your own energy dynamics is a key with which you can master your natural abilities, including your capability of manifesting that which you want. Just by upgrading your thinking and working to remove any false beliefs that you may have, you will allow your-self to step forward onto a path that will begin to change your life forever. That is, of course, if you have the courage to step out of your comfort zone, step out of that virtual box of thinking and take a step forward. Not easy at any time, but well worth the try. *It is your choice!*

We can attract the type of life we are meant to have when we understand how to achieve it within the fifth dimension. Once again, opening that unknowingly restricted virtual box of thinking is a major step forward in this regard. After reading this book, you may have a better understanding of some of the life challenges that we all face. Being aware of them will contribute to a reduction in any confusion that may arise. You will also have some techniques and processes to get to know your-self, or get to know it better. Of course, the big surprise comes when you strengthen the connection with your authentic-self. The range of choices you actually have in life will become clearer, and more than you think. To get to what you desire, you may have to deal with the clutter that is preventing you from attracting it. It would be unusual not to have a degree of clutter that clouds your perception, hampers your step forward to effectively meet life's challenges and stops you from manifesting what you are meant to have. Removing the clutter is a main part of the purpose of the next chapter.

Chapter 4

Turn your Life Around: Take Control, Let Go and Fly

If you are pained by external things, it is not they that disturb you, but your own judgement of them. And it is in your power to wipe out that judgement now.

Marcus Aurelius Antonius: Roman Emperor AD161 - AD180

Turn your Life Around: Take Control, Let Go and Fly

Time to Change?

What is stopping us from having a fulfilling, interesting and exciting life, however we would like to define what that is? What is stopping *you* from feeling happy with your life? This chapter and the following three chapters will help you to identify what you can do to attract the life you desire. Solutions are suggested to enable you to turn your-self around and increase your enjoyment of life. Moreover, the content of these chapters is designed to present you with what can be described as a 'new normal'. What is this new normal? It is about gaining a greater understanding about your-self and exploring life's big picture. It is about recognising that you have more choices than you realise. It is about being aware that you have a huge untapped reservoir of power (energy) within you. It is also about using this power for your benefit and for those around you.

Most of what follows I discovered while living and working across four continents. I like to think of my life as a large jigsaw puzzle. My task, as I journey, is to identify the different pieces of the jigsaw and connect them. Each piece of my jigsaw has three characteristics which represent something that:

1. helps me to achieve my personal and private goals (my hopes and desires) or
2. does nothing to interfere with my goals or
3. stops me from achieving my goals.

As I viewed my jigsaw and discussed it with others, I began to appreciate the generic nature of my findings. I also recognised how fortunate I was to be able to think outside of my own virtual box of thinking. It certainly gave me a broader understanding of how my belief system was affecting my life. My belief system was, at times, blocking me from achieving my goals and from having what I desired. These are energy blocks which had effectively cluttered my thinking and ability to achieve. Most importantly, I discovered that we all have an ability to work through and remove the blocks. This chapter identifies and provides ways to overcome a series of common blocks that we all face at some time in our life. My objective is to enable you to let go and fly. What do I mean by fly? Quite simply, to realise the life that you are meant to experience.

The question is, what is it that causes our consciousness to get cluttered with energy blocks, and what are these blocks? Diagram 4.1 shows a set of what I call seven major life drivers. The top five drivers are potential energy blocks. They are: automatic negative thoughts

(ANTs), self-esteem, beliefs, doubts and what I call the Triad (worry, anxiety and fear). They are like individual programs that clutter our mind. Some need to be dealt with and removed and some brought into balance. The bottom two drivers, Expectations and the Law of Attraction, are two key drivers that influence the process of attracting what we desire. We usually do not realise that these two drivers get affected by clutter. 'Getting affected' is like being infected with a virus which needs to be removed. The virus

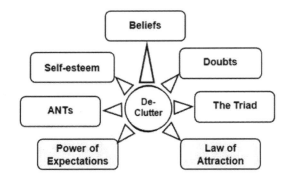

Diagram 4.1

creates what I call energy blocks and these are what prevent us from achieving what we desire. To get into a more satisfying and happier flow of life, removing the clutter is essential. Each of the boxes in diagram 4.1, from ANTs round to the Triad, represents a separate virus strain. My task is to bring each virus strain to your attention and to provide a method for you to use in the process of de-cluttering - removing the virus. Each of the boxes is explained in detail in this chapter.

We all have an internal barometer that indicates to us the state of our feeling of wellbeing. When we feel down I can guarantee that there are some energy blocks in the unconscious mind. But what is the barometer? It is the:

'thoughts we think and the words we speak'

The latter point - the words we speak - provide an indication of what is running in the unconscious mind when we are speaking freely without thinking. This is a very good measure of determining what personal issues are dominating the unconscious mind, as speaking without thinking discloses our hand. Not a good idea any time. The old maxim *think before you speak* rings true here.

Sensing emotions is also important, as they are the real power behind the words we speak. Emotions ultimately transform into the physical feelings behind something we have observed, or heard, or smelt, or tasted, or touched, or thought through or said during an experience such as a dinner engagement or meeting. The stronger the emotional response, the more powerful the energy behind the physical feeling we experience. This is something that we are not brought up to understand. Try to sense the energy differences that arise through physical feelings within your body while seeing, hearing, touching, smelling, tasting something, or saying something, or using your intuition. Words have much lower power content in terms of energy (not in ultimate effect, of course) in comparison with emotions.

How do you feel when someone says:

'you create your own reality in life'

How do you feel when they say that:

'you become what you think about on a regular basis'

When I first heard these things I felt angry, confused, and later on let down as no one had pointed this out to me when I was young. Slowly but surely, however, I began to take more responsibility for what was happening to me as a result of my thinking. After all, I was actually manifesting or creating what was happening to me. I also recognised that my thinking was driving my attitudes and behaviour (I return to this later). Realising that my thoughts are energy, and energy has an attractor (attraction) factor through my quantum bio-magnetic field (chapter 3), I began to accept the power that the world of energy wields. I also began to become aware of the contribution, both negative and positive, that I was making to my own life and to the lives of others.

Talking with close associates, they too had noticed that their thinking patterns had a lot to do with their reality. I have met some individuals though, whose lives are, to say the least, chaotic, in the sense that nothing seems to be going right for them. In such circumstances there is little, if any, chance of them maintaining a positive focus (or intent) on what they want in life in order that it could manifest. Their chaos was usually triggered by an accident or trauma which, upon investigation (for example, through a regression analysis), was found to have occurred at a very young age. Now, accidents can be a very sensitive subject and I was brought up to believe that they were random occurrences. Some accidents do appear to be random, but most are not. Non-random accidents can take the form of an injury, or an illness. It is possible to find out the reason behind an accident through regression analysis. What some find difficult to accept is that an accident is usually associated with a life lesson which the soul is trying to make the individual concerned become aware of. It also provides the individual with an opportunity to work through a life lesson while their illness or injury lasts.

If an accident or illness is life-threatening, powerful emotions can take over which prevent us coming to terms with what needs to be done. The last thing we want to hear is that we are actually being confronted with a life lesson! Nor do we wish to hear that the accident or illness is part of a process of learning. Both of these points can cause an enormous amount of anger, if not rage, to come to the surface. This happens not only within ourselves but also in those around us. Why? Because we may have a strong feeling of injustice such as: *why me?* or *why him?* or *why her?* We tend to ask these questions especially when we believe that the subject of such an illness, or accident is 'undeserving'. Such a belief gains expression in sayings such as 'only the good die young'. We are, of course, completely oblivious to the true reason behind the accident, or illness. Only now, with details being published from regression therapists' sessions, is the true nature and cause of some accidents and illnesses beginning to be recognised.

The apparent random nature of life used to disturb me, as there were times when I did not understand what was happening to me. An epiphany occurred when I began to consider myself a being of energy and what this meant. This led me to question what was driving, or guiding me as I journeyed along life's path. I noticed that whenever I made some changes that turned out not seeming to be in my best interest, something happened that brought me back on course. Every now and then I had a silent inner voice that would drop a word or a thought in my mind, or even fire up an inner passion at a most opportune time. This was, of course, my authentic-self coming into action. Now as my soul is part of my authentic-self/energy self, I wanted to find out more about what it does. And that was because I had some ideas about the spiritual dynamics of life and wanted to add some substance to those ideas. Ultimately, the intervention of our authentic-self helps us to deal with any clutter that may arise. The energy blocks causing the clutter that we may encounter can be viewed as interesting challenges (rather than problems) to overcome, that can lead us to enjoy a deeper sense of wellbeing.

Who Am I and What is the Purpose of My Being Here?
It is not generally realised that when we focus upon questions about why we are here and what is the purpose of our being here, it can create a block in our consciousness. The block is that, unknowingly, our consciousness gets trapped in the 2nd dimension of the second paradigm (chapter 1) and is unable to move out of this dimension. This effectively separates the fabricated-self from the authentic-self. Now we cannot dispute that we are here in a physical body! Programming our consciousness with these questions apparently distorts our consciousness energy field and limits our thinking. A challenge in life is for us to open our consciousness to think, from time to time, in the five dimensions of the second paradigm. To do so puts us on a path where we have an increased awareness of what is happening to us and around us. We will also have a clearer feel for where we are going in life.

As our mind assimilates the difference between the physical and sub-atomic worlds, it will empower us to think outside of our virtual box of thinking. The above two questions, though, are so important that I would like to repeat what I stated earlier in the book to ensure that you give the subject due consideration. Through my extensive travels, I have concluded that neither race, nor culture, nor gender nor religion affects the answers. Let me suggest the following to you as an answer to the first question: who am I? I am:

'a soul experiencing life in a physical body'

There is really no need to ask this question because, once again, this is what I am, what we all are, whether we want to believe it or not! Of course there are those who do not believe that they have a soul. There is nothing wrong with this for they are, in the scheme of things, where they should be. Part of their purpose may not require them to recognise that they have a soul. Whether they believe it or not, each soul has a purpose. And every soul has a contract which is like a directive containing its life lessons. The soul's purpose, therefore, is to work through the life lessons in its contract.

Looking at our lives from an energy perspective and from the soul's perception of reality, this leads me onto the second question: what is the purpose of my being here? I would suggest that it is for my:

'soul to grow in a physical body by experiencing and working through dfferent situations associated with life lessons that are played out through the relationships, activities and events I engage in'

The soul learns and grows by absorbing the essence or wisdom gained from the experiences of working through our life lessons, the emotions that arise from the situations we experience, and the choices/decisions we make in relation to those situations.

My own life experience, and the evidence that I have gathered to date, corroborate the two answers I have given to the questions about who I am and my purpose in being here. We are much more than just flesh and bones, economic performing units and consumers who require an infinite number of rules to keep us in line. We have a soul which has a contract with a purpose (life lessons) and we fulfil the soul's contract by:

- *understanding* why we end up doing what we do and by going with the flow of life instead of paddling against it. Most of us are brought up to fight against any resistance we come across. This is, in general, a misguided approach as the resistance is trying to tell us something. Of course, some resistance needs to be worked through but some may be suggesting the need for a change in course.

- being aware of how we *handle* ourselves (behaviour, attitudes, words spoken, tone of voice, body language and action taken) in different situations in which we find ourselves. Staying out of the dramas of life is essential and is in itself a life lesson.

- being *aware* of the choices/decisions that come up for us provides an opportunity to step back and to get a feel for the lessons that may arise, and then making appropriate changes to our lives, such as changing our behaviour, attitude, relationships, employment, residence, and so on is an essential step forward.

An important point about the soul contract is that the soul only has a bit of it to work with at a time. The soul purposely never knows its whole contract and its host's (spirit's) task is to ensure that the right life lessons are in play at the right time. This is an example of divine timing – things happen when they are supposed to happen!

It took until my mid-thirties to realise that I needed to open that invisible, unknowingly closed virtual box of thinking that I had accepted during my upbringing. As this box opened further, during my forties, I was made to face the reality of the statement that:

'we enter this life with nothing and leave with nothing!'

All we take with us when the soul departs is the essence/wisdom of the experiences gained. As a merchant banker at the time, this was a sobering thought!

Taking a moment to comprehend the world that we live in, it can be very rewarding to give some thought to what the quantum or sub-atomic world is about and how it affects us in day to day life because it can provide us with the mechanics to understand the human energy structure and supporting subtle energy body's fields. Once the full power of the attraction properties of the quantum bio-magnetic field is understood and what it does, life can move in a more interesting and rewarding direction. Fewer problems will arise in life, but there are, of course, lots of interesting challenges. Accepting the challenges we face and working through them brings success into our lives. What are these challenges and how do we deal with them? I will focus on seven of our major day to day challenges, highlighted in diagram 4.1, that have an effect on whether or not we obtain what we desire.

We can find some of the biggest energy blocks within our belief system. But guess what? To change a belief you only need to question it! We will now explore whether it really is that simple.

BELIEFS
It is to Your Advantage to Review what You Believe

An important aspect of ourselves is our belief system. Beliefs act like a filter for our perception. I define beliefs as 'what we accept as being true', and perception as 'how we see ourselves and the world around us'. It would be unusual for us not to review some of our beliefs during our lifetime. We usually add some new beliefs, lose some old ones, strengthen some and weaken some, as we travel along life's path. Whether we like it or not, we are programmed (conditioned) with beliefs from birth. Parents, brothers, sisters, relations, friends, school teachers, work colleagues, media broadcasters, authority figures and so on, all contribute to our set of beliefs. Some of our beliefs, of course, turn out to be false. Those who contribute to our false beliefs were most probably just dumping what had been dumped on them. This is of great consequence, however, for our beliefs are, as I previously highlighted, the filters through which we process (within our consciousness) what is going on in the world around us. Beliefs control what we think about ourselves, or about others, or whether or not we accept what someone has said to us, or whether we accept what we are looking at, or what we read, and so forth.

As beliefs control our perception, they can work for or against us. For example, at a young age, someone whom you looked up to perhaps made a cutting remark by saying that you were absolutely useless just because you did not do something for them, or perhaps in their view you did not do it well enough. In any case, if you believed what they said, the emotional impact on you could have been devastating. Even if you did not buy into it at the time, it still has potential to leave its mark within your consciousness. Why is that so? Because that experience of being so totally put down is stored within the brain and unconscious mind, permanently, for future reference. Examples of false beliefs that can be programmed into any of us, especially at a young age, are: you are always making a mess; you are useless; we never have any money; you have no ball sense at all; none of us in our family is good at science; you cannot dance for nuts; give up you can't draw, and so forth. All of these will have a negative emotional impact upon you if you believe them!

An important point to note is that at a very young age, up to about 7 years, the brain's prefrontal cortex is not developed. It has developed significantly by the teen years. This means that a child is unable to apply reason or logic to a cutting remark. A strong feeling of worthlessness, or low self-esteem may have been immediately programmed into the child because of a cutting remark and thus a false belief *I am no good* has been planted into the child's consciousness. This would remain with the child and continue to run within the unconscious mind. As the child grows through adulthood, their daily attitudes and behaviour would reflect a feeling of worthlessness and low self-esteem. It is advisable, as early as possible, for any false beliefs to be identified, worked through and removed. If they are not removed, then the individual in adulthood will go through life with a degree of low self-esteem which will affect their self-image, self-belief, self-motivation, self acceptance, and so on. We do not realise that our quantum bio-magnetic energy field is programmed by remarks made by others. What is also not realised is that this programming ensures that we are attracted to, or attract to us people, activities and/or events and situations that mirror our false beliefs. A key point to remember here is that the soul is in a physical body so as to bring any extremes it may experience into balance.

Diagram 4.2 shows a simple structure of how beliefs are formed. Beliefs are put in place because we buy into what someone has said to us, or accept what we see or read or feel. If a statement is made by someone who we look up to, a thought is generated in the mind. It

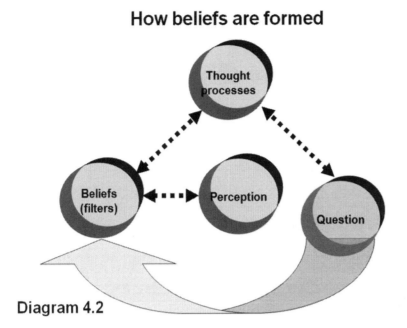

How beliefs are formed

Diagram 4.2

may also have an emotion with a strong physical feeling linked to it. If we accept what is said, then the thought can translate into a belief. The belief is stored within the unconscious mind, and any supporting emotion that arose is stored in the emotional subtle energy body (chapter 3). The information part of the thought is also stored simultaneously in the physical brain. Strong emotions that result from, for example, a trauma of some sort, also get stored within the weakest part of the physical body.

I met the son of a friend of mine a few years back who to my great surprise had taken up music. He was brought up in a professional family who disliked modern music. Many years before our meeting, I had been invited to a Sunday lunch with the family. During the lunch, their son asked if he could take music and a media subject as part of his 'A' levels at school. Both parents made it clear that they felt it was not befitting his educational background and status. They doubted that there was a future in his kind of music. He was attending a good private school. Although his passion was modern music, he was directed to take subjects that would enable him to read for a degree in journalism. Two things happened. The first was that his self-esteem took a big hit as he had initially felt his parents would support him to be a pop musician. He now felt completely de-motivated. The second is that he was not happy reading journalism. This had been decided for him by those who 'knew best'! His parent's belief system could not accept that there was any future in the music he liked. Their belief was that people of their social status should enter a reputable stable profession. To accept their son's choice, it would have been necessary for them to change their belief. The good news is that at university he was able to develop his musical talents with other students in the evenings. When he graduated from university, he set up his own band. He is now happy, but his parents would still prefer to be able to report to their friends that he was a journalist! How could they have changed their belief?

'to change a belief all that needs to be done is to question it'

It is as straightforward as that. But they were also required to look at their egos which got them into that state of affairs in the first place! Should you find your-self in a situation where you feel it necessary to reject someone's request, ask your-self why? Is it your ego in play, or is it that you really know best? Question your-self and go within to find out why you are not accepting the request. You will probably find a false belief and some ego persuading you. In the music example some typical false beliefs are: People in rock bands do not fit my social class, or, he needs to get a real job, or, he will end up being a drug addict, or, he does not know what he wants, and so on. All beliefs start with a thought and it is important to remember to question them if you want to change them. Otherwise the beliefs keep running in the unconscious mind, colouring your view of life and affecting what you experience in supportive or non-supportive ways.

Behind every false belief there is likely to be a strong emotion. When a false belief has been identified, it is highly important to also deal with the attached emotion. A technique and process to rid your-self of a false belief and its attached emotion is to:

1. measure how you feel in your body so that you can test the strength of the emotion.

2. get rid of the emotion by seeing it in your imagination as a large dark grey brick. Visualise the brick being attached to a balloon and then allow it to float away

3. re-script the old false belief and change it to something more positive

4. attach to the re-scripted belief a new, warm and happy emotion. To find a happy emotion, go into your imagination and think of something good that happened to you and attach that emotion to the new belief. You have now integrated the new belief and emotion.

As you will have gathered, the process and technique is basically re-scripting a false belief with a new one together with bringing the emotional content back into a positive balance.

DOUBT

As each of us progresses through life, there is a quiet and subtle destroyer lurking in the shadows, strongly supported by our belief system. It is a cause of most of the misfortunes that occur in life and it is called *doubt*.

Curtailing Doubt - a Destroyer of Happiness

Next to understanding the power of beliefs, it also helps to appreciate the power of doubt, which is like a creeping disease and a great destroyer not only of goals and ambitions, but also of lives. We never see doubt coming and it lingers quietly in the background waiting for an opportunity to slip into our consciousness to cause chaos. The power of doubt is unlimited and irresponsible. It can also subtly cause many disastrous outcomes in life; a few examples may be helpful.

Doubt:

- acts as a covert enemy at the gate of our consciousness
- prevents us from achieving success
- prevents us from connecting with our creative-self
- disconnects us from our authentic-self
- prevents us from seeing reality by corrupting our perception
- stops us from healing
- stops happiness and spiritual growth
- prevents us from having loving relationships
- most certainly locks us into a tightly closed virtual box of thinking.

Doubt is a trigger for energies/emotions such as anger, paranoia, hatred, jealousy, fear, alarm and so on. These are all destructive energies that affect our physical feeling of positive wellbeing and happiness. Doubt affects those with whom we come into contact, and even those on whom we may focus our attention within our mind. Yes, the energy of our thoughts affects others; as emphasised in chapter 2, our thoughts are all-powerful. It is important to always remember that:

'energy follows thought'

Doubt basically comes in three forms as shown in diagram 4.3.

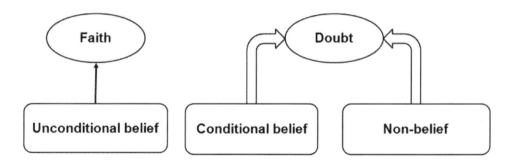

Diagram 4.3

It is all a matter of the belief system that has been set up within our consciousness. If we disbelieve in something like *'you have many lives in which to work through different life lessons'* this will be because we were brought up with that belief. We will automatically doubt the 'having many lives'. Furthermore, if we have a conditional belief such as we need top marks in our exams to get a top job, then we will doubt our ability to get such a job if we do not get top marks. Energetically, we push top opportunities away. In comparison, if we unconditionally believe that we can achieve whatever we want in life, then I can guarantee that we are more than halfway to success in our choice of whatever we want to do. I call unconditional belief *faith*. Think of John Major, the ex-Prime Minister of Britain, who was the son of a former music hall performer. What an inspiration to us all in terms of achievement. He believed that he could become prime minister and he did, in spite of strong competition. The important point here is not the range of actions and decisions he took in order to become prime minister, but that he did not doubt his belief and so worked towards his goal.

During our lifetime, it is wise to be ever vigilant against intrusions of doubt. The question arises, why should we even consider doubting ourselves and our abilities? The answer to this question may disturb some of you, and it should! We are usually conditioned (programmed) to doubt ourselves because of statements made to us by those whom we looked up to as role models and providers as well as other authority figures. Most of the time, the people subjecting us to this conditioning were just passing down what was passed down to them from their parents, relations, friends, teachers, authority figures and so on. I elaborate on this below when I describe what causes low self-esteem.

A lot of people I talk to have a degree of doubt arising in many areas of their lives. I discovered that one thing they all have in common is they usually have a limited of idea why they are here on this planet in a human body. There is little or no comprehension of what is the true purpose of their being here. Many also think that we are just a biological mistake, like some form of parasite, with no real purpose except to be consumers and to procreate. And most believe that everything happening in their life is mainly random. Others lose themselves in an intellectual debate involving different races, cultures, religions and so on.

If we raise our awareness by thinking within the world of energy and the second paradigm of the quantum world (end of chapter 1) we may discover that our curiosity about life grows. We may also be fortunate to discover that '*all in life is not as it seems*'. Problem here is that most human beings prefer life to be predictable and to stay in their comfort zone. Because of the massive changes that are occurring in this decade, life is becoming highly unpredictable. Staying in our comfort zone is becoming less certain. What does this do to us? It creates a self-destructive triad of anxiety, worry and fear! Like doubt, the triad has to be dealt with and brought to order, if we are to achieve the life we desire.

The TRIAD: ANXIETY, FEAR, WORRY

Move Out of your Stress Zone – Be Happy!

Anxiety, like doubt, has to be one of the most destructive forces and emotions that have been conditioned into us. Anxiety, stimulated by fear, leads to worry, and vice versa. These three form a Triad of supporting negative energy. Most of us could be awarded a doctorate in worrying. Worry can cause dangerous levels of neuro-chemicals to circulate around the body. As the mind influences the brain's and the body's cells, you can imagine that worry is not our best friend! I have many ex-colleagues, and some friends, who actually believe that they need something to worry about in their life to make it either less boring, or more interesting or challenging, or whatever. If you are like this, then I strongly advise you, and please note I am taking the liberty of not making it a request, to change your way of thinking and drop the word *worry* from your vocabulary and thinking altogether. This may be tough to do as the word worry is used daily by people on television, or radio, or by medical practitioners and just about everybody else in their conversations. Most are addicted to worry, and need to get real in life, for whether we worry or not, what is going to happen will happen! I pointed out in Chapters 2 and 3 that we affect what we focus our thinking upon. Yes, all that worry energy is either negatively affecting our state of mind, emotions and physical body, or affecting an external situation that we are focusing upon in the outside world, or some person we are focusing on. As an individual we are a powerful energy being. To realise this power in a constructive way, worry and doubt need to go (preferably into a recycle bin!)

The perils and outcomes of doubt have already been elaborated upon above. But guess what? Worry, anxiety and fear have a similar set of outcomes. They, too, are great destroyers! In today's fast-moving 24/7 world, we are all increasingly aware of the danger of stress. Anxiety, worry and fear are fuel to stress and cause any stress condition to intensify. Stress is a real killer and should be curtailed as early as possible when it arises. A little stress can be good for us, as it can keep us vigilant, but prolonged stress? Absolutely not!

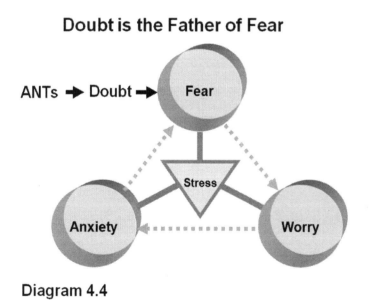

Diagram 4.4

Doubt and the Triad are triggers that lead us on to one of life's most destructive trails – the stress trail. Those unwanted negative thoughts that suddenly pop into our conscious mind - automatic negative thoughts: ANTs - are feedstock for Doubt, the Triad and Stress. In diagram 4.4, I show that doubt is the father of fear, which is the mother of worry, whose off-spring is anxiety. This Triad is a closed loop where if we are fearful we will worry, and if we worry we will be anxious, and if we are anxious then we will be fearful and if we are fearful we will worry and so on. The loop destroys inner energy, which is essential for creative self-expression and for an inner feeling of positive wellbeing and happiness. The loop also greatly reduces a natural healing process that we all have. It is most important to be conscious of the Triad, therefore, as a:

'closed loop, self-destructive and self-feeding, giving rise to high levels of stress'

We are just not trained to deal with the pressures of technology-driven, 21st century living. In case you are not aware of what triggers stress and the different types of stress which exist, plus the symptoms that evolve, I summarise them in the table below, and conclude with some techniques that you can adopt to help you deal with stress. Once stress has taken hold of us, there are two interrelated categories of symptoms: psychological and physical. The symptoms for each category in the table below can all interact with our consciousness to prevent us living properly in the present. They can also stop us from achieving our desires. And what are some of the symptoms of stress in this 24/7 lifestyle? The main symptoms are: insomnia, addiction, depression, anger, nervousness and pain. A more complete list of symptoms is shown in the table below.

Psychological symptoms	Physical symptoms
- worry	- breathlessness
- anxiety	- dizziness
- fear	- restlessness
- irritation	- sweating
- nervousness	- trembling
- anger	- nervous twitches
- tension	- sleeplessness
- panic	- muscular aches
- depression	- chest pains
- changes in behaviour	- constipation or diarrhoea
- changes in attitude	- cramps or muscle spasms
- food cravings	- fainting spells
- lack of appetite	- nail biting
- tearfulness	- pins and needles
- insomnia	- sexual difficulties such as erectile dysfunction or a loss
- tiredness	

There is no hiding from the effects of stress in today's world. We are confronted with stressful situations in four key life environments (amongst others), as shown in the next diagram, 4.5. Prolonged stress can lead to consequences such as the growth of tumours and heart disease. It will be helpful for you to be aware of different levels of tension and how it affects your wellbeing; to help you take care of your-self I present some measures you can adopt to make it easier to reduce your stress levels.

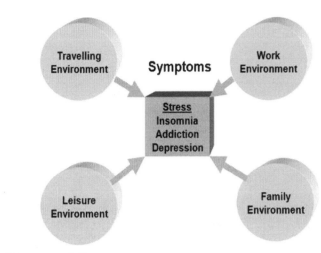

Diagram 4.5

Levels of Stress

Stress has been divided into four main categories by the medical profession. It may be helpful to understand each category and what you can do if you are ever diagnosed under a particular category.

1. **Acute Stress**: perhaps the most common type. It arises from the demands and pressures of life such as an event or activity involving, say, sporting activities, waiting for transport, driving, giving a presentation, experiencing anger or fear, engaging in an argument and so forth.

2. **Episodic Acute Stress:** occurs on a more frequent basis, especially in those routinely engaged in a busy lifestyle. It also happens to those whose minds are locked onto negative thinking. This is reflected in their life, which is usually fraught with conflict. They are usually anxious, short tempered, and may have a tendency to attract disastrous situations.

3. **Chronic Stress**: an accumulative type of stress that wears people down day after day, year after year, gradually destroying bodies, minds and lives. For example, people living in a war zone, or a violent neighbourhood.

4. **Post Traumatic Stress Disorder:** caused by emotionally damaging shocks such as an accident; physical, or emotional or sexual abuse; a natural disaster; the death of a loved one; experience of war or other conflict, being diagnosed with a fatal disease, and so on. This type of stress brings with it intrusive memories of events, or flashbacks which are associated with the event. It is typically accompanied by physical disorders.

There is a fifth type of stress that is now recognized which comes under the category of 'Geopathic Stress'.

5. Geopathic Stress

As we live in a world of energy, this energy can, at times, have a detrimental effect on us psychologically and physiologically. Our planet generates a powerful magnetic field which can sometimes become corrupted due to rock structures and/or stagnant water/liquids. The electric power grid plus its supporting transformers also generate harmful energy fields and cell phones generate energy that can cause damage to the brain if used for prolonged periods. Most of this can be dealt with by using the services of an energy geomancer and neutralizing devices. It is important to identify any Geopathic stress as early as possible to protect your long-term health.

The following has proven to be helpful in relieving stress:

De-stressing Your-self: Breathing to Reduce Stress
Who would have guessed that breathing, or rather how we breathe, would be of major importance in our life? If you are an athlete, or singer or actor, it is something you soon learn. However, for the rest of us, breathing is just something we do, like putting one foot in front of the other. Nevertheless, it is *how* we breathe that counts.

So how should we breathe? We should breathe in a natural deep rhythm from the diaphragm (stomach) upward to the top of the lungs. Most people breathe from the top of their chest leaving the bottom of their lungs with stagnant air. This is not beneficial for our inner feeling of positive wellbeing. To correct this bad habit, put a hand on your stomach and when you breathe in, your hand should start rising on the in-breath. If your hand does not rise, then adjust your breathing until it does. This is called diaphragm breathing.

If you observe your breathing when you are in a stressful situation you will notice that your breath flow is quick and shallow (called hyperventilating) and that you are breathing in at the top of your chest only. Such breathing only adds to the anxiety you feel, hence the need to breathe properly. There is a direct relationship between your breathing and your emotions. You can also be in another state, that is, using very slow breathing, which occurs if you are in a depressed condition, or sad, or in shock, or even feeling dejected. This, too, is not healthy. It is important for you to be alert to the many things that breathing affects, some of which are obvious while others are not, for example:

- the amount of oxygen in our blood that nourishes the brain and body
- blood pressure (can raise or lower it) and circulation
- digestion
- posture
- muscle tension

- how sensitive we are to colds or asthma
- the amount of energy we have.

The above shows us quite clearly that it is in our best interest to find a breathing rhythm that can help us to deal with any stress when it arises. Once again, a key to understanding what is happening within us is to recognise the reciprocal relationship between our emotions and our breathing. There are many different types of breathing rhythm that can be used to help us de-stress. I suggest that the following are worth a try:

The De-stress 6-3-6-3 Exercise
This is an exercise that can be done either sitting down or lying horizontal, whichever you prefer. There are four parts to the process which also involves seeing in your imagination different images and/or using your feelings.

Part 1.
If you can, find a quiet place with a comfortable seat. Sit down and get into a comfortable position, preferably with a straight back, and relax with your hands on your thighs or lap.

Part 2.
Either focus your eyes on something that is straight ahead of you or just close your eyes.

Part 3.
Breathe in through your nose and be aware of your in-breath as the air flows up through your nostrils. Using your imagination, see your-self sitting in a cloud of whitish, light-blue energy. As you breathe in, see your-self breathing in this whitish-blue energy. On the out breath, breathe out through your mouth and see your-self breathing out all the stress energy that has been trapped in your body. Imagine your out-breath as being a dark reddish-grey colour and see it dissolving as it enters the whitish-blue cloud surrounding you. Whitish-blue is a naturally calming colour and has an immediate effect on your inner feeling of positive wellbeing and happiness (state of mind and emotions). It helps in generating calming neuro-chemicals.

When our eyes are closed, the brain does not know the difference between our thoughts and the real thing. It creates the same neuro-chemical output to calm the mind and body. If you cannot see the image of the whitish-blue cloud in your mind with your eyes closed, try to sense, or just feel what is happening. If you cannot see, sense or feel, then just think the process through with your eyes closed. Either of these approaches will have a direct effect within your brain, emotions and body, producing good results. One final point, when you practise the following exercise, keep the tip of your tongue on the roof of your mouth just behind your front teeth. This completes an energetic circuit, thus enabling energy to flow through and around your body.

Part 4. Begin the breathing exercise and remember to:

- Breathe in through your nose, expanding your diaphragm (solar plexus area). As you fill your lungs, count slowly in your mind up to 6, seeing, sensing or feeling your-self breathing in the whitish-blue cloud of energy.
- Hold your breath for a slow count of 3.
- Exhale through your mouth for a slow count of 6 (seeing your stress being exhaled as a reddish-grey cloud).
- Hold your breath for a slow count of 3.
- Commence breathing in again for a slow count of 6 and see your-self breathing in the whitish-blue cloud of energy.

Do complete cycles 10 to 15 times for a few days then increase to a 20 to 25 cycle.

I would be remiss not to include diet as a potential substantial contributor to any stress that we may be suffering from.

Diet and Stress
In today's gastronomic world, a significant contribution can be made to your de-stressing program by being aware of what you are consuming in terms of food and beverages. Cutting back on your intake of salt, sugar, fats, caffeine, alcohol and additives (especially preservatives, emulsifiers, saturates, flavour enhancers, antioxidants and colourings) is an absolute must. A number of writers explore this in some detail. Robert Holden's book 'Stress Busters: 101 Ways to Inner Calm' will get you on your way. What we eat and drink is the main fuel for our body, which includes our brain. It affects how we feel physically and emotionally and that in turn affects our attitudes and behaviour.

The thought of cooking a good meal and having a relaxing glass of wine after work can have a major effect on our inner feeling of positive wellbeing. An important point to note, though, is that most things taken in moderation are usually good for our system. Excesses of any type indicate that we have a problem within our consciousness that needs to be investigated. To continue with an excess input of food (over-eating) and drink (binge-drinking) will lead to physical problems (damaged liver, kidneys and so on) and could also lead to further emotional problems. In short, our daily performance is affected by what we consume. What foods and supplements can we take to help us de-stress? Natural foods containing essential fatty acids and amino acids as well as minerals and vitamins, are recommended. Health food shops can recommend food supplements that may prove helpful to reducing stress levels. Relaxing music, videos and colours can also act as great stress busters.

One of the most powerful stress triggers is recurring negative thoughts, or automatic negative thoughts that circulate within our consciousness. Part of life's challenge is to identify and neutralise these.

AUTOMATIC NEGATIVE THOUGHTS - ANTs

Where Do ANTs Come From?

Like everyone else on this planet, I have both positive and negative thoughts. So while this is natural, we live in a world that regrettably promotes negative thinking. News media, many soap operas and films add fuel to our negative thinking by promoting false beliefs that ultimately affect our attitude and behaviour. This all lingers in our consciousness, and it is unfortunate that the mind seems to be geared to think in the negative. But why is this so? Quite simply, it is a part of our genetic makeup which is a throwback to days when we hunted for food and were hunted in our turn by flesh-eating animals. Hearing the roar of a sabre-toothed tiger or a lion did not promote a calm response if we wanted to stay alive! The brain is, therefore, naturally hardwired for survival and fear is one of our natural self-preservation attributes. In addition, from birth we grow up in an environment that trains our consciousness to be colonised by ANTs. This is achieved through the same path that built in the attributes of any doubt and low self-esteem that we may be suffering from. This path incorporates a belief system that has been a part of our socialisation and interaction with the changes in society.

Remember the old saying, supposedly made by Jesuit Priests:

'give me the boy before the age of seven and I will give you the man'

The importance attached to early childhood development, to the quality of child care and of early learning, is evidence that the foundations of our beliefs about ourselves, about other people and the world around us, are put in place at a young age. We add to and adjust those beliefs as we grow through the different stages of life. You are already aware that beliefs are the filters through which we accept what is put forward to us as truth by authority figures. Is there any wonder, then, about the ease which ANTs seem to be able to nest within us? Throughout our lives, ANTs work continuously behind the scenes in the unconscious mind. This produces ANT hills until we stop, recognise what is happening, and do something to eradicate them.

Recognising the Level of ANT Infestation

At this point I would like to remind you again, that everything in life (you, me, the car, house, money, thoughts and so on) is really different forms of energy. Any negative thoughts (and emotions) are just collections of negative energy. Because they are energy, we have the power to deal with them and to bring them into balance and/or remove them. In the world of thought energy, there are three separate energy states to consider if you are concerned about your ANT infestation. These states are:

1. **Primary:** where you have the opportunity to deal swiftly with a negative thought that has entered your mind. Just cancel the negative thought by thinking of something positive and supportive to replace it. Keep doing this until the ANT moves off. There is a chance here though, if the ANT is strong, that you will unconsciously enter into a mild form of depression if you cannot let it go.

2. **Secondary:** where a negative thought has taken hold and it is time to seek some professional support to remove the ANT, or ANTs, to help you get back into balance. The thought will have become hardwired in the brain. In this state you may be in a mild state of depression and require some therapeutic support and perhaps, at worst, a very short course of drugs and/or herbal treatment. This depends on how good the therapist/psychiatrist is. In such circumstances, practitioners who are skilled in helping you to get rid of any entrenched ANTs are definitely worth a visit.

3. **Tertiary:** where you could be in a deep state of depression and need to be under professional care, as you may well require a combination of drugs and/or herbal treatment to bring you back into balance. Ultimately therapy is the way to go, preferably with a minimal use of drugs. Some individuals are born with a chemical imbalance in their brain which leaves them clinically depressed. In this type of case, a course of drug treatment can only help them to minimise the effect of their depression, but by including therapy, and even self-therapy under supervision, this can help to minimise any drug dependency.

The most powerful attribute an ANT has is its supporting negative emotion. It is the emotion that causes any damage that arises from an ANT. Progressing through life, most of us find ourselves, at some time or other, within the secondary state of ANT infestation. Entering a secondary state of ANT infestation usually brings with it a victim mentality, as shown in diagram 4.6. Triggering a victim mentality can occur unconsciously and consciously. It is not generally recognised that we are surrounded by a victim energy field. ANTs automatically tune us into this energy field.

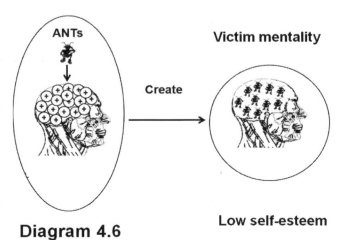

Diagram 4.6

The victim energy field is an independent energy thought-form. Imagine it as an invisible cloud of negative energy as shown in the diagram opposite. How did victim energy become an independent energy form? As an example, looking back in history to around the birth of Christ, humanity has been subjected to many, many wars, natural disasters and so on, where large numbers people died in great fear. They realised, while in a fearful state, that their death was imminent. In such cases the average person involved probably had last minute thoughts such as 'why me', 'it is not fair', 'I have been misled', 'I have been cheated' and so forth. All these thoughts are fear-based and are negative energy forms. They have huge stores of negative emotional energies attached to them. This type of energy operates and flows within the quantum reality (the sub-atomic level) of the surrounding atmosphere. As variations of this type of negative energy vibrate at a similar frequency, the thought-forms are drawn together into a cloud structure. It is the polarity of the thought-forms of energy that bind it together.

The victim energy field is like the air we breathe. We cannot see it but it is there. A problem here is that the density of the cloud allows it to have a thinking capability. I emphasised in chapter 1 that there are two types of energy. One has a conscious awareness and the other has not. Moreover, although we do not realise it, we attract the victim energy field through negative thinking associated with, say, low self-esteem. It is like turning the dial on a radio receiver to pick up a new radio station or frequency. Low self-esteem thoughts are situated along the wavelength of the victim energy clouds. When we connect with the victim cloud we also feed it, as victim mentality, low self-esteem and ANTs all feed off each other. This can make it quite difficult to shake off some of the negative thoughts that we generate. Usually, the ANTs are supported by false beliefs about our self. Nonetheless, recognising false beliefs is part of our soul growth and personal development in life. It is part of what we are here to do. It is all about raising our awareness of what is happening and bringing ourselves into balance. As you do this you will be confronted, once again, with the reality of the statement *'everything in life is not as it seems'*. This statement is important because of our belief system and how we flow with what can be called the *'river of life'*. Once this has been recognised, it is possible to exercise some control and begin to devise methods to counter any flow of ANTs that we may be experiencing. The suggestions below are intended to assist you in this regard.

Recognising the Damage Caused by ANTs - Depression
ANTs are key contributors to the state of non-clinical depression. If you have ever been in a

state of depression, you will understand how unpleasant it is. Being around a family member or friend who is depressed emphasises what a difficult condition it is. It affects the mind, emotions and body drastically. It completely cuts off an individual from their authentic-self, and can nullify any feedback from the body's sensor mechanisms. What the individual concerned may not realise is that the negative emotion behind the ANT may be a frozen emotion. This type of emotion can be difficult to remove. Getting into a frozen emotion is a huge challenge for anybody, including any therapist who may be helping to investigate the cause of an ANT. How do we recognise if someone is showing signs of being depressed? The symptoms can show up in many ways, but can also be easy to spot. For example, the signs and symptoms of a depression tendency can be a combination of:

- excessively low self-esteem that manifests in a lack of self-worth, self-acceptance, self-belief, self-motivation and so on
- withdrawal from usual activities such as socialising, sex, sport, going to theatre, cinema and talking with friends
- eating too much and putting on weight (or bulimia), or eating too little and losing weight (anorexia)
- being overly pessimistic; a strong feeling of guilt and of being completely helpless; nurturing a victim mentality that has emerged
- very low energy levels and always feeling completely fatigued
- poor concentration, loss of memory and poor decision making
- not sleeping properly (insomnia), unable to get back to sleep once awakened, resultant feelings of extreme tiredness, or over-sleeping and not wanting to get out of bed
- very restless and irritable
- persistent headaches, digestive problems and other physical problems that cannot easily be relieved or cured
- alcohol and/or drug abuse

You can see from the above that most people show signs of one or more of these symptoms during their life. Perhaps the most common symptom is the lack of ability to sleep properly. Popular statistics indicate that about 80 percent of the population suffer from poor sleep that is mild to severe insomnia. A major cause of this is an infestation of ANTs. Once an ANT has moved in, it doesn't take long for others to follow. For those of you who are suffering from any level of insomnia, I suggest an approach to help you reverse this situation.

ANTs are major contributors to heart disease, stress, obesity, relationship breakdowns, unhappiness, low states of an inner feeling of positive wellbeing, and so on. At the core of an ANT is a negative emotion which, as stated above, may be deeply frozen within your body. Dealing with this emotion can be a major challenge. So how do we do it?

To Remove those ANTs - Cut Off their Food Supply

ANTs need a supply of food. This is usually the negative emotions that are trawled up from within the unconscious mind through the emotional or second subtle energy body when an ANT is scampering around in the conscious mind. For example, in a heated argument we might suddenly have an unexpected thought that we want to beat the living daylights out of someone, or just smack them across the face. They may have said something negative that hit one of our sensitivity buttons. Our ANTs would immediately have had a feeding frenzy on the emotion(s) that were triggered, one of which was most probably 'anger'. Now if we suppress our feelings when in this state of mind, the anger will remain within our emotional subtle energy body waiting to come out at a later date. It can also become trapped somewhere in the physical body. As it is a negative emotion it should be discharged in some way as soon as possible. If the negative emotion is not discharged, two things can happen:

- first, the anger energy might unexpectedly find expression later, perhaps as a physical act of violence

- second, the anger energy may stay below the surface, accumulate and fester away, eventually affecting our physical inner feeling of positive wellbeing and emotional happiness. Our attitude and behaviour can also change negatively, which will affect those around us and our health.

Just look at individuals who are impatient and who have a short fuse (a quick temper). They have not learnt how to dissipate their anger. Not a healthy situation for them to be in, or for those around them! We are all like a biological tuning fork, resonating as a result of impulses, and we are typically affected by an impatient individual's very presence because of their energy field. If we are the focus of their attention, the effect of the energy projection of their negative thoughts can induce fear and erode feelings of positive wellbeing.

The quickest way for us to be free of negative thoughts or ANTs is for us *to accept our-self for who we are.* Self-acceptance is an important life lesson and it is essential to accept all of our-self, including the bits that we may not really like. It is only by accepting them as part of us that we can focus upon them as needing attention. This will enable us to prevent them making us less than we can be and from enjoying a fuller sense of wellbeing. Note that we are dealing with wholeness here. This is about getting our-self into a positive state of self-acceptance. We all have a dark side but it is part of our whole self. Carl Jung referred to this side as the Shadow-self, a part that is important for us to recognise, accept and work with. I cover the Shadow-self in the next chapter.

In the day to day work environment, there are two quick ways of cutting off the food supply of a negative thought, or ANT.

1. The first way is that if you do not have a feeling/emotion associated with the ANT, just disregard it and throw it into an imaginary rubbish bin. Replace it immediately with a pleasant positive thought. Keep doing this until the ANT has moved out. Should the same ANT come back again, then go through the same routine. In time, the ANT will get bored and leave you alone.

2. The second way is if the ANT has a strong emotion attached to it and you feel the emotion in your body. If this is the case, it is advisable to pay attention to it. Why? Because it is trying to tell you something about your-self. Your ANT could be triggered after a verbal attack of some sort arising from discussions with another person. Or it could be that an issue has been triggered within you following someone's quite innocent comment or statement. In each case if there is a strong feeling/emotion it will have to be dealt with. The task here is to neutralise the emotion. Use the method to remove the feeling/emotion suggested in the de-stress process above. Keep in mind that if you resist working with an issue, it will persist. In other words it will continue to run within your unconscious mind and affect your attitudes and/or behaviour. This is a classic case of:

'what you resist persists'

To Get a Life – Stop those ANTs!
Diagram 4.7 provides an outline of some of the different types of ANTs that set out to build colonies (ANT hills), unknowingly, within our consciousness. These ANTs are extremely cunning and multiply when given the chance. To initiate action to get rid of all of these ANTs, I would suggest that it is important firstly to recognise them, and secondly, to starve them of their food. The grey circles represent worker ANTs that scamper about doing their daily tasks. They can be easily removed. The black/white circles represent soldier ANTs, the defenders and attackers. They may be more difficult to remove. A brief description of what these ANTs do and how to get rid of them may help.

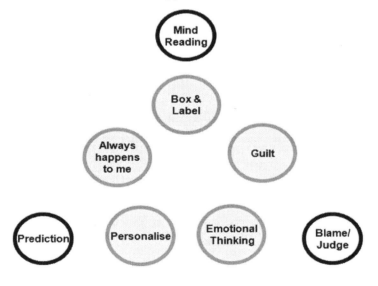

Diagram 4.7

1. Worker ANTs

- ### *Box and Label ANTs*

Part of our upbringing is to observe, sort out people and unconsciously put them into boxes with respect to how we see them. Once we have done this we tend to leave them there. Some example of the types of boxes we use are: describing somebody as being a workaholic, or materialistic, or having plenty of money, or little money, is working class, is sophisticated, is attractive or plain, and so on.

Labels are basically the same as putting someone in a box. A person can be labelled as being stingy (tight-fisted), unreliable, not numerate, stupid, an introvert, unworthy, a womaniser, and so on. In fact, a common set of labels is established and used with different boxes that we set up in our consciousness. The trouble with boxing and labelling is that we not only do it to other people but we also do it to our-self.

Process to Starve Out *Box and Label ANTs*

First step here, and for all of the ANTs, is to recognise that we are doing it. This is a common human trait. One thing which is helpful to recognise is that we tend to mirror each other to a great degree, through the boxes and labels we assign to someone. This provides us with an indication of the programs that are running in our unconscious mind. So try to stop doing it as it clouds the real characteristics of the person concerned. You may not realise it, but your thinking transmits the negative energy of your thoughts to them, which is not helpful. Do not forget that at the sub-atomic level we are all connected. When you think about someone, you open a link to their subtle energy bodies. Just like tuning into a radio station. You too are affected by your thoughts, so keep them neutral at worst, or positive at best. The unconscious and conscious mind has surprisingly dynamic characteristics, allowing great opportunities to change your thinking patterns. So try to keep an open mind. Take those whom you think about out of their box and de-label them. Do the same for your-self. Look at how you label your-self and change the negative labels. Take the image that you have made of your-self out of its box. You are an amazing being and have so much to offer. Go within and start bringing your talented inner-self out for everybody to see.

- ### *Always/Never Happens to Me ANT*

If we are in this state of mind, we are always waiting for something negative to happen to prove it to our-self. Out of one hundred, ninety good things could happen to us but we only focus on the not-so-good remaining ten, waiting for them to happen to prove our point! In this state of mind, we will increase the potential for negative things to happen to us.

The word *never* is such a powerfully negative word and it programs us not to achieve or receive. Just remember, if you are thinking 'my boss will never promote me', or 'she will never let me go on holiday', and so on - you are sending out these thought energies to him and he will most probably automatically comply with your thoughts. If you say to your-self that you will never be good at maths, or drawing, or running, or swimming and so on, then you are programming your mind and body to deliver your request. It will oblige you by complying one hundred percent!

Process to Starve Out *Always/Never Happens to Me ANTs*

It is so important to recognise when you are using *always* in a negative way. *Never* is also such a destructive word. Banish 'never' from your vocabulary. Use the word 'always' in a positive context. For example, use affirmations such as: I am always lucky, I am always looked after, I am always doing well in what I turn my mind to, or turn my hand to, and so on. Accepting that you are a quantum bio-magnet and that you program your energy field to attract success (or not), it is advisable to adopt this positive approach to thinking if a negative thought or ANT creeps into your consciousness. That will starve them out. We attract what we focus upon. Through the words we think, plus their associated emotions, we are programming our bio-magnetic energy field. So choose carefully the words you think.

- ***Personalise ANT***

A neighbour, or friend, or family member, or work colleague, or teacher at school, or ticket attendant, and so on may ignore you, causing you to feel that it might have something to do with you. Alternatively, your son may have had a surfing accident and you feel that you should have paid for him to have some professional lessons. Everybody's life is different and you never know fully what is happening in other people's lives. Unbeknown to you, they may have just been having a bad day for reasons that are nothing to do with you. What happened has nothing to do with what you should have done. It was to do with themselves and what was happening within them. It may have been a life lesson. If someone ignores us or a stranger suddenly loses their temper, it is all about what is going on in *their* consciousness though also to a degree within ours. Sometimes, someone may mirror back to us what is running in our unconscious mind, but at other times it is not connected with us at all. It is important to stop personalising things!

Process to Starve Out *Personalise ANTs*

People are as they are, and they attract into their lives activities, events and situations that match their quantum bio-magnetic field. Do not take things personally. Should something happen and a thought arises that causes you to take it personally, or you have called into your conscious mind a personalised ANT, try to recognise that it has nothing to do with you and let it go. If the thought comes back again then try to let it go once more. Plant a positive supporting thought about your-self, and keep the thought in your mind in place. Do this until the ANT goes away. You will also have made a positive contribution to the energy state of the consciousness of any individual who may be involved.

- ***Emotional Thinking ANT***

The old saying 'think with your head and not your emotions' is so true. Emotions/feelings can be misleading and it is best to have tangible, concrete evidence to back up any strong emotion/feeling we may experience. You may feel that you have not done well in an exam. If you have answered all or only part of the questions, then just 'wait and see'. Do not dwell on any negative emotion/feeling. You might find your-self in a position where you feel that your partner does not love you anymore. Your feeling may be telling you this but he or she may be feeling the opposite. Try communicating in a non-aggressive way and ask them. Tell them how you feel and try to resolve the issue that is running within you.

Process to Starve Out *Emotional Thinking* ANTs

In chapter 2, I showed that we can affect something just by thinking about it. Change any negative thoughts derived from negative emotions into positive, supporting thought energy. See the opposite of what your negative emotion is telling you is going to happen. Keep going around that loop until you feel the opposite is in place and you have neutralised the feeling. If we dwell on the negative feeling we will add to its strength. Victim-consciousness energy is just waiting for such an opportunity to enter. Ask your-self, what is causing the negative feeling. Go within your-self to try to locate the cause. Or better still, if you are in a partnership, communicate with your partner in a constructive way to get an answer.

- ***Guilt ANT***

So many people are swamped with guilt ANTs which need to be removed. Take the surfing example above where the parent may think 'I should have given in to his wanting extra lessons', or, 'I ought to have . . .' and so on. Guilt is very invasive and sneaks in when we least expect it. It can of course, at times, have what may appear to be a benefit. It could cause us to do things that we would not normally consider doing, such as clearing a disorganised study at an unplanned time because we feel we have to. When we believe we have to do something, then that feeling or decision is usually guilt based. This will most probably have a negative effect on how you feel, resulting in a bad mood or some other negative attitude. Stop thinking or saying 'I have to' and 'must do'. The word *must* is a subtly-based guilt word. You might say that you 'must visit your mother in law'! That is a sure sign that you feel guilty for not visiting her. When the time is right you will make that visit. Do not do it because of a guilty feeling, otherwise your attitude and behaviour will reflect your feeling of guilt. Your inner feeling of positive wellbeing and state of happiness are negatively impacted by feelings of guilt; let's appreciate that we are all here to learn lessons.

Process to Starve Out *Guilt* ANTs

It is in our interest to starve out any guilt ANTs as quickly as possible. We should of course use common sense in doing this. In the case of the untidy study, we could build into our work routine at home regular times during the year where we stop what we are doing and tidy up things. This creates a routine and minimises the chance of guilt slipping in. A couple of important points to consider are that an untidy study blocks the energy flow in the room. It is also a reflection of the state of your consciousness. Think of the benefits of tidying your study; visualise that in so doing you are creating a constructive energy flow and de-cluttering your consciousness. These are all great, positive and supportive benefits derived from the energy field that you are setting up. Visiting your mother in law because you want to is a positive and supportive step forward. She will feel the difference. If guilt is well established, your energy field will keep bringing you more of the same until you change it!

2. Soldier ANTs: Attackers and destroyers

- *Mind Reading ANT*

Here is yet another practice that we all indulge in from time to time. You glance at someone who may give you a sour look in passing and you believe that this look has something to do with you! Young people have sometimes been known to act violently in such situations, occasionally with fatal consequences, having interpreted that look as a sign of 'disrespect'. Looking at body language and listening to the tone of voice that someone is using, is one thing, knowing the cause is another. You are experiencing the effect of something that probably has nothing to do with you. My boss, when I worked in merchant banking, once shouted at me at a Monday morning meeting. He shouted at me because I turned and said a few words to a colleague sitting alongside me and wasn't at that moment listening to him. I looked at his facial expression (he had a look like thunder!) and felt, goodness he doesn't like me! When I talked to his PA during the afternoon she mentioned that he had been arguing with his wife for most of the weekend and she just would not listen to him! My mind reading was totally wrong and persuaded me of the folly of attempting to read someone else's mind. We simply do not know what is running in another person's head!

Process to Starve Out *Mind Reading ANTs*

Try in difficult situations to do two things. The first is to recognise that, even though you may know the individual well and are aware of what is happening in their life, you do not know what is running in their consciousness. Take a step back in your own mind and say to yourself *'what is it that I have to learn from this situation'*? In reality, you are probably mirroring your own issues in them! This is not easy to accept at first, because most likely, you have not been brought up to understand mirroring. Avoid reacting to the situation if you can, for it may not have anything to do with you. It may just be an unfortunate occurrence and you simply happened to be there. Mind reading can cause you to react in totally the wrong way, thereby adding to the other person's level of anger, for example. See the person in your mind in a happy and content way. Keep doing this until the mind reading stops. This will not only benefit them, it will also enhance your inner feeling of positive wellbeing and happiness.

- ***Blame/Judge ANTs***

Strange as it may seem, blaming is tantamount to having a virus infection. Some aspects of the way we judge are no better. This might not sound so odd if you think of your physical self as a biological computer (your brain and body) which has a virus infection. Because most of us blame and judge, we believe that it is a correct way to think and behave. Parents do it, grandparents, relations, friends, teachers, authority figures, and so on, all do it. In fact, most people do it. There are two sides to the way we make judgements. One is essential for day to day activities and survival, but the other is where we make a judgement to blame others for what is happening to us. We also blame others for what is happening around us in terms of activities and events (for example, the prime minister, or the president, or the neighbour, and so on). Once you raise your conscious awareness to consider and think within the 5th dimension, and recognise that you are like a quantum bio-magnet, you will soon realise the futility of blaming and judging. Guess what, though? If you blame someone, you also unknowingly tune into the victim-consciousness energy field and become a passive victim. This muddies the water and makes it difficult to solve any problem (or challenges) you may have perceived. Until you tune into the fifth dimension you are, once again, unknowingly in a state of denial: 'it's them not me! How could it possibly be me?'

Process to Starve Out *Blame/Judge ANTs*

To get away from the state of thinking where we blame others and/or make judgements about them, it is advisable to recognise that '*all in life is not as it seems*'. We do not really know why someone has behaved in the particular way that has offended us. We do not know their history or background. You were not aware (probably until now) that you are a quantum bio-magnet attracting everything that is happening to you and vice versa! This may seem to be too much to swallow, but it is true. The first step is *acceptance*. Accept that some of our thinking patterns are not in our best interest, or are just wrong! The next step is to deal with the way we think. We are all beings of energy, and if we consider energy as the fifth dimension and accept what this means, in time our awareness will change. Understand that there is a purpose for our being here; this understanding then has the capacity to make a major contribution to removing any blame and refine the way we make judgments.

- ***Prediction (fortune telling) ANT***

Negative predictions should be avoided. Remember, once again, that we are a quantum bio-magnet and our thought energy contributes to what we are predicting. When you listen to people during a conversation, note those who offer you a negative statement about a forthcoming outcome of something that you are discussing. Some will always give you a list of the negative things that you should expect. And that ranges from talking about getting your house repaired, to travelling somewhere, to what's going on at work. This gives you an insight into the belief system that is running in their unconscious mind. When I worked in investment banking in the Gulf Region, I noticed that most of the Arabian executives invariably predicted negative outcomes if they were asked to assess a project. When they were faced with a question such as *'what could be added to allow the project's performance to improve? Give me a creative suggestion'* there was usually a stunned silence! This was all the result of left-brain hemisphere thinking, without any access to the creative right-brain hemisphere. It was also a symptom of the strong tribal structure which is predominant in Arabia. Although this structure has some great benefits, its weakness produces a lack of creative thinking and a focus on the negative.

Process to Starve Out *Prediction (fortune telling) ANTs*

There are individuals who use a degree of prediction (hunch) abilities in their profession (commodity traders, derivative traders, stock brokers, and so on). They combine an objective analysis with a subjective assessment. There are some psychics who have a remarkable track record in getting their predictions right. The other side of prediction is where, in a negative frame of mind, we try to guess how someone is, or how they will behave when you see them, or what the outcome of a situation will be, or whether or not they should do something or continue to do something. In this negative state of mind it is advisable to stop such prediction, because you can actually strongly affect the energy field of the person you are giving advice to, as well as your-self. What is more, your prediction could be wrong! Transform the negative prediction in your mind into a positive, supportive thought of some sort. Keep doing this until you neutralise the negative prediction and can hold in your mind a positive outcome. Replace any negative emotion with a positive one. This is always the way to go.

When the above types of ANTs are recognised, it becomes easier to understand why we so readily drop into a prolonged state of negative thinking. There is little chance of a motivating and happy ambience being created when people's consciousness is suffering from an infestation of ANTs. The key here is to put every effort into preventing any negative thoughts growing into ANTs, as those ANTs will multiply at great speed. It is a kind of negative trap that prevents us from experiencing positive wellbeing and happiness. On the left side of diagram 4.8 an ANT (negative thought) is about to enter the individual's head.

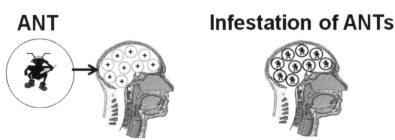

Diagram 4.8

Very quickly that negative thought becomes the main focus of attention. This thought might attract to it a strong negative emotion. When this happens the negative thought just goes round and round in the conscious mind and gets hardwired into the brain's neuro-cells in the right pre-frontal cortex, creating an ANT. If you happen to get into such a situation, you have the choice not to make the negative thought the main focus of your attention. Certainly, acknowledge and review the thought, but be prepared to let it go. Ask your-self *what, if anything, is there for me to learn from this thought?* Sometimes you may be able to immediately recognise that there is a lesson to be learnt and other times you may have to work with the ANT to discover that lesson. In such situations, we are entering into the gymnastics of consciousness for which few of us have received any training!

The right-hand side of Diagram 4.8 shows an individual who has been consumed by an ANT infestation which has taken over the conscious mind. If you are unfortunate to be in this type of situation, and most of us are at times, you will probably go to bed with the negative thought(s) in your mind, only to wake up and it is waiting to continue where it left off. It goes round and round and round until you deal with it. You can see why in this type of situation the thought is called an 'ANT', an Automatic Negative Thought. If you feel that you are being affected by ANTs, then it is important to recognise what has happened and to seek help in dealing with the ANTs. Otherwise, those ANTs will play havoc with any inner feeling of positive wellbeing and happiness. What can help to get you out of a negative rut is Cognitive Behavioural Therapy (CBT: Appendix 2). Today, Western society is plagued with ANT infestations. You can deal with this your-self provided you recognise what is happening and act immediately to get rid of ANTs as they arise. If your ANTs are deeply embedded, then you may require the help of a good therapist and/or medical practitioner. So how can you deal with your ANTs your-self?

Eradicate those ANTs and Get a Grip on Depression
It is vitally important to be able to cut off what fuels depression. ANTs are, in my opinion, a substantial part of this fuel supply, so let's go back to the beginning of how ANTs are created. How thoughts are created has been covered in chapter 2. Nevertheless, such is the destructive power of ANTs, which are created through our thoughts, that it may prove helpful to take you briefly through the subject again. Thoughts are created from many sources as shown in diagram 4.9. Examining these sources, thoughts are created internally by:

1. Our five senses (sight, hearing, touch taste and smell). These sensors take in external energy to generate an internal thought.

Other thoughts created within us are much more complicated. They come about through:

2. inner-self (internal influences): the ego, different beliefs, different personalities/sub-personalities, masks, the Shadow-self, intuition, the soul and higher self.

Thought Creation

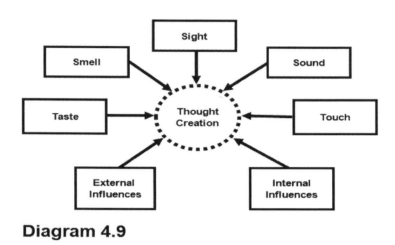

Diagram 4.9

There are also influences that come from outside of us:

3. external influences: such thoughts use the sixth sense, which has the ability to pick up energy changes like the atmosphere in a room or building. There is also a constant bombardment from the communication media - TV, radio, internet, newspapers and so on which affect mass mind thought. The energy-supporting, collective mass mind thoughts affects us more than we care to think. And individuals who think about us affect our energy field. The really spooky one, though, is that we are also affected by energy forms that roam the astral plane (discarnate souls, negative thought forms, thought parasites and so on).

Although the above sources of thought creation may appear to be rather complicated, each of us has the power to control whether or not we accept a negative thought that enters our conscious mind. That is provided you are not suffering from a clinical abnormality of the brain, or a non-clinical heavy depression where exercising such control can be a much more difficult task.

ANTs that keep recurring need to be explored either through self-exploration (preferably with someone who knows you well), or with a therapist. We have the power of reason with which to question an ANT. The approach used to question a random negative thought here is part of an investigative task. Dealing with the emotion supporting an ANT, which may be frozen, is another more difficult aspect of this task.

To get into this type of investigation, start by having a dialogue with the negative thought in your mind. Do not just accept the negative thought as it is most probably untrue. Some of the false beliefs that you were conditioned to adopt by authority figures in your life may still be influencing your thinking. Your negative ego, or a shadow part of a personality can also influence you, especially if it is trying to teach you a lesson. Take note of how you feel as you explore where the negative thought originated.

I have emphasised that the negative emotion supporting an ANT can be removed and replaced with a positive one. Most of the work to remove the ANT will probably be in dealing with the negative emotional content. If the emotion is frozen, then you may require some professional help to unlock it and remove it. If, however, you can get into the negative emotion easily, how do you reverse it? Try remembering a happy time you had in the past, and sense the emotion and physical feeling associated with it. See, or sense this emotion in your imagination as a ball of pure, golden, radiant sunshine (or some other form that you associate with warmth and happiness). If you feel the ANT's negative emotion in the pit of your stomach, move the radiant ball with your mind down into that area. Imagine its golden radiance dissolving any negativity that may exist there. If the negative emotion supported by the ANT is not in this region, move the ball to where you feel the emotion is located. Hold the ball in position, letting it radiate its energy until the negative feeling is reduced and, if possible, removed altogether. This exercise may have to be practised several times. Applying this approach is designed to prevent, or minimise, any damage to the body's cells as well as to activate a natural healing towards any damaged cells.

Removing ANTs can also be approached in other ways. A subtle approach is to not see an ANT as a problem but as a challenge. Accepting that part of life is to work through challenges, rather than problems, will put you into a solution-oriented frame of mind. When you focus on what you perceive as a problem, you become less solution-oriented. This is because the words you use in your mind, while you are taking a problem or negative thought apart, have enormous power due to other negative emotions that they attract. Analysing a negative thought usually leads to bringing up other negative views and comparative thoughts which can add fuel to the internal negative emotions that are running within you, and may divert you from a solution. In Western society, the brain has been hardwired to approach problems in a mechanistic way. Such an approach is geared to drill down to look for similar negative problems in the hope of finding a solution. Whether or not you are looking at a problem/challenge, you may have a choice to make with respect to the solution. You may not, of course, like the solution to the challenge or the choice that you have to make.

ANTs may be indicating the necessity to change something in our life. Most people have an unconscious fear of change and may be hesitant to take action. This is because they may have to move out of their comfort zone! It is important here, if you are facing a change, to get out of any blame and judgement cycle that you may be indulging in. We are all well schooled in operating within this type of cycle. After all, you may say, everybody else does it! They do not, of course, but it is perhaps one of the more difficult cycles to get out of. Once you are aware of this cycle, you can begin to make a step by step change that does not involve apportioning blame and making judgements.

ANTs ensure that we entrap ourselves in low self-esteem, and once low self-esteem takes hold, it is guaranteed that we are entering into some state of depression, albeit a minor one. Victim-consciousness also jumps in wherever possible. In this case, negative ego will always be making sure that we are confronted with situations that substantiate the negative thoughts and feelings. Such situations are just reflecting back to us our low self-esteem. The task here is to notice what is going on, not to comply with it, and to reverse the situation running in our conscious mind. We do this by working on our thoughts and changing them from patterns of negative thoughts to patterns of positive thoughts. Affirmations can be beneficial here and I suggest some below to get you going. An affirmation is:

'a strong positive statement that is always made in the present tense'

An affirmation is a way of manifesting and making real to you what you are visualising (seeing in the mind/imagination). You may find the following affirmations beneficial:

- I am bright, intelligent and creative
- I am very good at whatever I want to do in life
- I am a loving person and love all those whom I come into contact
- I am able to achieve whatever I put my mind to
- I am able to sense what is good for me and others
- I am always able to find a solution to the challenges that confront me
- I am attracting as much wealth to me as I desire
- Every day in every way I am happier, healthier, wiser and wealthier
- I am able to heal myself whenever I need to.

Select an affirmation that counters the ANT that may be disturbing you. If the above do not cover your particular ANT, then make up your own positive affirmation. Always begin it with "I am". When the ANT enters your mind, keep repeating the affirmation until it leaves. A good time to use affirmations is when you wake up in the morning or just before you go to sleep at night.

It can be seen that the approach to stop ANTs is relatively straightforward, but difficult when dealing with frozen and strong emotions. But even though, at first, it may be difficult to reverse the ANT, persevere, because you are probably working on a lifetime of entrenched patterns of negative thinking and their supporting emotions. Developing your own process to deal with ANTs is recommended. Those ANTs that are associated with frozen or excessively strong emotions may require some professional support to work through them (see Appendix 2). For your average ANT you may wish to consider using some of the following:

- Keep a journal and note down every negative thought you have during the day, for about a week. Arrange similar negative thoughts together as they arise so that you can see a pattern. Start working on the patterns by substituting your negative thoughts with positive ones. You may be quite shocked by the end of the week at just how many negative thoughts entered your consciousness, for example: being impatient in a supermarket queue or with the checkout clerk; someone beating you to a seat on a bus; a waiter or waitress not noticing you; someone speaking loudly close by; someone cutting you up in traffic or tailgating you, and so forth.

- Visualisation: if a negative pattern is the outcome of a bad experience, then re-write the opposite of this experience by seeing it and working through it in your imagination. Keeping the same actors (people) in the scene but change the scene to a positive one. See the negative emotion in the scene in your mind as a dark-grey energy form like a rock which you have loosened. Attach the dark-grey rock to a balloon large enough to allow it to fly away. See the rock flying away into the distance. If the balloon does not lift the rock, the emotion may be frozen. Go back in your imagination and work through the scene a few more times. If the rock still refuses to fly away then you will require some professional help to remove it. Bring into your consciousness a positive emotion that you experienced in the past. If you cannot find a positive emotion, make one up by thinking of something that will fill you with happiness. See this positive emotion taking the form of a golden rock to replace the grey rock that has flown away. Let this emotion fill the spot previously occupied by the old negative emotion. This exercise will ensure that the original scene and emotion are over-written and the gap left by the departing negative emotion being filled with the positive one.

- Talk to your-self during the visualisation, where you are reversing any non-supporting statements to supporting statements. Some of you may not be able to see pictures in your mind but can have a discussion/dialogue in the mind. Recognise that the negative thought(s) is most probably false and reverse what it is telling you. Doing this will over-write the negative thought, leaving in its place a positive, supporting thought.

- Using affirmations similar to the ones given above (or make up your own to reverse your negative thought), make sure they are always in the present and include 'I am' where you can. Just keep repeating your positive affirmation until the negative thought gets bored and leaves you alone.

- Stay away from negative media, negative soap operas and negative films, especially at the end of the day before you go to sleep. This is because the negative imaging or words can trigger deep-seated fears from within your consciousness which will have to be processed and neutralised while you are asleep. If the processing is incomplete or does not happen during the sleep state, you may wake up feeling less than your usual positive self. Stay out of any dramas, when they arise.

The above methods are increasingly used by individuals to help them alleviate their depression, or to heal themselves more quickly after, say, an operation, or from a traumatic incident. Because of the structure of consciousness, our awareness is communicated down to the cell level of both the brain and body. It is possible, therefore, to create miracles (spontaneous remission) within the physical body and at different levels of consciousness. That is, of course, when we realise and accept the link between our thinking, belief system and the effect it is having on our inner feeling of positive wellbeing and happiness as well as on those around us. Only when we are ready to believe in the power of thoughts will we be able to utilise an appropriate healing thought to its maximum potential. This is part of the process of 'getting it'. Now it is your choice, your decision; the door has been opened!

Thanks to the dedication of a few far-sighted doctors, surgeons, psychiatrists, psychologists, therapists, healers and so on, the power of an individual's consciousness (the mind) to create a spontaneous remission (a miracle) while in a state of disease is no longer front-line news. Science too, slowly but surely, is beginning to recognise the power of a thought within an individual's consciousness to affect the functioning of feelings of wellbeing and happiness. Most people tend to be intention-driven (focusing on an outcome or purpose). This being the case, the power of thoughts can be used to strengthen their creative purpose and ability to manifest what they desire. That includes self-healing and alleviating a depressed state of mind. To do this, it is important to control those ANTs and deal swiftly with any intrusive negative thoughts that appear to come from nowhere.

Activating a spiritual dimension (connecting with the authentic-self) is recognised as an essential component in strengthening an inner feeling of positive wellbeing and happiness. How we *handle* ourselves when an inner crisis, or an external difficult situation arises is a key measurement in terms of personal development and inner growth. If there is an infestation of ANTs and any low self-esteem, the chance of tuning into the authentic-self is greatly reduced. Handling an inner crisis, combined with difficult situations, is made more difficult. Unless our fabricated-self is sufficiently merged with the authentic-self, we deny ourselves a chance of tuning into and working with a spiritual dimension. It is a bit of a 'catch 22' situation! Given the importance of self-esteem, let us examine how to handle it in the various situations we find our-selves in.

SELF-ESTEEM

Victim-Consciousness: an Infiltrator Causing Low Self-esteem

What exactly is self-esteem? It can be defined as:

'an individual's overall evaluation or appraisal of their own worth'

Self-esteem is located at the core of the inner-self (or authentic-self). It's about self-acceptance, which is about self-worth. It is not a fixed state, it is dynamic. It can grow or decline, over time, depending on how aware we are of it, or not. It can also grow or decline if we are purposefully working on it, or not. Before looking at the causes of low self-esteem in detail, I want to make a small but important digression. When self-esteem goes through a change, due to what is happening in an individual's life, it can attract *victim* energy (ANTs, page 160) which infiltrates into the unconscious mind. This infiltration pulls self-esteem down to a lower level. It also results in victim situations (being discriminated against or treated unfairly) actually being manifested in many areas of life. If you discover that you are being, or are acting out a victim situation in your life, then you can guarantee that you have experienced a change in your self-esteem which has attracted victim energy infiltration to cause the situation. Such is the power of the quantum bio-magnetic field and manifestation.

I pointed out earlier that over time actual victim energy thoughts reached such a high energy density that they formed a massive, independent negative cloud of energy. The density of the cloud is such that it vibrates at its own discrete frequency range and also *thinks* within itself. I call this a *victim-consciousness energy field*. Why is it important? It is important because consciousness and the brain are like a transmitter/receiver of energy. Certain states of consciousness, such as a change in self-esteem, create a frequency change within our consciousness that attracts the victim-consciousness energy field. Because of this change in frequency a channel is opened to receive from and also to add to the victim energy field. Hence it is able to grow in strength and propagate itself. When victim energy consciousness is attracted, it programs the quantum bio-magnetic field to attract people and situations where we experience being a victim. As soon as a victim pattern has been recognised it is possible to take remedial steps. These steps involve a change in our thinking. The purpose is to clear the victim situation and prevent it from happening again (it is a false belief). Therefore, because of the energy status of the victim cloud, I would suggest that low self-esteem is something which we should do all we can to work on and bring into balance. A question that is in our interest to ask, as early as possible in life, is, how do we recognise self-esteem in all of its different disguises?

The first thing to say is that Self-esteem is either positive (High) or negative (Low). For example:

Positive (High) self-esteem	Negative (Low) self-esteem
Like and love themselves	Do not love or like themselves
Love life itself	Dislike life
Have an open and creative mind	Have a closed mind
Love being on the planet	Do not want to be on the planet
Can take criticism	Cannot take criticism
Have a progressive view of the world	Have a limited world view
Interact honestly with people	Do not interact honestly with people
Can receive constructive feedback	Their feedback is usually non-constructive
Feel in control of their life	Feel not in control of their life
Have strong integrity	Have limited integrity
Action orientated and like to make things happen	Avoid action due to fear and prefer to stop things happening
High expectations about future	Have low expectations about future
Are flexible and not rigid	Inflexible and rigid

The earlier you begin to identify the level of self-esteem you have and, if required, make appropriate changes to bring it into balance, the better your life will become. Self-esteem sets us up to behave in different supportive or non-supportive ways through our attitude, behaviour and the experiences that we attract to ourselves. The goal when dealing with any of the challenges we face that are due to low self-esteem, is to bring self-esteem into balance. In reality, we probably fluctuate from either being in too negative a state or to being in an overly positive state where our self-esteem, is concerned.

How Self-esteem is Conditioned Within Us

Each of us has come into this lifetime with our own personal issues (life lessons) which also include issues that have been passed down to us through the ancestors (through the genes). The ancestral line (diagram 4.10) includes mother and father, both sets of grandparents and great-grandparents, aunts, uncles and so on. Although a major reason for our being here is to work through our life lessons (issues), another reason is for the healing that takes place in

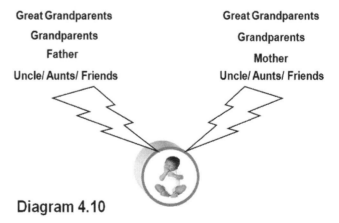

How we are conditioned and influenced

Diagram 4.10

the process of creating a positive closure to them. Once each major life lesson has been identified, accepted, worked with and cleared, we do not pass it on to the next generation, which would be the case for life issues not otherwise cleared. It is also possible to clear a life lesson only for it to return again if we fall back into old habits, attitudes and behaviour. This should be looked at as a test to see if we really did 'get it'.

In energy terms, once a life lesson is worked through in our consciousness, we have basically changed the programming within the subtle energy bodies and also the programming within the physical body's gene structure. The latter is important as the programs in the genes are passed on from generation to generation. This is because the body's cells are aware of our consciousness. A change, therefore, can be made to programs that are already stored and running at the cellular level. Furthermore, as time and space are coincident in the world of energy (the quantum reality), not only do we clear major issues within ourselves but we also clear the issues back up the ancestral trail and for future generations. This is difficult to believe, if your consciousness is trapped in your intellect, which runs on a four-dimensional, fabricated-self understanding of what life is about at best. I personally still find the healing effect at the sub-atomic level of reality quite mind blowing.

Progressing through life, the quantum bio-magnetic energy field goes through a continual process of change, due to what happens with the life lessons/issues that are attracted to us. This energy field strengthens our positive thinking or further weakens our negative thinking. The energy field, therefore, depends upon how much control we are exercising over the thoughts that are running in our conscious and unconscious minds. Balancing the body's energy fields is without doubt the name of the game! Diagram 4.11 includes various scenes that most of us act (or live) through as we follow life's path. All of the scenes have a direct effect on our self-esteem. These scenes can take place anywhere - at home within the family; at work and with colleagues; at a place of study with fellow students and lecturers; where and with whom we socialise; within personal relationships, and when we are travelling.

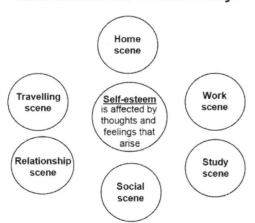

Diagram 4.11

Self-esteem is constantly being affected by those with whom we come into contact and the communications we enter into. It is also affected by the events, activities and situations we find ourselves in. The task is to always try to keep everything in balance. Of course, from time to time, our feelings and/or reactions to events may become extreme through arguments, disputes, rudeness, hatred, anger, fear and so on, but we are nonetheless masters of our own destiny. So, when things get rough, we can either dwell on the negative aspects of what is happening to us or view it as a challenge. A rather tricky but important tactic to learn in life, as soon as possible, is to:

'stay out of the drama'

This is by no means an easy task. It is essential to try to grasp the significance of what is happening and to learn from it. But once we are engaged in a drama, emotions fly and the mind becomes clouded. Most times we may be unable to see the wood for the trees. What we may not realise is that all of this is driven by our ego, for ego flourishes on dramas. If we buy into what appears to be an attack on our-self, and make a negative response during the attack, then we will be buffeted by the negative energy flow that will occur between our-self and those involved. It is important to recognise in life that:

'if you do what you have always done, then you will get what you have always got'

Recognising, during an attack on our-self, our own attitude and behaviour, including body language, tone of voice, and thoughts, is a step forward to safeguarding and strengthening our self-esteem. Our thoughts have great power. If those thoughts are negative, this power can have a detrimental effect on our feelings of wellbeing and happiness and negatively affect those around us. Alternatively it can stimulate the opposite. Quite simply, the opposite contains a balancing effect that has the power to create an inner healing within our-self and those around us. Our energy fields are all interconnected. So which would you rather have, conflict or healing? It's your choice!

What Low Self-esteem Does to Us

Low self-esteem has destructive capabilities and is endemic throughout not only Western populations but also the rest of the world. For a happy, contented and successful life each of us is required to do something to reverse any patterns of low self-esteem that exist within ourselves. Some approaches to bring self-esteem into balance are given below for you to practise.

Diagram 4.12 summarises some of its major effects. Next to Doubt, that great destroyer and enemy at the gate, and victim-consciousness that attracts miserable situations, you can see that low self-esteem deserves a similar rating. Looking at my own family (father, mother and grandfather) I could certainly see a connecting thread of low self-esteem. Could there also be a genetic link that was passed on to me? There certainly was, and I can recall a childhood experience which contributed to lowering my own feelings of self-worth. This happened when I was eight years old. My father had a dairy farmer visit the family hotel once a day. His name was Colin Lamont. I was a naturally happy child (which surprisingly

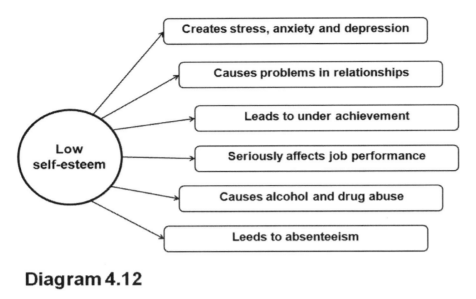

Diagram 4.12

was the cause of many of the future challenges I was to face) and the farmer and I got on well together and used to chat as he delivered the milk. After a particular visit, when Mr Lamont and my father were coming out of the back door of the hotel carrying a large empty milk churn, he happened to say to my father "what a great wee lad you have here, he must be a boon to your business". To which my father responded (he was in a bad mood at the time) "him, he's the most useless boy in Christendom, he doesn't do anything to help me". I was truly devastated by this, as part of my job at that age was to entertain the hotel guests from time to time and to wash endless numbers of dishes and cutlery. What is in one little word? I would suggest - everything. I did not know at the time that I was being set up (conditioned) to experience and to deal with two important challenges, namely, victim-consciousness and low self-esteem. This indeed has been part of my soul's growth process in this lifetime. What I find really interesting is that all of the negative experiences that knocked my self-esteem, unknown to me, were setting up false beliefs within my belief system. These false beliefs had an effect on my thought processes and what I attracted to me as I advanced along my life's path. My quantum bio-magnetic field did its job well!

Sins of the Father Beget the Son – Including Self-esteem
Ultimately, the negative effects of low self-esteem have an effect on what happens to us in a career, social or home environment. It is vitally important to recognise that parents have a major effect on the development of their children's self-esteem. It took me some time to make a connection between my parents' and my own self-esteem. For example, my father was a very hard working Scotsman. He was popular and excelled in anything he put his hand and mind to. And yet, he had low self-esteem. When my parents migrated to Southern England, after about six months of settling in I just loved being there. By then, I had started to make friends with local teenagers my own age and have some fun. But my father never really adjusted well to the change. He somehow felt out of place, although he certainly was not. It was my mother who pointed this out to me much later. I mention this because in life

the *'sins of the father beget the son'*. Little did I realise that back up the ancestral trail, low self-esteem must have been an issue which was passed down to him and thence to me.

Both sides of my grandparents (one side Scottish and the other English - with a German background) had been through pretty tough times. My English grandmother's parents had escaped persecution in Germany (about 1890) and settled in England. Most certainly, because of the persecution they would have had issues related to low self-esteem and victim-consciousness. My Scottish grandfather's mother became a widow at 45 years of age with five young children and had to survive in the years before a welfare state was even thought of. She did not put her children into an orphanage. Instead she managed somehow to travel to England for employment in service, taking her children with her. That was most unusual for that time period and I simply do not know how she did it. My grandfather was the fifth child and from what I can recollect from him, he had a pretty miserable childhood. Times were very difficult and he did not get on too well with his brothers and sisters. I can see from this how the seeds of low self-esteem and victim-consciousness had been well and truly laid. These would have been duly passed on to his three sons, one of whom was my father. And, of course, those parts he had not dealt with himself would have been passed on to me to deal with.

Even though I was born a happy soul and in the end have succeeded in doing nearly everything that I set out to do, I still had a low sense of self-worth. Notwithstanding, I am always willing to help a fellow soul on their journey. From time to time, this led to people taking advantage of me, especially at work (when I unconsciously let them). It took me a considerable time to figure out that something within me was, at times, sabotaging what I was doing and that my low self-esteem was responsible. Slowly but surely I began to figure out that at the core of my being, something felt not quite right. It turned out to be the imbalance in my self-esteem. Only when I was in my thirties did I begin to contemplate life and to take time to step back and examine what was happening in my career. The next two examples shook my professional foundations, occurring when I was working in the United Nations (UN) in Rome and the other when I was working in the World Bank in Washington DC.

Let me set the scene for my UN job at the Food and Agricultural Organisation (FAO) and World Food Program (WFP). The first thing you have to understand about the UN is that it has a quota system when recruiting people and recruitment is made only from member countries. The number of people the UN hires from a specific country is related to the financial contribution the member country makes to a particular agency. Second is, therefore, that your boss is most likely going to be of a different nationality from your-self. Third, there are different races, cultures and religions at play in the operating environment.

Being a Scotsman, and British, I was well honed at working in different Western environments but ill equipped, at the beginning, to handle the diversity of protocols that were running in this truly international environment. Even though I was very diplomatic, when it came to making a point which I believed should be made, I did not always see that I was infringing upon the cultural sensitivities of professionals from other cultures. Unwittingly, I was having an effect on their self-esteem and they in turn were having an effect on mine. Some of the things I did and said innocently, out of a lack of cultural understanding, caused their negative reactions.

When I was making a point very forcefully during a meeting, I did not at first truly hear or feel the subtle tonal differences in the voices of the various non-Western UN professionals present. It was easier to get the feel for European and United States professionals, but for other nationalities – well, it could be difficult! Nevertheless, I did begin to gain some wisdom when a good UN friend said quite bluntly after an important meeting, "look John, you certainly won the battle against that Division Chief, but I can assure you, you have lost the war!" "What do you mean?" I replied. "You caused him to lose face (lowered his self-esteem) amongst the participants at the meeting and in his culture that is an unforgivable sin". "Lose face?" I replied, "What has that got to do with driving home the changes that are essential to be made?" "Everything!", came the response. Needless to say, the Division Chief did not implement the changes that I had recommended and driven home so forcefully. He easily found reasons and excuses to say why he could not. His ego had been bruised and he clearly subordinated the logical changes I had argued for, to his ego and loss of 'face'. This too had an effect on my self-esteem. My ego was strong, so strong in fact that it prevented me from being alert to the effect my way of dealing with matters in meetings was having upon those around me. Their subsequent failure to do what I felt they should, affected *my* level of self esteem.

As the years progressed in Rome, I noticed that my own Swedish boss and other colleagues were, from time to time, also going on the attack towards me. Little did I realise that my quantum bio-magnetic field, programmed by my consciousness, was causing this, including of course my attitude and behaviour. They were simply mirroring back to me some issues I needed to learn from. It never occurred to me that I should look within myself to find the answer! I just blamed other people who did not want to accept what I was saying or doing and also blamed my boss and colleagues for their unsympathetic attitude – nothing to do with me, I felt! How wrong I was. During this time period, two issues were running in my unconscious mind. The first, that I was infected by a victim-consciousness which was linked to low self-esteem. As you will have gathered from the example above, this had been put in place at a very young age. The second issue was that a lack of sensitivity was running within me, perhaps because of too much ego? This caused me to be faced with situations which indicated that I had more to learn about the sensitivities and ego not only of others but also my own.

In the West we are not encouraged to look into our emotions or feelings. And we are conditioned from childhood to believe that on no account should we show them in public. Ultimately, this causes a lack of sensitivity to other people's reactions to what is being communicated. In my UN working environment, I later realised that a lot of the time my colleagues and I were mirroring our issues between each other. They too had something to learn. I believe that it would have helped me enormously then, if I had understood the phenomenon of mirroring and the quantum bio-magnetic field. Now these doors have been opened for me, I handle things differently and hopefully with a lot more sensitivity.

In my second example, when I was working in the World Bank in Washington DC, one of my bosses accused me of losing my analytical capability. This was due to the way I had assessed a project. I felt that his statement was wrong and told him so, but to no avail. Because of my dyslexia I had honed my analytical capability to a level higher than normal. Nonetheless, my self-esteem was shattered by his statement, though thankfully only for a short period of time until I thought through quite carefully what he had said. There is always something of great value to be learned from such experiences. In my view, he was wrong because of the situation caused by the project I was working on, but he was right from the Bank's perspective.

So what were the issues? The project had a loan agreement which had covenants that the country in question had agreed to. One covenant was to ensure the fair retention of crops produced by the farmers (landlords had been taking too much in the past); another was development of a suitable supporting crop distribution system, development of cash crops, and so on. The actual project was an enormous irrigation scheme which had a large, newly-constructed dam. Unfortunately, the dam started to move downstream and later had to be drained to be repaired. This left about 20,000 small farmers and their families with a limited income and with a shortage of food supply for at least a couple of years. Any such failure of the dam was not covered in the loan agreement. Because I put the farmers and their families' wellbeing first, I was accused of losing my analytical capability! Of course there were great lessons for me here, which I learnt, especially within the area of contractual agreements, report writing, and in the psychology of large organisations. Once again two issues surfaced with respect to what I was attracting at the World Bank. The first was victim-consciousness through low self-esteem. The second was about being too open and forthcoming. In addition, a bit more reserve (keeping my own counsel) and careful listening was called for.

Wisdom comes to those who listen and hear what is being said before responding. During my childhood in the family hotel in Scotland, I was always very open and outgoing with the guests. This was part of ensuring that the visitors felt comfortable and enjoyed themselves. As I ventured forward on an international career my characteristic trait of openness had to be tempered. This meant that the program which was running in my unconscious mind with respect to being innocently open had to be modified to protect myself from overly aggressive working environments. There are individuals in any working environment who are always eager to use another person's openness against them. Keeping my own counsel was also an important lesson for me to learn. It was all about creating a balance through sensing the situation I found myself in. I certainly needed to hone my sensitivity to handle a broad range of self-esteem-related challenges in different work situations.

Self-esteem has many attributes that can have an unsettling influence on our lives if we allow it to happen. I am sure that the reader may also have been affected by some of the attributes of low self-esteem and/or victim-consciousness at some time in your life. What are these attributes and how do they show up in your life?

Attributes of Self-esteem

In diagram 4.13 I introduce the concept of a quantum bio-magnetic field energy wave. The energy wave is made up of all the components of self-esteem such as self-motivation, self-belief, self-worth, and so on. When there are changes taking place to self-esteem, victim-conscious energy is attracted into the subtle energy bodies. As we project the negative energy wave around us, people pick up on it and reflect it back to us. The victim energy field gets further nourishment as the negative projection is received, thus making it stronger. This results in self-esteem becoming degraded.

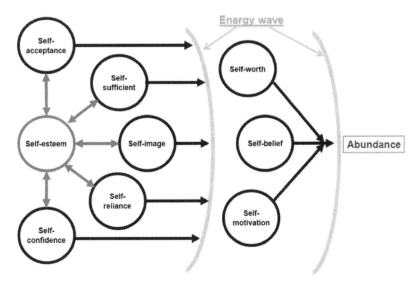

Diagram 4.13

In the work environment I have talked to many successful people across a broad spectrum of employment, from super models to medical practitioners to news presenters to CEOs and so forth, and I am always surprised when some exhibit, usually in private, traits of low self-belief, or low self-acceptance, or low self-worth, and so on. From the outside they appear to have everything going for them, but on the inside this is certainly not always the case. What is also interesting is that they may be smiling and looking happy in a gathering, but if you are a sensitive individual you will sense that this outward expression does not reflect their inner reality. You will feel that there is something not quite right behind the smile. Something is going on behind the image that is being projected to you. Sometimes that something is a great deal of emotional and mental turbulence.

Whether we like it or not, low self-esteem affects self-image, which affects how we project ourselves. It affects self-confidence and self-worth. It affects self-acceptance and self-sufficiency. It also affects self-motivation, self-reliance, self-belief, and so on. So does self-esteem matter? Absolutely! If we do not believe in our-self, how can we expect other people to believe in us?

You can see from diagram 4.13 that low self-esteem will have an effect on its family of attributes. This happens from within the unconscious mind. It pollutes the conscious mind and programs the quantum bio-magnetic energy field to attract to us relationships, activities and events that provide us with an opportunity to recognise and to change the causes of our low self-esteem. That is, of course, if we are actually aware of what is going on within us and around us, and why it is happening.

It is important to take a step back and to recognise, once again, that from an energy perspective to a great degree:

> *'the outside world we perceive (people, places, activities and events) acts like a mirror reflecting back what is actually going on within ourselves'*

Now there's a challenging concept to accept and to work with. It is a concept that is missing from our education and is definitely worth considering because it provides a principle key to enable us to steer our life in the direction that we desire. The concept is also most important to understand if we find a requirement to explore the causes of any low self-esteem we may have. There is so much going on in the world around us that we tend to limit our perception to a selection of what is happening. This limit is affected by the beliefs (our filter system) that are running in our unconscious mind. Getting into our belief system to change any false beliefs requires us to engage in a process of self-exploration. Self-exploration is made much easier when we become aware of the synchronicity of what is happening around us, because life is always trying to tell us something.

Balancing your Self-esteem

There are definite steps that can be taken to work on balancing your self-esteem. First of all, let me remind you that the secret in maintaining a happy life is to keep, where possible, everything in your life (for example eating, drinking, sex, sport, travelling, and so on) in balance. If you have low self-esteem, it is important to identify, accept, and work through what is causing it, so that you can bring it into balance. As you work towards the causes of low self-esteem, and there may be many, it is necessary to step back for a moment and recognise that the cause is *false*. This is because it is based upon a false belief! It is simply not true. How come? Because most probably the false belief was actually dumped on you by someone else, a family member, relation, friend, teacher, authority figure, and so on. My task is to help you to neutralise your false beliefs. We all have them! In carrying out this task it is too easy to forget that we are dealing with a thought and most importantly trapped (perhaps frozen) emotions, all of which are energy. The thought and emotions are running unknowingly in the background within the unconscious mind and within the subtle energy bodies and physical body. Western culture has trained us to focus primarily upon the power of reason, logic, the intellect, and of course, consumption! We have not been encouraged to understand emotions and feelings. Only during this century is the importance of the power of emotions and feelings in driving feelings of wellbeing and happiness becoming (slowly) more accepted by the medical establishment, and it is certainly more evident in popular awareness although the link between the effect of the emotions on the physical body is still less well appreciated, let alone the subtle energy bodies and vortex energy centres.

There are different approaches that can be used to help in the task of neutralising false beliefs so as to bring low self-esteem into balance. It is a process of self-exploration, and I will take you through two approaches to enable you to take action to identify, accept, work through and balance any low self-esteem that may exist. The first looks at the outer indicators which you can use to detect low self esteem, whether in yourself or someone close to you. The second approach is self-therapy, which is a process. If you take the self-therapy route it can be useful to have someone suitable to help as you are going to explore the depths of your unconscious mind. This could be upsetting as you may bring up some powerful negative emotions, perhaps from some disturbing childhood issues that have been long buried. Such an approach is not for the faint hearted, and unless you are prepared to take full responsibility for your-self, I would recommend that you use a qualified therapist (see Appendix 2). At times, it may take several sessions to unearth a trapped or frozen emotion that you are working to release. Persevere!

Identifying Outer Indicators that Reveal Low Self-esteem

Listen carefully to the words that you use when talking openly with someone, when you are engaging in a free-flowing conversation where you speak without consciously weighing your words. If you are using a lot of negative words and/or your tone is negative, or your words are not self-supporting, ask your-self *'what is it that is causing me to use these particular words and/or this tone of voice?'* In conversation, listen to how you describe your-self and what you are saying. Are you always expecting the worst? Do you run your-self down? How often do you run other people down? Are you a negative gossiper? Do you play the martyr role from time to time? Are you playing a victim role? and so on. This can be helpful in directing you towards any causes of low self-esteem. You may detect a series of negative words that you use which are non-supportive. Note down these words in a journal and aim to stop using them. Begin to replace the negative words with positive ones, or at least with some neutral statements.

It can also be helpful in relationships, or in company, or when you are listening to a conversation, to home in on the words that other people are using. This will give you an insight as to where their self-esteem is. I would like to remind you here that they may be mirroring back to you certain aspects/issues related to your-self. If there is any negative verbal repetition in conversations, together with a strong feeling in your solar plexus (either positive or negative), these are helpful indicators for you to determine what they are mirroring back to you. No feeling means that what is being said may not be relevant to you. A feeling means that what is being said is relevant. Observing others, and your own body language (ask someone that you can rely on here) is also a good indicator of both your and their level of self-esteem. Look at their facial expressions when they talk. How do they hold themselves, their poise - are they round shouldered, do they walk with their head down, and so on. These are all external indicators that can give you an insight as to the level of their self-esteem. Remember, it is also necessary to explore what is happening within our-selves too, to bring any low self-esteem back into balance.

Identifying Inner Causes of Low Self-esteem
To find the inner causes there are two directions that you can follow. The first direction is where you may choose to go to a qualified therapist or counsellor. Why? Because a skilled therapist can help you transform a negative emotion into a positive one and to re-integrate it. (that is to replace the old emotion with the new emotion). If you are not familiar with the range of emotions that influence you, I provide a detailed list in Appendix 1.

The second direction is where you may chose to explore what is causing your low self-esteem by your-self. This I call self-exploration, and if you decide to follow this route then I would recommend the following:

Preparing to Deal with Low Self-esteem
Find a close, sympathetic and patient friend, or partner, or relative, who you trust and who can be with you throughout each session of self-exploration. This is necessary because you

may bring up some powerful negative emotions at times which can translate into a strong physical experience with the release of tears. Sometimes it can take several sessions to release a trapped emotion. Great patience is required here. I was asked during a workshop that I attended to write down as many emotions as I could recall. I found this exercise rather difficult as identifying, thinking about and understanding different emotions was an area in my education and upbringing which was missing. To get you thinking about emotions and feelings (feelings being the physical experience arising in your body from an emotion), the table below provides an indication of five basic emotions and their opposites.

Basic Emotion	*Opposite*
Love	*Hate*
Fear	*Anger*
Trust	*Distrust*
Surprise	*Anticipation*
Hope	*Despair*

(source: Wikipedia)

Some emotions can be broken down into secondary and tertiary emotions as shown in the table below. This is helpful to know if you are not sure which part of an emotion you are working with.

Primary emotion	Secondary emotion	Tertiary emotions
Love	*Affection*	Adoration, warmth, fondness, liking, attraction, caring, tenderness, compassion, sentimentality
	Lust	Arousal, desire, passion, infatuation, hunger
	Longing	Longing

It is important here for you, and whoever is helping you, to identify and isolate the negative emotion; to then work with it to remove the negative emotion; to identify a positive emotion; finally to make sure that the positive emotion is re-integrated to the same location as the negated emotion.

Other basic steps to consider, if you follow the self-exploration route are:

- take a journal with you that can be used to write down the steps to be followed and record the results of each session. You may decide to use some positive affirmations to help you to re-script some of the false beliefs that you have unknowingly accepted. That is, after you have worked with and removed the attendant negative emotion(s). Sometimes it is preferable to record the affirmations on separate cards so that you can read them, or have them read to you, when you are in a most relaxed state, for example while listening to some music, or in bed before you go to sleep, or when you wake up. You could also make an audio recording and play it back at an appropriate time. To begin a self-exploration session, it is advisable to:

- select a convenient time period and find a quiet spot where you will not be disturbed.

- practise each step involved with whoever is helping you so that you both understand and can deal with what is going on.

Getting into the Process of Changing Low Self-esteem

The purpose of the next steps is to shift you into a position where you can investigate any causes of any low self-esteem. Most importantly, once you identify a cause, accept it, work to neutralise it (I show you how to do this below), re-integrate the supportive new script and emotion, and move on. There are six steps:

1. Make your-self comfortable in a place that you have selected. Either sit or lie down. I want you to get your-self into a relaxed state of mind. Once you have done that, I will take you through a deep rhythmical 6:3 breathing exercise. Before doing the breathing exercise, do make sure that you are breathing through your diaphragm and not your chest. To check if you are breathing through your diaphragm, put a hand on your stomach and as you breathe in your hand should be rising. There should only be a minimum of movement in your upper chest.

   Once you are comfortable and breathing through your diaphragm you can begin the rhythmical relaxation breathing cycle. The procedure for the 6:3 cycle is to breathe in slowly through your nose for a count of six, hold your breath for a count of three, breath out through your mouth for a count of six and hold your breath for a count of three. Keep repeating this cycle about twenty times, always in a slow, rhythmical way, and try to do it unconsciously (without thinking).

A worthwhile addition to this breathing exercise is to imagine that as you are breathing in you are standing in a whitish golden coloured fog of positive energy and that you see your-self breathing it in. As you breathe out sense your breath and see your-self breathing out all the stresses and negativity of the day as a reddish dark grey cloud. See this cloud dissolving in the surrounding whitish golden cloud which has strong healing properties.

2 Begin a process of *visualisation* (seeing/hearing/sensing something within your imagination and senses). It is important to clear any negative thoughts from your mind, and also to still your busy mind while going through the relaxation breathing exercise. Try projecting a favourite positive image into your imagination that gives you much pleasure: say a tropical beach with a calm emerald sea, some golden white sand and green palm trees; or another image could be your favourite forest, or snow-capped mountains and so on. Some of you may be more oriented to sound, or are kinaesthetic (physical sensing ability) oriented. It is important to use whichever sensing ability you prefer so as to hold whatever it is you are focusing on in your imagination. Be aware that you may have to change the scene several times if the negative thoughts or busy chatter in your mind do not go away, or creep back in. Repeat this exercise until you can hold your attention on the image that you are visualising while keeping your mind as still as possible. The energy emitted by a busy mind that has a lot of chatter going on and/or negative thinking interferes with you connecting with your unconscious mind. When you enter your unconscious mind you are in a position to access any false beliefs with their attendant negative emotions that are causing low self-esteem. Your task is to be able to access these beliefs as quickly as possible and to neutralise them, plus the attendant negative emotions.

Steps 1 and 2 above put you in a position to use a powerful process called *guided visualisation* in support of searching for any false beliefs and negative emotions. You may prefer to develop your own after some practice. Experiment and go with what works for you. An important point here is that you are going to use your imagination, which is one of your most powerful attributes. The following is designed to stimulate your imagination:

3. Once in your relaxed state of mind, the guided visualisation process involves using your imagination to see your-self in your mind walking along a path in a forest with the sun shining through the trees. The air is fresh, birds are singing and you feel the relaxed atmosphere. You come to a clearing and there is a cottage in front of you. The

cottage has a carved wooden door with a large brass door knob. You walk up to the door and turn the knob, pushing the door open. As you enter the cottage you see a comfortable chair in the centre of the room. Close the door, walk to the chair and sit down. As you relax in the chair you see a large flat screen television in front of you. This television operates through your thoughts and you are able to switch it on and off by merely thinking it. You are also able to project your thoughts as images onto the television set and view them like a reel of film. Switch the television set on with your mind.

4. In your relaxed state of mind take your-self back to when you were born. Move ahead until you reach a time when someone said something that upset you, maybe:

   o saying you are a naughty/bad boy or girl
   o shouting at you aggressively, telling you to stop what you were doing, which may have frightened you
   o shouting at you because you were playing a noisy game
   o saying something negative after you had made a drawing that you felt proud of, for instance 'you are just like the rest of your family, they cannot draw for nuts either'
   o telling you that you are useless, and so on.

   Project the incident with the different player(s) onto the TV screen with your mind. It could even be your parents fighting each other in a heated argument that made you feel insecure and you thought it was your fault. When you do this you have identified a *false belief* that will lower your feelings of self-worth. Feel the emotion that you are sensing when you locate a cause. Record in the journal or make an audio record of the event and the emotion/physical feeling you felt. The emotion is most important for it needs to be worked with, changed and re-integrated.

5. After a cause has been identified it can be worked through to remove it. Whatever the cause, it affected you emotionally in some way or another. All you wanted to do was to please those big giants (parents, relations and so on) whom you depended upon, to receive some praise and perhaps a warm hug or even a kiss. As you review what you have recalled, recognise that at a young age you were just like a recording machine with no way of assessing what was being communicated to you and therefore unable to reject the information as being untrue. Most importantly, appreciate that those communicating with you did not know any better. No one had taught them the basic psychology of parenting, or if they did, they had little clue about its application. Even professional psychologists have been known to treat their children in appalling ways! It is important to realise the fact that there was nothing wrong with you! Once again, the person communicating with you just did not know any better.

They were probably responding to you the way their parents and grandparents had responded to them. Nonetheless, how do you reverse the cause? There are three steps here:

i. When you recall the incident back into your mind and onto the TV screen, see it as a stream of images just like a film. Wind the film back to the beginning and delete each frame of the film. Now go into the emotion that went with the film scene and sense how it feels. If it brings up tears, allow them to flow out as this is dispersing the emotion. After you have released this feeling, take the emotion and see it being put into a recycle bin or box to completely dispose of it.

ii. Make a new film in your imagination of the previous scene on your TV screen, this time seeing the person (or persons) that made the damaging statement(s) filling you with praise for what you had done and encouraging you to do better. See them giving you a warm hug and feel the warm emotion that arises within you when someone gives you praise and affection. If it was just your parents (or other people arguing negatively which affected you) then see them being friendly and having a supportive conversation (together). Add the warm emotion to the new film.

iii. The final step is to put the new film with its attendant positive emotion back into the spaces that were occupied by the old film and negative emotion. This is called re-integration and involves putting the new film in the third subtle energy body (chapter 3) and the brain (hardwiring), and the new emotion in the second subtle energy body). All you have to do here is to simply run the film and the emotion in your imagination. By doing this in your imagination you have filled the empty information and emotional spaces that were left. Try to feel the new warm emotion from the praise that has been given to you (or arising from a warm conversation) not only rising within you but also streaming out into your quantum bio-magnetic energy field. You now feel good about your-self and have a warm feeling in your solar plexus or somewhere else in your body.

You have just removed a false belief with its attendant negative emotion and replaced it with a positive, supportive one, deleting the old energy from your quantum bio-magnetic field and replacing it with a positive supportive energy.

Repeat the above exercise each time you recall a negative incident that has affected your self-esteem. This exercise can be used to work through difficult life experiences. The key here is to always ask the question:

'what is it that I have to learn from this experience to enable me to move on?'

Sometimes you will know instantly and other times you may have to wait until you get an answer from within your-self, or for an outside incident to occur to make it obvious to you.

6. It is often helpful, after the above exercise, to repeat in your conscious mind some positive supportive affirmations. The affirmation will be recorded in your unconscious mind and it is an easy way to help you to change your attitude and behaviour to create a happier and better life. It also means if you are faced with a difficult situation, making regular use of affirmations can help you to handle the situation well, rather than just reacting to it.

Affirmations also have a powerful effect in contributing to what is manifesting in our life. Repetition of positive statements has great power, just as repetition of negative statements do. Most of us in the West are conditioned to repeat the negative thoughts in our conscious mind. Just look at the news media for a start, and all those soap operas that are pumping out negative messages. These negative messages are programming our unconscious mind and quantum bio-magnetic field. So why not practise repeating some positive messages for your-self and reap the benefits in terms of changing what you are manifesting in your life. Remember the old saying:

'if you do what you have always done then you will get what you have always got'

And also,

'if you think what you have always thought then you will attract what you have always attracted'

Such is the power of the Law of Attraction. A major key for success in repeating affirmations is to actually believe what we are stating. I had a friend who was having a difficult time in his life as nothing was going right for him. I asked him if he wanted to come for a session where I would look into his childhood to identify what was causing his present difficulties. He had a negative feeling about psychology, thinking it was all rubbish, and preferred not to. He did realise though that it was in his best interest to do something about his negative thinking and said he would consider using some positive affirmations to help him. I took him through the steps involved and gave him some powerful affirmations to state on a regular basis to contribute to turning around his life. I emphasised that the best time to repeat them was last thing at night before going to sleep and first thing in the morning when he awoke. After about three months I asked him at a barbeque in the desert what was happening in his life, had things changed? 'Nothing' was his response, 'everything is just the same'. Interestingly, I had also taken his wife through the same process, including giving her the same affirmations that I had taken her husband through. She had been writing some children's stories and had had no success in getting them published. When I took her aside at the barbeque, she was full of excitement as she was about to sign a contract with a well-known publisher. I asked her about her husband and she confessed that her husband had confided in her that he had been stating his affirmations for the last three months and nothing had changed. He then concluded that he was not surprised as he did not believe that such things could work. To him, it was a lot of rubbish!

It is important to remember that beliefs are the filters through which life flows. If you do not believe in something, then you set up a guarantee for it not to work! Such is the power of beliefs. You cannot hide from the effects of your quantum bio-magnetic field, part of which is programmed by the belief system. I have a close friend who is an engineer and is totally mechanistic, form-based and linear-time-biased in the way he looks at life. Such people are locked into their unknowingly biased virtual box of thinking. This is probably quite right for his life to date, and the way he handles his challenges. But if it is not, then he may have to go through some situation that stops him in his tracks (for example, illness or an accident) so that he is forced to review just where he is in his life and to consider alternatives in how he handles what is happening. Ultimately, thoughts, words and especially emotions have great power, so make sure that your mind is filled with positive supportive words, supported by positive emotions/feelings. It is the negative thoughts/words/emotions/feelings that create misfortunes and a less than acceptable lifestyle. I provide some typical affirmations that may help. Be aware that you should only practise a few affirmations at a time. Do not fall into the trap of using too many at one time. Like most things in life – keep it simple and short (KISS).

Here are some affirmations for you to consider and practise during times when you may be feeling uncomfortable because of some change:

- Every day in every way I am better and better and better.
- I am grateful for the financial prosperity that is flowing to me in great abundance every day.
- I am attracting to me the best job that suits my talents and soul growth.
- I am releasing any fears that I have and draw in energy of peace, love and light.
- I am releasing any anger I have within me in constructive and helpful ways.
- I am transmuting any negative emotions that arise within me into positive creations of love.
- I am attracting partners into my life who are supportive, compassionate, considerate and loving.
- Every day in every way I am happier, healthier, wiser and wealthier.
- I am a loving, sensitive, understanding, considerate person.

It is important to be aware that even when different causes of low self-esteem are removed, some of them may creep back into our life again through interaction with other people. That is, of course, if we let them! If our day to day thinking is biased in a negative direction we are setting our-self up to strengthen any low self-esteem that may be running in the unconscious mind, and to attract victim-consciousness energy! This is where building a strong foundation of inner confidence about our-self provides us with the strength of mind to prevent us from falling into a downward negative spiral that reinforces low self-esteem. Stating regularly appropriate affirmations is a powerful way to neutralise any negative remarks or negative thoughts that we may pick up from time to time. As always, if we feel that we are under attack, it is helpful, once again, to ask our-self:

> *'what is it that I have to learn from this experience or thought?'*

If nothing comes up, then state a positive affirmation to neutralise the effects of what may be a false remark from someone. If, on the other hand, a particular situation or a series of negative thoughts keeps repeating, then it is advisable to go deeper to find out why we are attracting it, and then neutralise the cause. Catching negative thoughts and disposing of them before they become deeply embedded in our consciousness and hardwired in the brain is essential to maintain an inner feeling of positive wellbeing. Our level of happiness will also be given a boost.

Only when I reached my 50s did I come across a miraculous, quick acting process that we can all easily apply. It is called the Power of Expectations. This is a process that has the power to overwrite elements of low self-esteem which cause us not to achieve the greatness we have within our-self. Every family member, teacher, professor, leader and so on should be schooled and trained in this process. It has not only the power to take those who are thought of as 'poor performers' right up to the highest level of achievement, but also the power to raise the population of a nation to achieve greatness for their country. Expectations (see below) can be a real placebo to enhance achievement.

Time for a Shock - Are You Sitting Comfortably?
Nothing really prepared me for how I would feel when a close friend said to me, many years ago at a meeting in the UN:

> *'do you know, John, that you are 100 percent responsible for what happens to you in your life?'*

This was like red to a bull to me, and my mind exploded with all the reasons why this could not possibly be so! After all, like most Western people on this planet, I had been well schooled in the art of blame. It's nothing to do with me, it's them! How could I possibly be responsible for my frustrations and misfortunes? It took some time for the smoke to clear, and as it was clearing I began a quest to prove my dear friend wrong. This took many years. I attacked the statement from different directions, but each time I had to agree, as I recognised that the choices/decisions I had made led me to where I was at the time. I finally stopped challenging the statement, once I understood the power of each human being's quantum bio-magnetic field and how it is programmed. Yes, my dear reader, it is wise to consider that we are, in general, indeed 100 percent responsible for what happens to us in life. We can be precluded from understanding this due to the separation of our fabricated-self and authentic-self. If there is no bridge between the two selves then only our physical reality will be recognised. We attract to us and are attracted to all that happens to us in one way or another. The words used, tone of voice and body language all make their contributions too. They mirror what is running in our quantum bi-magnetic field. That being said, what a splendid gift my friend had given me. It shook my belief structure to the core and substantially raised my awareness of what is really going on around me and in my life. It also provided me with an understanding that it is within my own power to be able to change my life for the better. I am responsible for making my own choices/decisions: no one else. People may force their will upon me, but I make the choice/decision as to whether or not I agree or buy into it.

There is another part to this story which also shook my belief system (a double whammy, as some of my friends would say). After I calmed down, my friend went on:

> 'I hope you don't mind, John, but the anger you have just displayed is a measure
> of the degree to which you unconsciously see your-self as a victim.'

'Victim!' I responded, 'I certainly do not see myself as a victim!' With my background, I secretly believed I was a bit of a 'master of the Universe'! Of course, once again, my friend was absolutely spot on. But the question arose: when did my unconscious victim mentality get programmed within me and how did it show up in my life? In addition to the above situations, there is one further incident that stands out in my mind as sowing yet more seeds for my victim-consciousness when I was five years old. This also contributed to the way my self-esteem was affected.

I was in Scotland, five years old, and it was during the summer season at the family hotel. My Scottish grandparents were staying for a week. I never felt comfortable with them, as I detected that they did not like children and were not particularly happy people. My grandmother never really liked my mother, who was English, and had made it quite plain to her. One morning, I saw my older sister (she is three years older) and grandmother in a little storage room. What fun, I thought, I'll close the door and lock them in. As I did so they shouted angrily 'let us out!' Because they were so angry I said 'no – not until you ask nicely'. I turned to run and tell my mother what I had done. As I turned, it was just in time to catch the full force of my grandfather's hand across my head, which sent me reeling. I picked myself up, in tears, and ran to my mother, who came to my defence. My grandfather's response was that I was a stupid and ignorant little boy and that both my sister and grandmother could have suffocated in that room. This was certainly not true for there was a large gap under the door and even at five years old I sensed what he said was wrong. The punishment for having what I considered fun and being called stupid was immediately programmed into my unconscious mind. I felt victimised, and my self-esteem was dented. Most of us in fact have our self-esteem undermined as we journey along life's path.

When self-esteem is in balance it means that our quantum bio-magnetic field is more likely to attract us to, or attract to us, a happy supporting environment. Learning how to use the law of attraction is a must for us if we are to experience the life that we desire.

LAW of ATTRACTION

Change your Luck: Change your Attractor Energy Field

In chapter 3 I developed the concept of the quantum bio-magnetic energy field which has attraction properties. It obeys Universal Laws, which are different in comparison with the physical laws that we are used to. Diagram 4.14 shows an outline of a set of typical quantum bio-magnetic fields which are made up of all the subtle energy bodies that are part of the whole human energy structure. The frequency at which the quantum bio-magnetic field vibrates determines what it attracts and what is attracted to it. Our physical self, as part of the different energy fields, follows suit of course.

Field of Attraction (Quantum Bio-magnetic Field)

Diagram 4.14

Before giving you the good news about the law of attraction and how to use it in your favour, let me also offer a warning. There is some potential danger that can arise when we use our quantum bio-magnetic field for manifestation purposes. Life is not a series of random events where we must rush to grab as much as we can. Each of us has a unique purpose. Some people's purpose may appear grand in material terms (plenty of money, houses, cars, boats and so on) and/or great in social terms (prince or princess, titled, a celebrity, footballer, senator, and so on), and others may appear to be insignificant (poor, unemployed, gypsy, manual worker, and so on). The grand, great or insignificant part has nothing to do with an individual's real purpose for being here in a physical body. Such titles or labels only represent a platform that is used for souls to work through their life lessons, together with the associated tapestry that goes with it. We have been conditioned to understand that the grand, great and good are what life is about, yet it is not so. There are some who appear to have everything (materially and socially) and yet tragically exit this earth plane early by taking their own life. This indicates they have not understood the purpose of their being here. Also there are consequences in exiting this way. My investigations have shown that those who take their own life return again in a different body and repeat the same life lessons. This time, however, the soul may chose a less fortunate manifestation - it all depends on the life lessons we chose before we were born.

Each of us has the inner resources, the ability and stamina to complete the experience of our different life lessons, so how is it, then, that some people choose to exit their life at a young age? It would seem they have not completed a particular life lesson, such as addiction (for example drugs, alcohol, money, sex, work, and so on). Over this last ten years, I have seen so many young talented people who come from wealthy backgrounds with famous parents and who went to the best schools and top universities, overdose on drugs. Such a waste of talented souls! Sadly, they did not understand the real purpose of their being here. Their academic training did little, if anything, to give them any sense of the true meaning of life, or any direction to satisfy their real needs and passions. An inner gratitude for their position in society and for the opportunities which were put before them was clearly absent; the gifts and talents with which they were endowed were taken for granted. They had not received sufficient guidance and the opportunity to become aware of all that we really are. It was likely, therefore, that there was a large gap in their emotional intelligence (chapter 5). Life's real purpose has little to do with money, or the hoarding of it. That is unless it is associated with a specific life lesson such as to learn to let the money go. Keeping money flowing and using it wisely is also a life lesson. Recovering from losing it is another. On a brighter note, how can we use the attraction factor to bring to us what we are meant to have?

Understanding the Attraction (Attractor) Factor
Now, the law of attraction is one of those deceptively easy laws to use. So why does it seem to work for some and not for others? It all depends upon where we are in our own inner or self-development. It also depends upon how we have programmed our quantum bio-magnetic field, which is a key to the law's power. If we are destined to amass a fortune and collect many material things, there is a strong chance that we will do so. If it is not a part of our destiny then there is a negligible chance that we will do so. For most of us, amassing money and material things is not the true purpose of life. This does not mean to say that we should not be comfortably off with what we desire. The quantum bio-magnetic field is always a perfect match to its attraction factor. Until now, we may not have been aware that we are consciously and unconsciously programming this field. How can we influence the

programming of our quantum bio-magnetic field and its attraction factor? There are five levels of input which we need to be aware of. These levels arise from:

1. pre-programmed issues (life lessons) that are a part of our growth and self-development in this lifetime.

2. additional issues (life lessons) that we take on through false beliefs that we unknowingly accepted.

3. the effects of the intention that we have set up (for example: the material goods we want; what we want to do in terms of a profession, or hobby, or sport, or the type of partner we want, and so on).

4. our authentic-self acting as a referee to ensure that we are attracting what we should be attracting. When we are outside of the natural flow of our life, we are not responding to messages from our authentic-self. There will be resistance to what we are trying to do, or quite simply, nothing seems to be happening.

5. miscellaneous effects caused by our being too-single minded in our thinking, or resulting from not being in tune with our creative self, or shutting our-self away from taking any action, and so on.

I highlight the above so that you can appreciate that sometimes it can take extra time for the law of attraction to work, and sometimes it will not work at all. By 'work', I mean attract to you what you desire. In this chapter I take you through the steps involved to clear the energy blockages that prevent the law of attraction from working.

Western society is heavily conditioned to believe that money is the cornerstone of society. This is a false belief that is constantly blasted to us from all directions, especially from the media. But, while money is clearly important, it is nevertheless just another form of energy. And all energy needs to flow, otherwise it becomes stagnant. Some apparently lucky individuals use the law of attraction to manifest a lot of money; some others will attract enough money to be comfortable, and for the remainder it may not work at all. The latter group indicates that there are those whose life lessons are not about making or attracting money. Amongst this group, though, there may be some who have not identified, accepted and worked through the appropriate life lessons that will enable them to attract enough money to be comfortable. In this case there will be attraction factor blocks in place within their energy structure.

Attraction Factor Blocks
In life's journey, when things are running smoothly everything has a natural flow. If any difficulties are experienced there are two messages that you may wish to take note of:

- first, is that you are probably going against the flow, which is akin to paddling or rowing against the tide or a river current. It seems to be a struggle to get things to work in life. It would be useful to rethink your goals and strategy.
- second, is to examine any negative thoughts and/or influences. Negative thoughts cause doubt, which has the potential to push you off your path. They also significantly affect your quantum bio-magnetic field.

Strong negative thoughts need to be worked with and brought into balance as their energy over-rides what we are trying to attract through the law of attraction. Some examples of this are where we may have some strong negative thoughts about our-self, or another person, or about a forthcoming event, or perhaps we are becoming overly self-important. Powerful thoughts can take over the conscious mind and we can quickly become fixated on a particular thought or train of thoughts or a particular outcome. It is important to realise that these thoughts have lives of their own, for they will have become hardwired into the brain. Attraction factor blocks which affect manifestation requests are covered in detail in this chapter and also in chapter 7.

Working on the Attraction Field
Now that you are aware of the attraction field, you can begin to consciously change it to your benefit. I have pointed out that this field is responsible for you being attracted to, or attracting to you, everything that enters your life. Once you 'get it', life becomes much more interesting. So, too, should all the different types of situations you may find your-self in, whether good or challenging. There are three outcomes that arise because of the interaction of our quantum bio-magnetic energy attraction field with the energy environment surrounding us.

- First, where we identify, accept and work through the life lessons (issues) that arise from the people and situations that we have attracted to us or us to them. When the life lessons have been worked through and cleared, we automatically move on, if we need to, to our next destination for a new set of experiences (life lessons). These new experiences will be in line with the changes that we have made to our quantum bio-magnetic energy field.

- Second, where we feel an urge, perhaps to move our home location and/or employment – this is because we are not recognising and working through the experiences/issues (life lessons) confronting us and learning from them. In this case, other opportunities will be attracted to us for us to recognise what we need to change within our-self. These changes are more likely to occur in the new environment. Some people change their home every two to three years, which is an interesting example of unconsciously trying to balance their energy field by working through their life lessons and/or challenges in a new location.

- Third, we may stay where we are and keep repeating our life patterns by going round and round the same experiences/issues with the same people, until we learn whatever it is we are required to learn from them: that is, until we finally 'get it'. There is no short-circuiting this process, we all go through it. If we do not 'get it' by working through life lessons, we will repeat a similar set of experiences and challenges in another lifetime. So is it important to recognise what is happening in our lives and to deal with the issues? Absolutely! In the end, we are architects of our own destiny.

As you will have gathered, life can get rather complicated and it is small wonder that many people find it difficult to use the law of attraction to their benefit. So many courses that are given, and much that is written, fail to present the big picture behind the law of attraction. It is much more than just chanting some affirmations on a continuous basis and using the power of positive thinking with its supporting emotions and controlled visualisation. It is in our best interest to explore what is causing the doubts that arise within us and the false beliefs that we have been unknowingly conditioned to accept. So, to work to change your attraction field to your benefit, I recommend that you consider the following:

1. Because our fabricated-self separates from the authentic-self after birth, using the law of attraction to our benefit may prove to be elusive. Once these two selves are merged, manifesting becomes much easier. I take you through this task in the last chapter.

2. Learn and regularly practise a breathing/visualisation technique similar to the one presented in chapter 2, page 86, to get into the other 90 percent of the brain/mind system. Following this technique will help to slow down your busy mind and body. The next part of the process is much more effective when it is carried out in a relaxed state.

3. Create an intention in your conscious mind to have what it is you desire, for example: a sum of money, or a relationship, or a happy life, or the perfect job, or to get top exam results. Focus on your intent and bring in a strong positive emotion (feeling) that you can remember. Hold this emotion with your intention for about 18 seconds and then let it go. Now see your-self with what you desire and being very happy with it. It is important to recognise that you have just programmed your quantum bio-magnetic field and you only need to do this once, especially as you have used a powerful emotion to back it up. If you planted some vegetables in the garden you would not keep digging them up to see how they are doing, you would trust that they are doing well. The same trust is required when you have processed your intention. It is growing in some shape and form. You can, however, bring the images of your having been, and being happy with what you desire, back into your imagination from time to time. This will strengthen the attraction field and the process of manifestation.

4. What is it that interferes with your intention and the arrival of what you desire? The reasons are given in 'understanding the attraction factor' above. If you work through any blockages that you may have, you will be able to manifest your desires fairly quickly. Working through some of your blockages (we all have them) may take some time unless you seek professional help. I have provided an approach to removing blocks in the Self-esteem section above. Some people try to use affirmations to over-write the negative belief, but this can leave the supporting negative emotion component in place. The emotion component needs to be fully discharged to remove the block and to bring about a balance. When you get into the emotion you will more than likely find some anger attached to it. This too needs to be dealt with. You can release the anger by shouting, drawing, walking, playing tennis or other sport, and so on.

Certainly life is never straightforward for long, and this is especially true in relationships. Such is the importance of relationships in your personal development, I take you through how the law of attraction affects them below. Relationships are also covered in depth in the next and final chapters.

Law of Attraction and Relationships

There are two important attributes that we, as human beings, have that affect the relationships we enter into. These attributes are the quantum bio-magnetic field and its attraction factor effect. Diagram 4.15 shows two people who are attracted to each other. Their energy fields resonate at a frequency that is mutually supportive (in terms of their needs and goals), and the quantum bio-magnetic-field attraction effect draws them together. The biological response to this will be a release of appropriate hormones such as pheromones that ensure both are definitely attracted to each other. There will be unconscious goals representing some life lessons through which both parties have an opportunity to grow.

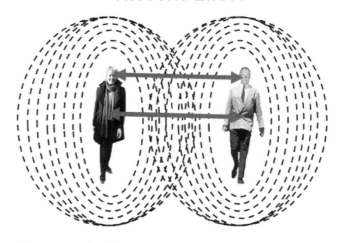

Diagram 4.15

In the quantum world and indeed in life itself, especially within relationships '*all is not as it seems*'. It took me many years, and much travelling around the world experiencing different cultures, to understand this statement fully.

During the early stages of any relationship, everything will most probably be running smoothly. However, after the honeymoon period (all relationships have one!) has ended, things may appear somewhat different. What has happened? The challenges (needs, goals and life lessons) within a relationship will surface and demand to be worked through. This is a necessary part of the growth requirement of the souls of both the parties involved. If the challenges are not worked through, there is a good chance that the relationship will break up. If this happens, it is an indication that the energy fields of each of the parties' have become non-compatible and their attraction factors are repelling one another. The needs, goals and life lessons running in each of the party's unconscious minds have not been fulfilled. After a suitable period of time, when the separated parties' emotions have recovered, they may choose to look for another partner. What is usually not recognised here is that they will unconsciously attract a different partner, but one who has a similar set of needs, goals and issues. These may be disguised but they will nonetheless be there.

Divorce rates are high in the United States and United Kingdom (about 60 percent of marriages/partnerships), because of a lack of compatibility in the relationship between the two parties. Such situations are, in general, really a reflection of the couple's lack of ability to work through their combined unconscious needs, goals and issues/life lessons, or even a lack of desire on their part to recognise and work through them. Some examples of unconscious needs are, if a couple marry, or join together in a partnership mainly because they look good together, or only for good sex, or one has plenty of money, or they need the security, or social status, or simply to have a child, and so on. In these types of situations the probability that the relationship will not last is high. Unfortunately, today, many relationships have passed their *'time to separate by'* date, but both parties stay together for all the wrong reasons such as money, assets, feeling insecure, fear of change, the children, social position, lack of courage, stubbornness, and so on. Happiness, in these types of situation, is a distant memory. If the couple's concerned were to recognise:

1. *why* they had incarnated;
2. that working through their issues life lessons together is a major part of the relationship, and therefore
3. that they have a purpose in being together,

then there is a good chance that their lives would change for the better. This can be done with mutual goodwill and an ability to be honest and non-judgmental, or it may involve seeking professional help.

What's Happening in your Relationships?

The words used and the tone of voice with which two people communicate are an important measure of the state of their relationship, a good indicator of the ongoing attitude and behaviour of the parties concerned. It can be an indication of whether or not any abuse is going on within the relationship. Words have energy which can have a constructive or destructive effect within each party. These characteristics are part of the communication process. Each of us can choose to be patient, to be understanding, to be honest, to be compassionate, to be sympathetic, to have integrity, to be a good listener, to be supportive, and so on. Each choice/decision we make in communicating within a relationship has two outcomes. We are either:

'contributing to the relationship or *contaminating the relationship'*

There is no third way! Nevertheless, most of us are brought up to believe that there is a third way, which is, quite simply, to blame the other person when something goes wrong: the 'it's them not me!' syndrome. Invariably, this is accompanied by 'let us punish the other person as well', or just 'sulk'. Understanding relationships in more depth is covered in the next chapters along with how to deal with the blockages that can affect relationships.

Diagram 4.16

When two individuals come together, their attraction is affected by their energy polarity (North and South pole). All biological material has an energy polarity. At a sub-atomic level, there is an interesting phenomenon where like poles attract (diagram 4.16). Quite the opposite effect to what we observe in the physical world. When two people join together as partners they are primarily drawn together because of the attraction between their quantum bio-magnetic fields. As mentioned above, these fields incorporate a matching requirement of needs, goals and life lessons that are running within their consciousness. I was certainly quite oblivious to this concept.

In diagram 4.16, the matching requirement running in each of the parties' consciousness has generated a bio-magnetic field where the energy structure is more concentrated towards the North poles. The two North Pole magnetic fields' attraction properties keep them bonded together. If they successfully work through the challenges that arise from within their relationship, then both energy fields will begin to merge, forming one common bio-magnetic energy field with a true North/South polarity as shown in diagram 4.17. Alternatively, if they do not realise what is happening within the relationship, then discord between them may arise. In such situations, both may subject each other to blame, criticism,

Diagram 4.17

degradation, abuse, and so on. There is now a high probability of a break in the relationship (since they will be energetically repelling each other). Each will believe the other is incompatible, instead of recognising that they are mirroring each other's matching requirements between themselves. In such cases the two North poles may finally repel because their energy fields have not merged (they have failed to 'get it').

To summarise, the first step towards improving any relationship is to recognise that each party is drawn to the other for the purpose of enabling both their souls to grow. In a marriage, most people believe that procreation is mainly what it is about. But in a marriage, or a partnership, the real substance lies within the inner growth potential between the two souls involved. If children are part of a relationship they will also be contributors to the growth challenges. Differences that arise within a relationship are not really problems, for they represent challenges that provide a growth opportunity. For too long there has been a lack of acknowledgement, let alone understanding, of the spiritual dynamics (soul growth) within relationships. This spiritual dynamic includes such characteristics as the ability to be compassionate; to listen and actually hear what is being said; to offer unconditional patience and assistance; to offer unconditional love; to be considerate, not to be attached; not to form a co-dependency, and so on. Attachment is interesting as it is usually based on insecurity. In relationships, strong bonding is a key to success. Attachment gives rise to problems such as abuse of all sorts.

Parents' Effect on their Children's Future Wellbeing

When a couple conceive, the future child's mental (Intellect) subtle energy body's (SEB) field can start to become programmed by what is happening in the surrounding environment. Usually, this begins after a child is born but that depends on the soul's life lessons. The couple's behaviour, attitudes, words spoken and thoughts, are all being picked up by this SEB. In addition, the future child's emotional SEB field can also pick up the moods and emotions/feelings arising from what is happening between the parents and

Field effect on a child

Diagram 4.18

from, once again, what is happening around them (diagram 4.18). When a child is born, the parents' characteristics, such as motivation, or a lack of it, can be transferred through their genes. One of the parents, or both, may also have not wanted the child at the time of conception. This would be transmitted to the unborn child through its energy field. The result would translate into a strong feeling of insecurity and of rejection.

Most things that happen to us in life are not random, and the feeling of insecurity and rejection would be enacted during a child's lifetime as part of their life lessons through the situations they find themselves in. If the parents do not see themselves as being lucky, there is a high probability that the child will take on this attitude. It is all in the mind (the consciousness part of their subtle energy bodies). Should parents have less than optimistic habits and attitudes, they can do much to contribute to their child's or children's future positive wellbeing by recognising what they are doing to them and taking steps to change it. Adopting a genuine positive attitude in front of their children is essential for their sense of wellbeing. For parents, choice, as always, is the balancing factor here. Each chooses what thoughts they wish to focus upon. To get into the world of thoughts we are entering an arena of mental gymnastics. Yes, just like any athlete, it's advisable to train ourselves. But this time it's training our thinking. And that is because the energy of our thoughts affects the health and wellbeing not only of ourselves, but also of those around us, including any unborn child/children in their mother's womb. Thoughts control attitudes and behaviour. So chose your thoughts well.

By now you will appreciate the effect we have on unborn and young children. As a parent, siblings and other family members are the main contributors to the programming (conditioning) of your children's quantum bio-magnetic fields until others add to this when they go to school. Their future career and progress in life is greatly affected by this. Most importantly , by the time a child has reached 18 years and above (if and when they finally leave home) they take on full responsibility for their own programming and their life. This means that they are responsible for attracting, or being attracted to what is happening to them. I hear parents blaming themselves for what is happening to their young adults after they have left home. What such parents do not realise is that they have given their children the gifts (yes gifts!) to enable them to meet their life's challenges for their souls to grow. So, dear parents, do not beat yourselves up for you are, or were, responsible (amongst other authority figures) for programming their quantum bio-magnetic field. This is a gift which enables them to attract their life lessons after they leave home (and even before) on their own life journey. In spiritual terms, your children chose you in spirit especially for the gifts (programming) that you gave them. They may have to undo some of this programming, but that is part of their life challenge and soul growth.

Power of Expectations - Miracle that Empowers Success
If we believe we can achieve a particular goal that fulfils a passion, there is a high probability that we will. What is it then that stops us from achieving great feats in life, whether sporting,

artistic, academic, engineering, scientific, or any other? The prime causes are doubt, low self-esteem and victim-consciousness, all of which it is necessary to deal with and remove, as I have shown you above. You can also help others to do it. There is more good news, as sufficient anecdotal evidence exists to show that it is possible to neutralise elements of low self-esteem through a process called the *'Power of Expectations'*. As I researched the Power of Expectations, it took my breath away. And applying it is simplicity itself.

When I was 17 years old and living in Eastbourne in East Sussex (England), I needed to upgrade five of the nine subjects on my Scottish Junior Leaving Certificate to an English Ordinary Level certificate standard to be able to obtain entry to a college to study for 'A' levels. To help me pass the subjects as quickly as possible, I had two private tutors. A Mr Shaw and his daughter, who was a recent Oxford graduate. He was headmaster of the local Grammar School. At each tutorial, both of them filled me with confidence in a quiet, unassuming way and were always warm and complimentary as they worked with me. I achieved 4 x As and a B in the subjects I studied with them and that was in spite of having a dyslexic handicap! Moreover, I attained those grades in double quick time! Such is the Power of Expectations from both sides that is my own high expectations and my tutors' high ambitions for me. The results speak for themselves. But what is it that guarantees such success?

Expectations: It is all About the Integrity of Communication
In Chapter 2 I indicated that in the world of quantum physics, it was proven that a scientist can interfere with the results of an experiment just by thinking about it and/or observing it. I pointed out that thoughts plus emotions/feelings are energy, and that this energy is subject to the laws of a quantum reality (the laws of the sub-atomic world). What this means to us in everyday life is that thoughts are instantly communicated through the 5th dimension (energy), to the consciousness of the individual/individuals that we focus upon, and/or to the situation/situations focused upon. It does not matter how far away we are from whom or what we are thinking as time and space are co-existent in the quantum world of reality. There is an instant connection with whomsoever or whatever we are thinking (see quantum entanglement and non-locality in chapter 1). Why am I bringing this up here? Because the sincerity of a communication, or lack of, will be sensed by any individual we are working with, from our thought energy.

When we are in a face to face communication with someone, they are also working in an energy reality which operates within the 5th dimension (diagram 4.19). During communication, the words used, tone of voice and body language also play an important part from a 3rd dimensional perspective. In the diagram, the woman has spotted the man, who is an old friend, and greets him. Her conscious mind is processing the communications made between them in two different ways. The first is by visual observation and by hearing his greeting. This takes into account the man's body language, tone of voice and words used. Second is that her unconscious mind will be responding to the man's thoughts. Both of their energy systems, through their second (Emotional) and third (Intellect) subtle energy bodies (chapter 3), will be communicating together (remember we are all connected at a sub-atomic level). But, like a telephone, it is necessary to dial in to communicate with someone.

Communication affects body language, voice, words and thoughts

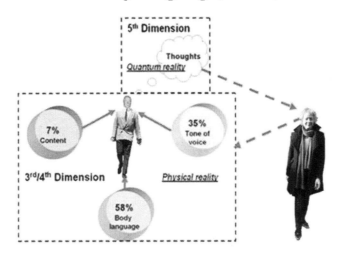

Diagram 4.19

There is some degree of privacy when a connection is made by thinking about the individual concerned. Most of the time, they need to agree to receive the communication, as both people in the diagram do. The effects of this connection will be relayed through to her as a gut feeling about him and perhaps an inner knowing of what he is actually thinking. He will also be going through the same process, mainly unconsciously. A social psychologist in Canada made an interpretation of the proportional split of the automatic analysis within our consciousness that occurs when we communicate. He put forward that, as the conscious mind processes what is going on, it allocates about 58 percent of its time observing body language, 35 percent to the tone of voice and 7 percent to the words used to decide on the authenticity of the statements being communicated.

For the miracle, and it is most certainly a miracle, of the Power of Expectations to work, the *integrity behind the communication* is absolutely essential. We cannot fake it to make it work. Ticking boxes of what to do and putting a smile on our face will not be convincing enough for this process to work. It has to be natural and come from the heart energy centre. Why is this so? It is because those with whom we are communicating pick up through their own sensors, including those sensors that operate within the fifth dimension, the integrity of our communication. These sensors are our:

i. eyes, to observe body language; ears to hear the tone of voice; the words themselves

ii. second subtle energy body (Sacral – Emotional), third subtle energy body (Solar Plexus - Intellect) and fourth subtle energy body (the Heart) plus their supporting vortex energy centres (chapter 3). These sensors pick up the information energy and the emotional energy (negative non-supportive, or positive-supportive) behind the communication. The truth (Intention) behind the words used is also sensed. An individual's intuitive response is affected by all of this, as they sense whether the communication is sincere or not. Ultimately, there is no hiding the truth.

Having explained the subtle way the Power of Expectations functions, what follows is a short process that includes all the necessary steps for practising it.

Applying the Process of the Power of Expectations for a Successful Outcome
It may be helpful to understand the psychology behind the process associated with expectations from the position of the communicator. In today's world every parent, teacher, lecturer, professor, manager, CEO, authority figure, and so forth would benefit from an understanding of the power behind expectations and how it works. It would also be in their best interest to understand the effect that their own thinking and belief system is having on the individuals they are working with. Those receiving a communication (students, employees, family members and so forth) may also benefit from knowledge of the power behind expectations.

Part of the process is to communicate to the individuals concerned, that they have hidden talents still to be uncovered (we all have them). Moreover, it is essential for them to feel that you are going to provide help and support to bring their talents out. Tell them that they are the best (you know that they have hidden talents!) even though they may not recognise this and might feel inferior (low self-esteem). Let them feel your passion with respect to the support that you are giving them. Your task, like any teacher's, is to show them that they can do it, whatever 'it' is. Another part of the process is to spend some quality time with them. That is to show them that you care, and encourages a feeling of belonging. A few minutes of quality time is like a bar of gold to the individuals concerned. Most of all, encourage them at any and every opportunity. Never criticize except in a positive, uplifting manner. In reality, you are activating a placebo response within the consciousness of the individuals concerned. Through this approach you are also causing them to be self-motivated. So, what is the psychology involved in the process which activates the power behind expectations? The process is deceptively easy and can be broken down into four distinct parts:

1. People can be motivated effectively when they look up to you and have a sense of your *sincerity* when you communicate with them. In this type of situation, you will be regarded as a role model. What is happening here is that in physical reality, the energy content of our three-dimensional world (involving seeing and hearing) affects them both consciously and unconsciously. In addition, the communication's unseen energy of the fifth dimension transmits the degree of integrity and intent. It's the individual's *belief*, or more accurately their inner understanding of the truth and feeling behind the communication that allows them to buy into what has been said. The communication could be about succeeding in their exams, or teaching a specific subject, or expressing their creative abilities, or promoting their ability to succeed in activities such as sport, or acting, or public speaking, or events that they relate to, and so on. They will succeed because they believe what is being communicated to them. This belief is confirmed by their senses, which feel the truth behind what is being communicated. Included here is the overall supportive energy content behind the communication (the sincerity). I use the word sincerity, for to promote a sincere statement it has to come from the Heart energy centre.

   If you are the person doing the communicating, then you actually have to believe what you are saying and also feel it. The words should not be coming solely from the Intellect (mind or left-brain hemisphere). On no account must you express a negative comment as this will de-motivate anyone concerned and contribute to a false belief. Always take any negative comment that may surface before communicating and turn it into a positive, supportive one. This may prove to be difficult at first, as we are all well trained in the art of criticising, judging and blaming. I expect we could all be awarded an honorary doctorate in the ability to criticise, judge and blame! The communication needs to come direct from the Heart energy centre. A simple way to communicate words from the heart is to practise visualising your consciousness moving down from around your head into your heart. See your-self doing this in the imagination. We are not taught to do this at school and you may find it both difficult and strange at first. But do persevere, for the benefits to be derived could be enormous. Whoever you are communicating with should *believe* with certainty what is being said to them. They will then be self-empowered to accomplish their task, as their expectation will be that they will succeed.

2. When an individual is moving forward, fully in the flow of 1 above, they usually show their expectations to the outside world by achieving what they set out to do. This can be achieving top academic results, excelling in some creative activity, stopping smoking, being successful in some sporting competition, being an empathetic manager, an effective leader, and so forth. This is important as it is also confirming

their success to themselves. It is a key part of the process and is crucial for their self-motivation.

There can also be a dark side to an individual's motivation which could arise from the negative ego part of their Shadow-self. Their motivation could be derived from an inner drive arising from a powerful negative emotion expressed through a thought such as 'I'll show those miserable "bas***ds'!

3. At this part of the process, where you may have been helping the individual(s) to achieve, it is essential to maintain continuity and respond to their performance with more heartfelt (sincere) support to further help them on their way. Such support is important as it strengthens their motivation. It is the quality and sincerity behind the communications taking place that is important and not necessarily the time spent helping them. Most of us are brought up to believe that it is the actual time and effort we put in that will bring the rewards. The power of the psychology of expectations proves this is not the case. Of course, if you want to follow a workaholic route you may also achieve success, but at what a cost! This cost is not only to your-self but also to those in your life. Life is for living and work supplies the means to live. Balance is the name of the game. Use the power behind your expectations to help you to create a balance. Expect life to flow with ease and expect to have some fun.

4. You will have now entered a circle of self-fulfilling prophecy and have the confidence to produce more of the same with other different individuals or groups.

Fathers/Mothers/Corporate Managers, Please Note
Psychologists have proven that high expectations produce higher performance and low expectations produce lower performance. In business/commerce/public sectors, managers would benefit greatly from recognising that raising their colleagues/members of staff expectations is a major key to increasing their level of motivation, performance, productivity and inner feeling of positive wellbeing. It is not about just saying the right words and ticking personal development boxes. The same is true at home in the quest to motivate family members. For the Power of Expectations to work, what is said must come from the Heart energy centre! Most people (especially children, teenagers and new employees) sense when words are coming from the head (Intellect) and not the Heart. The fact that the words we use are all-powerful has not been emphasised enough in either our upbringing or our education. In Western countries we tend to abuse ourselves and other people all the time, albeit sometimes unknowingly. This happens through the words we use and the emotional/feeling content behind those words. People are de-motivated, including family members, because words are used carelessly without thinking about their feelings. The art in the psychology behind expectations is to take any negative comments or criticisms and turn them into

positive supportive statements. This requires patience, a genuine concern for the individuals involved and a passion for them to achieve greatness.

Expectations Create the Outcome

What is the process running within ourselves when at the receiving end of a communication flow? What is it that is driving our expectations? There are five steps involved in this flow process, including the outcome (diagram 4.20).

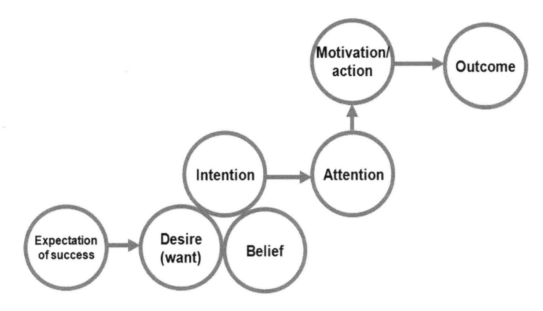

Diagram 4.20

Expectation of Success

Step 1. Everybody operates like a quantum bio-magnet obeying the Universal Law of Attraction. There are no exceptions! The bio-magnetic field is programmed in part through our conscious thoughts, allowing us some flexibility to change what we are attracting into our lives. In diagram 4.20, an expectation is communicated to you with sincerity (that is a communication from the Heart energy centre which fills you with an inner warmth and confidence) from an individual you look up to. You feel recognised and supported and consider that you have been given an opportunity to succeed.

The other person is communicating to you that they are confident about your ability to perform outstandingly well in what you are doing. They have stated that every effort will be put into ensuring that you will achieve top results. Alternatively, you might enter into an event feeling confident that you will do exceptionally well, and actually *do* exceptionally well. Whatever it is, you will be in a highly self-motivated state. Another aspect of motivation could be that you have a passion for what you are doing. Yet another aspect is where someone may have insulted you at a young age saying how useless you were, and you are determined to show them and the world that you are not. This can trigger very powerful self-motivation. In addition, a bio-magnetic energy field is transmitted from you that make a substantial contribution to the manifestation of what you desire. Strong emotions are a major contributor here.

Desire, Belief, Intention

Step 2. Here, because of a communication from someone, or from within your-self, you believe that you can do what has been communicated to you, or follow through with more of the same from the experience you had at some previous event. Within you is a desire (a feeling that needs to be satisfied) to follow through to show that you can do it. Belief and desire are two powerful forces that have been brought into play in a positive context. These forces contribute to a positive intention (the focus and direction of thought). Intention is like an energetic seed that has been planted and it waits to manifest into what is desired.

Attention

Step 3. Attention (the power of concentration within the conscious mind) is focused upon what is desired. This is a very powerful state to be in, as it actually energises the seed that has been planted. Desire and belief empower you, in time, to manifest what the mind (consciousness) is focusing upon. If whatever is being focused upon has a harmful, revengeful negative component, then it can throw the mind and body out of balance. This can lead to a state of dis-ease (that is, you can make your-self ill). It is essential to ensure that your thoughts are kept positive (or at least neutral) and that there are no elements of doubt arising within the mind. It is important to remember that we attract what we focus upon.

Motivation and Action

Step 4. The communication received, or an experience in some sort of activity or event, will have filled you with great enthusiasm. You have entered a highly-motivated state. A powerful inner-energy to perform well has been stimulated within you. It has given you direction and you move ahead convinced that you will achieve great things. Obstacles and difficulties melt away as the focus you have adopted attracts supportive influences. You perceive that there are no problems, only challenges which stimulate you to find win-win solutions. You are, one might say, in the natural flow of life and not struggling or fighting against it. If you face continual difficulties, on the other hand, it usually means you are pushing against the natural flow of where you should be going. Any difficulties that arise should be easily dealt with, otherwise consider changing course.

Final Outcome

Step 5. You sail through any challenges with ease, achieving the goals that have been set. Motivation is high, having affirmed that you have really 'done it, whatever 'it' is.

Applying the power behind expectations on a regular basis is a must, not only in formal education but also in sporting, professional, business, social, family and other environments that involve people who need to be motivated. Now you know, why not try it out?

Each of us, as we journey along life's path, is working with the seven attributes of our Self, highlighted at the beginning of the chapter, either consciously or unconsciously. The five negative drivers: False Beliefs, Doubt, the Triad, ANTs and Self-esteem, require constant attention to bring them into balance. The two positive drivers, the Law of Attraction and Power of Expectations, also require careful nurturing. Once we recognise and work with them, we are well on our way to take off and fly. The chapters that follow will add some rocket boosters, to enable us to take off to reach the life we are meant to have. We are invited to choose to *'make it so'!*

Time to Take Off and Fly

Imagine your-self to be the captain of an aeroplane parked off the runway. You are going through the pre-flight checklist before starting the engines. As you go through your checklist, you receive a radio transmission from the control tower (your inner-self) stating that the airline has discovered there are some dangerous passengers on board who need to disembark. Each of us is like that aeroplane, and unknowingly we have some dangerous passengers on board. It is in our best interest to identify and disembark them (get rid of or neutralise them). Once they have left the aircraft we are in a state where we can start up our engines, take off and fly with ease. In this chapter I have clearly identified some unwelcome passengers that may have boarded your plane. They had certainly boarded mine!

I was helped in recognising my unwelcome passengers thanks to books written by some exceptional authors, such as Dr Barbara Ann Brennan, Dr Daniel G Amen, Louis Proto, Dr Wayne W Dyer, Phillipa Lubbock, Eckhart Tolle and others. Plus all those to whom I have been privileged to give some coaching. As I explored getting to know my-self, the pursuit of self-knowledge revealed a host of unwelcome passengers. It took me some time to appreciate that some of these passengers were there to help me work through a particular life lesson. It would be unusual not to have these unwelcome passengers on board, who are probably quite familiar to you by now! They are:

- o   Mr and Mrs Doubt
- o   The Triad family - Worry, Anxiety and Fear
- o   Their Relatives - Automatic Negative Thoughts (ANTs)
- o   Senior Citizens Mr and Mrs Low Self-esteem and Mr Victim
- o   Mr and Mrs Over-Positive and Negative Ego.

Any of the above unwelcome and potentially dangerous passengers can stop you from taking off, or force you to land unexpectedly at some time during your journey. You may be wondering why I have chosen Mr and Mrs as part of the titles. As beings of energy, we all have a male (positive) and female (negative) energy structure. Each attribute of our persona has a male and female characteristic. Do not take the word 'negative' in its traditional meaning, for in this case it is just part of our energy polarity (chapter 3) at a sub-atomic level. It is part of who we all are. In our energy form we are a combination of both male and female! That may prove a bit of a shock to some of you?

Being aware of the dangerous passengers we may have taken on board is half the battle in life. That is because once identified we can do something about them. Sometimes, the unwelcome passengers can be stopped from boarding, or off-loaded after de-briefing. This chapter is like a de-brief and provides us with an approach to deal with some of our more prominent and unwelcome passengers. In the end, how we deal with them is up to us.

There are many books written about the 'Law of Attraction' and sometimes a book or course is useful in helping us find our way towards what we want, which could be a satisfying relationship, or new job, or more money, or a new home, or peace of mind, and so forth. Where the exercise can go off track is when our ego is the main driver behind the reason for what we desire. Ego has infinite wants and it will push us into satisfying its wants. In doing this, ego can effectively push us away from what we really desire. The exercise can also go off track due to negative programs running in the quantum bio-magnetic field. These programs form energy blocks to prevent or hinder us from attracting what we desire. I have already shown the different types of energy block that can arise and how to remove them. The following chapters will also help in this regard.

To investigate what is blocking us from having what we desire requires us to take a step back to look at our-self. Doing this puts us in a position to find the cause of an energy block. It also means that we take personal responsibility for our life (if we are not already doing so). There is an interesting concept! Psychologists tell me that most of us dislike ourselves. This implies that the last thing we want to do is to explore our inner being! Very few approach the subject of why we are here in a physical body and explore what our life is really about. Who would want to do that? Yet, the rewards in doing so can be enormous. To explore and to become aware provides opportunities to ensure that not only are we in the flow of life, but that we are also on our life's best path. Abundance/manifestation in all its forms then becomes a natural occurrence.

The real journey through life includes being aware of our personal development needs (personal growth and inner, soul growth). Of course, work to have that house and/or car and/or boat, or whatever. Recognise, though, that these are the stage props on the different scenes/acts of our life. Each scene/act enables us to refine the choices/decisions we make by reflecting on the experiences we had in different situations. If we experience any resistance and we fight it, then we are pushing what we desire away from us because we are generating negative energy! We may also discover that the resistance we are experiencing could be trying to tell us to change course. The resistance will also be telling us to look for any unwelcome passengers that we may have inadvertently taken on board (False Beliefs and so on). Identify them, work with them, bring them into balance and disembark them. Above all, life is about achieving our goals and having fun - lots of it!

Flying is also about stimulating that internal *placebo* capability we all have - the power behind an expectation. We can get rid of so many unwelcome passengers (those false beliefs) just by recognising that they are not ours! They were directed to us by other misguided, lost and sometimes unwittingly dangerous souls (authority figures). Look not sternly upon, nor judge them, for their task was to contribute (unknowingly) to the programming of our quantum bio-magnetic field. Their contribution helped to program in us the issues (life lessons) that are here to help us grow. Some of our issues can be swiftly dealt with by accepting that we are a unique soul with an infinite number of possible directions to follow. The choices/decisions made will determine which direction we follow and the intensity of our life lessons. Recognising and working with our authentic-self and the gifts that we have brought with us in this lifetime is a major step forward towards achieving what we desire. In the end, flying is all about going with the natural flow of our life. We are captain of our own aircraft, so take off and fly. At times, inevitably, we may have to land to take on some more fuel (energy) and perhaps to take on some more passengers, some of whom may be bad for us!. The cycle then begins again . . .

The challenges facing us all, including the planet, in this 21st century, require each of us to take a very good look at ourselves and what is happening around us. It never occurred to me that I should actually question the way I was brought up and educated. I certainly saw lots of strengths, but I also felt that something was missing. My educational background fell short in my ability to answer the question, do I really 'know myself'? Only when I entered my forties did I begin to ask myself questions that put me on the path to really getting to grips with this.

My understanding of relationships began to grow as I noticed that I seemed to attract certain types of relationships and situations. Moreover, I began to take a step back to listen more carefully and observe my own behaviour and attitude along with those with whom I was in a relationship. I realised how important relationships were to me in terms of personal development and for my inner growth. Knowing my-self was indeed a quest worth pursuing for it changed my life. The next chapter will I hope contribute to your efforts to understand *your*-self and also improve how you understand and handle your own relationships.

Chapter 5

Understanding Relationships and Self-Empowerment

We need to find the courage to say 'NO' to the things and people that are not serving us, if we want to discover ourselves and live our lives with authenticity.

Dr Barbara De Angelis

Understanding Relationships and Self-Empowerment

How are your relationships: excellent, indifferent or poor? Do you have a goal to create a loving relationship with a partner? It would be unusual to not have such a goal in life. The same goes for good relationships at work, or maintaining good relationships within the family, or within a sports team, or social gatherings, or with neighbours and so forth. At times, a relationship may not go smoothly. All sorts of situations can arise that seem to prevent this goal from being achieved. Is there a way to turn relationships around if they are not working? There is, if you are prepared to spend some time looking a little closely at your-self and at those who are involved with you in a relationship. To know your-self is a major step forward in understanding what is going on within your relationships. For, if you know your-self, then there is a good chance you may gain an insight into those who are in a relationship with you.

This chapter is designed to promote a greater understanding of your-self, and your relationships with others, mainly through a focus on the 'persona'. The persona is the diverse elements of your personality. I break it down into its diverse elements to give you an insight into some of the drivers which affect your attitudes and behaviour. Most importantly, it will provide some suggestions as to how you can change your quantum bio-magnetic field so as to attract better relationships as well as bring you your heart's desire. A note of caution here - be careful about what you wish for, because if you genuinely wish for something, there is a reasonable chance you will get it! There would seem to be nothing wrong with this statement. In fact, it seems to be very good news indeed. Except that in life there are times when *'things tend to be not as they seem'*, and that includes people!

Each of our personalities has a light and a shadow side. Both are equally important and I explore why later in the chapter. The most important relationship arenas we experience are the family, the workplace and our social scene. These arenas are important because such captive environments enable each individual to face and work through their life lessons, and I explain how this comes about. At the end of the chapter I explore what is called the culture of the workplace, whether private or public sector, and how it affects relationships. As we are beings of energy, I also look at the effects of land and building energies and how they too affect families at home and people in the workplace.

I have found that, for me, half the battle in creating good relationships is to understand what caused me to say what I did, or behave the way I did, or what influenced my attitude, in the various situations I have experienced. Gaining an understanding of what was driving my conscious and unconscious minds, which caused my attitudes and behaviour, certainly opened a door to improving my relationships. Just 'being me' was no longer an excuse, if things did not go well. Consider, if you do not know what is unconsciously influencing you in your life, how can you really understand what is causing your attitudes and behaviour? Or for that matter, how can you really understand the influences that are causing someone else's attitudes and behaviour?

Sometimes my approach in discussions was to criticise others with little, if any, understanding of the mechanics of what was going on within me, or within them, or between us both. In previous chapters, I may have created a bit of shock and awe when I put forward the concept that at the sub-atomic level of the environment of our authentic-self *we are all 100 percent responsible for what happens to us in our lives*. As I indicated, it took me quite some time to come to terms with this statement. Well, there is a bit more shock and awe to come, because in this environment we are also 100 percent responsible for our *attitudes* and *behaviour*. Even this statement caused me to feel angry until I understood more about the real me. Who is the real me? The real me is my authentic-self, but I was constantly and unknowingly being run by my fabricated-self - until I learnt to merge the one with the other. More on this below. What follows can help improve the map of life you have which is set within your consciousness and brain.

It is enormously beneficial for our wellbeing when we realise that the process of 'getting it' includes recognising why we are here in a physical human body. As I put forward for your consideration in the previous chapter, a major part of being here is to acknowledge that we enter life with life lessons and issues we need to grow from. These are challenges, and it is imperative for us to work through them to create a balance, as we journey. When you choose a partner, they too will have fragments, or more, within themselves of the same life lessons and issues that you have. It is a part of the invisible attraction field.

What are these issues and life lessons? They cover characteristics of fear, anger, patience, abuse, trust, acceptance, addictions, honesty, hope, forgiveness, insecurity, abandonment, intimacy, poverty consciousness, integrity, money, sex, love, ego, and so forth. A major part of the soul contract, that we agreed to work through before we were born, are the issues and life lessons that we are to face. Yes, in case you missed it in previous chapters, the soul does have a contract, which is really more like a directive. Accepting this responsibility can have a powerful and beneficial effect on how you perceive the various relationships that come into your life. The key thing here is to focus upon the challenges that arise in your relationships, and taking time out to really get to know your-self in this regard is essential.

Some of the life lessons and issues that arise as we mature can be minor and, hopefully, worked through easily enough. For example a minor issue may be to stay in contact with friends, or to be polite and communicative with awkward people, or pay bills regularly, or take action on personal projects without being prompted by others, and so forth. Sometimes though, a minor issue can prove to be difficult and end up turning into a major one. It all depends on how the issues are *handled*. A major issue can be as it implies – difficult! Such an issue can be abuse of some kind or another, or alcoholism, or addictions and so on. As soon as issues are categorized as problems, their dynamics unfortunately change for the worse. Why is this so? When something is considered to be a problem, a negative mindset kicks in (it's already hardwired in the brain) which generates a negative perspective. This is the way the mind works. Trying to find a solution by drilling down into the problem means taking it apart bit by bit, looking for what is wrong, but this invariably just adds to the problem. Remember, all issues are really challenges and should just be seen as such.

When 'challenges', as opposed to 'problems', are faced, the conscious mind usually jumps immediately into solution mode with a positive orientation which has a supportive energy format. We are looking for what is right, not wrong. This is how it needs to be because any personal judgement made on what is wrong is usually coming from a biased perspective. Why is it biased? It is biased because we only ever actually see a small part of what is actually happening. This is quite normal, and in neuro-linguistic programming there is a term or presupposition *'the map is not the territory'*. How come? Each of us will experience a situation in life slightly differently, in comparison with others. Our belief system filters what we see, affecting what we believe to be true. In other words, our perceptions are different – truth is never absolute!

Attracting a partner into your life means satisfying both parties' needs and goals. We all have personal needs such as for love, financial security, status, to procreate, social acceptance and so on. One of my close friends, a very attractive model called Jane, to whom I was giving some life coaching, used to say "once I find the right man who loves me, my life will feel complete. I just feel incomplete at present". If you take a look at what this statement means, it basically shows that her problem is a lack of self-love and of self-worth. At the time she made the statement, she was looking for someone to plug this lack within herself. All her close boyfriends turned out to be unsuitable, for they too were looking for someone to love them so as to plug their lack of self-love. Her sex life was good but in the end she felt empty.

From an energy perspective, both Jane and her various partners were like quantum bio-magnets resonating at a similar frequency. The attraction factor here was really to show each of them that something was missing (self-love) and not that they had a true love match. Because of her physical attractiveness she caught the attention of a few partners who had high self-esteem and strong self-love, but they fled because they found her too clinging. At the core of her lack of self-love was low self-esteem. The reality of Jane's situation was that until she changed her own low self-esteem, developed strong self-respect, self-acceptance, self-worth and in the end self-love, then there was little chance of her having a happy and long-lasting relationship. She finally recognised that she was in denial of these facts and worked through the issues with a therapist. After a relatively short time, she attracted a man who matched the changes that occurred within her bio-magnetic field and is now in a warm and loving relationship. The issues she had that were stopping her from having a true loving relationship were put in place during her early childhood. Her mother had divorced when she was only two years old; there was also some abuse from her stepfather and a relative as well as manipulation within the family as she was growing up. These had to be acknowledged and worked through before there was any chance of her having a successful, warm and loving relationship.

Ask Your-self – Who am I?

Some of the research for this book was prepared after discussion with some regression therapists (therapists who used a hypnotic regression approach to take their clients back in time to explore and to bring into balance some of their deepest issues). Another part was through the channels Messrs Chou, Chan and Lama Sing, all of them beings in spirit. At this level of communication I am able to access higher levels of knowledge. I wanted to get answers to some questions such as – 'are we all born with a blank slate for a personality, a Tabula Rasa?' I was quite blown away with the findings. The answer to this question is quite unequivocally – no! We are born with a personality structure which is made up of a core personality that has different elements/characteristics supported by different sub-personalities. For example, an element/characteristic can be: critical or non-critical, controlling or non-controlling, abusive or non-abusive, patient or impatient, nurturing or non-nurturing aspect. These are all in place and usually in balance when we are born. The 'usually in balance' statement covers cases where a soul enters a foetus at birth.

There are situations where the soul needs to be conditioned by what is happening within the parental relationship and/or surrounding environment before birth. In this case, it is necessary for the soul's growth. It is important to recognise that life as a human being is about the soul's growth, a fact that is missing from educational curricula. After birth, we also develop what is called masks. These are additional elements of our personality which allow us to fit into the different social/work environments we engage in. The elements/characteristics of the personality/sub-personality are an intrinsic part of who we are. I will refer to personalities and sub-personalities as the 'persona' and elaborate on its characteristics below.

An important feature of the persona is that each part of it has a positive and negative aspect. This makes sense when you consider that each personality, sub-personality and mask is in effect a small module of energy that interacts at an appropriate time with our thinking process. These energy modules have a North and South magnetic pole, plus a polarity, with a positive or male and negative or female side (see schematic diagram 5.1). I use an oval shape to represent an individual persona module of energy for demonstration purposes.

Characteristic of a Personality/ Sub Personality

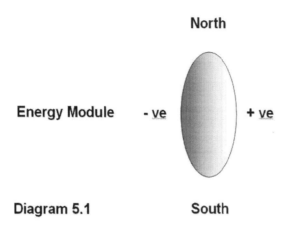

Diagram 5.1

These modules of energy operate at a sub-atomic level. After birth, the balance of the different elements of our persona is affected energetically through what is happening in life, due to those who interact with us. This affects elements of the persona's polarity, changing its original form (see chapter 3). One of the life challenges that we all face, in terms of personal development, is to bring those characteristics or elements of the persona which are out of balance back into balance. The spiritual dimension here is how we *handle* bringing them back into balance. I use the term 'back into balance' a lot in this chapter. At times this task may be reasonably easy, but most times it can involve a lot of hard work. We are forced into the world of emotions and it is necessary to understand their significance to our inner feeling of positive wellbeing and happiness. Strong emotions, especially anger, require careful handling as they usually have an uncomfortable effect on those we are communicating with and also within ourselves.

Elaborating upon the energy structure of the persona, each of its different elements/characteristics is really like a constellation (a cluster) of energy modules. Each element/characteristic, therefore, contributes to its particular personality which ultimately makes a contribution to the quantum bio-magnetic field. As you are aware, this field is like a bio-magnetic key that makes sure we are attracted to and lock on to the most suitable relationships/partnerships/experiences to learn and to grow from.

The polarity of an element/characteristic indicates its strength. It can have a strong positive or strong negative polarity depending upon how it has been affected as we journey through life. Life is full of contrasts, especially in relationships. And life is seldom black or white, which means that it is through learning from the contrasts which we experience in relationships that personal development (personal and inner spiritual growth) is accomplished. The strength or weakness within the persona provides opportunities for us either to clash, or to come together in a warm supportive relationship. They represent an important component to work through life's lessons.

Attraction Energy in a Relationship

The basic attraction model (diagram 5.2) that I use has at its core two key influences that affect a potential relationship, both of which are easy to recognise. These influences are our attitude and behaviour towards others and to oneself. Yes, how we treat our-self is important! What is it that drives these two key influences? They are driven by the belief system, individual needs, the persona, masks, and what is called the Shadow-self. They are all an integral part of the programming mechanism of the quantum bio-magnetic field. Collectively, they are important influences that help us to determine whether or not we chose to enter into a

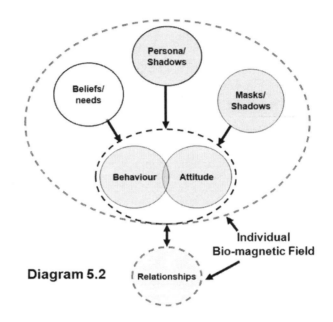

Diagram 5.2

close relationship with someone. An explanation of the persona, masks and Shadow-selves is given below. This will give you a better understanding of how they affect the relationships you enter into and the relationship you have with your-self, for better or worse. From my own perspective in the workplace, I have found that the attitude of the people I hired was a key feature that determined how much they achieved and how well they got on with their colleagues. Attitude is a great influence on our own behaviour and on those around us. Personalities have a life of their own as well as energy needs. These energy needs, and their demands, can have a powerful effect upon us. Some of the effects are shown in diagram 5.3.

Getting acquainted and working with the persona, masks and Shadows can help to bring any detrimental effects that may emerge into balance. And how can this be done? Mostly, by acknowledging and working to change any attitudes and/or behaviours that are causing a problem. In diagram 5.3, stress level, well-being, perception, attitude, behaviour and outcome are affected by the energy influences of a range of various elements/characteristics of the persona that surface as we engage with the different experiences we face in life.

The persona, the Shadow-selves, masks, belief systems and their supporting emotions (diagram 5.2) work hand in glove, all contributing to create what I call a *relationship attractor/attraction factor*. That is an energy setting within our quantum bio-magnetic field that draws to us, and draws us to, our day to day relationship experiences. It is important to remember that how we *handle* the

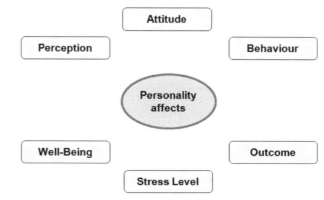

Diagram 5.3

situations and experiences we attract is a main part of what our personal development and inner growth is about. It can also give an indication of how well we have worked through a life lesson. If we have a reasonable degree of sensitivity we will be able to identify a good deal of our own persona, Shadow and mask traits. I will call the persona, Shadow and mask traits 'personality traits' from this point on. When we recognise our own personality traits, it is obviously helpful in relationships as I believe that one of life's lessons is to be sensitive to the effect we have on our partner and those around us, in order to bring any personality traits that are causing a problem into balance.

The son of a friend of mine, who came down from Oxford with a first class degree, was quite unaware of how caustic some of his personality traits were. He could not form meaningful relationships with women and found his work environment quite hostile and exhausting much of the time. He had an intellect second to none, but he also had very low emotional intelligence. His work environment is the main platform at present that will help him to become more consciously aware of the changes he needs to make within himself. Looking at where he is, learning when to tone down his sharp intellect, is certainly a necessary first step. Raising his level of emotional intelligence by tuning into his own feelings (for a start) is a second. Recognising which personality trait he needs to work on and bring into balance is a third important step if he is to prevent himself from developing a stress-related illness. Such an illness could arise if he continues to be in denial about what is happening within and around him. It would be in his best interest to 'get out of his head' and recognise the imbalance between his intellect and his emotions/feelings. When I met him again he had already made some positive changes within his personality; his life is improving greatly.

As I was exploring the structure of my own persona, two important parts of it stood out, namely: *ego* and *free will*. The research I was involved in highlighted that when the structuring of the persona is at the completion stage before birth, ego and free will are the last two components that are put in place. Ego and free will operate behind the scenes within the unconscious mind. In the dynamics of what is going on within our consciousness, ego and free will are like managers. They have a control over our personality traits that enter the conscious mind via the unconscious mind most of the time. All of this depends upon what is happening in our day to day life. The energy interactions caused by thoughts related to our personality traits within our consciousness are translated into the thoughts that we receive in the conscious mind via the physical brain. Please note, once again, that thoughts are not generated within the brain itself. The brain translates thought energy from consciousness energy fields into the thought that we experience. Having identified two key managers in our consciousness, what are the different aspects of our persona? Do they have the power to take over the conscious mind?

Who's Pulling your Strings?
Understanding personality traits and how they relate to attitudes and behaviour, increases the chance of appreciating what is going on in your relationships. Such an appreciation also provides an insight into the activities/events that we are involved in. Diagram 5.4 shows someone who is going about their day to day life within the context of their persona.

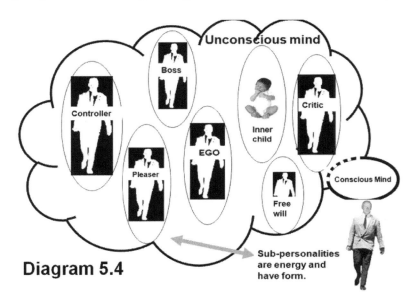

Diagram 5.4

Located within the unconscious mind, the various elements of the persona are waiting for an opportunity to enter the conscious mind to gain experience. Now opportunities/situations are attracted to us because of our quantum bio-magnetic field. This provides the prospect for some of them to enter the conscious mind. Ego and free will manage those elements of our persona, which pass from the unconscious to the conscious mind to gain experience from the opportunities/situations that we connect with. Ego is the most powerful of the two and operates solely through thought. Free will operates solely through energy. The purpose of having a manager is to control the energy flow of all the elements of the persona that are in use. When each has had their experience, they return to the unconscious mind to await another opportunity to perform.

At times a personality, Shadow-self or mask, can push ego aside and take over the conscious mind, because of the type of situation we are in. This is a bit like having the conscious mind hi-jacked. For example, we may have a very strong Controller personality (see below). As soon as any opportunity arises that requires the Controller's presence, it will immediately push forward to gain influence. If it has been ignored in the past, it will have built up a powerful energy, like a head of steam, and will push aside anything in its way, including ego. We may also have a strong Critic personality which feels the need to criticise at every opportunity, and so forth. From an energy perspective, each personality trait needs to have its chance to perform. They are like actors who create the experience that we have an opportunity to grow from. They feed from the energy exchange between the interactions of what is going on around us. When they are fed and satisfied they return to the unconscious mind to wait for their next opportunity (feeding time!) to arise.

If the ego is swept aside by a personality, Shadow-self or mask demanding its opportunity to perform, there can be a battle between the two. This, of course, has a direct effect on our attitude and behaviour. As the battle calms down, free will, acting as an intermediary, can be activated to bring about an energetic balance to what is going on and/or to point to other opportunities. Free will always has to wait until the energy exchange has played out to a certain level before it can be effective. A major point to make here is that any extreme attitude and/or behaviour caused by a personality trait needs to be brought into balance. Part of the challenge for each of us to grow emotionally and spiritually is to bring extremes of attitude and behaviour into balance. It is important to note that the soul also engages with the various personality traits from time to time through the conscious mind, when appropriate. When we 'get it', together with an understanding of why we are here, then there can be no excuse to say "well, this is just how I am"! We are responsible for who we are and our attitudes and behaviour. Acknowledging this can help with the process of changing ourselves for the better.

Understanding the nature of some of the personality traits can help us to change. Personality traits are especially helpful in not only understanding the type of relationship we attract but also how a relationship progresses.

Recognising Personalities
I highlight five aspects of our persona, in diagram 5.5, which all play a considerable role in our lives. I was introduced to the work of a psychologist/therapist Louis Protto who wrote a book called 'Who's Pulling Your Strings?'. In his book he elaborates further on personality

traits. A good exercise to carry out from time to time is to monitor these five aspects of your persona, as they emerge from within your-self and also from those around you.

Selection of Main Personality

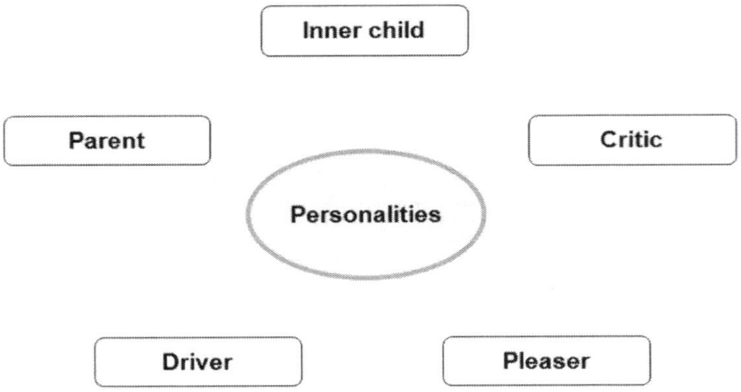

```
                    Inner child

    Parent                                  Critic

                    Personalities

            Driver              Pleaser
```

Diagram 5.5

If a personality is playing itself to an extreme, it's advisable to investigate why, and make an effort to work out what it is trying to teach us. It's basically calling on us to learn something. The goal here is always to bring it into an acceptable balance (for our own comfort and those who we are interacting with). I will begin with the Inner Child personality, which is the only one to have a twin. The twins are:

1. the individual Inner Child

2. a separate Inner Child related to the energy body's system that links us with the soul. This I call the soul's Inner Child or Energetic Inner Child, a part of the soul's structure.

Inner Child Personality
Within the persona structure, the Inner Child personality enables us to enjoy life, to be happy, to be intimate in relationships, to be creative, and so forth. These are all part of its important attributes. I must emphasise here that the Energetic Inner Child does not relate to the years we have as a child maturing into an adult in a physical body, it relates to the child years (early development) of our spirit through each soul's incarnation (chapter 4). This means that the Energetic Inner Child grows as the soul grows through its experiences of working with the different subtle energy bodies (SEBs, page 104). Which of the subtle energy bodies that are being worked with depends upon the experiences/situations arising from the soul's contract. The Inner Child personality too is a fixed part of our personality structure throughout our lifetime. It can have an influence on how we react and behave in different situations.

The Inner Child is recognised by psychologists as perhaps one of the most important personalities that we have. When we are born, our authentic-self is made up of different personality traits which can be affected by the mother's thoughts, those individuals who are interacting with the child, plus what is going on around the child before birth. All of this contributes to the fabricated-self. If the baby, while in the mother's womb, has been subjected to difficult energy experiences such as arguments between parents or relations, abuse between mother and father, this can have an effect on the Inner Child's personality. In this case the soul will have entered the foetus's development at an early time for the experience. This effect can form the creation of a pre-birth mask (additional identity) which will influence the physical child in terms of their attitude and behaviour from time to time. As the physical child develops, it is important to recognise that it has no logic and reasoning ability to help it figure out what is happening. This ability develops from the age of about 7 when the child's prefrontal cortex (the home of logic and reason) grows in substance. Without the support of the pre-frontal cortex during its early years, a child (including its original Inner Child) only operates through feelings and emotions.

It goes without saying that children are very sensitive and innocent; they need intimacy; they need gentle words, understanding, nurturing, and so forth. If some of the physical child's needs are not fulfilled as it is maturing, the Inner Child will seek to have these needs fulfilled at some time in the future. It does not matter if you are a parent, a chairperson or CEO of a company, a lecturer, an admiral, a prime minister, president, prince, or princess, if the Inner Child personality is not in balance it will affect your performance during adult life. How does it do that? It does it through your attitude and behaviour in the diverse relationships you are attracted to or attract. If any of the various characteristics of the Inner Child's personality are suppressed, they will surface at some time or other in an attempt to be acknowledged and brought into balance. What are the characteristics of the Inner Child?

The Inner Child's personality is made up of several different important characteristics. These characteristics are the individual parts of its character which themselves are like modules of energy. The modules form an energy constellation, as shown in diagram 5.6. The individual parts emerge to express themselves when a particular experience demands their presence. They also form a part of an individual's inner needs. In the drive to strengthen the intellect, as we grow into adulthood, the needs of the Inner Child, just like the development of emotional intelligence, tend to be ignored, and even at times suppressed. As the Inner Child is very sensitive and innocent, it comes out in an individual in situations where they seek approval from others. The Inner Child also loves to be spontaneous. You can see from the different characteristics in diagram 5.6, why it is so important to make sure that the Inner Child in its totality is alive and well throughout our life, and is not being suppressed. A point to emphasise again, is that the Inner Child does not grow into

Examples of Inner Child's Energy Constellation

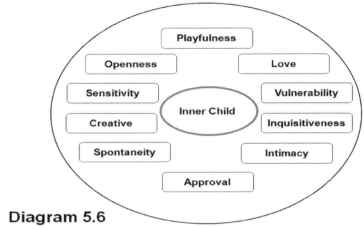

Diagram 5.6

adulthood. It stays as an Inner Child representing an important characteristic of our persona.

In any relationship, the Inner Child needs to feel held. Doctors have shown that babies who are dumped in an orphanage and not physically cuddled (held closely) die, even though they are well fed. As adults, we too need physical touching and to be held if an emotional relationship is to flourish in a healthy way. The Inner Child is innocence personified, and wants to be intimate. To express or show intimacy in a relationship, the Inner Child needs to be active and not suppressed. The ego does not know how to handle, or to protect the Inner Child.

In its bid to try to stay in the front line (not to be suppressed and pushed back) within the unconscious mind, the Inner Child will attempt to seek the support of other persona energies which include the Inner Parent, Pusher and Pleaser. They will try to strongly defend the Inner Child from any perceived attack. Always remember that the Inner Child is not able to look after itself because it is a *child* and needs support. If the outside world breaks through the Inner Child's outer defences, it will cause a problem. If a young child is subjected to a negative atmosphere that lacks feeling, it can eventually result in the actual child, or later the adult, becoming ill or having a breakdown. This is because the Inner Child operates solely on feeling energies, just like any baby. It has no logic or reason to defend itself!

Four Inner Child Characteristics

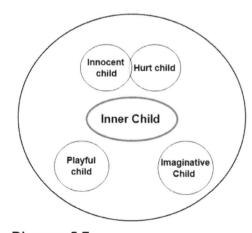

Diagram 5.7

As we journey through life, there are some characteristics of the Inner Child's structure that are of great value to us. I have chosen four, as shown in diagram 5.7: the innocent child, hurt child, imaginative child and playful child.

Recognising these characteristics of the Inner Child helped me to understand why, at times,

I felt and behaved the way I did in the situations I found myself in. Everybody has these four characteristics to a greater or lesser degree. If they do not manifest at all, it would be beneficial to establish why not. If they are too strong, they again need to be investigated and brought into balance. Once I recognised which of my Inner Child personality characteristics was either suppressed or too powerful, I worked to balance them. This helped me attract a more stable, close relationship. It also improved my relationships with friends and colleagues.

Innocent Child

If the characteristic of the Inner Child is suppressed it can lead to real problems in close relationships. For example, an individual may lack the ability to allow themselves to feel vulnerable, to be sensitive and could be capable of being wounded or susceptible to attack. If a baby is surrounded by a negative atmosphere with, say, parents having a quarrel or shouting match, then it will turn inwards for its own protection. The baby recognises the voice tones around it and feels the energy exchange going on. If it is subjected to continuous periods of any of these negative tones/energy, it will retire into the trait of Hurt Child. As explained in Chapter 3, the baby's energy sensors (the Emotional and Solar Plexus sensors) pick up the energy of others 'emotions, thought and intent, thus adding to its distress. If a child's vulnerability has been suppressed, later on in adulthood they will find it difficult to allow themselves to feel vulnerable in a close relationship. This is because they will have built an invisible emotional protective barrier around themselves. If this continues over a period of time, the negative energy that is generated within will cause the adult to experience the Hurt Child.

Hurt Child

The Hurt Child characteristic represents part of the foundation for many of the problems faced in the teenage and adult population today. When a child is subjected to continual hurts in the form of abuse, control and manipulation of any kind, then much psychological/emotional and physiological damage can occur over the medium to long-term. As the physical child matures, there will be a tendency to continually attract abuse, or to give abuse in different relationships. This is a slippery slope where unless the individual concerned can reverse the situation, the negative energies can become locked in (frozen) causing a blockage until a way is found to release them. As we are all quantum bio-magnets, we attract to us or are attracted to any imbalance of personality issues that are running within us. This is not only a part of our personal development as we journey along life's path, but also how the soul learns to grow.

Entering the realm of the Hurt Child, at any age, sets up conditions which make it easy to enter into a state of depression. In this state, any emotional intelligence we have is virtually switched off. If you happen to be in a primary (early) state of depression, you are probably not aware of this. You may also not realise that it would be beneficial to raise your level of emotional intelligence to counter the depression. Taking a look at binge drinking or the drugs problem that is endemic, especially amongst young people, in the UK, USA and elsewhere in the world. There is a common cause, but like most major social problems, politicians and their medical advisers are not really in a strong position to identify the cause. They are good at identifying symptoms, but certainly not causes, which is because they are locked within their limited, left-brain-oriented virtual box of thinking. Of course, the politics and economics of the problem are also a part of their approach. The cause of the serious binge drinking/drug problem is identifiable for everyone to see. I would suggest that it is one of an *emotional deficit* within the individuals concerned. They basically have an unconscious inner feeling of a lack of love (arising from low self-worth, self-acceptance, self-esteem, and so on) and have little idea of how to be naturally intimate and vulnerable.

If parents do not understand what intimacy and vulnerability truly mean, then how can their children? To rectify this situation, it is necessary to explore what happened within the family (and relations) as well as during the years at school and time spent amongst friends. This will help to identify when it was that an individual may have been hurt as a child. Look at today's 24/7 families who have little, if any, free time. Look at the negative media bombardment - the high adrenalin suspense films, video games, soap operas and so forth, that are played out on a daily basis. These things are now seen as 'givens' in modern society. There is little meaningful attention paid to the ability of children to sift these powerful visual and emotional influences and impulses and to articulate the effect they are having upon them, especially on the child's capacity to separate fact from fiction. Depending upon their level of self-esteem, self-worth, and self-discipline, children and adults might well hang onto and copy attitudes and behaviours depicted in such media, which are intensely damaging. Is it any wonder, therefore, that there is a lack of emotional intelligence and an emotional deficit in children and young adults?

Those with a strong Hurt Child (both children and adults) can also have short fuses. They lash out at someone verbally and/or physically with little provocation, and often with no remorse or sense of compassion. Many a dictator like Hitler, Stalin, Franco, Bonaparte and brutal kings such as Frederick the Great of Germany or Peter the Great of Russia, all had a mega Hurt Child. It is interesting to note that they all suffered from severe verbal and physical abuse as children.

Playful Child
On a more cheerful note, when you go on holiday, or have a relaxed and fun weekend with friends, it is the Playful Child characteristic that surfaces within your consciousness. If you

are unable to relax, then you have a problem with the negative side of your Playful Child and you would be well advised to investigate why. Somewhere in the past, your Innocent Child may have been attacked and it's advisable to identify when this occurred. Take steps to rectify the situation first of all within the conscious mind and make sure that you change your attitudes and behaviour accordingly.

Today's 24/7 lifestyle, including long working hours, subdues the Playful Child and leads to an increase in stress. There is also the potential here to slip into a downward spiral where everything in life is taken too seriously. As with all the personalities and their different characteristics/elements, acknowledging and keeping them in balance is the name of the game. If we are having a really bad day but we can see some humour in the situation, then the Playful Child has definitely come into play. If not, try saying to your-self 'step back, you are on Candid Camera!', and see if the Playful Child will kick in. I have worked with many a boss whose Playful Child was locked well and truly in its room. Heaven knows what life at home must have been like with their families. Emotional intelligence must have been sadly lacking, thus leaving little, if any, scope for improvement in their working and home environment.

Imaginative Child
Part of the foundation of the creative self is, believe it or not, the Imaginative Child characteristic of the Inner Child. Imagination and intention are energy links to our creative abilities. If the mind is full of busy chatter, or jammed full of facts, or over-laden by a strong intellect, or negative thoughts, or involved with a drama of some kind, there is little chance of us bringing in our imagination. It is necessary to first still the mind, which can be accomplished through the breathing and/or visualisation exercises given in the previous chapters. Once the mind is stilled, we can empower the Imaginative Child to emerge. In energy terms this approach also grounds our energy system, allowing the imagination and creative thoughts to flow in a stable manner. People who daydream and are lost in space tend not to be well grounded. Nevertheless, there are times in life when this state is to be welcomed, especially during harsh conditions.

As you will see from the other personalities and their varying characteristics that follow on from here (for example the Parent), they can have a grounding effect on the Imaginative Child. Such a grounding effect enables the Imaginative Child to function in a balanced and productive manner. Creative thoughts can then begin to flow on a regular basis.

Parent Personality
There are three main characteristics of the Parent personality that are still major players in my own and most individuals' lives, namely the Protector, Controller and Nurturer

Three Characteristics of the Inner Parent

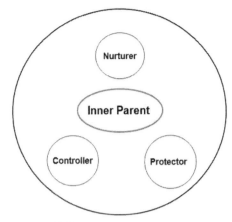

Diagram 5.8

(diagram 5.8). Like all major personalities the Inner Parent has a constellation of individual energies or characteristics. It is recognised by psychologists that the main function of the Parent personality is to protect the Inner Child if its vulnerability is threatened.

Protector
Living and working in four continents around the world, I became aware that I was always being protected by some inner/outer force. Yes, we do have a Protector in our personality bank. If I inadvertently strayed off the path I should have been following, this force always pointed me in the right direction. In New York, when I walked around the centre of the city, I would always make a detour if the direction I took did not feel right. I am pleased to report that I did not have any bad incidents in that great city because I was tuned into my Protector. The Protector is our very own survival guide, if we chose to tune into it. To keep us out of danger the Protector is able to use intuition, dreams, premonitions, hunches, sixth sense and so on. The Japanese Samurai developed their Protector personality (amongst others) to improve their fighting skills and self-defence. Another example, which I still dine out on today, is when I left Kuwait. I had worked there for a five-year period. My professional slot had been localised (nationalised) and it was time to move on. I left Kuwait on July 4th 1990 and Saddam Hussein invaded the country on August 3rd 1990! In this case my Protector was working through other people as well as myself to obtain this outcome. Normally I took the month of July off and would return to Kuwait from my vacation on August 1st!

Such is the power of the Protector that it ensures conditions are set up to pull us out of pending trouble spots, if we are not meant to be there. Of course, if we find ourselves in a tricky situation (including life-threatening), whether we like it or not it will be for an experience to enable the soul to grow. The Protector can even cause us to have an accident, or to be ill in order to protect us from a potential future danger. That is why I usually say that some accidents or illnesses are not as random an occurrence as they appear to be, as there is always some meaning behind them. For example, if we catch the flu we may be forced to stay home in bed, and the reason could be that we have been overworking and require a rest, otherwise we may become seriously ill! Whatever the cause, there is usually a good reason.

Controller

We live in a rule-based society and the Controller is an element of the Inner Parent that makes sure our behaviour conforms to what society expects of us. It helps to make sure that we are acceptable - or not, as the case may be. Like the Protector, the Controller is there to ensure we are kept out of danger, enabling us to continue with what we are doing. The Controller and Protector energies are quite similar and they are often found to work together. In addition, if deep down in our unconscious mind we feel that we are not in control of our life, we may find that we are always trying to control other people's lives. We may even attract others, perhaps in relationships, whose lives appear to be chaotic. The solution here is to first recognise our behaviour and that what is happening within our unconscious mind is perhaps mirroring what is happening around us (it is being reflected back to us). This is part of the quantum bio-magnetic field of attraction in operation. It is bringing to us a situation, or situations, which reflect an issue (life lesson) that is running in our unconscious mind. In this case, it is advisable to look at the issue(s) as it is part of our personal development and spiritual growth. To change the energy program in your unconscious mind which is causing a problem, the following may be helpful:

1. go back within your unconscious mind to find the cause of the issue. This is usually a negative incident or series of incidents that probably occurred in your childhood. Therefore, go back to your birth and work forward from there.

2. re-write (re-script) the scene that you find which is the cause of the issue (life lesson). This will allow the Controller/Protector to get back into balance and off its defensive stand. Work to discharge any attached negative emotion. When you have done this, bring in a positive emotion which you should associate with the new script to replace (integrate) the negative one which you have worked through and discharged.

It is best to work through these either with a therapist (see Appendix 2) or with someone who is close to you and whom you trust. You may find it helpful to revisit the detailed approach I provided in chapter 4 on the methodology for changing the energy programme in your unconscious mind, The Protector/Controller are the Sumo wrestlers (real heavyweights) of the Inner Parent and need to be carefully monitored.

Nurturer

Diagram 5.9 represents four characteristics of the Nurturer's energy constellation. The Nurturer is the personality that looks after our wellbeing. It tries to make sure that we do everything in moderation - have the right diet; take a rest when we are working too hard; be happy within ourselves when things are a bit down, and so forth. How much we like our-self is also affected by the Nurturer. People who are concerned and care for others have a strong nurturing Inner Parent. In a relationship, it is the Nurturer that ensures we are

Four Characteristics of the Nurturer

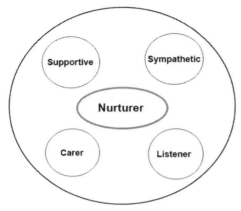

Diagram 5.9

sympathetic, support our partner and listen to them when they need us to. I first really noticed the Nurturer personality when I was in the United Nations. I had a girlfriend whom I absolutely adored, but the relationship fizzled out after about four months. This was mainly because she was never very responsive to what I was doing, lacked empathy and was quite narcissistic. Had I known about the Inner Parent status then, if she had agreed I could have worked on her weak nurturing side to try to bring it back into balance. Of course, I too had to learn from *my* need to be nurtured, as that was also out of balance! I accomplished this in later life, however, and am confident I have brought the need into a healthier balance.

The Nurturer is one of the Inner Child's protectors and will always attempt to come to the Child's aid if its vulnerability is being threatened. As each of our personalities has a positive and a negative side, if the negative side of the Nurturer is strong it will be insensitive, lack understanding and lack empathy. If the result is an over-caring Parent, we get fed whether we want to be fed or not, or we are told to wear a crash helmet when we cycle, not to climb trees and not to go out by our-self and so on; we are over protected, not to say stifled. Such situations can create a lot of negative feelings within the recipient of the attention. The Parent, who has all the good intentions in the world, is unknowingly creating a hostile reaction. Guess what? The Parent, because of the rejection they inevitably face, will most probably also develop a *martyr* syndrome. This will create such reactions as – *you never appreciate anything I do for you; nobody loves me; you just take me for granted;* and so forth! Lots of balancing to do here!

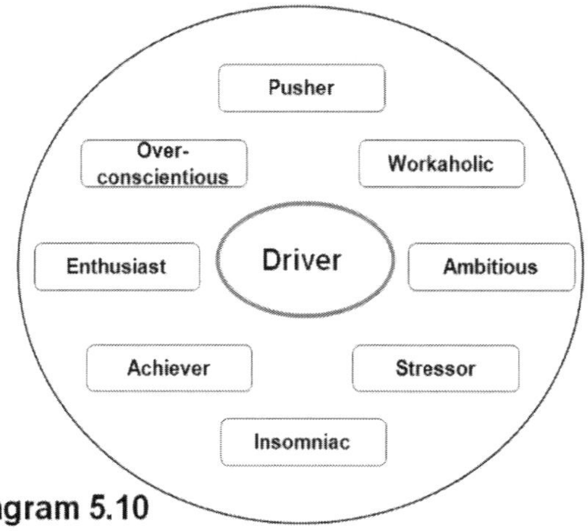

Driver Personality

Diagram 5.10 represents a selection of the constellation of energies/characteristics that can be found within the Driver personality. The Driver is a powerhouse that gets us going where we want to go in life. It can push us forward without any remorse, thereby increasing levels of stress. If we discover that we are overly

Diagram 5.10

ambitious and enthusiastic, the Driver is to be thanked for this, as it has fired up these parts of our persona. If we had a financially deprived childhood then the Driver can push us to extremes to achieve in this area. The Driver can also push us to becoming an insomniac through burying our-self in our work. In such a state, we would most likely begin a downward slide of sleeping irregularly while at the same time finding it difficult to rest, which of course can lead to our becoming quite irritable.

The Driver is just like an inner Boss who sees his job as being to protect the Inner Child from hardship of any kind; to push us to provide comfort and security for our-self and others; to be of service, and so forth. However, when the Driver is working flat out to protect the Inner Child, it will prevent other characteristics such as the Playful Child or Imaginative Child from coming out. A touch of 'all work and no play makes Jack (or Jill) a dull person'. Other personalities such as the Parent can intervene to rein in the Driver in this type of situation. If the Driver is not reined in, it can become a relationship destroyer. When the Driver is in balance we will be well motivated, enthusiastic and empowered to achieve our goals.

Today's society values the high performer and emphasises success. Both high performance and success incorporate Driver characteristics. These are Ambition, the Pusher, Achiever, and the Workaholic (diagram 5.10), all probably running flat out. They will not be in balance. Like any machine, running ourselves flat out will cause us to experience a breakdown of one sort or another. This is why it is advisable to bring the Driver into balance. The same is true in situations where the Non-Performer and Non-Achiever are running us. Here, where the Driver has been suppressed, we need to give it as much attention as possible. Crucially, this is because individuals with a weak Driver are more likely to drop out of life. In such cases it is necessary for them to generate an inner *hope* and *belief* that something better exists.

To invoke such inner hope, it would be advantageous to stimulate the amazing placebo attribute that we all have within us. This is the increasingly recognised 'power behind *positive expectations*' (chapters 4 and 7). By using the power of positive expectations, sufficient inner energy can be generated to kick-start a strong inner motivation in the individual concerned. The choices/decisions are theirs to make so long as they themselves acknowledge the need to move on to a more uplifting path. Improving the choices/decisions we make is one of the great areas of learning as we journey along life's path. And we should always bear in mind that there is never a wrong choice/decision! It is the lesson(s) learnt from making the choice/decision that is important.

Pleaser Personality
The Pleaser's characteristics are shown in the energy constellation diagram 5.11. Its function is basically, once again, to protect the Inner Child. We can see from the Pleaser

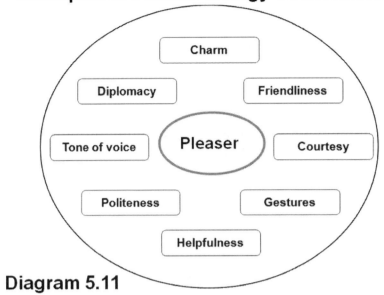

Examples of Pleaser Energy Constellation

Diagram 5.11

characteristics that it has all the traits we need to be popular. It is the Pleaser that helps us to attract lots of friends: or perhaps very few. The Pleaser can persuade us to be a good listener to such an extent that people talk about the same problem with us again and again and again. That is because we have not set up boundaries within ourself that stops them dumping their problems on us! We may be unconsciously trying to please them in case we lose their friendship. We may also be over-empathising and refusing to let them know that they are using us as a sponge to absorb all the things they keep wanting to throw at us. If the Pleaser is in balance, then we will probably be good at relationships and do well in our job. If it is over the top by being too strong, people may see us as being insincere and perhaps untrustworthy. If it is weak, then we may appear to be a bit of a wimp.

A friend of mine was always complaining to me that one of his wife's girlfriends who visited her regularly would bring a present for her, which she did not want, each time she visited. The friend would then stay for about three hours dumping the same set of problems on his wife each week. Even though his wife gave her good advice, she only heard the words but did not get the message! The wife's Pleaser was weak here which allowed her friend to dump on her. After some counselling the wife recognised this weakness as well as a requirement to set up some *boundaries* with her friend. She recognised that listening was not enough to help her friend and that it would be advantageous to get her friend to change her thinking. In order to do this, she brought to her friend's attention that (metaphorically) her record was stuck! She did this subtly by saying to the friend that she wanted her to talk about something positive that had happened to her in her life. Her friend found this very difficult at first, as she could not think of anything. She was also asked not to bring any more presents when she visited as she did not need to be afraid of losing the wife's friendship. As my friend's wife began to act more like a therapist, her friend began to recognise her present-bringing and dumping behaviour and her ANTs (Chapter 4) for what they were, and slowly but surely began to change. After much persuasion her friend agreed to see a proper therapist.

Critic Personality

The Critic personality is powerful and has many characteristics, some of which are shown in the constellation of energies in diagram 5.12. The Critic provides us with the power to reflect on what we are doing and to discriminate on the quality of our work in comparison with others. If properly managed, it has the ability to contribute to our state of excellence. The Critic is, of course,

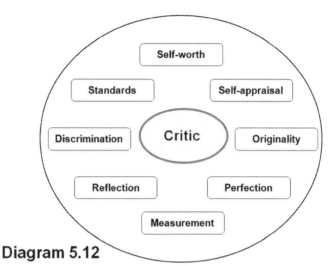

Diagram 5.12

the great perfectionist and could drive us crazy with its eye for detail in the quest to produce perfection. It has very high standards and will compare our work with the work of experts. If we are fortunate to have a balanced Critic then we will do a good job to acceptable standards without getting addicted to the detail.

Negative characteristics of the Critic can be seen by observing people who attend course after course on such subjects as personal development, or work on themselves through self-therapy, or meditate continually for hours on end. This can be due to a low sense of self-worth through feelings of inferiority (low self-esteem). The problem here is that the Critic can be so powerful that it could shut out other personalities, such as the Inner Child. This can cause an individual to slip into a dangerous negative state where they may harm themselves, or someone else. The Critic is humourless and cold, enabling the individual to identify when it is present and has control over them.

As mentioned at the beginning of the chapter, all of the personalities have both a positive and a negative side. They are there to teach us lessons so we can learn to bring them into balance, especially if they are operating at an extreme. As quantum bio-magnets, we attract scenes/situations on life's path that allow different personalities to show themselves. Such situations provide an opportunity for us to recognise those different personalities, work with them and thus grow through the experience of doing so. Not recognising what is happening within relationships, and failing to deal with the situations that arise from them, puts us in a position of getting stuck in a continuing cycle of similar circumstances: until we 'get it'!

But life is not at all straightforward. As different personalities work through us, we can also develop additional ones. They are called *masks (additional identities we create within ourselves)*, which we take on perhaps to fill a gap in our personality structure or to supplement a weak one.

What Masks are YOU Wearing Today?

The process of creating these additional identities begins from childhood onwards (diagram 5.13).

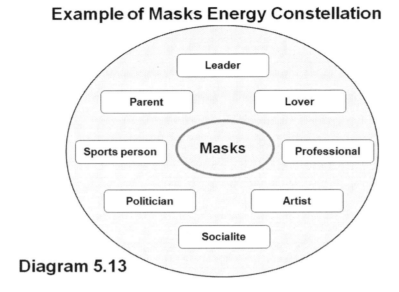

Diagram 5.13

Development of masks continues as we journey along life's path. Masks are much simpler than a personality in that they do not have a constellation of energy. They have different intensities, however, from strong to weak. Masks are a part of the personality that may appear from time to time as we work through the day. Masks are projected onto other people as part of a communication to establish an image of ourselves in another person's mind. Much later in life we go through a process of shedding our masks.

When I left Scotland at the age of 17 I had a broad Glaswegian accent. All the close friends I made in England found this amusing. I quickly integrated into southern English society and I admired so many of these new friends who I found quite sophisticated, that I began to act like them. This meant that I was growing (unknowingly) some new masks (identities). I continued to develop my sports personality mask through sailing; I was taught squash; I did a lot of competition shooting; I went beagling, and so on. My professional personality mask went from electronics, to nuclear physics, to computer science, to operational research, to international consulting, to development banking, to merchant/investment banking, and so on. My leadership personality mask became stronger when I was commissioned into the Royal Naval Reserve, got promoted in my professional life, and so on. I developed some social masks by attending a number of magnificent parties, which arose from my business, military and diplomatic contacts. Now you can imagine that as I started down the road of personal (and spiritual) development I thought that I was most certainly on my way in life and in a strong position. That is, until at one seminar/workshop I was asked the question: 'who are you?'

To begin, I started going through my masks, those different identities of myself that I have just described to you. At that time, I did not know anything about masks and their development. As mentioned in the previous chapter I was stopped in mid flight and told: "John, you are not your titles, your qualifications, your job, your clothes, your house, your car and so on – so who are you?" Needless to say, I was completely speechless. This was most unusual for me! That particular question 'who are you?', was to cause a major shift in my consciousness, as I had just been stripped of all the things (the masks) that I believed in and regarded as 'me'! They showed where I was in society's structure, but that is just about all, because masks really only describe what I had fabricated over my authentic-self during my lifetime. It was a most humbling experience and it gave me much food for thought as I discovered that there is a lot more to me (and my close friends) than I had ever realised. But to get there, I had to step out of my virtual box of thinking. The further I delved into the latest psychology and understanding of what life is about, separating what made sense and was meaningful to me, the more I began to understand what caused my attitudes and behaviour. My tutor and spiritual teacher master Chou also offered me valuable advice here. Life then became much more interesting and happiness was no longer a dream, it became a reality. In this book I come straight to the point of *who are you*?'.

A psychologist like Carl Jung, I regard as yesterday's man, today's man and tomorrow's man. Freud, who is another great psychologist, I consider as yesterday's man. Why do I make this comparison? Jung understood, and was not afraid to promote, the spiritual dimensions of life. He also recognised that taking psychology into the laboratory to add a scientific label to it created limitations. And that is because this takes us, once again, back into that limited mechanistic, form-based and linear-time-biased, virtual box of thinking that we are all conditioned to accept, which focuses on the left-brain hemisphere. Jung's thinking belongs to today's
paradigm shift of thinking which takes into account the sub-atomic or quantum world as he brings in the intangible world of spirit into certain aspects of his work. Jung also recognised that we human beings have a Shadow side to our personality, which has different characteristics, and that these characteristics need to surface in the conscious mind to be worked with. A most important part of the growth challenge in life is to work with our Shadows.

Houston: We have a Shadow!
Just what is this 'Shadow' that many psychologists have written about? I define the Shadow as:

'the collection of all the dark (negative) parts of personalities/sub personalities and masks within the unconscious mind'

Each personality and mask has a Light and a dark (Shadow) part, which is stored in the unconscious mind. Either part can flip into the conscious mind to create an attitude and behaviour during day to day situations/experiences. The type of situation dictates whether or not the Shadow or the Light part comes into play.

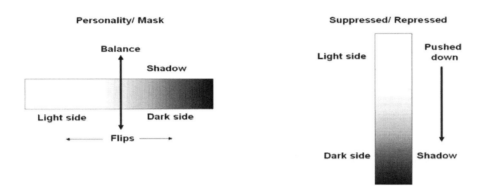

Diagram 5.14

In the left-hand side of diagram 5.14 a personality or mask is represented by the horizontal rectangle. When the Light part (left-hand side) is in the lead, people experience the positive or happy you. In this case, everything is going well in our life. The right-hand side of the diagram is shown when the dark (Shadow) side is in operation. When we show the Shadow-self we are usually unhappy and our attitude and behaviour is most likely less than acceptable to those around us. We need to bring the Shadow into balance with the Light part. We do this by being sensitive and sufficiently aware to recognise that we are causing a disturbance and perhaps creating an unpleasant atmosphere. Having recognised an unfortunate attitude and behaviour, it is necessary to investigate the cause. A process of how to do this is given below.

There is a tendency not to allow the Shadow parts to come into play, for fear of being rejected by those who matter to us if we reveal it. Our Shadows *need* to come forward, as they are a real part of who we are. They are part of the life lessons from which we grow. If we suppress/repress a Shadow, it will be pushed down. In the second diagram above on the right, a Shadow has been pushed down. If the Shadow continues to be suppressed, it will explode like a volcano at some time in the future, because it is meant to be heeded and worked with. The same is true of everything that we suppress, from a personality and mask to a particular form of attitude, or behaviour, or talent, or emotion, or idea, and so forth. Everything that we suppress has the potential to erupt, probably at a most inopportune moment! Because we tend not to investigate Shadows, they can build up a surplus of energy which can manifest in a form of negative projection at someone or something. Some examples follow on the next page.

At Birth Shadows are in Balance
The light and dark parts of our personalities are in balance at birth, that is, there is 50 percent Light and 50 percent dark (Shadow). Nevertheless, the soul may have a requirement to enter the foetus before birth. This would be to purposely pick up some experiences (energetically) from what is happening around it. In this case, some of the personalities will change – some may grow more positively and some more negatively (diagram 5.14), thus increasing the Shadow. Some personalities will also change as we mature. This is due to the experiences that we encounter. At any time a parent, relation, teacher, friend, boss, person in authority, and so forth, can create a change in the balance of a particular Shadow within us. Whoever is involved, it is important to understand that they will be unknowingly projecting their own Shadow in us. Remember, it is not ours, it is theirs! They are sowing the seed of a false belief in us. The Shadow is probably created from something that they dislike about us. What they do not realise is that they are most probably mirroring themselves in us. They need to pause and look within themselves. With regret, this is not part of our education. What they dislike is most probably an issue within their own unconscious mind that needs to be acknowledged and worked through.

Shadows can have a powerful effect upon us, as they are like negative energetic beings within our consciousness. The intensity of their energy will ensure that they surface within the conscious mind to have their say, and to feed off the energy of the situation that is being experienced. How we handle ourselves is crucial here if we are to create a balance. Suppression of a Shadow or its opposite Light part, or even a mask, is not recommended, so there is no need to be overly diplomatic! If we are, this could cause the build-up of pressure like a head of steam within us that needs to be released. Such a situation easily results in a spontaneous outburst with unfortunate consequences with respect to the emotions/feelings of those involved.

Any suppressed or repressed parts of us will form part of our personality energy dynamics. As described in previous chapters, from birth we construct what I call a fabricated-self around us, building over the authentic-self. In so many cases individuals live their whole life through their fabricated-self and they have no idea who their real, authentic-self, is! When we want to please, or to be accepted and not rejected, or want to be loved, or want approval, this can give rise to the suppression of a particular personality, or Shadow, or mask. In such cases, we accept what is happening to us. There may not have been a choice here, because we may have been too young and/or not been in a position to challenge the perpetrator(s).

However, from late teens onwards and on leaving home, life enters its adulthood phase. In this case there is nearly always a choice/decision to consciously accept or reject what is being said and/or what is happening to us.

How do Shadows show themselves? Some examples may be helpful (names changed, of course). A former next-door-neighbour called Bert had an attractive wife whose name was Sandy. When I visited them, or when we met at a party, both were very civilised, and behaved in nothing but a 'sweetness and light' manner. He was an IT consultant and international yachtsman. She was a social worker, and like him, travelled a lot. My bedroom was adjacent to theirs (I lived in a terraced house). At regular intervals, when Bert was home, late in the evening I could hear her screaming at him (abusing him) and treating him like a piece of dirt. He did not respond and took the abuse like a boxer's punch bag. They had a son, and when he finally went to University, Bert sued for divorce. In their case, Sandy was projecting her Shadow-self onto Bert. I heard that she had been abused as a child and had, therefore, not dealt with the issue. During her early years, she had repressed her feelings and chose not to respond to the perpetrator (probably for good reasons). Living with Sandy, Bert allowed the Light part of his response to be suppressed. He retreated into his shell.

Both Bert and Sandy were not learning from the experience, as they did not have a clue about what was really going on psychologically, emotionally or spiritually. Bert needed to ask himself why he was retreating into himself and she needed to look into her Shadow-self to determine what was causing the outbursts. A therapist could have helped both of them had they sought help. They did not. When Sandy had recovered from the divorce, she attracted another partner and after a short honeymoon began the same cycle of abuse with him. He left her very quickly and she sold up and moved on. In both cases her Shadow represented the dark part of her personality energy structure and her partner's the Light part of his personality's energy structure. Both needed to be worked through them to bring them into balance. Each of our lives is purposely full of situations of varying contrast, for it is through experiencing the contrasts that we can learn and grow a great deal.

In another case, my friend Paul's son Peter told me a tale about someone who had tried to bully him on his school bus (he was twelve years old). The bully, who was bigger and a year older than him had pushed him around twice before and he had asked him to stop doing it. The third time when it happened the bully was more aggressive so Peter whacked him (unexpectedly) on the jaw. The bully fell back onto a bus seat, and Peter walked on. He was never disturbed again. In this case the bully's Shadow represented a young insecure person who was projecting hostile emotions onto those around him (a dark energy). He picked on Peter as he represented the Light energy side to his Shadow. Peter was strong enough to defend himself and dealt with the situation. Interestingly, the bully later became one of Peter's friends.

Paul told me that Peter's mother had been bullied by her mother many times and she had not dealt with the issue. She bullied her son from time to time and even tried to bully Paul, but he would not accept the situation and told her to stop it (his Light side was stronger than her dark side). What happened here was that although she did stop trying to bully both men, she did not deal with her Shadow-self which caused her to want to be a bully from time to time. Her Shadow-self was a victim-consciousness which she had taken on because of her mother's behaviour. How should she deal with this, to bring the Shadow personality into balance? The steps involved are crucial for anyone who discovers a Shadow characteristic within themselves and need to work with it.

Shadow Hunting – They're in Season!
You will have gathered by now that yes, we all have Shadows, whether we like it or not! To find out what the Shadows are can be a reasonably straightforward task. On the other hand it can also be a rather tricky one if the Shadow concerned is hostile and/or very deeply embedded. In this case, the support of a good therapist can provide guidance through the experience. Because we project our Shadow-selves onto the outside world and they are reflected back from those around us, or the situations we are involved in, it is, once again, in our best interest to work with any Shadows we may have in order to bring them into balance. I have broken down the task of finding any Shadows that may exist into five steps as shown in diagram 5.15.

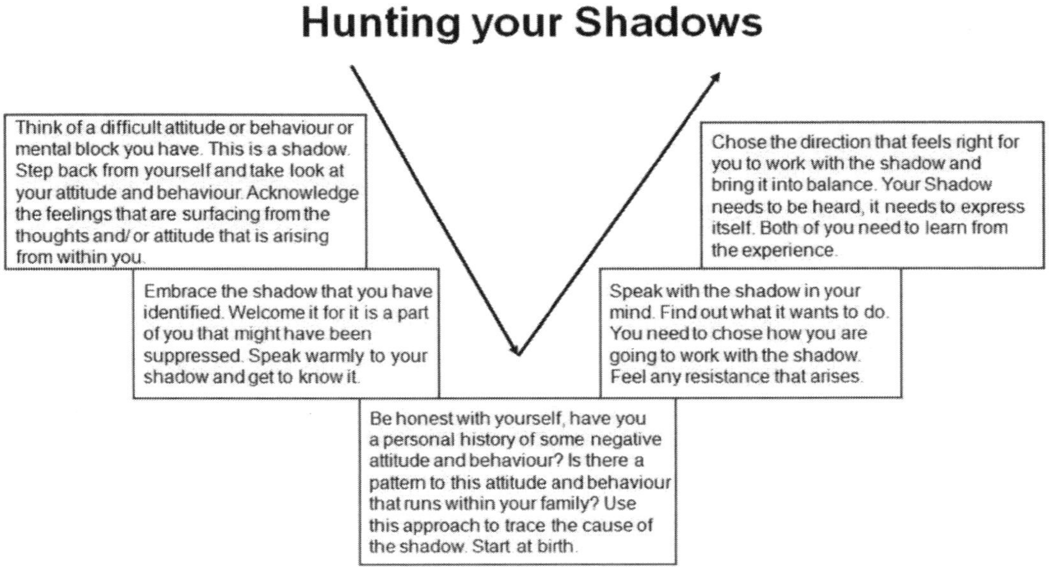

Hunting your Shadows

1. Think of a difficult attitude or behaviour or mental block you have. This is a shadow. Step back from yourself and take look at your attitude and behaviour. Acknowledge the feelings that are surfacing from the thoughts and/or attitude that is arising from within you.

2. Embrace the shadow that you have identified. Welcome it for it is a part of you that might have been suppressed. Speak warmly to your shadow and get to know it.

3. Be honest with yourself, have you a personal history of some negative attitude and behaviour? Is there a pattern to this attitude and behaviour that runs within your family? Use this approach to trace the cause of the shadow. Start at birth.

4. Speak with the shadow in your mind. Find out what it wants to do. You need to chose how you are going to work with the shadow. Feel any resistance that arises.

5. Chose the direction that feels right for you to work with the shadow and bring it into balance. Your Shadow needs to be heard, it needs to express itself. Both of you need to learn from the experience.

Diagram 5.15

If you have a sympathetic and understanding partner, a lot of this work might be done with them. I elaborate upon each step below, starting from the top left in diagram 5.15.

Step 1.
Make sure that you have a journal to record what is happening. If you are going through the process alone, then record the details at the end. It is preferable to have someone with you as you may hit some sensitive emotions. Tell them what you are doing and give them a list of the steps involved so that they can take you through them. Relax into a comfortable position in your favourite chair, or sofa, or lie on the floor, or bed, or whatever. Be comfortable and chill out. Take your-self through a deep breathing exercise (like the 6:3 technique –chapter 2, page 86) to enhance your relaxed state. When you feel ready, move into your imagination and see your-self stepping out of your body in front of your-self. Turn around to face your-self so that you can observe how your physical body is behaving. If you cannot actually see your-self doing this in your imagination, go through the motion in your mind and sense it happening. It's important to observe your-self within your mind, or just sense it. Maintain the ability to see, sense and to measure how you physically feel while going through the exercise. This will enable you to get a physical feeling and sense of how you behave in different situations.

Take your consciousness back to your birth and then move forward through some previous experiences that had a negative effect upon you. How did you behave and feel? Where within your body did the feelings register? Now travel forward again and see your-self (in your mind) at a time when you felt bad because of your behaviour. Let the actual experience behind this behaviour resurface within your mind. Check if it relates to a situation that keeps coming up in your life. If it does not, then clear your mind and go further forward until you find one that keeps repeating itself in your life. You have just found one of your Shadows.

Step 2.
Greet the Shadow that you've located for it is a part of you. Embrace it. We all have parts of ourselves that we like and parts that we dislike. A principal key in this personal growth work is for you to love the parts you like and dislike equally. You may find this a bit difficult at first, but I ask you to persevere as the negative Shadow energy needs to be brought into balance – a neutral state. It is important not to feed the Shadow with more negative feelings (this is negative energy). You are trying to bring the Shadow's emotional energy into balance. Start a conversation in your mind with the Shadow and give it a sympathetic hearing. Listen to what the Shadow is saying to you. Try to reach an agreement as to where you are going and give your Shadow *'quality time'* to help each of you to get into balance emotionally (energetically).

Step 3
The Shadow that you have located represents a regular pattern of the attitudes and

behaviours you exhibit in a specific situation. It will have different characteristics that contribute to its whole self. Your task is to work towards finding the reason for it being there, which may be buried deep within your unconscious mind. Take a further step back and recall if your attitude and behaviour are a pattern that exists within your family. An interesting point to make here is that if your Shadow is a family trait, then as you bring it into balance you will have a direct effect on other family members! We are all beings of energy and by the Universal Laws we are all connected at a sub-atomic or quantum level. When you create a balance within your-self, you will also be creating a balance within your family with respect to the Shadow (the issue) you are working on. You are in effect not only healing your-self but also family members.

Step 4.
It is time now for you and your Shadow to begin working together to explore what made your Shadow reach its present level. As you begin a dialogue with your Shadow, it is important to maintain a connection with your feelings. Agree a strategy with your Shadow for how you are going to work together. Decide who is going to lead. Will you swap leadership with your Shadow at an appropriate time? I recommend that you do this. When you begin, suggest to your Shadow that you will go back to the time when you were born and then to move forward until you find the situation, or situations that caused it to start changing. If it is a family trait (you were born with it), investigate the reason within your family for it being there. In this case, ask your Shadow to identify how it came about within your family? If the change in the Shadow arose during your lifetime, work through the incident and similar incidents in your life which contributed to its change. You may find varying degrees of resistance as you do this. Try to work your way through any resistance. If you get blocked, even after going back to it at different times in the future, I suggest that you get some help from a therapist.

Step 5.
When you locate the first incident within your consciousness where the Shadow started to grow, tell it that you are going to re-run the situation or incident again as you need to change the experience. You are going to take a positive stand and respond to the perpetrator, or attacker, to show that you are not going to be abused, or manipulated, or put down. You are not taking on their Shadow, or false belief as they are projecting it onto you. You know that the problem is within them and is not with you. When they projected their Shadow onto you, you were only expressing your-self. You were happy within your-self and did not intend to upset them. You only mirrored back to them their Shadow, but if you have done something that has upset them, apologise and move on. Your Shadow is now free to begin rebalancing (that is re-integrating) itself within you. Search for other situations where the same Shadow may have been repressed or suppressed; re-script each scene with a positive outcome and work on the emotion to rebalance the Shadow's energy. The important thing here is that the Shadow gets re-integrated with the personality where it can participate as an equal member

of your personality team. You are no longer in denial. This means that the Shadow can be called into play, not in an extreme state as you journey along your life's path encountering diverse situations and experiences, but as part of the normal you.

My purpose in bringing to your attention the complexity of the personality structure is to give you a feel for what is going on within your consciousness and the consciousness of those around you. We are complex beings. But if we gain an understanding of what is going on within us, it can help to smooth out our relationships. You will now have a better understanding as to why the ancient Greeks put that famous statement above the entrance to the temple of Apollo in Delphi: *'Know thy self'*. In today's language it is simply *'know yourself'*. For if we do not have a basic understanding of ourselves, how can we understand someone else? This becomes painfully obvious when we begin to recognise that we are, in general, mirroring our personalities, masks and Shadows back from other people! As the concept of mirroring enters mainstream education, we should witness more and more a reduction in the practice of blaming those in a relationship with us, arising from heated exchanges on account of what is happening. There is really no blame, only a learning experience! Staying *out of any drama* is what we should be striving to do.

I used to see a lot of apparently dysfunctional families around. I now realise that they are not dysfunctional. What I was reflecting was my own lack of understanding of the dynamics of human relationships, what the purpose of the Shadow-self is and the process of mirroring in the pursuit of personal and spiritual growth. There is not really any dysfunction and those involved are working (usually unconsciously) through their life lessons. They are also contributing to the conditioning of one another's quantum bio-magnetic field, through their interaction, to make sure that they are attracted to or attract exactly what they are meant to experience, learn and grow from.

Boosting your Relationships
Have you at some time in your life been friendly with a couple who seemed to be made for each other? Such couples have their disagreements and perhaps, at times, some heated arguments, but they always seem to quickly make up and are happy to be with each other. However, I see so many couples and families who seem to be in turmoil with very little purpose. Well, in reality, this is not the case. Rather, it is their not being aware of what is really going on within and between them. What I find interesting is that the dynamics of a commercial company is similar to human dynamics. The reason for this is more complex than the obvious fact that they both involve people. There is also the energy effect of the land site and the building structure to be taken into account. I comment more on this in a separate section at the end of this chapter. Some companies appear to be quite chaotic, dysfunctional and unpleasant to work in. Other companies have a great culture and are

pleasant to work in. The laws that govern a harmonious partnership, or happy family, or a great company to work for, are the same. Once you begin to get to know your-self and get a feeling for why you behave the way you do, with all the attendant attitudes and behaviour, you are well on the way to understanding what is really going on within a relationship of any type. I explore below how to improve four types of relationships which are a major part of life:

- **Personal Relationships** - finding a partner, wife, husband or friend.

- **Family Relationships** – developing a harmonious family atmosphere.

- **Professional Relationships** – hiring the right people and creating a constructive working environment.

- **Relationships with the Environment and Buildings** – recognising the power of a building's/land's energy, its effect on the occupants and their contribution to the energy structure.

My purpose here is to provide you with indicators that will help you appreciate what is really happening in the various relationships in your life. Diagram 5.16 is similar to the one shown at the beginning of this chapter. Crucial elements of the quantum bio-magnetic field are the *needs/goals* and *beliefs* that we all have. They run continuously in the unconscious mind, and are part of the bio-magnetic attraction factor that contributes to bringing about personal relationships. The good news is that we can actually identify the needs/goals and beliefs that may not be in our best interest and make changes where appropriate. This will also change the programming of the quantum bio-magnetic field and, therefore, change the type of partner we attract. We only have to know how to do it.

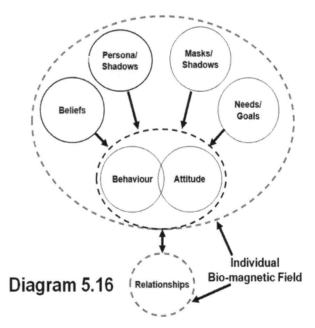

Diagram 5.16

Personal Relationships

In all relationships, including a lot of what else happens in life, I have found that *'all is not as it seems'*. When you consider entering into a relationship, there is what can be described as a set of conditions which have to be consciously/unconsciously satisfied. These conditions represent our needs/goals, which are running continually in the unconscious mind. We rank our needs/goals, which are passed through to the conscious mind, according to what is missing in our lives. For example, money, companionship, sex, status, and so on. As these needs/goals surface in the conscious mind, we think about them regularly, which adds strength to their contribution to the quantum bio-magnetic field. Nevertheless, some of the needs/goals may not surface and we can be quite oblivious of their existence. In this case we may, therefore, be unknowingly in denial of them.

I have spoken with a few people who actually believe that we should not have any needs or wants! Personally, in such cases, I believe that they are in denial, and it would be in their interest to explore why they believe this to be so. One thing is for sure, we can all have infinite wants but we have only a finite number of needs. I believe that part of Western society's life challenge is to bring the *'want more'* syndrome into balance. A syndrome of this type can quite easily lead to uncontrollable greed. Greed is a personality, or mask. It has a light and dark characteristic, with the latter contained in the Shadow-self. And it is in our best interest to bring the Greed personality into balance, should it ever surface.

The dark or Shadow characteristic of greed is the part which induces an individual to do anything to satisfy their insatiable appetite for, say, money, power, material goods, sex, and so on. In such cases they will plunder everything, from pension funds to antiques, to weak-minded individuals, to get what they want. An example of an excess of the Light characteristic would be someone who collects things like paintings, or coins, or books for the sake of hoarding them. They have a surplus that they do not require. The Light element, like the Dark, should be worked with and brought into balance. When greed is brought into balance, the individual concerned will have realised that there is no scarcity or lack in their life. Scarcity or lack is usually running in their unconscious mind, controlled by a strong fear. If they operate from the authentic-self with the right intention and focus, what they want will manifest at the right time. Removing the fear, which is coming from a feeling of lack, is the key.

Attracting a Rewarding Personal Relationship
If you intend to look for a partner, there is a simple process that you can use which involves three steps. Like all the processes in this book, they are most effective when you are in a relaxed state. The steps are:

1. Focus in your mind the type of partner that you are looking for. Use your imagination. When you are doing this it is important to recall a strong, warm, positive emotion (feeling) to energise the thought you have in mind. It is the supporting emotion that increases the power of the energy attraction factor. The supporting thought is information which carries only a limited energy. A word of caution. To attract a harmonious partner, it is absolutely essential to disable your ego. If your ego is

engaged in your drive to attract a partner, then you will be in for an unwanted experience. This is a life lesson associated with ego!

2. After completing the first step, let the thought go. Do not keep going back into the process as that will render it much less effective. Should the thought keep popping into your mind then just recall something positive to ease it out again. You would not dream of digging up a seed that you planted in your garden each day to see how much it has grown! The same holds true for an energised thought.

3. Last but not least, take some action. Get your-self out and about – play some sport, go to classes where you will meet like-minded people, travel, and so on. Another note of caution on the action part – do not go out with the specific purpose of finding someone. Energetically, you reverse the whole process into one of searching, and searching begets searching, which becomes a never-ending cycle. In this situation you are coming from lack. Go out to have some fun and enjoyment, not to find a partner. Enjoy, and your quantum bio-magnetic field will do the rest! Trust is a most important ingredient here as well as a life lesson.

You may meet someone quite quickly or it may take some time. Take action by keeping your-self in circulation and watch for synchronistic events to occur. These could be an unexpected party, or an urge to go shopping, or to accept an invitation to go off with some friends on an outing, or on holiday, and so on. Just stay in the game!

Behind the scenes in your unconscious mind will be some basic needs/goals which require being satisfied (energetically) when you meet a potential partner. Basic needs/goals are fairly straightforward to understand. They can differ depending on your culture, social status, financial status, religion, and so on. Some of the basic needs/goals which most people in society have and which those seeking to form a relationship typically look to have satisfied are to:

- feel valued
- be listened to and understood
- belong to a social group in which you feel comfortable
- feel part of a family
- feel secure
- have a home

If there are issues of financial insecurity running within either one or both parties, the following will be dominant:

- the need to be financially secure
- the need to have lots of material goods and large property

If you are within the right age group a major need will be to:

- get married, procreate and raise a family

When you meet someone and you both feel that there is a connection, there will most probably be matching needs/goals. These needs/goals will be part of your quantum bio-magnetic field and your two fields will connect. At times, during your search, physical attraction (ego and hormones) may be the dominant feeling. In this case, the relationship will most probably end up being short-term. Sometimes, a strong financial insecurity or lack of social status or other need/goal in one of the parties can prolong such a relationship beyond its natural conclusion.

When both partners have matching needs/goals, some of them will also be in the Shadow side. This could be matching levels of abuse of some kind. They may remain hidden until both partners have gone through what can be called the honeymoon period, during which both of them will be trying to please each other. The Pleaser personality will have been in full operation. Certainly, once the honeymoon period is over, some of the positive masks that each of them may be hiding behind will drop, and their Shadow sides will begin to show at appropriate times. Their task is to recognise this and to work through the issues (life lessons) that come to the surface, preferably in a harmonious atmosphere.

If the atmosphere in a relationship is disturbing or aggressive, then it is advisable to ask why. Is it a fear, perhaps a repressed victim-consciousness, that is arising from within one or the other partner, or both, which is causing angry outbursts? Sometimes a couple may be required to seek professional support as neither of them will have the skills to unlock the emotions involved. They may be too close to each other and require external support. In today's society, a therapist can be of great assistance to unravel personal issues and emotions and help bring a relationship back into balance. In the final chapter I elaborate on how to manifest a harmonious relationship, by showing you what may be blocking this.

Invisible Relationship Challenges

Everybody enters a personal relationship with their own baggage (that is their life lessons or issues) including their needs/goals. Little do parents realise that they are major contributors to the strength or weakness of their children's particular needs/goals (and future baggage). The strength of basic needs such as the love we desire, physical contact, security, home, food, money, a job and so on, is all affected by the parents' interaction, or lack of, with their children, and by other authority figures. A point to note is that if parents have not worked through their own personal growth issues, some of which may be a carryover from their parents, who in turn carried them over from their parents and so on, these issues will unknowingly be taken on by their children! Should this happen, it could also strengthen or weaken the intensity of some of the children's specific needs/goals. As my American friends would say, the big whammy here is the mirroring that is taking place. The quantum bio-magnetic field's attraction factor within family members ensures that the life lessons are put in place and ready to surface at an appropriate time. This broadens the belief that a marital or close personal relationship is only about procreation, camaraderie, sex, money, having lots of material goods, sharing and so on.

When I was in my teens, twenties and early thirties, my main focus (representing some of my inner needs/goals) was on ambition, sex, material possessions, earning a good salary, camaraderie and so on, somewhat similar to all of my friends. As I matured, I slowly but surely began to understand that there was more to forming a close relationship than I was brought up to believe from my parents, friends, the media and so on. Life really became much more stable (in the long-term) and interesting when I broadened my horizon. My needs/goals began to change when I passed my forties. What I was looking for then was a like-minded soul interested in exploring, travelling and seeking out the truth in its many forms.

Once both partners 'get it' and understand what a relationship is really about, it becomes a rich and rewarding experience with minimum stress.

People's needs/goals vary enormously as can the pressure (usually unconscious) that society is subjecting them to. A live-in partnership can be described as one of the best human laboratories for personal development which includes spiritual growth. Both partners are in close contact with each other. Their task, for life to be agreeable and harmonious, is to work at balancing any issues (life lessons) which will arise between them, as they journey along their life's path. Once they understand the principal dynamics involved (that is, what is really going on) in the relationship, this task should be much easier.

Getting on with Each Other
In a relationship, the underlying raison d'être is the growth potential (both personal and spiritual) that exists between both parties. I put forward, for your consideration, the secret of success of not only personal relationships but all the types of relationships that you may develop during your lifetime. In Diagram 5.17 I use two terms to describe the energetic forces that contribute to making or breaking a relationship. The first is that for both parties to successfully navigate life's challenges, both are required to be 'responsive' to each other (the green line in diagram 5.17 represents a high probability of success).

Secret of a Successful Relationship

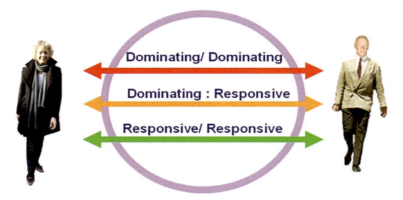

Diagram 5.17

This requires each to understand him/herself, and also what makes the other partner tick. Both people in this case 'get it'. They recognise the different attributes of their persona, masks and Shadows that arise within the relationship and are able to discuss them with each other to bring those that are out of balance into balance. Issues and conflicts are no longer a battleground but a platform to achieve much personal development and spiritual growth.

The second term is 'dominating'. When a person enters the realm of domination they are in the arena of control, of power, of authority, of much criticism. A dominating partnership (the red line above representing danger and instability) can be a living hell as each party tries to control the other. Abuse and manipulation are two of the main tools that are used in what can be described as a 'battleground' relationship. The abuse and manipulation can take many forms. Verbal, emotional and physical abuse can be applied at the same time, but verbal and emotional tend to be the most widely used. Personal development in these cases cannot occur unless one party splits to join with another partner, or alters their behaviour as they come to acknowledge what is going on. It requires one, or preferably both of the parties involved to be willing to step back because they acknowledge what is happening and recognise that it is in their best interest to make a change within themselves. If they do not, and terminate the relationship, there is a high probability that they will attract another partner who will give them *more of the same* until they 'get it'.

Perhaps the most common type of relationship is the dominating/responsive type (the orange line in the above diagram represents a state of caution). Either partner will attempt to dominate the other from time to time, but they may recognise, or have brought to their attention, what is going on within the relationship. There is potential for much personal development in such a relationship as each person attempts to create a balance arising from any conflict. If one partner constantly dominates the other, who acquiesces every time, then there is no potential for a balance to take place. The probability of a split in such cases is high. If the partnership remains intact, there will be little if any personal development and spiritual growth. Insecurity may be a major reason. The weak partner may remain in the relationship due to a fear of becoming homeless, or without sufficient finance to have an acceptable lifestyle, or loss of social status, or for the children's sake, or for fear of not finding another suitable partner, and so forth. If one partner understands what is happening but the other doesn't wish to, the relationship will probably become a minefield, to put it mildly. Good communication between both parties is a must, together with an open mind and - above all - a strong emotional intelligence.

Whoever you Partner with – You are Right for Each Other!
If you are looking for and find a live-in partner, or a girl/boy friend, or marriage partner, who likes you, then you most probably have a good energetic fit. This means that your needs/goals and, of course, personality structure (including differences) are compatible. You can both expect some personal development and spiritual growth. If you chose for reasons that solely satisfy physical/material sides and your wants, for example, or combinations of 'must be good looking, be tall or short, be well-built and strong, have a great figure, have plenty of money, be a great lover, be socially well connected' and so on, you may still succeed in finding a partner. The problem here is that the chance of your staying together for the right reasons is most likely going to be small!

As mid-life is reached, it can be a crisis time! Besides the hormonal changes that occur, in a relationship where only one partner has gained a broader understanding of what life is about and the other is just not interested, there is potential for the relationship to break up. For what was meaningful in the past may no longer be meaningful. Each may have developed totally different interests in life, adding to their non-compatibility. That divorce courts are bulging at the seams is a testament to these facts. In many cases, couples only stay together for the children's sake, or for material or social or prestige reasons. But even though a relationship may be emotionally barren and miserable, couples may choose to stay together. It may surprise you that in every case, the underlying reason for staying together is, unconsciously, about life lessons involving personal and spiritual growth. Taking this point into consideration highlights an interesting conclusion that:

1. there are no wrong relationships!

If this was clearly understood, it could raise the energy dynamics within a partnership for the best of all those concerned. This includes any children belonging to that partnership. Acknowledging the issues and life lessons that each is carrying, and working through them, would make a significant impact on their personal development and spiritual growth. Without this we are back to being like a hamster on the wheel going round and round and round with no apparent purpose. That is, of course, until we 'get it'!

After the Honeymoon

I had a close friend called Dan in the United Nations who had had three wives, all of whom looked exactly alike. One sadly died leaving him with a son, and the other two divorced him. By the time he reached fifty, he found a new partner who better fitted his needs. Nature usually makes sure that the chemistry of a matching couple (that is the pheromones they give off) is strong enough to bring them physically together. And, of course you can be sure that they have matching needs/goals. When this happens, the couple can choose whether or not they wish to enter a permanent relationship. If they do, once the honeymoon period is over, both partners in the relationship will have begun to expose their true selves, warts and all. This is where the compatibility of personalities and matching of needs can form a positive bonding force to keep the relationship going. If there is some negative incompatibility, this is not necessarily a bad thing. It just means that the lessons to be learned will most probably be a bit more challenging and perhaps a bit more painful and stressful.

Most people who enter difficult relationships usually do so unconsciously for the growth potential that exists. It is what their soul desires. Sometimes it can be driven solely by the ego, which is guaranteed to end in disaster of some kind or another! Ego, at times, can have sufficient power to over-ride the soul's desire. Each soul has the ability to read the energetic personality profile and needs/goals of the partner in a relationship and its purpose is to play out the relationship to learn the life lessons that arise from within it.

Guess what Lasting Relationships Need?

The great energy-balancing force that acts like pouring oil on troubled waters in unhappy relationships is the level of emotional intelligence (EQ – Chapter 6) and diagram 5.18. Without a reasonable EQ, couples in close relationships can spend a considerable amount of time sailing through stormy waters together, arguing and sniping as they interact. Not a good idea, as it will add to the stress levels of both parties concerned. EQ joins the ranks of a principal relationship builder, as shown in

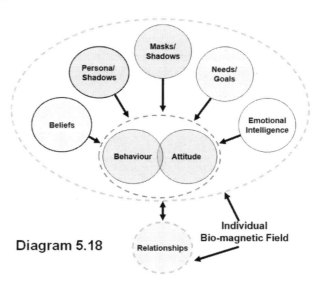

Diagram 5.18

diagram 5.18, and has a strong effect on whether or not a relationship will stand the test of time. There tends to be a problem in the West where society prizes the development of the intellect and knowledge at the expense of emotional intelligence. A great deal of analysis of relationship experiences has been carried out and a handy checklist of what to do or not do is available. This does little to strengthen the bonds between two people. Good relationships are not obtained by ticking the relevant boxes of some expert's checklist. Strong foundations are put in place through developing such characteristics as:

- Empathy and Diplomacy. Developing empathy focuses on the ability to identify with and understand a partner's feelings, motives; the situation they are in, and the personal issues and lessons that they are working through. Diplomacy focuses upon the skilful and sensitive handling of situations that arise in a relationship. Personal and spiritual development in life is about the way we *handle* ourselves, our partner and those involved in a relationship with us.

- Compromise and Accommodation. These are great builders that strengthen the bonds between those involved. It is also an excellent test to see if we are over-controlling or weak. The key is to remain in balance.

Acting on the above qualities, which are a major part of emotional intelligence, can lead to acceptable attitudes, behaviour and genuine acts of denial which should not be seen as weakness. It is a sign of someone who feels strong within their identity and who has the ability to keep the peace. They have a high level of emotional intelligence. It is always so much easier to simply let a negative personality or Shadow flare up, or cause the ego to give rise to unfortunate attitudes and behaviour, without thinking about the consequences. Both the perpetrator and receiver of an outburst suffer from the flow of negative energy and words that ensue. Each individual is affected by increased levels of stress and the emotional consequences which arise from a negative outburst. When difficult situations are handled well, those involved experience personal and inner (spiritual) growth. If a situation is not handled well this will cause the attraction of similar occurrences until they learn the relevant lesson(s). Not learning from the situations we find ourselves in effectively puts us back onto the hamster wheel until we 'get it'.

Can you Sense your Partner's Feelings?
In a relationship, sensing how our partner is feeling is a big plus. If we can read our partner's moods we will be an absolute star! That is, of course, provided our EQ is also strong enough to deal with the cause and effect of any difficult moods, or mood swings, that they may be experiencing. The good news is that it is a reasonably straightforward task for us to sense our partner's mood. Psychologists have shown that when we are looking at someone, the conscious mind allocates a certain amount of its time to analysing the other person's behaviour, including body language, tone of voice and the words they use. Apparently about

55 percent (diagram 5.19) of the conscious mind's processing time is used to assess body language; about 38 percent in analysing the tone of voice and about 7 percent in analysing the words used. Eyes and ears are the obvious sensors here, but there is another sensor that you are now aware of. As both partners in a relationship have a quantum bio-magnetic field, this too is a part of the cross-examination process which operates through the Solar Plexus sensor. How can you tune into it? In your imagination, move your mind down into the solar plexus region. How you feel within your solar plexus is important. Do you feel a tension there? Do you have a warm or cold feeling, or do you feel nothing at all? Keep practising this until you pick up sensitive feelings in the solar plexus, or elsewhere.

Psychology of communications in a relationship

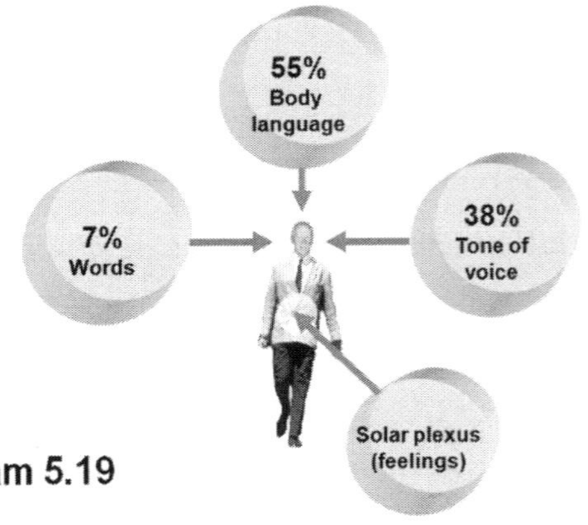

Diagram 5.19

I was fortunate to be able to strengthen my own solar plexus sensing in different business environments. I used this sensing mechanism in international business negotiations while sitting round a table, by focusing (in my mind) on the solar plexus of each of the business persons attending. This gave me a feel of how they were (tense, not interested, angry, and so on). Some were able to hide their natural behaviour well by keeping an expressionless face, placing their hands on the table and speaking in a smooth, monotonic voice. They could not, however, disguise their bio-magnetic field which, when accessed through the solar plexus centre showed how they really felt. In Arabia, I found that people there have a natural ability to hide their behaviour and to control their voice tones. Tuning into their bio-magnetic field via the solar plexus during a meeting was a distinct advantage because I was able to sense where the opposition was coming from and whether or not they were bluffing; frequently this resulted in more favourable terms being obtained through a compromise.

Sensing the truth in communications

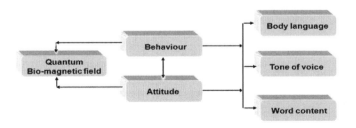

Diagram 5.20

Diagram 5.20 shows the energy links caused by an individual's attitude and supporting behaviour as well as the link to the quantum bio-magnetic field. Although people can be trained to disguise their voice tones or body language and to be careful with the words they use, they cannot disguise their quantum bio-magnetic field which provides a true indication of what is running within their consciousness.

Tuning into your Partner's Feelings

There is a short process that you can use to quiz your partner's Solar Plexus sensor. When you do this, I would ask you to note that you are really operating at a sub-atomic level (within the quantum world). When you start thinking of what happens in the fifth dimension (energy) and within the dimensions of the second paradigm (end of chapter 1), you unconsciously open the possibility of connecting with the laws that operate within the quantum world. The statement *'it's all in the mind'* is a crucial key here, and so true.

The steps involved in the process to connect with the Solar Plexus sensor are:

- Prepare your-self by getting into a relaxed position and begin to focus on your breathing. Get into a regular rhythm of breathing through your diaphragm before you begin and keep it going automatically. You can do this with your partner or someone else. I would suggest that a 5:3 breathing rhythm would be good in this case. For example, breathe in for a count of 5, hold for 3 then breathe out 5, and hold for 3. Continue until you get into a natural, deep, breathing rhythm. Remember to always breathe through your diaphragm and not your upper chest.

- Clear your mind of any clutter! If you have lots of different thoughts roaming around your conscious mind, use a visualisation technique to tune out those thoughts and to strengthen your mind's focus. For example, see in your mind a favourite scene, and if the chatter in your mind interferes, keep changing the scene, or focus more on the detail until it stops.

- You are now ready to begin the connection process to the other person's solar plexus. Just see in your mind a pipe of light moving from your solar plexus to their solar plexus. You are now connected. It really is that simple.

- Now move your *awareness* down to your solar plexus (you have energetically positioned your consciousness within your own solar plexus sensor). Notice how you feel. Do you feel tense or relaxed? You may have to practise to fine-tune how you interpret the feelings you pick up.

- Remain connected while you are in conversation and for the duration that you are discussing an issue, or some problem, or negotiating something, and so on .

- After you have finished, it is absolutely essential that you disconnect from them. In your mind, see your-self cutting the connecting pipe at their solar plexus and retract it back into yours. See your-self putting a cap over it to seal it. Do the same for them.

You are protecting your-self here as you do not want to be walking around picking up their feelings, which you would do if you do not disconnect, and vice versa.

This process will be recorded within your unconscious mind when you practise it. The more you practise the easier it should become. When you are interested in someone, this connection automatically takes place. Usually, there is so much clutter in our mind that we do not realise it. The above process will help you to connect and especially to disconnect.

The Truth about Relationships!
In any relationship, what happens between two or more individuals is affected by their belief system and needs/goals. During the last two decades, technology (thanks to the influence of quantum mechanics), the structure of society, social interaction, travel, and telecommunications, have advanced at an exponential pace. To keep up with the reality of what has been happening and to be able to meet the challenges of the 21st century requires a *belief system upgrade*. This is especially true in relationships and the challenges that they present. Such challenges are made much easier to appreciate when we have a clearer idea about why we are here, who we are and that we have a definite purpose. There are also good reasons behind the diverse experiences that we encounter on our life's path. Learning from the choices/decisions we make is a crucial part of our growth.

An individual's belief system can get corrupted by many false beliefs, related to themselves and the world around them, that they have been conditioned to accept. We are generally unaware that so much of what happens to us is activated through the unseen world of energy (the fifth dimension) by the quantum bio-magnetic field. Great artists, scientists, writers, engineers, athletes and so on naturally tune in to the fifth dimension. Some are quite unaware, but others know that they are doing it. Now that you have upgraded your understanding of what we are, a physical as well as a being of energy with a bio-magnetic field and a soul, there should be less of a mystery with respect to relationships. Accepting that relationships are a key learning platform for life's lessons, I would suggest that:

2. there are no bad relationships!

'How can this be so?' many of you will be thinking. I hear again and again in workshops and seminars where participants say 'I know of so many people who are in miserable and unhappy relationships. What you are saying is absolute rubbish! No one in their right mind would enter into such dreadful relationships'. Those who make such statements do not realise the whole truth about why they are here in a human body, or why their lives actually play out the way they do? If they did, then things would look quite different and the experiences of those involved would be interpreted as being constructive rather than destructive. Take for instance, in our authentic-self's environment (the sub-atomic world), we are 100 percent responsible for what happens to us in our lives and by increasing our awareness of what life is about we can quickly learn to make better choices/decisions. How can I make this bold statement? Quite simply because, once again, we are:

- a soul in a physical body that is growing spiritually through the experiences caused by the choices/decisions we make.

- a quantum bio-magnet field generator, attracting to us and being attracted to people, situations, activities and events which are to be a part of our learning experience.

Of course, procreation of our species is important, but our growth as a soul is just, if not more, important than procreation. Buying a house, cars, clothes, jewellery and other material things are a part of life, but these are only the tapestry or stage props. They accompany us as we work our way through the different acts/scenes of life that help us to gain our life experiences. Satisfying our needs and reaching our goals is fine so long as we can also hone up on our life skills along the way.

I use throughout the book the concept of our life taking place on our own personal theatrical stage. The actors, different acts/scenes, stage settings and props are all there because we have attracted them to us or us to them through what is running in our consciousness (that is conscious, unconscious and higher conscious minds). They are all there to teach us something! The problem is with the education and training we have been exposed to which has unknowingly restricted the way that we perceive life and the way we think. Fear is a powerful driver in our virtual box of thinking, which has caused us to strongly focus upon the material and physical characteristics (the stage settings and props) of life. We measure people's success by such features as their titles, money, possessions, intellectual ability, fame and physical attributes. I always remember my Scottish grandfather saying when I talked about buying and collecting things as a young man, 'always remember John that you cannot take them with you when you go'. So true, but hey, why not enjoy some of them while we are here! Everything in moderation is absolutely fine.

The more I work with people trying to unravel their life lessons and what is happening within their relationships, the more I am drawn to say to them:

3. your relationship was meant to happen!

You will have gathered by now that whether or not we enter any short- or long-term relationship, the unconscious reason for each party's involvement is for personal development (personal, emotional and inner (spiritual) growth). A characteristic of our persona, which I would suggest we need to recognise and correct, is that we are addicted to judging. Certainly, making judgements is a part of life's experience, but not to the extent to which the practice has become common place within society over the years. It can be said that our judging capability is completely *out of control*. How can I make such a bold statement? I make it because I realise that I usually do not know what is happening in the life of the person or people I am making a judgement about. I was also helped in this quest by being able to step back and to learn from what was happening in my space. To do this I had to make an effort to upgrade my awareness. Since then I have seldom looked back, and am continually learning how the Universal Laws of the sub-atomic world affect me at a physical, four-dimensional level. This is especially important in understanding the reasons behind my behaviour and the different attitudes I show. Was my upgrade difficult at times? Absolutely, I had to ease myself out of my comfort zone and shed the many false beliefs I had taken on from childhood as well as throughout my life. Has this affected my views about making judgements in a relationship? Most certainly, especially after realising that I am 100 percent responsible for what I attract. To summarise some of the key issues, we are:

- growing through life's challenges as we learn to make better choices/decisions from the situations/experiences we have attracted to us or are attracted to in our partnerships.

- a form of bio-magnetic mirror. This means that our partners, at times, reflect our issues back to us and vice versa (it is not them it is me!). The world around us and every person we meet is, from time to time, reflecting back, to some degree, the challenges that we're required to grow from. We only need to recognise and acknowledge them. But sometimes the mirroring can be so subtle that we miss it.

- human beings born with a self-correcting capability. What does this mean? It means that we are always given an opportunity to make a choice/decision to initiate a change. That is, if we have identified the need and have the stamina and courage to do so. A problem arises when we lack the ability to see the synchronicity of events that are occurring in our life. This happens because of the clutter in our mind. The clutter, together with any false beliefs, prevents us from understanding what is really happening.

- not given an understanding that in order to achieve a happy and content life, it is important to stay out of any *drama* that may confront us. This may prove to be difficult, as doing so is a major life challenge and life lesson. The task here is to absorb the essence from what is going on, and not to become involved in the details of the drama. A drama just heightens negative energy exchanges, which reduces the chance of a diplomatic solution. Dramas are addictive, leading us to want more. TV soap opera ratings rise with every increase in a family crisis, which helps to promote a drama culture. This is not exactly good for audience stress levels and health, nor are some of the role models conducive to creating a harmonious family life.

- o not taught to understand the subtleties of the ego and how it can work for or against us in a relationship, or elsewhere. Ego can be a great destroyer until an understanding of its purpose is gained. A life lesson is to bring the ego into balance.

- o not taught to understand the synchronicity of different activities and situations that happen in our lives, nor why people enter our lives. Life is usually viewed as a series of random occurrences. Upgrading our awareness to accept that this is not so is essential. A major discovery here is that there are few, if any, random occurrences. This can make life very exciting indeed.

All of the above has helped me to be less judgemental in relationships and I believe that I have become more understanding and compassionate. For I have learnt that much of what is happening in my relationships is teaching me something about myself. This has led me to the conclusion that:

4. every relationship has a purpose!

There are no exceptions to this statement! The essence of why there are no bad or wrong relationships lies in understanding that the experience gained is for personal, emotional and inner (spiritual) growth. That is why every relationship has a purpose. We are all given the power to make our own choices/decisions. This dictates whether we enter a relationship or not. When we enter a relationship we are given a choice as to how long we stay in it. If a relationship is stagnant, we can try different ways to revive it. If this does not work, then there is no growth, probably because real communication and understanding has ceased. In such cases, it is time to consider a change. Making this choice is reasonably straightforward, provided there are no children involved. Life can become much more complicated when children are brought into the world. I waited eight years before I sued for a divorce, for family reasons. The emotional cost to my-self was enormous and 'hanging on in there' is not a decision that I would recommend. With hindsight, in my case, it would have been best if I had made a clean break as soon as possible. I had a son though, and making sure that he was looked after was my first concern. I chose to do so and I do not regret that decision, for I have learnt much more about myself and what relationships mean.

If you are in a relationship and it is proving to be difficult, take a good look at your-self first. Try to figure out what is going on within your-self. You may not realise it, but your partner is presenting you with some gifts. Some of you of course may be thinking that this statement is absolutely nuts! Well, it is most certainly not, for you are actually mirroring your issues back from your partner. Your partner is simply reflecting them back to you through their communications, behaviour and different attitudes. On the other hand, you are also reflecting your partner's issues back to them. Both partners need to understand what is going on, otherwise the relationship may become fraught. If this happens, and in the end there is no communication, then it is time to consider moving on as there is no growth. An important key to success here, for both parties, is to 'know your-self'.

Family Relationships

My Western education and culture provided me with only a limited understanding of the real purpose of my being here in a physical body. Why should this be important? From my perspective, it is particularly important when we enter into the realm of families, and especially raising a family. We are much more than 'I am my father's son or my mother's son, my father's daughter or my mother's daughter'. These statements focus upon our biological status (blood line) and, to a degree, emotional status. Most of us may be firmly entrenched with the view that the bloodline is an all important feature in life. It may surprise and even shock you to know that this is not so. For the soul and its experience in the physical body (it is a bit like 'rent a body' in spiritual terms) is what life is really about. The progression of the soul has little to do with the blood line as the body is the vehicle used for the soul's experience.

A soul may be a king or president in one lifetime and a taxi driver or farmer in another. The physical body is the soul's vehicle for experiencing life through the different choices/decisions we make. Groups of souls can incarnate together in families in the same country for the purpose of mutual soul growth. My research has shown that we change race, culture and so on to meet our spirit's growth requirement! Because of the way we have been programmed to think, this is a statement that will no doubt seem unbelievable, if not ridiculous to most people. But in one lifetime you may be European, or American, or Chinese, or Indian, or African, and so on. In another lifetime you may change country, religion, race and culture. It all depends on the growth a particular spirit needs.

We need to understand some basic facts about the phenomenon of bringing a baby into this world. You may already be aware of some of them. Diagram 5.21 starts with a baby at birth in a state of innocence, which represents its original authentic-self. From birth to seven years of age is crucial as this is when the child is programmed by all those individuals (parents, siblings, relations, friends, teachers and other authority figures) that they come into contact

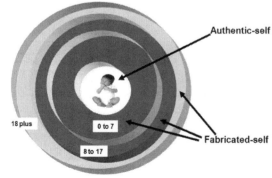

Authentic (inner) Self and Fabricated (outer) Self

Diagram 5.21

with. A baby runs purely on emotions until its prefrontal cortex develops substantially from about seven years onwards. It uses all its sensors including its energy ones (vortex energy centres – chapter 3) to get a feel of what is happening around it. Very quickly, the baby/child realises that its job is to please, as this brings rewards. After all, if the giants surrounding the baby/child reject it, then it instinctively knows that it will die. As the child grows, between ages 8 and 17 its capacity to use logic and reason also grows, thanks to the development of the prefrontal cortex. Of course, when the child enters the teenage years, hormones start circulating and the young individual begins to not only flex their muscles but also claim or assert their independence.

Children too mirror our issues back to us! In the relationship between us and our children lie many surprises. From an energy perspective, children are little:

- o quantum (energy) mirrors reflecting our own issues back to us (and vice versa)

- o energy tape recorders, storing everything that is being said to them and around them within the unconscious mind part of their third (Intellect) subtle energy body (Chapter 3) and physical brain

- o energy tape recorders, storing the emotional energy/feelings behind the thoughts and verbal statements of those communicating with them within the unconscious mind part of their second (Emotional) subtle energy body and also the physical body

So, when they hit puberty, do not be surprised if some of your children's behaviour is outrageous. Parents and siblings , relations, friends, school, authority figures and the media have all contributed to how our teenagers are, energetically, emotionally and physically! Maturing from childhood through teens into adulthood, logic and reason develops rapidly and we become much more rational (hopefully). Let me suggest to you some more food for thought that you may already be aware of:

'we are all driven by our emotions'

I make a point in describing the Shadow-self above, that suppressed emotional energy affects our unconscious mind and physical body. This trapped energy forms clusters within a child's second subtle (Emotional) energy body and their physical body. Such clusters can grow to cause blockages to the natural energy flow around the child's energy body circuits that need to be released at some time in the future. As a child is like a little quantum bio-magnet, they will unconsciously and automatically attract to them similar experiences to the ones that caused the trapped emotions. Unless they find a way to *release* this trapped energy, they will carry it through to adulthood until they experience an energetic explosion within. When this happens it can cause an accident, or an illness, or an emotional problem.

Most parents usually do not realise the extent to which they are constantly conditioning their children. There is another important concept that parents may not be aware of. A baby takes on a pattern of both the mother's and father's issues which are imprinted within its energy structure. These tend to have been passed down to both parents from their parents who had them passed down by their parents and so on. An interesting process occurs here. In adulthood, if a parent works through an issue and clears it, something short of a miracle occurs. They automatically clear the same issues within their child (or children). It is part of a healing process which results from the invisible connections that exist at the sub-atomic or quantum level between the individual concerned and family members. The healing process obeys Universal Laws which operate outside of the physical reality that we understand.

All members of a family's energy structure are inter-linked. They automatically tune in energetically to one another. I call this the energetic links Through these links, information and emotions (including issues and life lessons) are transferred at a sub-atomic level. This is not generally understood and is only slowly becoming recognised. Accepting the energy links, you can begin to see why clearing any blocks with or without a therapist's help, is enormously beneficial for everybody concerned. As we are all connected at an energy level, understanding the quantum physics law of entanglement (non locality – chapter 1) can be of great help here. This is because gaining an appreciation of what is going on at the fifth dimension (energy) will help us to have a better understanding of what is going on within our-self and within those around us.

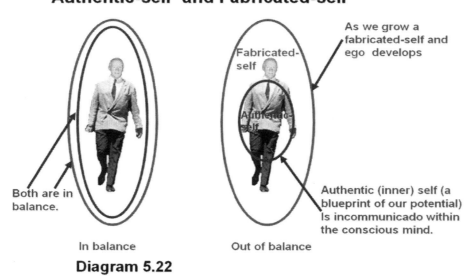

Diagram 5.22

In diagram 5.21, I showed what I call the fabricated-self which begins to develop from birth. Looking at the right-hand side of diagram 5.22, the fabricated-self is in control. The individual's authentic-self is nearly always cut off from their awareness during adulthood, because of the overwhelming power of the fabricated-self. When the fabricated-self is in control it gives ego free reign to do its thing, and ego is the strong influence here. A principal lesson in life is, first of all, to acknowledge that ego is a strong driving force and a dominant feature in our attitude and behaviour. A second important point to make is that it is to our advantage to acknowledge when a mask (identity) is a main feature controlling our attitude and behaviour, because the mask is not who we truly are. Finally, other parts of our persona may also be out of balance, causing a variety of unfortunate attitudes or behaviours at times.

The left-hand side of diagram 5.22 above (this is an energy representation of our self) shows an ideal state where the fabricated-self has merged with and is in balance with the authentic-self. In this case, the individual's awareness is able to communicate with their authentic or inner-self. Why is this important? It is important because in this state there is an intuitive understanding of what our purpose and life path is. It also means that there will be an ability to naturally sense our partner's and family's needs and to *act* accordingly. If the fabricated-self is solely doing the driving, then we will mostly *react* to demands placed on us. This is not a healthy situation for all those concerned.

As acceptance of the reality of the sub-atomic or quantum world and the power of the Universal Laws that operate there grows, a transformation within you will take place. This transformation is caused by:

- the opening of doors in your consciousness to raise awareness of what is really happening. This may take some time as a new brain map is being put in place
- an increase in perception of what is really happening in your life
- a better understanding of your family's dynamics, your contribution to them and vice versa.

Children are put under a lot of pressure to conform. Consciously and/or unconsciously, a parent wants them to comply with their wishes. The danger here is that a parent may not realise that it is their own ego that is causing them to put pressure on their children. It is in a child's own best interest to feel what is best for them. Most can, if given the chance, though some may not. Children are in touch with their authentic-self which will give them direction. If ego is running the parent, then they are operating from their fabricated-self. In cases such as this, status (for the parent and child) rears its head and demands recognition, usually much to the detriment of the child concerned. For example, the parents speak of prestigious professions like neurosurgeon, or medical doctor, or chief executive officer, or lawyer, and so on. When a child hears the reverence that the parent holds for such positions, they will want to please, so they say –' mummy or daddy I would like to be a neurosurgeon (or a. . .) when I grow up'. This is only to please the parent and does little to help the child inform the parent with any confidence what it really wants to do. But do parents know best? This is an interesting question, and the answer depends on the parent's perception of what life is really about! A parent so easily projects their unfulfilled needs/goals and/or fears onto their children. The child or young adult then enters the world trying to fulfil the parent's needs and goals and not their own.

Many surveys have been carried out in Britain and in other countries to measure how people feel about their job. A shocking statistic emerged from the results of one of these surveys. Taking London (UK) as an example, it was apparent that 80 to 90 percent of the population hated their jobs and are only really there for money to pay the bills. Each of the participants had parents, so what was missing from their upbringing that caused them to be so unhappy and unfulfilled? This book contains some answers and solutions to help the reader to understand various changes that they may wish to consider. Making these changes is a step forward to ensure that you and your children have a more fulfilling and happy life.

Addictions Start Within the Family
Two important challenges in life are associated with addictions. The first challenge is to try to avoid them, and the second is to get rid of them by recognising and working through them. Addictions, to which we can all fall prey, come in many forms, for example work, sex, alcohol, drugs, food, beauty, power, fame, sport and so on. Addictions can start at an early age and arise to satisfy a need/goal. Right at the core of the need is usually the failure to satisfy an emotion. So many families have not been brought up to appreciate the power of emotions.

I believe that most of my generation and previous ones have had no training in emotional intelligence. It was not thought of, and certainly not discussed, or even called by any other name throughout my entire education. Emotional intelligence is talked about much more today, especially in the context of the way people treat one another without regard to the impact of their conduct upon others. Nevertheless, the understanding of emotional intelligence tends to be limited only to how individuals interact with one another. If I look back along my ancestral trail, most certainly, my grandparents, great grandparents and so on would have had little if any training in emotional intelligence. And if they did understand it, it would have been through a natural intuitive understanding. Strong emotional intelligence is important because:

addictions are caused by an emotional deficit

What do I mean by this? As human beings, and as beings of energy, there is a need to experience an inner positive emotional connection with the surrounding environment (people, locations, buildings, situations, activities, and so on). Such an emotional connection contributes to an inner feeling of positive wellbeing, security and happiness. As pointed out, from birth and during early years of development, everybody has a need to connect with others both physically and energetically (emotionally), otherwise they will get out of balance. A minimal energetic connection creates an *emotional deficit*. To ensure that a child has a strong emotional connection and foundation within, the child needs to be given plenty of physical contact, including hugs, positive voice tones when communicating, reassuring smiles, encouraging feedback about its achievements, and to experience a positive energy atmosphere at home. Similarly, the child also needs to be made aware of the part they play in creating that positive atmosphere, or its opposite, especially as they grow older. This is a tough order given the social, media and consumer pressures on parents today.

For individuals who are emotionally out of balance, they will turn to something (booze, drugs, sex, food, work and so on) to plug the energy (emotional) gap which has unknowingly been created. As quantum bio-magnets, they will be attracted to something to enable them to fill that gap. It is essential to ask why they may be behaving in such a way. Are they in *denial* of something? Yes, for they are. But what has caused this denial?

I once worked with a businessman called Jack who had some personal problems that were bugging him. As I got to know him better I discovered that his mother had denied him a close supportive love and used her controller sub-personality to keep him doing extra homework. She had wanted him to get top grades and do well in the world. He of course wanted to go out to play with his friends but was denied the opportunity. I asked Jack if he had received lots of hugs and warm embraces while he was growing up. He couldn't remember any! He was not only in denial about his playful side (the inner-child which was suppressed), but also about his emotional needs. He tended to go over the top with respect to alcohol and to feel unfulfilled, even though he was successful enough in business to afford himself a grand house, fast car, and so on. Throughout his life, Jack was very success-driven in terms of getting qualifications, getting promoted in the company, standing out in the social scene, gaining material possessions, and so on. Prolonged inner happiness, though, had always eluded him. Jack's story, like that of so many others, is a clear demonstration of the fact that:

'when ego is the main driver in life,
true inner happiness becomes a distant dream'

Because of the conditioning experienced in life, a large proportion of the population is bereft of an understanding of the true meaning of the word *'love'*. There is certainly a lack of understanding of the power (energy) behind the word love. There is also a lack of awareness that *intent* can corrupt the power of the energy behind love. How can this be so? Sex has been increasingly substituted for the word love, more than ever since the 1960s and what some have called 'the sexual revolution', the mantra of which was 'make love not war'. Now there is nothing wrong with sex as it is usually the physical manifestation of love. When it is not, however, the intent behind the desire can be merely to satisfy a want or a frustration – in other words, a lack!

I have had several experiences of people where because of a growing emotional deficit, sex was being used, unconsciously, like a currency. It allowed them to feel needed. They gave themselves freely and believed they felt loved. In this context the feeling is not really love. It is a feeling of being needed. Many people grow to love sex and it becomes an addiction. This happens to the extent they don't too much care who they have sex with, or how little they know about the person(s) they give themselves freely to. Nor do they care if they never set eyes on them again. They rationalise their love of sex and are adamant that it has nothing whatsoever to do with their need for love. When one is allowed to look behind that sexual activity and explore with the individuals concerned what their early childhood and general upbringing was like, you invariably find that they did not experience a natural love in its true sense from their parents. Consequently they did not feel needed within the family. Out of this grew a limited feeling of self-love and self-acceptance, which arose from low self-esteem. How did this happen? It happened sometime after birth. It happened because their parents had limited (if any) understanding of emotional intelligence and may well have suffered themselves from a lack of it in their own upbringing. Furthermore, only recently has an understanding developed about the power of the fifth dimension (energy) and how it relates to relationships. Is this important? Certainly, because it enables those concerned to have an idea of what is going on unconsciously between both parties and also energetically within the person concerned. In this new millennium, there is a growing appreciation of the deeper parts of our being and the effect we have on one another through the medium of the fifth dimension. Understanding the power of emotions, or lack of, is a key in this dimension.

When I reflect upon the emotional deficit and emotional burden that so many individuals are carrying today, I can only repeat *'all is not as it seems'*. The downslide probably began with grandparents and parents (if not with those who went before them) who carried a huge emotional burden from the First and Second World Wars. The emotional shock and horror of these two wars, which includes the 'Holocaust', have not yet been fully dealt with and integrated within both an individual's and a country's national psyche. When I look back at the 1950s into the 1960s, the general outlook in Europe and the US was *if you did not talk about it, it did not really happen or it did not matter.* It was also a period which marked the beginning of the end of the social norm which held that *children should be seen and not heard.* All of us to some degree, whether we like it or not, carry an emotional block from these two wars and their aftermath. Unlike today, there was no general mechanism or approach to enable those who lived through the two World Wars with all their dreadful outcomes, to fully release the trapped emotions. These negative emotions became unknowingly repressed and have been passed down from generation to generation until even today.

To make sense of any un-dealt with or suppressed emotions, it is important to recognise firstly, that there is a life lesson involved and, therefore, a challenge. Second, understanding what is going on at an energy (sub-atomic) level can help us to come back into balance. In adulthood, to deal with an addiction challenge (we all face addiction challenges from time to time), it is necessary to acknowledge that we take responsibility for what is happening to us. The next step is to go within to find the cause of the challenge, accept it, work with it and bring it into balance. To create a balance, it is necessary to work through the issue, re-script it and remove the attached negative emotion. Both should be replaced with a positive outcome and a positive emotion respectively. Should you choose to do this by your-self you should do so preferably with a close friend. Otherwise, do it through a therapist.

The word 'love' is greatly misunderstood by many. If I said 'what we need is love' in a public forum, a considerable number of people would not know what I meant. Some would think immediately of sex. Some, especially macho males, would cringe and walk away. Others see love as being conditional. Some would have an image of an ideal couple that are happy, content and in harmony with each other. Others may even envisage it as nations coming together and bonding. I came across what was suggested as a universal definition of true love as an:

'unconditional attachment resulting in a harmonious permanence'

Alas, nothing could be further from the truth for the above definition is totally ego driven! At a sub-atomic level, love is an all powerful force, or energy, that can bring extreme chaos into balance. Most importantly, it should be unconditional with *no* attachment associated with it; this is true love - unconditional and unattached. If an individual is unhappy and experiences love, they can be uplifted to uncharted levels of an inner positive feeling of wellbeing and happiness. This type of love always comes from the heart. Successful healers operate from the heart.

In a *healing environment*, someone who is ill with a tumour is affected by the words that pass between them and the healer (whoever the healer may be). They are also affected by the energy that is channelled through to them from the healer. A spontaneous remission, in today's medical terms, can be experienced. In this case, what in layman's language would be termed 'a miraculous recovery' has occurred. The chaos experienced in the patient's body's cells that caused the tumour (an energy block) has been brought into balance by the patient themselves. An energy transfer transmitted through the healer to the patient has also contributed to accelerating the change.

To explain the above example further, three key conditions are required for a spontaneous remission (miracle) to occur within someone in a state of dis-ease. These are that:

1. the patient must believe that they are going to be cured

2. the healer's intent is unconditional, and that there is

3. there is no attachment to the outcome on both sides (healer and patient).

You may be wondering, why I chose the above example in this exploration of family relationships? Basically, for two reasons. The first is that the energy transfer channelled through a healer is on the same wavelength as the energy from a family member associated with love, and the second is because in a family relationship, or even a relationship between two individuals, behind the scenes at a sub-atomic level, the relationship is really all about healing in one form or another (emotional, psychological, physical and spiritual).

How can this be so? Because in a family, each individual is mirroring their own issues in other family members who are reflecting them back, and vice versa. In dealing with an issue, you are unknowingly either creating a balance from an over-negative energy state or an over-positive energy state. It is that simple. Each member of the family, in time, will hopefully bring their issues to the surface so that they can be recognised. Once this occurs, the issues can be dealt with and brought into balance by working through them. This will create order out of an energetic imbalance (chaos) within the individual family member. It will also create a more fulfilling relationship. There are three laws within a family relationship that are essential to strengthen the relationship. They are similar to those of the healing example above. The laws are that each family member:

1. believes that they are in a loving relationship

2. knows that the love is unconditional

3. experiences a strong emotional bond with no attachment to other members of the family.

These laws make or break families. Attachment can be a huge issue for many and it is often greatly misunderstood. Attachment means that one or both partners or family members are clinging onto each other. This is normally caused by those with the attachment unconsciously feeling insecure. And the insecurity most probably arose during their childhood. It would also form part of the attraction field that brought the soul of the child into a particular family at birth. The family provided the home base for the life lesson of insecurity to be instilled within the child. As the child's life progresses, other people such as authority figures, siblings, relations, friends, and so on may also contribute to the life lesson. The issue can be addressed, and brought into balance, if not during childhood, then through the teenage years or into adulthood.

Strong bonds between loving couples are not necessarily an attachment. They can be a pure energy bond of love, and all too infrequently, unconditional love. If an attachment issue arises in your life, it is necessary for you to acknowledge it, find out the cause, bring it to the surface and work with it to bring it into a state of balance (non-attachment). You may find my argument that there should be no attachment in a relationship a bit odd. Now you know the reason, hopefully you will have a better understanding of what an attachment issue is.

Once again, the strength of a lasting relationship lies in an unconditional bond of love. This bond has a powerful energy structure associated with it. It has the type of energy structure that can overcome great hardships and difficult situations. So many couples live in a conditional love relationship. Such a relationship functions very much along the lines – 'you do this for me and I will do that for you' - 'you conform to my expectations, irrespective of what might be going on for you and I will be understanding and loving'. If the condition is not met, punishment can follow. The code of practice to aim for in any relationship is, therefore, unconditional love which includes non-attachment.

Cutting the Ties that Bind
Perhaps the biggest attachment we may carry in life is with respect to children. This can unfortunately continue after they have left home. Most young adults will be dependent on the family until they are about eighteen (or possibly earlier) and even into their twenties. After this they need to employ the skills with which their parents have hopefully equipped them to face the challenges of the outside world. It is important for parents to slowly but surely cut the ties which have bound them and their children together. If you cannot let your young adults go, you will have an attachment issue (a program running within you) that you may wish to investigate, bring to the surface, work with and balance. In a good many cases, the attachment issue is caused by guilt and it is a life lesson for the parent. The guilt would probably be centred around feelings such as 'if only I had done this, that or the other, they would have been better, or they would have made better choices . . .' There is no need for you to go there because you, dear parent, have doubtless equipped your children to make sure that they meet their life lessons. So, unburden yourselves and forgo the guilt trip!

When children reach adulthood and have left home, they will grow through their own experiences, influenced by the choices that they make in life. If we interfere with the choices they make, then we are affecting their growth. At best, we should be wise counsellors who give advice when it is requested, irrespective of whether the advice we have given is what the seeker wants to hear. The likelihood anyway, if the advice is given when it has not been requested, is that it will most probably fall on deaf ears. Regarding those times when children may require financial support. However genuine the request, this type of support needs to be given with a watchful eye. This is to make sure that a co-dependency is not being set up. It can be difficult to accept that young adults need to leave home to forge their way through life. Staying in their comfort zone at home can prevent them from doing so. In such cases they are denying themselves the challenges that life has to offer. For those of you who are having difficulties in letting go of your young adults, Phyllis Krystal has written a book called 'Cutting the Ties that Bind'. This book will help you to deal with attachment issues. My task here is to bring the issue to your attention so that you can appreciate the importance of dealing with it.

Relationships in a Work Environment
Why would I want to look at relationships within the work environment? Next to a marriage relationship, relationships at work are powerful because they are forged and developed in a captive environment. There is no escape, unless we resign from our job, or get promoted, or move to a different division/department. Relationships at work provide an important opportunity to observe our own attitudes and behaviour and those of our colleagues, if we care to do so. You may think that the work environment is just about work. I can assure you that it is much, much more. After the honeymoon period during the first several months of employment, just as in any marriage relationship, the masks that you and your colleagues have been wearing will begin to dissolve. All of the parties involved will have an opportunity to have a glimpse of the real person behind the mask. On top of this, the intensity of mirroring personal issues and life lessons between you and your colleagues and vice versa will probably increase. This is done unconsciously amongst those concerned. If you are able to take a step back and observe what is going on, there is great potential here for personal development. Accepting your own role in what is going on is crucial, even more so when things are tough as your colleagues are only reflecting back to you your personal issues and/or life lessons to a greater or lesser degree.

You may not realise it, but some of the work colleagues you come across will be there as teachers. Such men or women tend to remain in the organisation as they are there for that purpose - to teach. One thing is for sure, they will probably not know that their role is to be a teacher, nor will the company. In the world of energy, our quantum bio-magnetic field draws us together for a reason. Personal and spiritual growth through resolving issues and life lessons is the reason. Making money is secondary. We are all brought up to believe that making money is the primary reason why we join the workforce. Money, like everything else, is energy that enables us to do what we wish to do and to pay the bills. The teachers we meet can be pleasant or unpleasant individuals, depending on the issues that are running within us.

How do you recognise the teachers in your work environment? The teachers who come into our life can have a positive and/or negative influence on us. For example, the negative ones may be there to act as a bully, or a critic, or devious controller, and so on. What can be difficult to accept is that they will be reflecting back to us an issue and/or life lesson that is running within our unconscious mind. This will probably come as a bit of a shock as it certainly did to me! The test, and it is a test, is to bring out our ability to deal with the issue. If we handle the situation poorly it could cause us to get engulfed by a victim-consciousness. How we handle what is going on is the key measurement of how well we are doing with respect to our personal and spiritual growth. If we adopt and nurture a victim-consciousness this will, in general, be an additional issue that we would do well to work through.(Most of us suffer from victim-consciousness at different times on our life's journey.) A teacher, who may be one of your colleagues, or a manager, or some person in authority, is there to stimulate and bring to the surface a particular issue for you to work with and bring into balance. I can assure you that when you have successfully dealt with the issue, the teacher will no longer inflict themselves upon you. They will either pick on someone else, or you will move to another position in the company, or will seek employment elsewhere.

The bully is perhaps one of the more difficult types of manager or person in authority to work with. Such people could be your worst nightmare, and they have the ability to push some of your buttons and stress level off the scale. The bully is a persecutor, but so are the devious controllers, or critics, or other abusers who can have a negative effect on you. These types should be an exception, but that depends on the leadership style in your workplace. Successful CEOs, or directors, or managers usually know how to build supportive and effective relationships. They can build a work environment or culture (see below) where employees are happy and therefore give their best. If you work in an oppressive environment it indicates that those who run the business, including their supporting managers appear to be doing a rather poor job! The bottom line of the profit and loss account may be weakening, or look good, but at what human cost? Millions of pounds (or dollars) of productivity in the leading economies of the world are being lost because of stress-related ailments. The human cost and strain on the health services on account of these ailments is also enormous. They are usually due to poor management skills in the workforce. Another important issue involved in the work environment is a lack of emotional intelligence.

There are of course brilliant chairmen, CEOs, directors, managers and so on but they are in short supply. Why is that so? This, too, as in the examples I have given above, is the result of the type of conditioning they have been subjected to from childhood through adulthood. Such conditioning includes the development of the intellect and requirement to recall facts (which is seen as 'knowledge'). It pervades management thinking and training to a great extent even today, except for a magnificent few. Rational thinking leads the way! And that is in spite of the fact that a growing number of people in management circles now understand that:

'if you do what you've always done, then you'll get what you've always got!'

Human beings are still regarded to a great extent in the work environment as a form of commodity. Such conditioning lacks a semblance of emotional intelligence. Without sensitivity towards emotional intelligence, real progress in managing people is inhibited. Surveys continue to show that there is a gap in awareness about the power of emotions/feelings, and how this power can be used to the benefit of all concerned. If handled properly, it can result in a significant increase in productivity on account of inner feelings of positive wellbeing and happiness among the workforce. The organisation's success will in turn induce deeper feelings of positive wellbeing and happiness and give workers and managers alike a greater sense of purpose, if not job security.

Your work environment, its location whether outside or more typically building-based, the building itself and your colleagues, all have a key energy signature that matches your own to some degree. The working environment is like a captive, archetypal, quantum energy field. As I have demonstrated above, everything in life is energy and certain types of energy have an attraction capability. Therefore, in general, most of what occurs in life is not really random. If we are not meant to be where we are then we will not stay there for very long. Either we will leave or the company will dispense with our services. There can be, of course, the odd exception where, because of strong will power and narrow thinking we stay, but remain very unhappy. I have seen this latter scenario in many situations, from the United Nations through to investment banking. It is usually caused by money (a good salary), prestige (ego) and the individuals concerned having low self-esteem.

Employees' Needs to be Happy

Diagram 5.23

Relationship Needs in a Work Environment

Just as you have needs in a marriage, which your partner tries to satisfy, the work environment also has to fulfil your inner needs in one way or another. If needs are not met, then this may cause you to move on. You might move even if the job market is depressed and unemployment is high, because you are not meant to be where you are. Dealing with the uncertainty about your next job could well be one of your life lessons. Collectively, your needs form an essence which a good leader instinctively senses. Five key needs pertaining to any employee are shown in diagram 5.23. Starting at the bottom and working up:

1. If the job does not cover basic expenses to support living, then this need will not be satisfied. In such circumstances there is a tendency to be unhappy and to feel insecure. Other ways of making money to compensate for the shortfall will be a priority. 'Basic expenses to support living' could be the equivalent of 'how long is a piece of string?' until the individual concerned clearly defines the standard of living to which they aspire and why. A point to note once more is that we all have infinite *wants* but only a few real *needs*. A major fallacy that most of us have been socialised to believe is that having money is essential to create an enjoyable life. Certainly, some money is needed in today's society but how much and to do what?

2. It is important to feel that the company or organisation appreciates you. This will satisfy the essential need to belong. Such a company or organisation will have a culture that creates an atmosphere where you feel that you belong. In this case, you will tend to be proud to belong to the company. A caring company or organisation can be described as a supportive family. There is a general feeling of caring for the wellbeing of each person in the company or organisation.

3. If a job is perceived as menial or apparently trivial it can have a detrimental effect on your self-esteem, morale, motivation and overall inner feeling of positive wellbeing. It is beneficial for you to appreciate that every job has its part to play in meeting the organisation's goals and contributes to the success of the company or organisation. Each job, from mail delivery to chairman is important otherwise it would not be there. Most importantly, a job is what you care to make of it. When you make a job meaningful, it satisfies a particular need. Taking pride in a job shows that someone is balanced within themselves. Your attitude and behaviour with respect to a job is a reflection of your character. No job is ever too trivial! In energy terms the job is a gift to you. You make the job, the job does not make you. Each job is a platform to grow from both personally and spiritually. It is what's going on in your mind that counts and, of course, how you handle circumstances surrounding your job. These include:

    o the expectations and reactions of those who know you and who feel are under-employed or wasting your talents;

- your own work colleagues treating you with less respect than you deserve because they equate you, the person, with the 'menial' job you are doing;
- your own work colleagues perhaps being jealous and uncooperative because they do not consider that you should have got the level of job you are doing, and, of course, the way you discharge the responsibilities that the job carries.

4. You will want to feel that you are being listened to and understood. So many problems can arise because people feel, either that they are not listened to, or that what they are saying is not understood, or a combination of the two. If this is the case there will be little, if any, feeling of connection, or inner feeling of positive wellbeing between the company or organisation and your-self. You may feel that there is little point in working there. If you find your-self in this type of situation, you may wish to consider the following:

    - look into your style of communication. Are you getting across what you want to communicate in the best way possible, or does the style put people off and prevent them from getting past their dislike of your manner, or tone of voice, and engaging with what you are actually saying? How well are you understood? Are you a mainly visual person or communicating in a mainly audio style, or are you a feeling-centred person, and so on? Re-adapt your style of communication to match the person who is communicating with you:
    - if you are communicating with others in their preferred style, you may still at times have a communication problem with them. If you do, there will be a program running within your unconscious mind that requires identifying, accepting, working with and bringing into balance. This will stop such situations recurring:
    - that it is time to move on as you have tried the above and nothing is working.

5. Do you feel valued? If a company wants to capture your heart and mind it is essential that you feel valued. This is such an important need. If you feel that you are valued you will also have a feeling of importance. Your self-esteem will soar and you will radiate a high degree of self-worth. A good leader will create a feeling of your being valued. If you do not feel valued then it may prove difficult to fully support the company or organisation, or for you to do your best. Your self-esteem will be low as well as your self-worth and sooner or later that will be reflected in your performance. Your below-par performance will further depress your self-esteem, especially if your managers identify it and decide to make it an issue. The whole thing thus becomes a vicious circle of negativity and such situations can cause you to look for another job.

Nonetheless, if you do not feel valued, it is also advisable to look within your-self. Ask your-self, how much do I really value myself? How strong is my self-esteem? If you feel that you place a low value on your-self, then this will be an issue that you need to work through and bring into balance. Once you value your-self the company or organisation you work within will also value you. Seeking an external source such as a company or organisation to boost your value and self-worth is the wrong way round. The Power of Expectations (chapters 4 and 7) can act as a self-worth placebo in certain circumstances. Using expectations purposefully depends upon the excellence of the management style where you work.

You can, most certainly, have successful relationships in a work environment. It depends not only on your needs being satisfied but also upon your attitudes, behaviour and rapport with:

- your-self
- your colleagues
- your bosses
- the physical environment (land and building energy)
- the type of job that you are doing and your attitude to it.

Once again, 'know your-self' is a prime starting position when you enter a work environment. If you do not like your-self on account of low self-esteem, how can you expect your colleagues to like you? In this case it is advisable to investigate why your self-esteem is low (chapter 4). It is always important to remember that your work environment is mirroring bits of your-self back to you. *It is not really them, it is you*!

How do you Create a Successful Work Relationship?
Body language, attitudes, behaviour, words used and tone of voice will be the first things your colleagues see and hear. They will get to know your different idiosyncrasies and sensitivities very quickly. This is part of the fabricated-self which is driven by your ego. Now the fabricated-self focuses on a number of important characteristics, such as:

- professional growth
- professional status in company
- remuneration
- fringe benefits
- size of office
- job training, and so on.

Understanding the influence of ego here is a life challenge. There is a need to recognise ego's influence, work with it and bring it into balance. Merging the fabricated-self with the authentic-self is another life challenge. I provided guidelines on how to merge both in the last chapter.

The fabricated-self's needs are easy to see from the above list of characteristics. Notice how they are all quite mechanistic and form-based, a perfect fit within what has become the virtual box of thinking that most of us are conditioned to accept. They all fit within the physical (Newton/Descartes) laws of reality that we perceive. These laws condition us to only see this level of wants. But what about the authentic-self's (spiritual) needs that we all have? These are a bit more subtle and include satisfying the following. That we:

- are making a difference by what we are involved in
- feel we belong
- are being of service to the community
- are using our inner creative self from time to time
- are regularly using intuition (hunches) and intuitive intelligence
- perceive that there is true meaning in what we are doing.

Notice how the above do not really fit into a mechanistic or form-based framework of life. They do, however, fit within the Universal Laws of the sub-atomic or quantum world. How can I justify making this statement? Because the soul and spirit (see chapters 1 and 3) operate at a sub-atomic level. Everything we know of operates at a quantum level and is subject to the same Universal Laws. When we are on life's true path and going with the flow, each of the above authentic-self's needs is automatically met. These needs connect us, through the quantum bio-magnetic field, with the challenges that we attract or are attracted to and work on. They are a part of our life lessons and the soul's growth. What most people are not aware of is that at times we:

'cannot see or feel our needs because of our wants'

This is very much in line with 'cannot see the wood for the trees'. It is those infinite wants again that hang around causing a thick fog on a sunny day. A touch of 'cannot see the sun for the fog'!

A Company's Culture is a Key Part of 'Life's Stage'
Although in this section I describe the culture (the workplace environment, which has its own persona) of a private company, it is just as relevant to the public sector. This is a reflection, to a great extent, of the persona of those who are in charge, the persona of supporting employees, plus the energy signature of the buildings and land on which they are situated. Those in charge are responsible for contributing to the employees' motivation and wellbeing, something that, at times, is not recognised. Enlightened leaders realise that employees' lives

are affected by the culture of where they work. And the employees' level of productivity can be said to be directly proportional to how this culture makes them feel about themselves and about the organisation. Enlightened leaders also recognise that their most valuable asset is their employees. They come first. The cash-rich state of their company is viewed as a close second. Enlightened and successful leaders develop and maintain a strong and unified culture throughout. It may be helpful if I define a bit more what I mean by the company's culture. I will elaborate, also, on the term 'life's stage' in the above title and what it means.

Let us take a look at a simple model that I use which takes into account the challenges - life lessons – issues - we are born with and are expected to work through as we travel along life's path. Metaphorically, in this model, once again I see the world as a theatrical stage. The stage presents us with the chance to perform in different acts and scenes which are opportunities to work through our challenges. How does this take place in practical terms? Assuming that during the average lifespan of an individual there are about ten acts which represent different time periods in their life. Within each act there can be several scenes. Each scene presents us with different opportunities/situations for personal and inner (spiritual) growth. These various acts and scenes can include marriage, workplace promotion, changing home or job, social experiences, sporting experiences, and so on. From birth until finally leaving the parental home, they tend to focus upon home life, schooling, hobbies, sport, and so on.

Our life can be regarded as a story which is really a script that is being written and played out as we gain experience by working through the scenes in each act. We are the principal actor throughout. It is important to recognise that we are here to bring any extremes that occur within the different acts of our lives into balance. This includes attitudes and behaviours. How we *handle* what is happening is, once again, key to our spiritual progress. We have the ability to improve our life script as we go along. During our journey, the work environment, the clothes we wear, our place of work, the title we are given, constitute the stage props that set the scene. Now there is also a causal part of the workplace such as the diverse aspects of its culture.

The culture of an organisation gives it a life essence. It gives employees a sense of purpose. Five key elements of a company's culture are shown in diagram 5.24. How does each of these elements affect the overall culture?

Values
Right at the heart of a company's culture is its set of *values*. I define values as the very soul of a company, reflecting its reigning culture. In today's commercial world, a company's mission statement should be a reflection of its values. This is not always the case and can

Key Elements to a Company's/Organisation's Culture

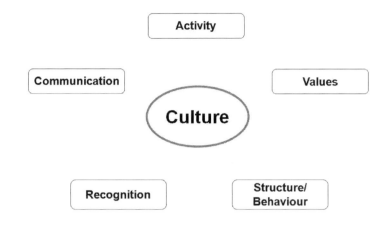

Diagram 5.24

sometimes be a form of window dressing. Those at the head of a company are responsible for setting its mission statement and values. But what are these values that are so important for a harmonious and successful company? Values are about the corporate persona, or character; this is composed of different personalities, each with their own individual characteristics. It is usual for the values operating within the corporate persona to reflect such characteristics as service, integrity, fairness, justice, compassion, respect, interdependence, belief, responsibility, responsiveness self-worth, and so on. All that is said about a private company's values is just as relevant to public sector organisations. A company is like a family where the parents are raising their children and moulding their character. Within a company the parents are the chairman, CEO, directors and managers. They are responsible for running the company. Through the directors, management sets the boundaries for how employees should conduct themselves in the workplace and also regulate how employees interact with one another. They influence the degree of motivation experienced by the employees.

Setting the Company's/Organisation's Values

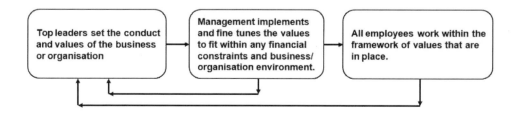

Diagram 5.25

Diagram 5.25 shows a structure that has the potential to generate success in any company which cares about its employees.

Activity

The *activity* of the company dictates the pace of work that an individual, together with the rest of the employees, will be confronted with. Sales orientated or commodities trading, derivative product trading or merchant/investment banking, entertainment, consulting, or research and development - companies will have, in general, a work hard and play hard culture. Knowledge-based companies such as the legal profession, accounting, architecture, or commercial banking, can be less frenetic. Spending time in a company will condition you to a certain pace of work driven by the culture. When you change your place of employment, it is essential to recognise the type of culture that you are joining. It is important also to observe how the company's activities, pace and behaviour, compare with your previous employment. If you do not, you stand the chance of being misunderstood, perhaps damaging your chances of promotion and maybe relationships with colleagues. Using intuition (your hunches) at work can play a strong part in helping you to navigate your-self around the new culture. So use your intuition, intuitive intelligence, and succeed!

The leader (Chairman or CEO or equivalent) receives feedback from both management and employees down to the lowest level. In this case, the leader has a good feel of the pulse of the business. They know what is going on. To build a successful company and achieve greatness, a leader needs to maintain such a system for receiving and giving continuous feedback about what is happening in the company. Without this feedback, it is more than likely that a leader will only react to events. This does not guarantee advantageous change. My own observation within the commercial and public sector worlds is that many leaders get involved in distractions that cause them to lose sight of where they should be going. This is dangerous as ultimately the organisation and its employees suffer the consequences.

A company's values can be divided into two sorts – external and internal. They are universal, variable and therefore, not set in stone. External values relate to how the outside world views the company. This is influenced by the internal values as described above. There are a set of core values such as integrity, compassion, responsibility, belief, honesty, self-worth and so on that should always remain the foundation of any company. It's the management's responsibility to lead by example and to send out strong signals with respect to the company's values. However, as stated previously, some values which may be related to the market, technology, material supply and so forth may change over time, necessitating reassessment. Employees' needs, too, will change over time and will require reassessment. All companies have a lifespan. Those which do not change will not survive. Once again, in a linear time-biased world:

'the only thing that is constant is change'

If some of a company's appropriate values do not change to meet variable market conditions, including its mission statement, then the company will face a short lifespan. Inter-relationships with employees, management, the board and other stakeholders such as suppliers also need to change over time. Just think about IBM's past. The company made the critical decision in the 1980s to move from making large mainframe computers to desktop and laptop computers. To survive and grow they went through a metamorphosis where they had to change from the top to bottom of management in quick succession. Today, wise senior executives and managers recognise that their relationship with respect to employees is a dynamic, flexible one if it is to ensure a harmonious and efficient workforce

Company Structure and Behaviour

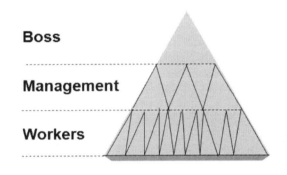

Diagram 5.26

The *structure* of a company/organisation affects the essence of its culture. The structure also has a strong influence on employees' attitudes and behaviour towards one another. A pyramid shape is the traditional structure within a company (diagram 5.26). This can affect how people communicate with one another within the structure. In today's work environment, formal ways of managing employees and the way they address each other are, in general, on the decline in both the private and public sector. The use of first names is becoming the norm, but old ways can die hard. What is important here though, is how the work force and management feel. When there is a comfortable feeling about the way employees are communicating with each other and with management, and vice versa, and there is a strong supportive culture, it is usually supported by higher levels of productivity and an overall sense of positive wellbeing.

Titles are part of the management structure and are very ego sensitive. The title you are given can have a major impact on your self-esteem. A title that you are happy with usually leads to an increase in productivity. Working in large bureaucratic structures can be very impersonal. If you work in such a structure, what you may discover is that the desk you sit at is the job and your personality may count for very little, if anything. Whoever sits at that desk will do the job. A very mechanistic approach! This can be quite soul-destroying for most people and generate a sense of not belonging and a felt lack of appreciation and so forth. It also means that those concerned may feel that they are easily replaced. The son of a close friend of mine, an economist, went to a major Government department for a job interview and was told by one of the interviewers 'we do not do humour here'. In such an environment the culture (if any) lacks a foundation of emotional intelligence and usually turns out workaholics. What would be lacking in this type of job is a connection with the authentic-self. The job would be driven by the fabricated-self where the ego is drawn to the title. It could, on the other hand, provide at least for a short time, good experience and remuneration. As we are all quantum bio-magnets, to work in such a job speaks a lot about the individuals concerned. Dare I say that low self-esteem is involved as well as ego! Why low self-esteem? Because the individuals concerned believe that they need a prestigious name in order to climb up the career ladder. The authentic-self knows exactly where they should be going!

As we take responsibility for our attitude and behaviour, each of us has our own opportunity to set a standard of behaviour within the culture of the company. It is a human trait to want others to emulate our type of behaviour. If the company or organisation that we join has a strong and supportive culture then this task is made easy for us. If there is little, then we have an opportunity to set a standard, even if it is only by our-self. The contribution that we make to the culture where we work is vital, for we are an important part of that company no matter what our level. Our attitude and behaviour will make a difference in one way or another. And guess what? Our quantum bio-magnetic field is working behind the scene in our favour.

Recognition

You have the ability to be a visionary. Just what do I mean? If you are operating from your authentic-self, you have access to your inner creative abilities. You will also have the ability to connect with your intuitive intelligence. This may gain expression in the form of a brilliant idea that can make a major contribution to the company. If you are working in an organisation with a strong culture, there are many ways you can be rewarded. You may receive *recognition* in a way that makes you stand out as a superior person in comparison with your colleagues. There are usually some customs and ceremonies where senior management and your colleagues come together to applaud your idea. The ceremony could be a celebration drinks and/or lunch or dinner where you may be given a certificate of recognition calling you a Champion, or Hero, or a Star of the company. The organisation's purpose here is to ensure that you are recognised in the presence of your peers and that you feel a *valued* member of the company. A word of caution here should your creativity be recognised in this, or a similar manner. It is important to be careful to make sure that your ego does not take over. If it does, it may cause you to overdo your reaction to your newly-found success and be off-putting to some of your colleagues. Such behaviour can be damaging to your career prospects over the long-term.

In a situation where you believe you have a brilliant idea but no one is interested, try to find a willing listener at a senior level. If you cannot, then you may have to find a company which is interested. Keep in mind that there can be a problem with overly rational thinkers in any position, whether of a senior or lesser rank. They can have a strong, blind side. Such thinkers will tend to focus upon meetings, memos, budgets, marketing numbers, glossy presentations, and so on and they can unknowingly lose the plot. This is because they probably lack the ability to think laterally (outside the box) as their world is driven by their intellect and recall of information. This is not their fault as their training would have focused on a rational approach which is mechanistic, form-based, and relies on numbers.

Successful senior executives, who succeed in climbing the corporate ladder, believe in themselves, are constantly using their intuition, intuitive intelligence and intellect to create their achievements. The secret is to know when to cut out the intellect. If you believe that your idea is a winner, then use the old maxim – 'if at first you don't succeed try, try and try again'. A good example here is the inventor of the MASER and LASER (a United States citizen). He was told by his two Nobel Prize winner bosses that he was wasting his time on the MASER concept - his idea did not fit their way of thinking - he should follow their wise guidance for after all *they* were Nobel Laureates! Unperturbed by their comments, he continued to feel within his bones that his idea was the way to go. Did he give up? Absolutely not, and he went on to develop the MASER and LASER. He received accolades of recognition in the end. He achieved success because he truly believed in his idea and in himself. He was working from within his authentic-self. Today, lasers are a part of the technological landscape everywhere.

Communication and Culture Communication
Communication happens at three levels within a company. These levels are:

1. the communication between two individuals which I have already discussed in this chapter (body language, tone of voice, words, and so on).
2. The flow of information that occurs through memos, emails, telephone, meetings, presentations, and so on.
3. The communication through the company's cultural network. This informal network is where things can get done very quickly without the delays caused by bureaucratic inefficiencies – provided, that is, the company has a strong culture.

As an employee, you are very much a part of the cultural communication network in one way or another. Your relationship with the communication network is important not only for your promotion prospects but also for the company's ultimate success. How you feel and how you express your-self within all three levels of communication is important. The first two levels of communication are easy to recognise. The third level has many characteristics and it may be useful to familiarise your-self with them. Looking into these third-level characteristics requires a step into the very essence or inner self of the company. Diagram 5.27 provides a snapshot of the different characteristics. A short description of each gives a flavour of what to look for.

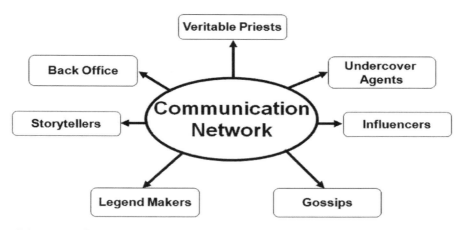

Diagram 5.27

Veritable Priests

To recognise a priest, look for a senior executive who is well established and has been in the company for a considerable time. They are usually wise, sympathetic, very knowledgeable and good listeners. Employees look up to them. They appreciate the power of the cultural network and keep a watchful eye on it, making sure that it works for the benefit of all concerned. They can usually be found in a staff position at headquarters, reporting to a top executive. Veritable Priests wield enormous power but operate from the Shadows. They are invisible to the outside world.

Undercover Agents

In the management world, most managers have what can be called their undercover agents. These are employees who listen in to the gossip, or moans and groans, or observe who is doing what to whom, or who may be a rising star, and so on. They keep the manager well informed and are invaluable in helping managers be effective, especially if changes have to be implemented. When you join a new company, a smart manager will ask you after perhaps a six-month probationary experience some leading questions. The questions may be about systems and procedures as well as whether or not you are happy with the colleagues with whom you are working with. Answer the questions well and you could rise up the corporate ladder with your manager when he is promoted.

Influencers

Senior executives are usually supported by such personnel as consultants, advisers and personal assistants. These people can represent the power behind the throne. To be in this position they will have built up an extensive network of contacts from a junior level all the way up through senior positions. Their intelligence feedback is such that they know more than anyone else about what is going on, and will have the best feel of the company's pulse. If you want to get on, try to find out who the influencers are and make friends with them. On no account fall out with them!

Gossips

Gossips are the daily news promoters who pass on what they have heard. The news may not be too accurate, but at least you will have some idea as to what is happening at the time. Gossips really tend to be the entertainers and can provide some respite if you work in a large company. As the news is passed around, it can get embellished. If this happens and it is about you, it would be in your interest to counter what is being said if you feel you need to. Negative gossip can do your image great harm, especially if you are new and have not established a name for your-self. Just make sure that if any gossip is circulating about you it is supportive. If you discover that the gossip is not in your favour then befriend a colleague who is a known gossiper and get them to reverse what was said. This may minimise any damage that may have been done. As a rule try to get into the habit of only passing on positive gossip as it is likely that 'what goes around comes around'!

Legend Makers

Who are the legend makers? They can be two or more people who agree to say supportive positive things about each, other at all times, to other colleagues. This is a strategy that will most certainly help them to rise to the top on a fast track. Senior executives are always on the lookout for those who have a positive supportive attitude and are good workers/professionals. The psychology behind this is powerful, especially taking into account the quantum bio-magnetic field effect. Like attracts like and senior executives are keen to pull in positive supportive influencers. If you keep saying something regularly enough, you will soon begin to believe it and it will affect your bio-magnetic field (a bit like an affirmation). Such behaviour also advances the perception of each individual. Nonetheless, if an individual were too-strongly promoting themselves, it could produce a destabilising effect because their ego would be pushing through too intensely. Political parties use the legend approach when they choose a leader and do their best to promote the leader to legend status. Of course, in the political arena you can fool people some of the time but not all of the time. The same holds true in the legend-making game in companies. A similar point to note here is that if an individual's bio-magnetic field is negative, positive statements made about them will be doubted. Call it gut feel!

Storytellers

Storytelling is similar to legend-making except this time the message being communicated is a story. What is important here is that it has a good punch line. Why, because most people will remember the punch line which will trigger a memory of the story itself. A good story can change the reality of what is happening within a company for the better. The outcome can change employees' and customers' perception for the better, without realising it. From this you will gather that a story is a very powerful medium to promote. This is especially the case when the story has an emotion which connects with the listener. Working for an organisation with a powerful image can have a strong effect on your self-esteem, motivation and productivity. Apple is a company that is a good example here.

Back Office
The back office can include Human Resources, budgeting division, management accounts, logistics support and so forth. It is an area where you can find some of the longest serving members in an organisation. If you want to find out the accuracy of stories, or legends, or just plain gossip, then this is where you may find the most exact interpretation. Senior executives can covet apparently junior staffs who are long servers. They do so because long servers are excellent sources of true facts that support any stories that are circulating. In the cultural network they are perhaps one of the best sources of intelligence, from the grass roots level upwards.

All of the above points, with respect to culture, are a part of the inner mechanisms, and what can be described as the energy (spiritual) dynamics of any company. They can also provide a mirror image of the needs of your own inner-self. If they are being met in the workplace, then you are in a position to perform to the highest standards. If they are not, then it is in your best interest to look within to find out why this is.

Each organisation has its own life and energy structure. A major part of this energy structure is contributed from the buildings and supporting land. These influences can actually make or break a company's success.

Relationships with Land and Buildings (both Work and Home)
Who would have thought that an energy relationship exists between us all and the land and buildings we live on and work in? Moreover, who would have thought it would be important? As your consciousness begins to operate within the fifth dimension, so the recognition of your being constructed of energy will trigger a change in the way you look at life. Each of us is a being of energy living within energy structures and surrounded by an energy environment. When something is out of balance in these structures, it interferes with the energy's flow and the imbalance can cause a blockage that slows down or stops the energy flow altogether. This blockage can result in the physical and, at times, emotional systems breaking down over time until the blockage is identified and cleared. When issues and life

lessons arise that we are in denial of and are not facing up to, a blockage is created and will remain until it is cleared. The same is true for a home and for the building in which we work. Energy blockages that arise are frequently created due to unresolved disputes. A building plus its land can actually work with us to help remove any blockages - or can add to the blockage. It all depends on where the building is located on the planet's magnetic energy grid. It also depends on what has happened in the past on the land. An outcome in balancing land and building energies is an increase in self-empowerment within all those concerned, and success in the organisation's operations.

Ancient Greeks and Romans knew where to locate their temples and cities by determining where a magnetic energy node was within the planet's energy grid. They may not have known what energy was in those days but they sensed it was there and, recognising its power had ways of measuring it. An energy node is highly positive when it is at the top of the magnetic field's cycle. And such a node will strengthen the success of a city or temple that is established over it. An energy node is highly negative when it is at the bottom of the magnetic field's cycle. There are also black spots energetically where stagnant water (or material) is trapped underground causing a destructive negative energy. These cause energy blocks. In addition, a high concentration of negative emotions, for example after a violent death, or massacre, or bloody battle, or the dumping of bodies of people who died traumatically or in extremely miserable conditions, can cause a black spot which creates other negative energy blocks. All these types of negative energy are absorbed by the land and by any building that is constructed on top of the affected site.

Another important point to make here is that a site could have absorbed many layers of negative energies over the years. In this case, each layer has to be removed and neutralised, just like peeling an onion. Move into a house, or start a business on top of a site that has dark (negative) energy and it is highly likely that the family will be very unhappy, or the business will fail. If an office building or a home is built on a dark energy spot, there is also a likelihood for someone to develop a terminal condition physically and/or that the occupants will have difficult times in life. So checking the energy status of where you live and work to see how beneficial it is for your feelings of positive wellbeing and happiness is a good idea.

As an example, when I worked in Rome I did not realise that there are a few dark energy sites still existing there. The church has consecrated most of the dark sites but a few still exist. I did, however, notice a lot of what I found to be odd occurrences within the United Nations building in which I worked. I was fortunate to have a job that took me around the different divisions within the UN agency. Although the energetic atmosphere did not feel supportive, some great works in the agency's field program managed to get implemented.

What were the odd occurrences? Some staff members had nervous breakdowns and had to be pensioned off; some died while still in their thirties/forties and there was a vicious political ambience in some divisions.

This may have seemed normal to an outsider, or a sceptic, or even to some who worked there. It was only in my later professional years elsewhere, when I became involved in investigating the relationship between energy and our physical wellbeing, that I realised there was an energy balance problem at the Rome site. Apparently, some of the buildings that the UN occupies were constructed on top of an ancient burial site where the bones and bodies of those who had died in traumatic circumstances (perhaps during the games at the Coliseum) were deposited. More likely, the strongest energies in the buildings were those left by the people who occupied them during Mussolini's time. Much of the dark energy is due to the hate which was directed to the ministry that occupied it during that time period. The buildings were the headquarters for administration of Italy's overseas colonies. Releasing these energy blockages would most certainly have had a strong beneficial effect on those who work there today. Such a release would not only induce a feeling of positive wellbeing in those who work and use those buildings, it would also result in an increase in efficiency and worker satisfaction.

Keep in mind that we are quantum bio-magnets and our field radiates in just the same way that a radio transmits energy. We also receive energy transmissions from the surrounding environment. The composition of the energy signals that are received mirrors what is running within our conscious and unconscious minds. Its power is proportional to the emotion that is attached to what is running in our minds. Once we start thinking about the fifth dimension and the dimensions of the second paradigm (the quantum world) we will be able to intuitively tune into concepts that will change how we see and what we believe about the way things are. Abundance and manifestation will begin to be more realisable on a regular basis. Illnesses may be recognised earlier, thus giving more time to take remedial action. You already have the power; you only need to know how to use it. Part of utilising this power is to live in harmony with your-self, to live in harmony with those whom you come into contact with, and to live in harmony with your surrounding environment. Although these are all subtle energies they carry enormous power and affect us greatly.

There are two other key facts that may help you to utilise your energy power effectively. These are:

1. to be careful with your thoughts and always keep them supportive (that is, strive to get rid of any ANTs). Keep out of negative gossip and dramas.
2. To recognise what is going on around you. Try to figure out what you are supposed

to be learning from what is being mirrored back to you from the surrounding environment. If you cannot, then park the incident and see if more of the same occur. Your attraction field and mirroring will have caused what is happening to you. When you are with other people they have the potential to hit a button within you to trigger how you feel via the mirroring process! Do not despair, as many times I end up scratching my head thinking 'what on earth have I to learn from this?' It can be tricky to figure out!

In the East, traditional customs made sure that a building was positioned and constructed in a way that the energy flowed though it in an optimal way. Each building was blessed just like at a christening. This is a good example of operating unknowingly within the fifth dimension (energy). It is unfortunate that as Eastern countries adopt more and more a Western consumer and cost-conscious approach, so they are inflicting upon themselves the limitations which go with it. In the West we see no limitations, but that is because our belief system is operating mainly within the four dimensions of the physical plane. You may not realise it, but this is very limiting. If a business collapses we relate it to the market and/or some accounting imbalances (cash flow) and so on. Using physical, ordinary, four-dimensional thinking (the fabricated-self), we are incapable of seeing the reality, which has to do with a combination of the energy state of the land and building, as well as the energetic state of those who are working there. Increasing awareness of the fifth dimension and what is happening at a sub-atomic level empowers us to see reality for what it is – expansive and with infinite abundance. This is just like the sub-atomic or quantum world where there is an infinite abundance of energy. And, of course, 'all is not as it seems'. Just like life itself.

Balancing a Land and Buildings Energy State
A new breed of professional is available for hire today. They are capable of seeing and feeling the energy state of not only land and buildings but also of human beings and animals. These professionals, who can be described as Energy Geomancers, are gifted in two ways. They know how to:

1. identify and to work with and clear energy blockages, bringing them into balance and getting the energy to flow again. Depending on the cause of the blockage this can be a complex task.

2. channel to the site in question forms of sacred geometry that are linked into what are called Platonic solids. Sacred geometry is a powerful tool used to help stabilise the energy state of land and buildings. Such a task is complex and is carried out on a case by case basis.

When geometry is used, the actual drawing of the sacred geometry begins within the conscious mind of the individual concerned and is translated onto paper (or a computer screen via a drawing software package). It is important to recognise that the thought process energy (at a sub-atomic level) actually connects the sacred geometry to the site concerned, for time and space are not on a continuum but are co-existent. This can be difficult to understand for those who only relate to their first or second thought dimension of the second paradigm (chapter 1) or can only relate to physical reality itself. In such cases their reaction is usually one of denial, basically through a lack of awareness.

There is another successful, well-honed and better known Chinese energy science approach called Feng Shui which is used to alter the energy flow through buildings. Many successful companies have hired a Feng Shui adviser to sort out the energetics of their building. Feng Shui is a technique and process that investigates a building's design, structure and contents to determine how the energy flows through it and where that energy might may get corrupted and blocked. What is fascinating about Feng Shui is that it is both a science and an art, which requires objectivity and subjectivity (just like quantum mechanics). To understand how it works, it is necessary to think outside of the conditioned virtual box of thinking we all have.

What is your relationship with the physical structures and their contents that you come into contact with? Have you ever thought about it? I certainly had not until the late 1980s. There are two main characteristics to consider when you want to determine your relationship with a physical structure and its contents:

1. Living in a house or apartment, and working in an office or factory building, you leave your energy imprint within the structure and contents of those buildings. Buildings are like solid state tape recorders. If you are happy with your life and your work, you will add to the building's energy. If you are unhappy you will leave a negative imprint. All of this is stored at a sub-atomic level within the building's structure and contents. Your energy field, therefore, affects the energy dynamics of the structure and its contents. From this you will have gathered that previous occupants will also have left their energy imprint within the building's structure and in any furniture, computers, and so on that they used. If you are buying a home, try to find out if it was a happy home! And if you are starting a new job, try to find out if the office building or factory has a happy working environment. You will then have some idea as to what you are letting your-self in for. As pointed out above, the land and building itself has its own energy characteristics. This can be either supportive or detrimental to your physical feeling of positive wellbeing and happiness. With the exception of black spot energies, there is a good chance that you can reconfigure the land and building energy to create a supporting structure.

2. The shape and structure of the building, the direction its entrances are facing, its contents and the ground it is built upon all have a powerful effect on the building's energy structure and dynamics (how the energy flows within it). The land and building, being like a large solid quantum magnet, will tend to attract people with a similar energy signature. If the building has a chaotic energy structure and dynamics, I can assure you that it will attract people who have a strong chaos paradigm running within their unconscious mind. Not the sort of place that I would feel comfortable, or happy to work or live in. It is important to use the higher sensors we all have to determine the feel (your gut feel) of an office, or factory, or home before committing (if you can) to being there. Most people do not, as they lack the background in energy dynamics. If force of circumstance pushes you into a building that you are not too comfortable with, there are ways to neutralise the energy around your space. To do this you will require the assistance of an Energy Dynamics professional.

Energy Empowerment

Many people do not have a true understanding of their full capability. We do not realise the energetic power each of us has to change our life for the better. It seems outrageous to consider that we have been conditioned with false beliefs, but we have. It happened to our parents and to their parents and so on. So do not blame them, but simply recognise that you are at a threshold where you can create a transformation within your-self. You can transform your life simply by changing your bio-magnetic energy field. You are all-powerful and you only need to recognise it. How do you make a change within your-self or home or workplace? The answer comes in three parts:

1. Be aware that you have been conditioned (programmed like a computer) with some false beliefs. Try to recognise and to change them. We all have them so you are no exception. Princes, princesses, presidents, leaders, 'A' list celebrities and all those whom you may look up, to all have them! Break out of the unknowingly closed virtual box of thinking and recognise that you too have infinite potential. Take a step back and recognise that you are a being of energy operating not only in the limiting four-dimensional space of the physical world, but also in an unlimited fifth-dimensional space. As you are aware, in the sub-atomic or quantum world, your thoughts have infinite power, so use them wisely. There is a basic law to remember that what you put out (thought energy) you get back tenfold, so be careful with those thoughts!

2. Love what you are doing for this is the most powerful energy of all that can affect change. If you dislike or hate what you are doing, you are polluting the energy environment around you as well as affecting your own physical and emotional state.

What is important here is to try to maintain a constructive thought process and a positive intention. This will permeate everything around you and contribute to a harmonious atmosphere. You affect energetically, through your quantum bio-magnetic field, the solid matter (material) and energy field of the land and buildings and their contents where you live and where you work. Your field also affects the people around you. Try to get rid of any ANTs that may be lurking around in your mind! Remember that the power of your expectations is vast. Use it, and do not let anyone extinguish it. You are your own guardian in this regard. Other people may try to pull you down. If this happens, see it as a test of your own resilience and pull your-self back up. What is going on within your inner-self in terms of your thinking, beliefs and perception is driving your field. It is also attracting the situations you experience in the outside, physical world. So keep your field shining brightly by losing the negatives and keeping it in balance.

3. Similarly, your outer physical-self affects people who are around you. What is your outer physical-self? It is your attitude, behaviour, body language, tone of voice and the words you use. Monitor these, as it will give you an indication of what is running in your unconscious mind and ultimately in your quantum bio-magnetic field. Other people will judge you by these characteristics.

There are a growing number of enlightened and successful business leaders in both small and large companies who are aware of and have an intuitive feel for the energy dynamics of the building in which they work and the home where they live. Some have used Feng Shui advisers to improve the energy flow within the building(s) and the contents used in their business. This has had an effect on the wellbeing of their employees. In such situations there will have been a trickle-through effect down to the company's bottom line. Energy geomancers can make an important contribution to top management and help them get the best out of their business as well as contribute to their employees' inner feelings of positive wellbeing and happiness.

Management, just like each employee, has a choice to either recognise and adapt to the changes that are coming into effect in this 21st century, or not. Effective life-leadership is essential to weather the challenging times ahead. Each of us will be pushed to make a choice. If you are a business person, are you getting into the flow of success or are you scrambling around trying to fix old commercial and corporate structures and systems that are past their sell-by-date? Government and International Agency bureaucracies face a similar challenge. By opening that virtual box of thinking the answer becomes obvious. The choice is real: grow or decay. You decide - it's your choice! The test for successful leadership has never been so great. Old paradigms or models need to be replaced. Change is the order of the day. As President Obama optimistically stated many times:

"Change – yes you can!"

The next chapter focuses upon some elusive characteristics and skills related to leadership. My approach, once again, is to look at leadership through a 'know your-self' perspective. If you do not know your-self how can you possibly expect people to follow you? Understanding self-leadership is akin to life-leadership. It is not a skill where you just tick boxes on your good management chart. Rather, it is about knowing what is really going on within your-self and within those around you. This can provide you with a process to lead and to succeed. Ultimately, everybody succeeds in such an environment.

Chapter 6

Life-leadership: Personal Responsibility and Inspiring Others

Waste no more time talking about great souls and how they should be.
Become one your-self!

Marcus Aurelius Antonius: Roman Emperor AD161 - AD180

Life-leadership: Personal Responsibility and Inspiring Others

At some time during your life you will most probably assume a leadership role. You may chose to raise a family, or take the lead in some sport activity, or get promoted at work, or join the military, the police or support services, and so on. You are exercising a leadership role when you ask one or more individuals to do something for you. You also lead your-self as you journey through life. Life leadership is the combination of leadership of others and self leadership. How we *handle* a leadership role, with respect to our attitude, behaviour and sensitivity, is a life lesson challenge that we will have to deal with. It is also about taking personal responsibility for our actions. I elaborate upon the different elements of life leadership capability in this chapter. Diagram 6.1 outlines the core elements of life leadership. When we are involved in life leadership we have an opportunity to engage in practising the various elements shown opposite. The conditioning that we are subjected to after birth can have a detrimental effect on our life leadership capability, because in the natural course of our life we are usually unable to avoid taking on a number of false beliefs (chapter 4).

Diagram 6.1

Life leadership and personal responsibility go hand in hand. Over this last two thousand years, although leadership has grown strongly in all its forms, the opposite has happened with respect to personal responsibility. There are to be found, of course, small pockets of those who recognise and take personal responsibility seriously, but in positions of power or authority, only a few, in church and state (governments), have fulfilled the role of being shining examples for us to follow. As I gained an understanding of the life leadership role in today's world, it showed me that ego reigns supreme. Who in leadership positions today is coming from the heart? We are surrounded by religious and political bigotry, leaving us to be pawns in the game of life. In the end, we are reduced to recognising that it is up to each of us to take responsibility for our-self. The more we accept personal responsibility, the more we become a shining beacon of light within ourselves and to those around us. In this case, rules are not required, for the individual leads by example, which is a must in this 21st century. We are, ultimately, personally responsible for how we chose to lead ourselves and how we affect those around us. We may choose to give our power to someone else or we may choose to be self-empowered. The decision is ours to make. As we adapt within a leadership role, when we are leading others we will find that it may affect our own self-leadership. This is because understanding the characteristics that are required to lead others can help us to understand our-self better. We are provided with an opportunity to 'know our-self' in different situations.

An important point to emphasise, when we take a leadership position, is that we must know when to step back from it. This allows those whom we are leading to get on with what they are doing without being micro-managed. If we are dealing with our-self, then stepping back or pausing for a few moments allows us to listen to our intuition and to be guided by our authentic-self. So many leaders do not recognise that their leadership is only required within an appropriate time period. And in self-leadership, it is most important to recognise when to take a step back from letting our ego run our attitude and behaviour and allow our authentic-self to come through.

What sort of an image do you hold in your mind when you think about a leader? Should the leader be good looking, charismatic, extroverted, clever, strong alpha male or female type? What is your focus when you are looking for or at a leader? Are the leadership characteristics you expect dependent on the situation? For example, would they be different at work, in a partnership, in a marriage, as club president, social secretary, teacher, lecturer, and so forth. Are you looking for elements of: intelligence (knowledge-based), empathy, intuitive intelligence (someone with amazing insight), political skills, popularity, integrity, network of contacts, strong personality and such like? What do you expect from a leader? Do you want your leader to make all of the decisions for you or just the major decisions? Do you expect to be consulted with respect to the decisions that are taken (a democratic process)? Do you want your leader to come up with innovative ideas? Do you want your leader to have empathy and be diplomatic? Most importantly, do you want a leader who understands your needs? These are all important questions to consider when you are about to make a decision with respect to choosing a partner, or joining an organisation, or company, or choosing a politician, or going to college/university, or selecting a business colleague, and so forth.

Scope of Leadership Possibilities in Life

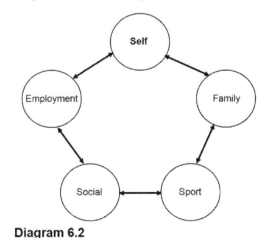

Diagram 6.2

In the diagram 6.2 'Self' (your-self in self-leadership) is at the top. An important point to note is that you are the most important person on this planet and Universe. For your soul is here to grow, just as your fellow travellers' are.

Each of them too is the most important person on this planet and Universe. Money, titles and position are merely the stage props used by other souls as a platform to face their life lesson challenges. If you have difficulty in leading your-self along your life's path, this will be reflected in other leadership areas of your life such as employment, family, social, and sport. A missing leadership attribute, until about the last two decades, has been an understanding of the importance of the emotional/feeling aspect required in a leadership role. This aspect is called emotional intelligence and is important with respect to motivation, self-motivation and confidence.

In the 1950s, surveys showed that about 3 percent of the population were regarded as natural leaders. As leadership became a subject of study by universities, it was found that about 80 percent of the population had leadership potential. It is believed that this potential could be realised by training individuals in the particular skills of leadership. As the last decade of the 1990s concluded, emotional intelligence was recognised as a key attribute that needs to be understood and practised if a leader is to be successful. Furthermore, the principles of emotional intelligence can be taught.

Emotional Intelligence (EQ) - A Key to Successful Leadership
Most of you will be familiar with the acronym for Intelligence Quotient (IQ). You have probably been subjected to IQ tests at school. It is part of the education process, that we are subjected to an IQ test, to determine our numerical, word association and spatial abilities. A score of 120 is considered to be fairly good. Because I am slightly dyslexic my score ranged between 40 (village idiot) and 160 (bright). The low score occurred when I felt confused and not supported. The high score occurred when I felt confident and supported. I bought a couple of books on IQ tests when I was 18 years old and practised the different tests. As soon as I was familiar with the broad range of questions that were asked I was filled with confidence and did well, whether or not I felt I was being supported. I managed to keep my score, in both difficult and easy situations, at about 140 without too much difficulty.

When I sat the 11 plus IQ examination during my last year at junior school, I think I must have scored about 40. Why, because I was put into a low-achieving first year stream at the senior school I attended, even though I had won two top prizes in the final year at junior school. Such are the rules in a bureaucratic educational environment! Nevertheless, within one year I was back in a high-achieving stream again. Why do I mention this? It shows what you can do with the support of good teachers who believe in you and most importantly who have the belief that you can do it on your own. Both are essential to generate self-confidence and motivation to achieve. Without the emotional support of my teachers and parents, I could have languished in a low-performing, apathetic stream of poor performers. The probability of dropping out in this case would have been high. Ultimately, it is all really about personal expectations, as we will see in the next chapter.

How important then is emotional support and encouragement in our lives? They are the key to helping us achieve the goals we set and to improve our quality of life. This emotional support usually needs to come from two sources. The first is external, that is from others, and the second internal, from within ourselves. Some exceptional individuals seem to be completely self-motivated, but I suggest that they, too, require some external support from time to time. Using emotions in a positive and constructive way stimulates motivation and confidence not only within ourselves, but also within those around us. Let us not forget that emotions are energy and energy follows thought (chapter 2) right down to the cellular level of the body.

What actually is EQ (emotional intelligence)? EQ can be defined as:

'the awareness of our emotions, and other people's, together with the ability to manage them in a healthy and productive manner'

A considerable number of people today are involved in training activities to enhance their Intellect (or IQ) by absorbing information. There is nothing wrong with that, except it is only a part of what we are really about as human beings. Developing the intellect and learning facts can certainly make a contribution to what I call psychological growth, but does little, if anything, towards developing our creative self and enhancing our inner (spiritual) growth. It is most unfortunate that society has been groomed to value the cultivation of the intellect and recall of information as perhaps the main achievement in life, and we are well rewarded, as I certainly was, for having and using that ability. The opposite extreme is celebrity culture where good looks, a particular talent and money are regarded as pathways to recognition and fame. Why am I highlighting both of these? Certainly not to knock them (each to our own chosen path to gain experience in life) but to point out that they both tend to lack the common ingredient of having sufficient EQ to be emotionally and spiritually healthy. They are driven by ego and in energetic terms are out of balance.

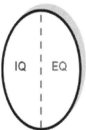

Diagram 6.3

Imagine the egg shapes in diagram 6.3 as a representation of IQ and EQ. The diagram on the left shows an individual with a healthy balanced IQ and EQ. The one on the right I suggest is a representation of the EQ and IQ of the average individual today. This shows, an individual whose EQ is out of balance and who has an emotional capability that is not in a healthy state. My task is to guide your EQ to move towards the left-hand diagram. That is, of course, if you want to or you are not already there.

Is EQ a missing attribute that must be put firmly in place? Most certainly, and this book will help with that task. At a physical level, emotions drive attitude, behaviour (including body language, tone of voice and the words we use) and how we feel (diagram 6.4). As we are all connected at a sub-atomic level, our emotions also affect those around us at a conscious and unconscious level. This is something that is being increasingly recognised and understood by scientists. There is certainly a great deal of evidence that was collected during the 'cold war' days (pre 1990), that show the power and effects of thoughts and emotions on human beings. To operate at a sub-atomic level means getting out of the head (the left-brain hemisphere - the Intellect) and tuning into the right-brain hemisphere (the Intuitive and Creative centre) as well as to connect with your authentic-self and imagination.

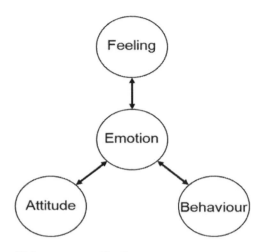

Diagram 6.4

In the West, most people are taught to hide or suppress their emotions. In British terms, that means to keep a 'stiff upper lip'! Emotions are seen as a form of weakness and something that should be curtailed. If you come from a Latin-based country, where showing emotions is part of the culture and behaviour, you are more fortunate and probably less stressed. As I emphasised in Chapters 3 and 4, emotions are an essential part of an individual's psychological and response makeup. When emotions are suppressed, those concerned are putting themselves into a state of dis-ease (imbalance) in the medium to long-term. Emotions and feelings are important inner indicators that let us know what is going on inside of us (physiologically). To recap, I define a feeling as:

> *'the physical manifestation (somewhere in the body, for example the stomach, heart, head and so on) of an emotion'*

And I define an emotion as:

> *'the energy form of a feeling that is being experienced within the physical body'*

Emotions can be enormously powerful and can work for us or against us. Understanding how negative emotions are formed and how to release them, if they have been suppressed, is an important key to developing a feeling of positive wellbeing and happiness. Negative emotions (chapter 3) arise from recurring negative thoughts, hate, prejudices, racism, intolerance, envy, fear, anger and so on. Emotions transform into electrical energy within the physical body flowing around muscle structures, the nervous system and so on. Negative emotions cause muscles to contract and over time that can lead to, for example, back problems, a common predicament faced by people in Western countries.

Identifying emotions and knowing what we should be doing with them is part of what emotional intelligence is about. I touched on emotions in the previous chapter and there is a list of them arranged in alphabetical order in Appendix 1. Do spend a few moments looking at this list which will give you some idea of the extensive range of emotions that we all experience. A key point to remember is that each emotion is like a cloud of energy vibrating at a specific frequency. As each emotion is formed, during different life experiences, so they will leave their own subtle physical imprint on us (a physical feeling). Because understanding emotions are not high up on schools' educational syllabus, or even at home, we tend to be ill equipped to handle them properly and probably are seldom aware how we feel when we experience different emotions. Most people are not aware that a major challenge in life is to bring each emotion into a state of homeostasis (balance) as it arises. This is true for both negative and positive emotions. It is usually the negative emotional energy that causes a lot of physical and psychological damage within us, although there are times when an overly strong positive emotion can also lead to a physiological imbalance and a heart attack.

I have selected six negative emotions (source: Wikipedia) which we most commonly experience and ask you to sit back, relax and try to recall how you felt in situations where each one arose.

anger	**boredom**	**disgust**
abuse	**loneliness**	**panic**

In which part of your body did you feel a physical sensation? Now look at the second table below (source: Wikipedia) where I have selected six positive emotions, and go through the same exercise. Do you feel the emotion in a specific part or parts of your body or within your whole body?

affection	**achieving**	**amused**
at ease	**empowered**	**in control**

This is a first step to enabling you to recognise what is going on energetically within you. Importantly, a prolonged level of too high a negative or positive emotion can be damaging to your-self and others. Your energy field affects those around you and vice versa. It is important to note that if your energy field is strong you will be less susceptible to interference from someone else's field. If your energy field is weak then you may feel uncomfortable around someone who is negative. Conversely, you might also get a buzz around someone who is very positive.

Surprise for Parents: Your Baby's EQ Starts from Conception
Having defined emotional intelligence and looked at how we may experience different emotions, how do emotions develop within our consciousness (and subtle energy bodies)? From conception, emotional intelligence begins to be conditioned within us through a simple process of absorbing the different energies arising from:

> parents, family, relations, friends and other authority figures and their relationship with themselves and us.

> the surrounding atmospheric energy created by the people around us and the physical location of the home.

This energy information is also recorded within the body's cells. From birth, a baby is a living energetic sponge conditioned to absorb everything from its surrounding environment (which is, of course, energy) as shown in diagram 6.5. The ancestral part in diagram 6.5 consists of all the issues within the family that have not been worked through and cleared, and are therefore passed on genetically and energetically from generation to generation until they are brought into balance.

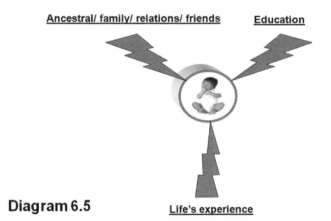
Diagram 6.5

When a baby sees a smiling face, it also feels the positive energy behind the smile. The baby's natural sensors (eyes and solar plexus) receive this information, which leave the baby with a positive, internal, physical feeling. The baby is able to experience the same internal physical feeling when words are used. The tone of voice and also the intention (the conscious thought that is being projected) behind the positive spoken words, are picked up by the baby's sensors (ears and solar plexus). When both match in a positive sense, the baby will feel happy and express this happiness in one way or another. The same internal feeling can be also generated through taste and smell (sweet tastes and pleasant smells) or being warmly held. A baby always needs gentle, warm, physical contact. A miserable expression on an individual's face supported by negative thoughts, tone of voice and words, will cause a baby to feel uncomfortable and/or unwanted, and can induce crying. Shouting and the use of negative words or verbal/physical aggression between two people who are around a baby, together with negative thoughts running in their consciousness, will also stimulate fear. This can cause a baby to cry. A baby will always feel threatened even though the negative exchange is not directed at it. As the baby's pre-frontal cortex is not developed, it cannot apply reason and will believe that it is to blame, or is about to be harmed. Unfortunately, this is the beginning of planting the seeds of low self-esteem and other issues such as abandonment, lack of confidence and insecurity.

As a baby develops it is confronted by parents and others subjecting it to words like 'good baby', or 'bad baby', or 'yes', 'no', and so forth. Because of a baby's or young child's lack of reasoning capability, great confusion can arise. This is because the baby/child may be being playful and does something which it believes would please the adult (and others). Let me give you a personal example. When I was about 7 years of age, my sister (she is three years older) and I cut out a couple of pages of a newspaper into fine confetti. It was a dull wet Sunday afternoon and our parents were sitting in the living room quietly reading the Sunday papers. We crept in with a handful of confetti and threw it over both of them singing, 'here comes the bride, fair fat and wide'. As it was such a dull afternoon, we thought that they would be amused and laugh! Did they? Absolutely not, they both exploded with anger. They instructed us to get a dustpan and brush and sweep up the mess. Our prefrontal cortices had not developed enough to allow for the possibility that they might get angry.

When we are met with a negative response we receive an emotional shock. The same is true for any child. This shock takes the form of a negative, internal, physical feeling and will be recorded as a negative emotion within us. Such emotions run continuously within a child's second energy body, unconscious mind and physical body, and can grow energetically as the child matures. They form part of the quantum bio-magnetic field. The negative emotions will require to be dealt with at some time in the future, because some represent issues or life lessons that we need to grow from. As negative energies and information are also stored within the body's cells, they need to be released at some time in the future. If this does not happen there is a chance that the energies will contribute to programming a state of dis-ease within the body's cells which can ultimately lead to illness.

Behind each emotion generated there will be an event or situation that will be recorded within the unconscious mind (and brain). If a child is told they are useless, or bad, or should give up, or will never be good at something, and so forth, it will contribute to a set of false beliefs (issues to be resolved) which will continue to run at all times within the child's unconscious mind. Each of the false beliefs will have a negative emotion attached to it. As the child matures to adulthood, these false beliefs are accepted as part of their status quo (beliefs about their own attitudes, their behaviour, abilities and the situations they find themselves in, which they accept as being normal). What does this do? It programs the child's bio-magnetic field and as the child matures it will attract relationships, activities and situations to others who mirror the particular life lessons/issues that need to be cleared.

Because we are not trained to recognise the effects of bio-magnetic mirroring, nor the significance of synchronicity of events/situations in life, we are usually quite oblivious to the reasons for what is happening around us and to us. Life lessons will keep recycling in our various relationships and the activities and events we are involved in, until we recognise what is happening and deal with it. A therapist can be a lifeline for help in discovering why certain difficult situations keep repeating themselves. What we thought were problems can become an interesting set of challenges to deal with and to bring into balance.

Identifying your EQ

I use three different approaches to recognise my own EQ level and those of others. You may wish to try them.

1. The first approach is to develop an ability to recognise what is driving our moods, attitudes and behaviour. Once I took time out to observe myself, I noticed certain recurring patterns of attitudes and behaviour surfacing from within myself. I began to notice what and who was able to hit my emotionally sensitive buttons, causing me to react. If this is too difficult for you to do by your-self, then I recommend that you use a personal development coach or perhaps a therapist. Key here is how you handle your-self (manage your attitudes, behaviour and anger) and those who are communicating with you.

2. The second is to be able to appreciate other people's realities and allow for what may be going on for them. After I had taken time to observe other people's moods, patterns of behaviour and attitudes, I then stepped into their shoes (in my imagination) and observed my reactions from their perspective. I gained an insight here on how they felt while interacting with me.

3. The third is to be conscious that communication is a two-way process and that I impact upon others in any interaction just as they impact upon me. Using this approach, I stepped back, again within my imagination, and watched myself interacting with others while they interacted with me. This gave me an opportunity to sense how I behaved with others and how they reacted to me.

I have found that working through the above three approaches forms an important part of measuring emotional and inner (spiritual) growth. In emotional intelligence, there are always two key words to note and they are *awareness* and *management*. Becoming aware of emotions arising from within ourselves, while being alert to other people's emotions, is a must. Management is all about practising to manage emotions, especially in challenging situations where it is important that we do not instantly react, but pause before responding. To think before we speak or react is a vital key to developing a high EQ.

We have natural sensors for identifying EQ which can be divided into two categories, as shown in diagram 6.6.

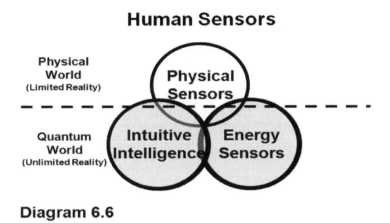

Diagram 6.6

> First, the physical sensors. These are the sensors we use to operate in the physical world - sight, hearing, smell, taste and touch. Sight and hearing are the two major physical sensors we use when we observe body language and listen to the tone of voice and words spoken in a discussion. Nevertheless, we have even more powerful sensors within the second category.

> This category operates at a sub-atomic level (within the quantum world). These are intuitive intelligence and energy sensors. You can train your intuition (part of your intuitive intelligence) to give you a 'gut feel' of someone's EQ and then use your physical sensors to verify what your gut is telling you. This is a much easier task than you may think, especially since, as I pointed out in chapter 1, we are all connected at a sub-atomic level. It is a bit like using an energy telephone. You just dial the number (that is, visualise the individual in your mind) and tune in (think about them). You are instantly connected. Do not forget that time and space is co-existent in the unconscious mind which is also the home of your imagination. Our energy sensors are basically the subtle energy bodies (SEBs) and their connecting vortex energy centres (VECs). The VECs act as information and energy filters through to each of the SEBs which form a part of the unconscious and conscious minds.

If you decide to work through the above approaches to measure your own EQ, you will be able to get a feel of what you are lacking. It will not only provide you with an indication of how you handle your-self in different situations, it will also provide you with an indication of how people might react to you. Plugging the gaps in EQ is an essential part of personal growth (emotional, physical and spiritual wellbeing). These gaps will most probably be related to how sensitive you are, how intuitive, how balanced, and so forth. Some questions that are worth asking your-self are, do you:

- contribute to an overall feeling of positive wellbeing, or do you leave a trail of unhappy people around you?
- have much control over your own emotions?
- have a short fuse whereby you just let fly by reacting without thinking about how the other person or persons may feel?
- stop and spend some time with your colleagues, or friends, or family members to find out what is happening in their lives? Or are you just too busy, with little or no time to communicate properly?
- know the degree of respect that people have for you, or not as the case may be, and can you find out why?

Looking at your-self and others in terms of EQ can help you to quickly build up an understanding of what EQ is about. It can also help you to identify the level of your own EQ. A framework, if you wish to look at your own level of EQ, is shown in diagram 6.7. It provides a structure for understanding the interaction involved and the consequences of what arises from communicating with others while going about your day to day life.

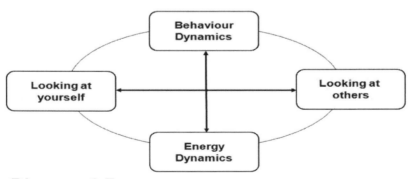

Diagram 6.7

1. **Looking at your-self** is about sensing how aware you are of your attitudes and behaviour. Are you an independent type or do you rely on others? Are you a leader or a follower? How sensitive are you? Do you recognise your strengths and weaknesses and are you a good communicator? Do you recognise your ego, and when you are being run by your ego?

2. **Looking at others** is basically looking at your people skills; are you able to form functional relationships; are you able to feel other people's situations and can you show empathy; can you function as a team member or in a social group successfully; have you diplomatic skills that keep a harmonious balance within a group of people? When you are looking at how others interact with you, it can also help if you put your-self in their shoes so you experience them looking at you. Do you recognise when other people are being run by their ego? Do you recognise when other people are mirroring your issues back to you or vice versa?

3. **Attitude and behaviour dynamics** is about how sensitive, understanding and flexible you are in your day to day tasks such as management tasks or solving people problems at work, at home within the family, or within relationships, or socially; in changing life circumstances or situations; in creating different approaches or solutions to the challenges you face. Are you in touch with your feelings and able to work constructively with them, or are you a rigid thinker unable to open your virtual box of thinking? Are you just not 'getting it'?

4. **Energy dynamics** is about your emotional state; are you a positive outgoing person; have you control over your stress level; do you create a stressful atmosphere; are you happy within your-self; are you forgiving or do you hold a grudge and carry around hurts that burden you like heavy baggage? Do you create a happy functional atmosphere wherever you are? These are some examples of where your emotions may require some work to bring them into balance.

As can be seen from diagram 6.7, all of the four EQ dynamics interact with and affect one another. They are not mutually exclusive.

Investigating life's challenges, I realised that being perceptive about what is going on around me, and aware of how I handled myself in different situations (self-management) were not only key components in the development of my EQ but also an important part of my personal development. As I travelled my life's path, a vital characteristic that we all have kept being brought to my attention. That is, as commented upon in Chapter 5, we all have *basic needs*. Of course, people often have an infinite number of wants, but we have only a limited number of basic needs for us to lead a happy and fulfilled life. What are these needs?

Basic External Human Needs
In the 1960s an American psychologist called Abraham Maslow put forward a theory of human needs. I call these basic, human, external needs, because they belong to the physical world and we access them mainly through the conscious mind. Maslow called them deficit needs and placed them in a five-layered pyramid as shown in diagram 6.8.

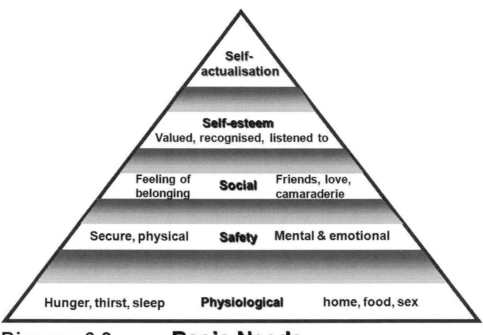

Diagram 6.8 **Basic Needs**
Source: Wikipedia

As progress is made through each level of need within this structure, so it is possible to advance to the next level of development as human beings. He reasoned that if we face changing and challenging times that cause us to lose a supporting need, for example a loss of employment, or accommodation, or money, then our conscious awareness automatically drops down to the appropriate survival level that offers security within the structure. The journey begins again from that level. As confidence is gained, step by step, progress is made and the next level is accessed. A summary review of Maslow's deficit needs in the diagram above may be helpful.

> The first level comprises the basic **physiological** needs. It covers the need to survive - eat, drink, have sex, avoid pain, have shelter and be secure and do all the other things which are required to survive. Today, this also covers the need for employment to earn enough money to pay the bills and get by at a basic level of subsistence. Once these needs are satisfied, advancement to the next level is possible.

> The second level satisfies basic **safety** needs (coming to terms with some inner fears). Here we are now in a position to earn sufficient money be able to buy or rent a property to live in and have enough to cover all the outgoings, including holidays; buying a car, and so on. We are in a happier state of mind, feel stable and are looking at the future in an optimistic way.

> The third level satisfies basic **social** needs. This is where emotional relationships and friendships are established. Consideration is given to raising a family. Clubs or societies are joined to meet like-minded individuals and to develop a feeling of belonging. At this level there is a susceptibility to being alone and to social anxieties such as being mugged or robbed. Recognising the plight of the homeless and giving to charity and doing charitable work is considered.

> The fourth level provides time to satisfy **self-esteem** needs. Respect from others is sought. Self-respect is worked upon, where effort is put into building feelings of confidence to handle life's challenges: personal competence, achievement, independence and freedom. Recognition in the private and public sector is sought. There is a need to be listened to and to make a mark on society.

> Finally, advancement is made to the level that satisfies the **self-actualisation** needs. And what is self-actualisation? Maslow called this 'growth motivation' needs. It is where there is a focus on achieving our inner desires/passions. An individual may be a successful businessman or business woman, or a doctor, or engineer but secretly has a desire to be, say, an artist but were stopped from following their passion by social pressures. They are now in a position to follow this driving inner need which they must satisfy for their personal and spiritual development. This is also allowing their authentic-self to come out and to be expressed. A real necessity in life.

Maslow's hierarchy is a useful indicator to help us recognise a pattern of needs in life. However, there are as always exceptions to the rule. What do I mean? There are those creative geniuses from the past and present like great artists, or poets, or scientists and so forth who operated at their self-actualisation level even though they were in exceedingly deprived circumstances. For example, they may have been living in poverty, or under repressive regimes, or in concentration camps, or gulags. It seems that some individuals are able to access their self-actualisation level without all of their basic needs being satisfied. In simple terms, a desperate situation or extremely adverse conditions can trigger an individual to escape from their harsh circumstances through self-actualisation. Such individuals will still have to deal with the cause of the situation at a later date. Maslow recognised that the sample size of individuals he reviewed to put together his theory was small. His hope was that others would take his work forward and elaborate on his findings.

Maslow's model of basic human needs is a general measure of what is required to get to a level of self-actualisation. Viewed from an external perspective it describes the physical and psychological requirements for growth. How is this achieved today? I will take my lead from today's business environment as some interesting changes have occurred there, slowly but surely, over the last 15 years. Companies, both small and large (that is, blue chip companies – Microsoft, BP, HSBC, BT and so on), recognised that the most important capital they have is their human capital, the people who work for them. Financial capital takes, of course, second but equal place! This has encouraged Human Resource divisions to take into account and to monitor the psychological aspects of a job. These aspects cover a wide range of an individual's inner feelings of positive wellbeing and personal development growth. They cover the individual's:

- professional status
- professional growth
- personal development
- awareness
- work/life balance
- remuneration
- job title

These can also be viewed as the psychological dynamics of the employee's position and can be taken into account in their employment contract and annual appraisal. It was hoped that this would stimulate employees to be more efficient and happier in what they were doing. Extra holidays, free membership to a gym, special courses on management and leadership, bonuses, and so on, have all been tried, with limited medium-term success, to create a more productive and happier work environment. But, something else was missing, what could it be?

There is a growing recognition that the material (and mechanistic) aspects of life do not provide anything more than short-term happiness. Through a broader understanding of human needs, thanks to the work of some enlightened psychologists and therapists over the last 20 years or more, the authentic-self's requirements are being given more recognition and a stronger emphasis. It is important to acknowledge that the authentic-self's needs are closely related to spiritual development and growth. This is where both external psychological dynamics (from a work viewpoint) and inner spiritual dynamics (from an inner personal development viewpoint) merge to produce fulfilment and happiness over the long-term. Growth in emotional intelligence is an important part of personal development. Company's Human Resources divisions are beginning to recognise the importance of supporting programs to increase the overall awareness of an employee's inner needs. This represents a low-cost approach to bringing large gains in employee productivity and feelings of positive wellbeing and happiness. Of course there will also be an increase in the company's bottom line (profitability). But what are these inner needs which operate at a deeper level of consciousness and what does it all mean?

Basic Inner Human Needs

If inner needs are not satisfied there is a lowering of motivation and productivity plus a lowering of ability to function in a socially acceptable manner. There is also a lack of ability to maintain interest in the work at hand. The downside effects of this can take the form of alcoholism, drug addiction and all other sorts of unacceptable social behaviour (bullying, abuse, and so on). Employers face low productivity as well as a poor attitude from employees. It usually follows that they also dislike their work. Taking Maslow's approach about understanding basic human needs a step further, there is a call for us to move to a deeper level of awareness which allows us to make contact with the authentic-self. To do this requires enabling access to the unconscious mind. Is this important? Absolutely, for attitude and behaviour operate from within the unconscious mind, as do such attributes as the creative self and intuition.

The instructions given to the unconscious mind through the conscious thinking mind can bring difficult attitudes and behaviour into harmony. Negative and limited thinking from within the virtual box of thinking that most are trapped in can cause attitudes and behaviour to be in disarray. All of this also influences what we do, when we do it, how we feel and how people will react to us Each of us has a set of deep basic inner needs, as shown in diagram 6.9, that enable us to function in a supportive or non-supportive manner. This applies not only in a work environment but also at home (in raising a family) or in a social environment. Satisfying these increasingly elusive needs within ourselves and in others is an important part of life leadership. When the above basic inner needs are satisfied, we operate in a stress-free, productive, creative and happy manner. Such an environment leads to an inner feeling of positive wellbeing and happiness.

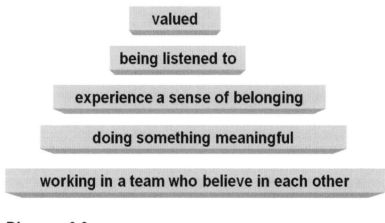

Diagram 6.9

To be empowered in such a way, each of us needs to:

- **feel valued.** Not feeling valued has a detrimental effect on our self-esteem, self-worth, self-image and so forth. Such a situation leads to feelings of depression and victim-consciousness. Feeling valued means receiving respect from others. But feeling valued also means generating that feeling from within ourselves. This must be a major goal, as seeking value externally can only offer a temporary veneer until we value ourselves. Each of us needs to feel self-respect and self-acceptance. Each of us is the most important person in the Universe, as we agreed to be born to grow through our own unique experiences and life lessons. Life will, in general, throw challenges at us to test if we really value ourselves. The outcome to strive for is 'yes I do absolutely value myself'.

- **feel we are being listened to.** So many people today feel that they are not being heard, especially the young who are lost in a world where parents seem to be arguing, about very little, at regular intervals, or are out socialising, or projecting their needs and fears onto them or just zombied on viewing television. No one seems to want to listen to what young people have to say unless there is the likelihood of some future business or political gain to be made. Listening to what someone is saying is of great importance and it is an art that is being lost to a substantial degree within Western society. People often seem to talk at or over one another. There is also a vital requirement to listen to ourselves, even as we develop the art of active listening to others. Only then can we recognise when our ego is talking over us and when our authentic-self is talking to us. The goal is to keep ego in balance and allow our authentic-self to guide us on our journey.

- **experience a sense of belonging.** Does your home and work environment promote a feeling of belonging? Each evening many people return after working late and perhaps after a long commute, close their apartment or house door, turn on the television, probably pour a drink and switch off for the evening. The community spirit that gave people a feeling of belonging seems to have evaporated. The transitory nature of employment has also removed a feeling of belonging. It has induced a fear that is keeping people locked into Maslow's 'Safety' level. And some young people aimlessly wander the streets and join a gang to stimulate a feeling of belonging. We all want to feel that we fit in. Two culprits that most powerfully prevent us from having a feeling of belonging are our ego and low self-esteem. They dictate to us what we should do and prevent the authentic-self from coming to our assistance to give the appropriate guidance that we require. So we lock ourselves up in our various boxes and search the internet for something that will let us feel that we belong.

> **be doing something useful.** Most people wish to be doing something they feel is useful in their lives or for other people. And yet, doing something useful is in the 'eye of the beholder'. The most menial of tasks can be an important part in a chain of tasks that produces something worthwhile. It is crucial to explain to individuals the significance of their task and how everyone involved is relying on each other. The feeling of not doing something that is useful generates a feeling of discontent. In such conditions people hate their jobs and only stay for the money, or because they feel it is a better option than staying at home as they might have even greater feelings of discontent there. The expression 'soul destroying' is appropriate here. The challenge is to recognise the significance of what is happening. Most people do not realise that the working environment is an opportunity for personal and spiritual growth. If this does not occur, then it is really time to move on. And when the soul judges that it's time to move it will happen whether we like it or not. It's all about fulfilling an inner need. Timing before such a move happens could be a month, six months, a year or more (even a lifetime). Only your authentic-self will know!

> **working in a team that believes in one another.** Not an easy task, especially with mixed age groups, ethnicities and nationalities. It is complicated by the different types of working environment, for example knowledge-based, scientific, engineering, banking, public relations, advertising and so forth. Even so, it is possible to put a harmonious team together, if the leader is sensitive and skilful. So many leaders have bought into the belief that it is in their best interest to be hard-nosed decision-makers with little, if any, empathy. This old-school approach can only produce success in the short-term, and at what a cost to all the individuals involved! Such an approach is really a cop-out. A team is not just a team, a random collection of individuals, as each team member is an individual quantum bio-magnet. They have, unknowingly, been attracted by their bio-magnetic fields to one another. Team members will also be mirroring their own life lessons with other team members. If this is understood, the chance of the members of a team believing in one another is greatly enhanced. And that is because they will realise the special circumstances of their meeting and that the end product is an enhancement of their personal development, including spiritual growth.

Manipulating the above basic needs has been used by leaders and governments in totalitarian and tyrannical states as a tool for control. When people realise that it is happening they are less likely to be disempowered by it. An extreme example of manipulation was in Germany in the 1920s and 30s when Hitler and the Nazi party managed to take over the mind and body of the German people and the country. Certainly, conditions were right for such exploitation. Germany was bankrupt after the First World War; it had lost the flower of its youth; the economy collapsed in the 1920s; there was mass unemployment; it had lost its self-respect and most of the population had lost their identity and pride. The country's focal point (the Kaiser) had gone - abdicated and retired to Holland.

With an understanding of basic human needs (both external and internal) Hitler, Goebbels and the Nazi party were able to quickly raise enough followers to take control of the country's parliament. They returned to the German people their lost values, personal pride and the illusion of personal power. They restored the people's love for their country. They promoted worship of their leader, honour, fear and blind obedience to achieving the party's goals. A major point here is that the leaders were feeding not only their own ego and personal needs but also the people's. Many German people did not realise they were being manipulated until it was too late.

The communists in Russia under Stalin ruled through fear, but also played on people's needs so as to stay in power. Why am I mentioning this? To show you that people are willing to give their power away when their basic needs are being satisfied. The problem here, though, was that by giving away their power they became trapped within a powerful and ruthless regime.

People's basic needs are, therefore, susceptible to ruthless manipulation. Adopting a positive approach to meeting such needs, however, true leaders can capture the hearts and minds of those working with them by satisfying their needs and allowing each individual to be self-empowered, motivated and to experience a strong feeling of personal development. Today's leaders/managers are responsible for their colleagues' feelings of positive wellbeing and happiness. Tolerating poor attitudes and behaviour can only be a mirroring of what is running in the unconscious mind of a leader/manager as well as in that of employees.

Getting More Out of Your Brain with Less Effort

Once it is recognised that honing the intellect and gaining knowledge is only a part of what life is really about, and that we are only using a small portion of our mind/brain system, a quite different 'thoughtscape' (the landscape of the conscious mind) develops. We enter a world where it becomes possible to 'do more by doing less'. We enter a world where life can be brought into positive balance with greater ease. We enter a world where truth is prevalent rather than illusions! We enter a world where it is increasingly possible to maintain a feeling of inner positive wellbeing and happiness. It is all a matter of opening a door in your consciousness and raising awareness to a higher level. This can be in two stages.

- ➢ The first stage is to recognise the need to use more of the right-brain hemisphere, because it is the home of the imagination, intuition and creative abilities, amongst other attributes.

> The second stage is to use various techniques that will help us access the other 90 percent of the brain and mind system (left and right-brain hemispheres plus conscious and unconscious minds). This is infinitely more powerful than just using the left and right-brain hemispheres. A key point to remember here is:

'if you think what you have always thought, then you'll get what you've always got!'

Einstein recognised that at best he was using about 10 percent of his mind/brain system. Nevertheless, he was able to naturally access his other 90 percent. Music was one of the tools he used to get there. As he played his violin, he may not have realised that he was increasing his level of alpha brainwaves to access the other 90 percent. An interesting point to make here is that if we actually think of certain types of relaxing music and silently play it in the mind, this too induces an increased level of alpha brainwaves, which represents a doorway to enter creative thinking. This happens because the brain cannot tell the difference between hearing the music and playing it in your imagination!

Normal day to day thoughts are filtered through the belief system which sets thinking boundaries within the conscious mind (that virtual box). Such boundaries are strongly in place today in the Western world and a great many of these boundaries are long past their sell by date. They have the potential to be upgraded slowly but surely through a natural process of understanding of what is going on at the sub-atomic level. Old ways die hard though, and the institutional structures that we all grew up with have been very resistant to change until the beginning of the 21st century. Change usually happens when the 'old guard' retire, which enables new structures and approaches within government, business, education and so forth, to be adopted. Economic downturns that put pressure on funding also play a major part in any restructuring. Change may appear to be unpleasant at times and not everyone wants to go with the flow. Nonetheless, nature's process of change is inevitable! We make our lives easier and more interesting by recognising, trying to understand, and adjusting to the change that is happening. As President Obama stated many times on his first election campaign: *'you are the change'*, and indeed we all are

Research into the effects of brain-training on people has progressed enormously over the last twenty years. Understanding brain plasticity is producing amazing results in helping people recover from such conditions as strokes and brain damage. Part of what this book is about is to recognise how the brain is used, about consciousness, and the link between the two. Amazing advances have been made with regard to honing the intellect, and the increase in technology has been breath-taking this last 100 years since the days of Einstein. That exponential increase in technological innovations is due to increasing numbers of scientists, engineers, business people and so on operating outside of their closed virtual box of thinking. What does this mean? Diagram 6.10 on the left-hand side shows the physical brain which is divided into two separate hemispheres connected in the middle by a concentration of nerve fibres called the Corpus Collosum.

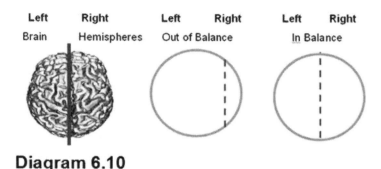

Diagram 6.10

To recap on the properties of the brain, the left-brain hemisphere is the part that deals with the intellect, reason, rational thinking, reading, writing, arithmetic, scientific method, detailed analysis (mechanistic approach), and so on (see chapter 2 for more details). In comparison, the right-brain hemisphere is responsible for the imagination, creative arts, intuitive intelligence, inspiration, dealing with the big picture, emotional expression and related behaviour, and so on.

The circle in the middle of the diagram shows the proportional use of the mind/brain system when we focus upon the intellect at school and in further education and absorb information during brain development. Here, the mind/brain system is out of balance having too much emphasis on left-brain hemisphere development. A problem with education today is that it still drives individuals to look at things from a mechanistic, material (form-based) and linear time-biased perspective. What is required is a balanced approach in education to develop individuals' abilities to produce an outcome similar to the right-hand circle.

Ultimately, the whole field of life leadership is affected by this out-of-balance perspective which we have been conditioned to accept. This cuts out the benefits gained from including right-brain hemisphere development. Leadership training, where boxes are being ticked as regards the things to do and the things to say, and we are being taught to work out strategies on a similar basis to obtain support, is the mechanistic style of leadership. We lead in this way, whether we like it or not, from within a closed virtual box of thinking which is left-brain (Intellect) hemisphere-oriented. In reality, this approach is quite limiting. At best, what works in one situation or company or country does not necessarily work in another. Using more of the right-brain hemisphere increases the level of success in what a leader is doing. It can easily raise the leader's level of achievement from mediocrity to excellence. Half the battle in using more of the right-brain hemisphere is to recognise what it does and then to get involved in activities that encourage its development. The emotional aspects involved in leadership training, such as bonding and camaraderie (a feeling of belonging) are well understood today, but successfully implementing this aspect can be challenging, especially within a mechanistic and form-based thinking organisation.

Dare Your-self – Use Your Right-brain Hemisphere!
Both left- and right-brain hemispheres have a natural aptitude for working together. When I worked in project finance and direct investments, I used to build integrated financial models of different projects (power stations, gold mines, manufacturing industries, petrochemical plants, dairy farms, retail outlets and so on) on my computer to check their feasibility over the long-term (5 to 10 years). My right-rain hemisphere would deal with seeing the whole project and understanding how it worked (holistic and non-linear). My left-brain hemisphere handled the detail and information I considered necessary as inputs for the financial model and to carry out the analysis required. Both hemispheres were required when I made an overall 'what if' risk assessment at the end of the project analysis. As I advanced in my career and took on more managerial tasks, the advice and guidance I gave to both clients and colleagues began to focus more on right-brain hemisphere activities, namely creative insights, hunches, and so on. Slowly but surely, the power of my right-brain hemisphere was increasingly being called into action.

To get our creative and intuitive thoughts to flow, a tactical change of thinking to encourage these thoughts is required. The thoughts are generally associated with:

- taking a broad overall view of what is going on (looking at the forest and not the trees).

- practising visualisation (Chapter 2 and getting into the other 90 percent and the Zone).

- using your imagination to think outside your current set of beliefs. For example, take ownership of the belief that you actually have infinite potential. Recognise that what you attract to you is caused by the programs running within your unconscious mind. And acknowledge that you, at an authentic level, are 100 percent responsible for what happens to you, and so on.

- practising use of your intuition. You can do this by disguising it as a guesstimate. For example, note down which of your favourite sports teams you feel is going to win; what time will you arrive at a particular destination; whether or not someone is reliable; whether or not you will win at whatever sport or game you are participating in. It is not really a guesstimate, for when you practise your intuition you are tuning into a 'what is', and 'what if' reality at a sub-atomic level (equivalent to making a telephone call at an energy level to find out the probability of what is already there).

Most successful achievers have an ability to work with both brain hemispheres. However, for others, the phrase 'being stuck in the head' is very apt. When you operate from your head, it limits your chances of success. What does this mean? It means that creative (out of the box) thinking is sparse except for a few naturally-orientated creative individuals. It also means that emotional intelligence is hardly recognised, and understanding the power of the imagination, intuition and intuitive intelligence to is almost non-existent. These attributes, as I have emphasised before, tend to be scorned in the world of the intellect! This results in most of what can be considered the really good stuff in life being left out. I say most of the good stuff, because in my own life, and in some of my colleagues', life became more interesting and satisfying as we created a balance by using both brain hemispheres. For many, using the intellect alone and recalling information did not give them the satisfaction and inner feeling of positive wellbeing that they expected from their working lives. I also noticed that other colleagues managed to compensate for the monotony of their careers through other activities outside of work such as playing a musical instrument, painting, amateur dramatics, or golf, or football, or sailing and so on. They were unaware as to how to integrate their creative abilities with their day to day work but managed to satisfy it through other activities.

A way to optimise your effectiveness as a leader is through your communication with others, and it is helpful to have an idea of their communication preferences.

What is Your Communication Preference?
How many times have you communicated with others and felt that they did not understand you, even though you were communicating something simple? How many times have you felt irritated because an individual communicating with you was not clear? And maybe you were also told at times by someone that if you do not understand what they are saying, you shouldn't be there or doing whatever it was you were doing? Clearly, that doesn't do wonders for your self-esteem! This happened to me once during a nuclear physics lecture where I was told that if I did not understand what was being explained, I should not be there. Sometime later, a different lecturer actually took responsibility for her communication by saying "if you have not understood these equations it is because I have not explained them clearly". What a great woman! Thanks to her patience I passed all my rather complex mathematics exams (in spite of being dyslexic). What is it that can cause a miscommunication?

Neuro Linguistic Programming (NLP) was put together, in the mid-nineteen seventies, by two interesting American psychologists, Dr Richard Bandler (a student) and John Grinder (a lecturer) at the University of California at Santa Cruz. NLP represents a technology of the mind. The foundation of NLP was laid down from transcripts of Gestalt therapists, and Dr Bandler observed certain structures arising. Both Dr Bandler and John Grinder noticed that they could model these structures, which represented what was going on within an individual's consciousness (conscious and unconscious minds). I use their models throughout this book, such as reframing, perceptual positions, representational systems, changing your cognitive map and so on. I was especially interested in why, during some of the business meetings I conducted, or in some workshops and seminars I gave, that not everyone appeared to have understood what I was communicating. NLP was enormously beneficial here, and I was shown how to improve my communication skills.

How we communicate is mainly affected by our sensory or receptor organs: eyes (visual), ears (auditory), kinaesthetic (feeling, touching, motion) and to some extent through taste (gustatory) and smell (olfactory) sensors. Communication is also affected by the inner dialogue that is running within the conscious mind. Each of us uses our natural sensory organs in a slightly different way as we translate what is happening to us and around us into actual thoughts and words. What does this mean? It means that some of us are more visually orientated, create images in the mind and use a lot of visual-based words when we communicate. Some individuals have a higher auditory orientation and will use more words in their communication associated with sounds. Others may be more feeling orientated with a natural emphasis in their communications that is biased towards words of feeling and emotion. We present, or represent, what we wish to communicate in a way that reflects our built-in individual bias. Many studies have been carried out which indicate that there is a natural bias ranking of visual-, auditory- and kinaesthetic-based words used in communication. One of these will be our primary style of representation and the others more secondary. A few simple examples are:

(Visual)	**(Auditory)**	**(Kinaesthetic)**
I see your point.	I hear what you are saying.	I feel that I am in touch with what you are saying.
I want you to take a look at this.	I want you to make this loud and clear.	I want you to get a grip on this.
Have I sketched this out clearly?	Does what I am saying sound right to you?	Are you able to get a handle on this?
I know beyond a shadow of doubt that this is true.	That information is accurate word for word.	That information is as solid as a rock.
That is pretty hazy to me.	That doesn't really ring a bell.	I'm not sure that I'm following you.

When people communicate with you, they will use words that reflect their dominant representation. All of us use a mixture of these three styles but one of the representational attributes is usually dominant. Those involved in catering may have a bias in the use of gustatory (tasting) and olfactory (smelling) words. A gustatory statement could be 'this whole situation leaves me with a bad taste'. An olfactory statement could be 'these facts do not add up and I smell a rat here'. Try to *mirror* their form of speech back to them as closely as possible. They will feel comfortable with you and also feel that you understand them. At first this may prove to be a rather difficult and too analytical a task. Persevere, because you will be well rewarded for doing so. Practise using a mixture of the first three sensors in your writing as it will make more people feel that you are on their wavelength.

How to Identify Similar Communication Preferences

If you are running a seminar or workshop and want to find out which is the preferred representation for each participant, here is a quick check. You will require a pack of three cards, one red, one yellow and one green. Ask each participant to choose one of those cards. The coloured cards are primary representations of different communication styles:

red: visual
yellow: auditory
green: feeling

Divide the participants into groups of two, each pair having chosen the same colour. Ask each one to speak to the other for three minutes describing their favourite holiday scene or music or sport or whatever. Both participants should feel comfortable with the session. Now mix them up with each going through a similar exercise with an individual with a different coloured card. Ask them how they felt? Was it as good an experience as their previous one? Individuals with a different representation usually feel uncomfortable with each other's communication style in comparison with the same style. Certain observations can be made to give you a clue as to what type of representation an individual is using.

1. Visual

It is said that *'the eyes are the windows to the soul'*. Eyes can certainly show you the thinking preference of the individual that you are communicating with. If you are in a one-to-one situation and close enough while in conversation, observe how their eyes move. This will give you another clue as to which representation they are following (remember to reverse what you are looking at as you are opposite them).

People's eyes will move in their own special way. Both drawings show an individual using visual representations (looking up to the left or right means 'yes'). As you are asking questions, the left-hand drawing represents an individual creating an image in their mind of what you are talking about. The right-hand drawing is where the individual is recalling an image from their long-term memory. However, if someone is recalling an image from their short-term memory they are more likely to look straight ahead during the thinking process.

Visual people usually:

- process their thoughts quickly
- speak quickly with a higher pitched voice
- stand or sit with their head and body erect
- sit forward in their chair
- breath in a shallow way from the top of their lungs
- like to dress well and are organized
- learn best from visual images

The next example is for auditory representation:

2. Auditory

Importantly here, the eyes will move either to the left or right horizontally. To elicit this eye movement ask a question that involves auditory sounds in the future like 'what would you think if the Prime Minister or President sang with a soprano voice'? Watch for the eyes moving to the right as in the left-hand drawing. If you ask them to recall a voice, for example a school teacher, or film star, or politician or friend, the eyes would move to the left as shown in the right-hand drawing.

Auditory people usually:

- speak in a rhythmic manner with resonant tones in their voice
- breathe from the middle of their upper body
- frequently talk to themselves silently with their lips moving
- sometimes tilt their head to the side while in conversation
- learn by listening
- want to hear feedback

3. Kinaesthetic

Feelings involve both inner feelings, that is emotions and the physical representation of them: gut feel – intuition, or tactile - physical touch. The left-hand drawing shows eye movement (down to the right) in response to a question which requires a feeling type response such as: imagine your-self sky diving or perhaps skin diving off a coral reef – how would you feel? The right-hand drawing shows the eye position (down to the left) where someone is having a silent internal dialogue with themselves, if you have asked a question that requires some time to think.

Kinaesthetic people usually:

- speak with a deep voice, talking slowly
- breathe from their diaphragm (bottom of lungs)
- appear to think more slowly in comparison with a visual individual
- Are quite physical and respond to touching and the feel of things
- stand quite close in conversation

All of the above eye movements indicate different thinking styles and primary representations. It is important to practise observing people over a period of time and in different situations to become proficient in using this technique. Sometimes the eye movements can be very quick and you will need to spot them when they occur. Individuals using the same representational and thinking styles bond together more easily.

Using your Communication Preference Power to Bond

Identifying how different individuals communicate, including how we communicate with our self, helps us to establish a bond with each other and our self. What many do not realise is that we need to form a bond with ourselves as well as with others, for if we dislike ourselves it is unlikely that we will be able to bond really well with others. The task here is to find out why this is so. Is it due to low self-esteem, or that we have been or are being abused in some way, or because we are feeling insecure, and so on? Diagram 6.11 shows ten communication attributes that we all use which affect our rapport with others. The outer five cover different styles that are used in external communication. I call these 'external attributes' meaning what you see, hear and feel. In comparison, the inner five attributes represent the inner drivers which are operating at an unconscious or sub-atomic energy level (I call these 'internal attributes'). Each of these attributes contributes to our communication rapport with others.

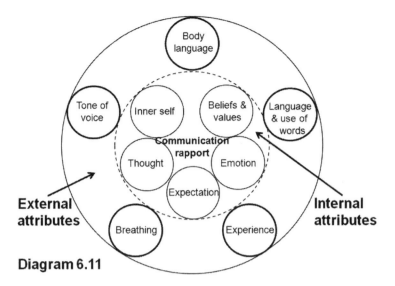

Diagram 6.11

External Attributes

Body Language

I pointed out in chapter 5 that 58 percent of an individual's assessment of a person on first meeting will be unconsciously focused on body language. Are they sitting upright in a chair, or standing upright? Are they round shouldered and bent forward? Have they a nervous twitch? Do they make eye contact when speaking, and so on? When you are communicating with someone you can strengthen the relationship with them by attempting to match their body language. Common sense rules here so do not overdo it otherwise they may think that you are being rude, patronising or mildly mocking!

Tone of Voice

Is their tone of voice uplifting, or depressing, or weak, and so forth? This represents 35 percent of the unconscious mind's assessment of an individual. The tone of voice used can tell you a lot about an individual provided you are listening (that is you are actually hearing their voice tones as well as the words used). If someone is speaking in a depressed voice, start at their level and lift your tone slowly to meet the tone that you wish to communicate with. You can lift a depressed individual out of their low mood to a higher and more positive level and so strengthen your relationship. If they are shouting, start at that level and ramp it down to a normal level. They should match what you are doing. If they are speaking too fast, start at that speed and then slow down your response or vice versa. Get them to adjust to your pace.

Language & Words Used

When you are observing and speaking with an individual, the words they use provide about 7 percent of your conscious/unconscious assessment. They also provide other clues which give you an insight into their thinking and communication representations. Nonetheless, what's in a word? Sometimes – everything, and we're immediately drawn into the reality within a relationship, once again, where you are either:

1. *contributing to the relationship* (with all the positive benefits that it brings),
   or
2. *contaminating the relationship* (with all the disadvantages that it brings).

This may come as a shock to most people, as we are conditioned to believe that there is a third way in relationships and that is to apportion blame: "it's certainly not me, it's them", or "I did not ask for this", and so on. This is all a matter of how we are conditioned from birth, and it shows little or no understanding of what is really going on at an energy and sub-atomic (quantum) level – that is the unconscious mirroring of issues (life lessons) between both parties. It is important to recognise that there is no third way in a communication with others, only the above two. Quite difficult to accept at times but true.

Breathing
Similar to getting used to recognising eye movements, this exercise may take some time to master. Watch the individual's shoulders or chest as they breathe and try to match their breathing. If they are speaking quickly try to get them to slow their speech down as this will help to help them to change their breathing. As you change your breathing rate you are also helping to stabilise your energy state and theirs. Like two tuning forks, you will be in tune and beat to the same frequency of the individual opposite, if you can get them to match your slow breathing, or vice versa.

Experience
If the person with whom you are communicating has a similar background or interests, both of you have some experiences which you can share. This will enable you both to feel comfortable as you will be on a similar wavelength. Two engineers, or accountants, or lawyers, or salespersons will have lots of experiences to share which can create rapport between them so that both parties will feel at ease.

The above external attributes contribute to enabling a harmonious relationship between a leader and those with whom he or she is communicating. What is it that stimulates these attributes? They are stimulated by the authentic-self and/or fabricated-self and by the thoughts running in the conscious and unconscious minds. In addition, there is another set of attributes - internal attributes, which are energy drivers that influence the external attributes at the sub-atomic or quantum level.

*

Internal Attributes

Authentic-self

The authentic-self usually has the disadvantage of being taken over by the fabricated-self. This fabricated-self has an infinite number of wants and also manages the personalities through the ego. In comparison the authentic-self has a limited number of needs which I elaborated upon earlier. Most important of all, the authentic-self communicates by providing us with strong inner urges to do something or not do something. It gets us to stop suddenly before something happens to us such as an accident. There is plenty of evidence to show this where an individual changes their mind about taking a flight and the plane crashes, or not catching their usual train which has an accident or breaks down. Many examples have been given by the survivors of 9/11 who got delayed, or missed a connection, or stayed at home, and so forth.

The authentic-self works through intuition and tries to nudge us back onto life's path if we have strayed too far off of it. It can also warn us about something that we do not need to experience. When we lead others, it can help us keep on the path which is of maximum benefit for all concerned. Be aware though, that a situation which appears to be negative, for example being made redundant, or the break-up of a relationship, may in the end be of major benefit. This is because we are being forced to move on and to start afresh in a new direction on our life's journey. This is because we have completed the growth requirement where we were and it is time to move on to the next life challenge. Or we were not learning the lessons that we were confronted with and are being moved along to a new location or situation to provide us with another chance to learn and grow. Finally, the authentic-self via the soul provides us with a thought that can give us the direction we are looking for. Provided we are listening.

Beliefs and Values

Once again, beliefs are the filters which colour what we accept as being true. They affect our perception of what is happening around us and to us. They affect our personal development and the development of others with whom we have some influence. So, too, do the values we hold. What do I mean by values? A value can be something that is useful, or important, or of worth (not only monetary worth). A value can also apply to moral principles. Just like beliefs, values come from the family, relations, friends, school, college, ethnic background, position in society (including economic), work colleagues, religion, and so on. As you can see, values are very important drivers in life. They are another set of filters that affect attitudes and behaviour. They have an effect upon the outcome of what we get ourselves involved in, and in the work we are doing. As such, they operate just like beliefs. The good news is that it is possible to change a value which is proving to be detrimental to us on our life's journey simply by thinking about it and re-scripting it in the conscious mind. This is similar to what we can do with a belief that is having a negative effect upon our life. The key here is to remember that we nearly always have a choice in life. And *we* are responsible for the choices we make, no one else, although before we are able to leave home and stand on our own two feet, strong elements of control by others, or lack of, can affect or limit the choices available. Beliefs and values are the main programmers of the quantum bio-magnetic field. Their input ensures that we face the issues/life lessons and growth challenges we have been born to meet, as well as to direct where this can best be experienced.

Thought

Energy follows thought and its effect on day to day living is covered in Chapter 2. Take some time to monitor your thoughts for a moment, as they provide an indication of what you are attracting into your life. Also note whether the thoughts are past, present or future. The past is only really of interest to us for the *wisdom* it offers, or for the enrichment we get from the conserved natural environment and the creative products of the generations that went before us. That is why we value cave art, the classical music of great masters, the pyramids, Shakespeare, and so on. If we focus upon past negative worries, anxiety or fear it will attract to us, through the essence of those thoughts, negative experiences in the present. Such experiences attract unpleasant encounters (conflicts) at work from colleagues or managers, or in family and social relationships, and so on. They can cause the attraction of a lack of abundance (relationships, money, opportunities, happiness). If this is happening, we can ask our-self:

'what is it within me that is causing me to attract . . .' (whatever is happening to you or what it is you are not happy about).

A considerable amount of time is also spent worrying about the future. This is such a de-motivating and destructive pursuit, for what we focus repeatedly upon has a high probability of manifesting in our life. So many people have bought into:

'live in the now!'

The above statement is fine, provided we know how to live in the now; *now* involves working through and clearing issues and/or life lessons so they will no longer be running in our field. This means that we should no longer attract to us or be attracted to such experiences. Sometimes the experience may return but as a test to see how we handle it. If we handle it badly, it will stay with us until we bring it into balance.

Part of the purpose of being here is to refine the choices and decisions we make so as to improve the quality of our life. Once we have done this, living in the *now* is the way to go.

Metaphorically speaking, there are no free lunches in life and we all need to work through our issues and life lessons, in one way or another! When we gain a basic understanding of the energetic or energy effects caused by thoughts, it is possible to influence and improve our future. Take charge of your thoughts, get rid of those ANTs and re-programme your quantum bio-magnetic field for success so that you are attracted to, or attract to you what you desire.

Emotion
Emotions are created from what we experience in life. They are the real energy power drivers that attract the different scenes in our lives. Emotions are the major contributor to how we behave, the attitudes shown, our feelings of wellbeing, the amount of drive we have to achieve our goals, how happy we feel, and so on. EQ, as described earlier, is an essential part of personal development for us to succeed in the 21st century. It is a major challenge to bring our emotional life into balance, similar to other challenges we face such as attempting to experience most things in moderation, without too many extremes, and being considerate not only to those around us but also to ourselves. We need to be able to control our own emotions, attitudes and behaviour so that we can find the path towards a fulfilling and happy journey with others glad to follow our leadership.

Expectation
Expectations are so important in life and I cover them in detail in Chapters 4 and 7. They can give us, and those around us, *hope* for today and the future; they can turn negative beliefs around, and they can provide us with an eager anticipation for life. Although much academic study has been carried out on the effect of the expectations a teacher holds for their students and the effect of their attitude and behaviour on students, so many appear to just not 'get it'. Expectations, rather than just being another academic subject, constitute a *state of mind and emotion* from which each of us would gain great benefits. What is this state of mind/emotion? It's a state where you recognise that each person has infinite potential and your job is to find how to release it. Raising the Power of Expectations can have a miraculous effect on those who may appear to be struggling with life's problems, or those who have come to demand much less of themselves. Such individuals have learnt to accommodate to other people's low expectations on account of class, racial origin, level of education, and so on. The psychology of expectations has the potential to raise individuals to higher states of excellence and achievement. Expectations are all powerful and can over-ride false beliefs and confound stereotypes.

Use the Power of your Expectations to Achieve Success
In life leadership, each of us constantly wields enormous power, if we only recognise it. What do I mean? In chapter 2, I emphasised that the physical brain and body act like a transmitter

and receiver. What we think about not only affects our emotions, motivation and physical state but also our inner (spiritual) state of being. Moreover, the energy of thoughts which are stimulating the brain and body are also being transmitted into the atmosphere. In communicating with someone, they not only hear the words spoken but can also pick up the thoughts behind the words through their unconscious mind (chapters 3 and 4). This usually takes the form of an inner sense, or feeling, that can strengthen or weaken an individual's acceptance with respect to what you are communicating to them.

Whether or not self-leadership or inspiring others is involved, what we think in our conscious mind is of major importance. If we have genuinely high expectations about an individual this will be sensed by them and they will respond accordingly, either immediately or over time. If we have high expectations about achieving our own goals, and we focus on the successful completion of that goal in the present, then there is a high probability that we will achieve it. Expectations play a very an important part in all leadership roles. Expectations have, as pointed out before, an amazing *placebo* effect on performance in the same way that criticism and careless words as well as negative tones of voice have an instant *nocebo* effect. If our expectations are high, we can be sure that these expectations will be mirrored back to us. If we allow doubt to creep in, I can guarantee that it will have a detrimental effect on ourselves and on those we are leading.

Part of the challenging task of 'getting it' in life is to recognise the Power of Expectations. Entering the world of expectations, the mechanistic world that we are used to is left behind. We step into the sub-atomic or quantum world in which thoughts operate. We are stepping into the world of energy and how it affects in a spontaneous manner biological structures such as the brain and body. We are also stepping into the world of emotions and how they affect attitude, behaviour and performance in education, work, home and play. In short, it is vital to learn when to get out of our heads (the Intellect – left-brain hemisphere) and move our consciousness more towards the right-brain hemisphere. It is also essential to take our consciousness into the Heart subtle energy body through the vortex energy centres (VECs chapter 3). The Heart subtle energy body is the emotional home of empathy, trust, compassion and sympathetic understanding amongst others. In addition, when setting goals, the power of intentions and expectations work well together, as they bring a common focus on what we wish to achieve in our lives.

Goal Setting: An Integral Step toward Achieving Success
Why should we consider setting goals? Is it because it focuses the conscious mind on an outcome that we desire? Most certainly, and this question is best demonstrated with an example. In the 1970s, Harvard business school started keeping detailed records of its graduates. During the late 1990s they wanted to find out how successful, from a monetary

standpoint, their graduates had been. One particular result involving graduates right at the top of the monetary scale surprised the professors. They had consistently set annual goals of performance for themselves and, of course, their business. They represented the top 3 percent and were worth in monetary terms about 90 percent more than the remaining 97 percent of the graduates. Some 13 percent set goals from time to time but the remaining 84 percent did not. From an abundance perspective, is setting goals important? Absolutely, and by abundance I not only mean solely financial abundance but also abundance in relationships, creative achievements, generosity, empathy, and so forth. Before delving into the mechanics of how goals work, let me define what exactly a goal is. A dictionary definition says it is:

> *'a state of affairs that a plan is intending to achieve and when achieved the behaviour intended to achieve it is terminated'*

Another and perhaps more practical definition is:

> *'a plan or target, or accomplishment, or action, or situation, or outcome and so forth that you wish to achieve, despite any inertia or chaos around you'*

From an energy perspective, and that is how I set my goals, I visualise what it is I want to achieve in my imagination in the present. I follow up in my thinking with a plan and then write it down to show how I am going to successfully it. At each stage of the plan I visualise it successfully completed in the present within my imagination. An important emphasis here is that I visualise my goal always being *successfully completed in the present*. At the level of the unconscious mind, this process is directing the energy from my thoughts, my intention and expectations towards the successful manifestation of the goal.

If you are in a leadership position in a company or other organisation, there is a major pitfall that most people do not recognise which is advisable to correct. A leader needs to learn when to stop leading and let the natural process of events work its way through to a conclusion. One of Britain's great leaders, Margaret Thatcher, fell into the trap of not knowing when to stand down. Probably unconsciously addicted to the power and control which the position gave her, she refused to relinquish her position and was removed by her colleagues. History will be less kind to her achievements because of this. Compare Mikhail Gorbachov, the President of Russia in a similar time period as Margaret Thatcher; he knew that it was time to resign, and after allowing for a natural process of succession to take effect he resigned. It is important to let goals come into fruition in a natural and effortless way. What usually happens is that we tend to micro-manage the process of achieving a goal, making it hard work and at times difficult to achieve. It is a bit like planting a tulip bulb and digging it up once a week during spring to see how it is progressing. Would you do that? Absolutely not!

Diagram 6.12 summarises the steps involved in achieving goals.

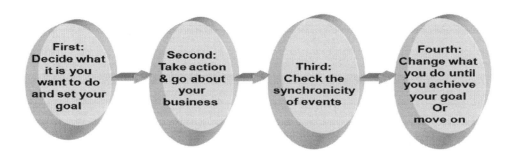

Diagram 6.12

There is a saying – *'go with the flow',* which is important once we have set up our goals. We need to not micro manage our-self, that is, we should avoid looking at every step in detail, for it just makes hard work of the process. We need to watch out for synchronistic happenings and try not to be blinkered. What do I mean? Sometimes when we set a goal, we may not realise that it is not in our best interest, so we should keep our eyes and sensors open and if we are experiencing difficulties (resistance), step back and review where we are and assess what it means. It can mean that the goal may not be one that is achievable and we, therefore, need to reconsider whether or not to continue in that specific direction. This is appropriate for business goals, relationship goals, monetary goals, and so forth.

Let us note the following Universal Law:

> *'whether a goal is for your-self or others, when you are in the flow, everything you do should be done as effortlessly as possible to achieve the goal'*

So the test here is that the challenges should be overcome without too much effort. There are times where we can force your goal into fruition but this can be at a great cost to our-self or others. Another behaviour that breaks up the flow towards achieving a goal, is to look back at some past negative experience and worry that it will recur (diagram 6.13). It is part of the human condition to worry about something that is going to occur in the future, for example a job interview, marriage, buying a car or house. Diagram 6.13 shows a process where focusing on a negative experience on a future outcome, or an actual past (historical) negative experience will cause us to fall into a trap so that the goal will not be achieved. Worrying is a powerful obstacle to achieving goals and it is advisable to remove any worries, if they surface. The opposite, where we focus upon a positive outcome, can contribute powerfully towards its manifestation.

History infiltrates the present and programs the future

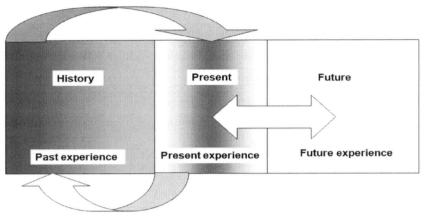

Diagram 6.13

The old maxim that we are generally not taught to recognise is, once again:

'history infiltrates the present and programs (or affects) the future'

What you choose to think is yours to make. It comes down to:

1. Have you worked through negative experiences from the past and brought them into balance so as not to keep repeating them?
2. Do you project a positive outcome for a future goal happening in the present (the now)?

If the answer to the above two questions is 'yes', you are thinking and moving in the right direction!

In life leadership, goals are important, as you are planting the energetic seeds of what you wish to achieve in the future. Through thoughts, intentions and expectations a powerful flow of energy is brought into focus to help in the manifestation process of your goal. Finally, the basic steps to consider when you are setting your goals:

1. chose a goal that is worthwhile and that you believe you can fulfil
2. put the goal into context
3. look at different strategies to successfully achieve the goal
4. evaluate honestly the effect of success
5. state the goal positively and express it in sensory terms (how you will feel when you achieve it).

There is a goal that I suggest we all need to consider seriously, which is to focus on bringing our authentic-self into our goal setting process (chapter 7). The principal reason we need to do this is because the authentic-self knows why we are here and what our purpose is. The authentic-self connects us with our happiest-self, confident-self, creative abilities, higher intelligence and intuitive intelligence. Most people tend to get totally involved in the dramas of life and cannot see the wood for the trees. This is our ego-driven fabricated-self in full flow. We think that the drama is what life is really all about! Certainly our virtual box of thinking keeps us in the drama because it is ego exercising its rights again! We see the drama as being real, and say 'yes of course it's real. Just look – it's happening all around me!' The task here is to consciously step out of the drama without engaging in extreme emotions or external conflict.

Measuring your success in achieving your goals is another step towards getting to 'know your-self'. I suggest that this is of prime importance and I do not make this statement lightly. I have extrapolated from sayings at the temple of Delphi, the following:

> 'know thyself and the wisdom of the universe and the secrets
> of the Gods shall be known unto you'

There is another important point that I would like to make here and that is:

> 'it's the journey through life that's important and not the outcomes'

Progressing through life, we change our identity many times by putting on different masks (Chapter 5) in an effort to cope with life's pressures. Masks take us further away from our authentic-self. What should we do? A first step is that we are required to extricate ourselves from any drama going on around us, to observe the players and how they are interacting with themselves and with us. From the above you will have gathered that an important skill in life leadership is to step out of the drama and ask your-self:

> 'what is it that I need to learn from what is going on around me?'

This is because what is happening to us will, in general, be a mirroring of the issues and life lessons that are running within our unconscious mind. The mirror will be what is happening around us with respect to people and events. This can be a bit challenging to accept, but with practice it becomes easier and most enlightening. An example might help here. I had a client who was divorced; she was always getting involved with divorced men whose children's lives appeared to be chaotic. Her goal was to sort out the chaos in *their* lives. She would jump into the family dramas and try to sort them out because she wanted to take control. This was not appreciated and the children's father did not welcome her good intentions. In this case, the woman was unaware that deep down she unconsciously believed that her *own* life was out of control. This was due to experiencing a chaotic family background as a child. Her boyfriend's chaotic family was just mirroring this back to her. Understanding that we are quantum bio-magnets attracting to us scenes and situations that reflect what is going on in our unconscious mind can help us to come to terms with this type of situation.

When we are setting our personal goals, do we ever give some thought as to why we are here in a physical body? Do we believe only that we are here just to earn lots of money, buy lots of stuff, get into a relationship, raise some kids, have fun and so on? Do we ever think that perhaps there are some deeper aspects to our life that we may not be aware of? Of course part of life can be all of the above, but there is another part which is what we take with us at the end of our life. And what is that? It is when we have completed our last goal in life - the fulfilment of the soul's contract, which is the real reason for our being here. Our authentic-self will guide us towards achieving this goal, if we let it. Part of our life leadership quest is to recognise this and to allow it to happen, or not, as the case may be.

It can be difficult to be optimistic about life, especially if we let ourselves become hooked into any dramas that are going on around us. Yet, being optimistic is an essential ingredient in life leadership and in attracting what we desire. Applying the psychology of expectations and intention for a successful outcome assumes an optimistic and confident attitude, and that is how we handle the experiences that come up as we travel towards the outcome. This is the important part of the goal exercise.

Confidence - Optimism: A Required State in Life Leadership
When we are leading others, and our-self, we are like the captain of a ship. A captain always has time to listen to the members of his crew. He will usually have a sympathetic ear and will always have a solution to help a crew member with any problems that may arise. Being optimistic, in this position, is an essential trait. Our attitude and behaviour will be infectious to those around us. Indeed our attitude and behaviour is also infectious to our-self. In this state of mind, as a quantum bio-magnet we will attract and be attracted to much more uplifting types of situations. Certainly, there will be challenges which will test the degree of optimism that we hold. Life is always full of contrasts - without them we would soon get bored!

Our life leadership is important for our wellbeing. During the day, if there is an incident where someone makes negative comments to or about us, or our capabilities, I would suggest two ways of handling it:

1. Give some consideration to what has been said. Do so because it's a good idea to check to see if there is something you need to learn from what has been said and what is happening. For what may be perceived as an unpleasant incident can have

some truth behind it. Some resistance in life can be simply a test to see if you really want to achieve a certain goal. At other times such incidents might be suggesting it would be in your best interest to reconsider what you are doing.

2. Walk away and say in your mind, *'cancel, cancel, cancel – I am fine, there is nothing wrong with me, I am good at what I am doing, I will succeed in what I am doing'*, and so on. Keep repeating this appropriate short mantra for as long as it takes for your conscious mind to stop disagreeing with you. I can assure you that your conscious mind will get bored and agree with you after a very short period of time! If a similar situation arises again, go through the same process. However, if it should keep repeating itself, then it would be wise to investigate the reasons. You may discover that your ego is misleading you.

A key to inspiring others when we are in a leadership role is through the example we set. Our ability to do this is affected by such states of mind as:

- do you feel good about your-self?
- are you happy about what you are doing?
- are you comfortable with those who are around you?
- do you feel secure?

If the answer is 'no' to any of these questions, then your quantum bio-magnetic field will ensure that you attract or are attracted to situations that reflect this state. To create a 'yes' from a 'no' means that you need to identify within your-self the cause of the block.

Most of us want to extract the best out of life. We want to attract the best experiences from the situations in which we find ourselves. This includes boosting the abundance in many areas of our life - relationships, material wellbeing, monetary matters, creative pursuits, continued good health, and so on. The next and final chapter is designed to help you to achieve what you really desire in life.

Chapter 7

Life's Journey: Re-awakening to Create an Inspiring Story

*Read not to contradict and confute, not to believe and take for granted,
not to find talk and discourse, but to weigh and consider.*

Sir Francis Bacon: 1561 - 1623

Life's Journey: Re-awakening to Create an Inspiring Story

How curious are you about your life? How much do you think you can change your life to your benefit? I have met and worked with some people who seemed to manifest most of what they set their mind upon. Everything in their life seemed to drop effortlessly into place. So different in comparison with my own experience! They created abundance easily and I was curious to know how they did it. Can we all get a slice of this abundance as we journey along life's path? The answer is 'yes', but it requires us to experience a reawakening and a shift. Each of us is responsible for writing our own life story, and by undergoing the process involved in reawakening, we take the power back into our hands to create that shift whereby we can write a more inspiring story.

What is this reawakening about and how do we do it, in today's uncertain climate? What is the inspiring story about? We do not easily realise that part of our consciousness appears to be asleep and needs to be awakened if we are to enjoy the full benefits of being in a physical body. Which part of our consciousness appears to be asleep? To answer this question I need to expand again on the concept that each of us is born with an authentic-self and that we gain a fabricated-self which develops from birth. It is the authentic-self part of our consciousness that appears to be asleep because the fabricated–self has grown over and blocked regular communications with it. In this chapter, my goal is to help re-establish regular communication between your fabricated-self and authentic-self. I do this by merging the two together. This will empower your natural ability to live an abundant life and to manifest what you desire with ease, through a shift in your energy fields. The inspiring story describes how you can handle the challenges/situations that arise while working towards the outcome.

At the beginning of this chapter, I examine a path that leads into the world of abundance. A natural human trait seems to be to dislike change, especially when it is forced upon us. I find that I am guilty, at times, of procrastinating when I have to make some changes in my own life. Yet change is an important part of our life's growth. I introduce you in this chapter to how President Obama envisages change and I elaborate on the change process that is taking place during this important time period. We all have the potential to make a constructive contribution to what is happening in the world. Our authentic-self can offer a major support to help us through the current changes, if we let it in. Explaining the difference between the dynamics of our physical (fabricated) and spiritual (authentic) selves, provides a framework to clear some false beliefs that are holding us back from attracting the life that we're meant to have. In meeting some of the difficult changes that confront us, it is advisable to tap into an energy reserve called our inner potential. I take you through what this means and elaborate upon the struggles that can occur between our ego and authentic-self.

Getting 'back to basics', to comprehend the challenges we face, is important, and I spell out what this means. I follow on with why life can be difficult, especially due to the influence of ego. A major part of growing through the challenges we face is to trust what is happening to us is for our personal and spiritual growth. The quantum bio-magnetic field around us will have attracted the situations we experience and at times we may get sorely tested in this regard. Life can be tough, and there is always a possibility of experiencing emotional and material loss. I reveal my own experience of what this is about. The experience helped me to come to terms with some of the difficult challenges I faced. All of this leads into the main part of the chapter which is about abundance in its many forms, their manifestation and how to boost them. What blocks us from being abundant in all areas of our life and how to clear the blocks is covered in detail. I conclude by acknowledging that we can all improve our life story if we truly want to.

To attract the good things in life, and to sustain a regular feeling of happiness, getting to 'know your-self' has to be the ultimate challenge that we all face. And this is because as I have pointed out in the book, we are all walking/talking quantum bio-magnets. Part of what we experience as we journey along life's path is a mirroring of the programs running in our consciousness energy fields. The programs are a part of our conditioning from birth through maturity. No matter what social level you are born into, it is the early conditioning that is put in place up to seven years or so of age which programs the unconscious mind with some of the toughest life lessons we are here to work through. Of course, the conditioning that occurs after seven years of age through teen years and beyond also gives rise to more issues and life lessons. These too will need to be looked at and worked through. Whatever our place in society we are all bound by the same Universal Laws. Laws produced by governments are mainly about keeping the population under control and can be shaped to favour different social groups. The Universal Laws on the other hand are by their very nature immutable and affect everyone equally. The titles people adopt are merely labels which add an extra tone to the different scenes/acts that we play out along life's path. We are all here to experience a variety of challenges which enable us to work through our life lessons.

I hear so many people say that if they had lots of money they would be very happy. My own experience from travelling around the world has shown this to be a false belief and one that is driven by the ego! Of course, money is an important ingredient in our lives but it does not buy long-term happiness and contentment. Certainly, attracting sufficient money to enable us to get a life and satisfy our desires without being a workaholic should be a goal. But how much money do we actually need to achieve an acceptable life? In the end, you may discover that the answer is - very little. For most of us to reach an acceptable balance, there is a necessity to enable a change in our thinking and feeling processes that will stimulate a transformation and make a shift in our thinking. Some of the changes to be considered may prove to be very challenging. This is a part of our life experience which can be made a whole lot easier by simply getting to know ourselves more intimately. In doing so, the process of re-awakening through the choices/decisions we make and the challenges/situations that we experience will guide us to everything we need. Happiness will become a regular experience.

You are the Change
In the United States of America, one of President Barrack Obama's main thrusts during his 2008 election campaign was for change. His words were not only timely but prophetic. His words were a call for all Americans to re-awaken and create an inspiring story for their lives. In reality it is a call for all of us to do likewise. We are all citizens of the world. This book provides many suggestions for processes and methodologies to help us make some necessary changes, strengthen the support we give our-self, and ultimately the support we give our family, friends and country. As individuals we need to lead by example, something that has been lacking to a great extent in today's fast moving, rule-based world where politicians believe that making rules to control as much of life as they can is needed to keep the population in check. On President Obama's rostrum, during his 2008 pre-election speeches, he sometimes used a slogan that stated this is:

'our time for change'

As individuals we are being confronted, at the beginning of the 21st century, with a need to not only change ourselves but also to contribute to progressive change in our country and the world. Have we the ability to change ourselves? This is a very personal question and it starts with each of us as an individual. I have always looked at politicians, whether male or female, as the leaders of our country. However, the current economic models used detract from their ability to offer us proper direction and a vision for the future. Instead we are encouraged to consume and to spend. We are regularly subjected to advertisements persuading us to consume more. Now there is nothing wrong with this provided it is kept in balance, but many people respond by accumulating more debt. The game continues until the market (those taking credit) becomes saturated with debt and can take very little more. Here comes the uncomfortable part; individuals who made use of excessive credit are ultimately responsible, as they had a choice. So, too, are those who promoted increasing debt. Where was the wisdom from those who should have known better - our politicians and bankers? They had an opportunity to offer sensible suggestions to guide people under their care on the dangers of taking on too much credit. Where was the fiscal guidance? Where was the leadership?

Notwithstanding the above, President Obama recognised the innate ability we all have to change for the better. Here is another slogan:

'change – yes you can'

All of this is very exemplary, but he knew and expressed his understanding of the people he addressed when he stated that we should all become involved in:

'change we can believe in'

There is a 'Catch 22' situation to this last change statement, though! It is necessary to believe what we hear for a successful change to take place. One of the greatest challenges in life is to recognise and change the *false* beliefs that have been conditioned within us from birth. These beliefs affect our perception of what is happening to us and around us. They stop us from making progressive changes. What are these false beliefs? Running in our unconscious mind may be false programs such as 'I'm not good enough', or 'I cannot do it', or 'nobody loves me', or 'I never win at anything', or 'money is hard to come by', or 'I will never have enough money', or 'relationships are always difficult', or 'nobody in my family can do maths or draw, or write, or spell'. Sociologist Wilfred I Thomas once famously said:

> *'things that are imagined as real become real as a consequence of*
> *believing that they are real'*

So, are the things you are telling your-self really true? Absolutely not, and you only believed it because someone you looked up to told you so. And you did not question it. Creating beliefs is covered in Chapter 4. The false beliefs we carry are not only about ourselves but also what we think life is about, what is happening to us, what is going on around us and in the world. Ultimately, false beliefs are disempowering. We are now in a time period where each individual has an opportunity to take back their power, to contribute to the greater good of themselves, family and their country. It is a time to engage in what President Obama referred to as the:

'change we need'

Some of your false beliefs will by now have been exposed, enabling you to work on them. My goal, once again, is to raise your awareness, by opening some doors within your consciousness to create a shift in your thinking so that you can strengthen the connection between your fabricated-self and your authentic-self. This will empower you to offer your authentic-self to those around you and to the world. Contributing your authentic value to what you are engaged in is a key goal in order for you to achieve what you desire. You will then be able to become involved in what President Obama described as the:

'change you have been looking for'

The essence of all of the above simply means that it is up to each of us to make a change within ourselves, to make a difference. You now know that through the fifth dimension you do make a difference not only to your-self physiologically and emotionally but also to those around you, to the planet and beyond. Without doubt as President Obama so nobly stated:

'you *are* the change'

You may already be aware that we are living through a most important time period. In this 21st century, raising our awareness outside of that limited virtual box of thinking is a must because thinking 'out of the box' means recognising that we need more than our intellect and recall of information or knowledge to meet the challenges that we are being confronted with. Our children's future and wellbeing as well as our own depends upon it.

Can our Authentic-self help us to Change?

Many years ago, I was fortunate to attend a talk given by a remarkable woman called Ivy Northage. She communicated in trance through a being in spirit called Chan. Chan brought to my attention that we all posses an innate inner-strength/inner-power or energy store within our consciousness (the subtle energy bodies - chapter 3). The inner-strength is a part of our authentic-self. It is a strength that enables us to meet the challenges that confront us. Recognising and using this inner-strength is a life lesson and it can be regarded as a natural resilience for us to come through a life-shattering experience. Martin Luther King referred to the inner-strength in a speech where he stated:

'there is a power in us more powerful than bullets'

What is this power? It's an energy reserve which operates from the fifth dimension. So where does the inner-strength come from? In my research about the characteristics of the soul, I discovered that it comes from past lifetimes where the soul was able to successfully endure and work through very difficult life-threatening situations. An interesting feature of this strength is that it continues to travel with a soul each time it incarnates. Every lifetime experience presents a soul with an opportunity to not only use this strength but also to add to it. Such a strength can be described as our inner potential to handle and work through the most difficult challenging experiences (mental, emotional and physical) that we may face in life. What's important to understand here is that this inner potential prevents us from giving up on difficult situations/challenges under extreme circumstances. We are surrounded by so many amazing examples of individuals who have demonstrated using their inner potential, their physical and mental ability to survive a period of extreme cold, a long period without food or water, climbing down a mountain while injured, sailing around the world alone, surviving long periods of isolation and torture, and so forth. These are things that would ordinarily be considered to be beyond human capacity to endure.

In chapter 1 I demonstrated how for most of us, the conscious mind is unknowingly locked into a form-based, mechanistic and linear-time-biased mode of thinking. This reduces our overall awareness which becomes infected by false beliefs. Removing the false beliefs is an essential step towards transforming our lives. One such false belief which needs to be weeded out is being presented with a situation or life lesson that is beyond our capacity to deal with. We are never confronted with such a situation - unless we become an addict of some sort - for example on alcohol/drugs. In this case we cut ourselves off from our inner-strength which is there to help us to deal with what is confronting us. The results of this can create a fatal outcome.

The inner-strength's power is subtle yet potent. It is so potent it is what greatness is made of. Do not confuse will-power or self-discipline with this energy reserve. These two attributes are important characteristics of the fabricated-self. A strong will-power can stop you procrastinating or being lazy. It can help you act on something. It can be your staying power to meet a particular goal. My own self-discipline certainly helped me pass my physics degree. Self-discipline gives us an ability to put off what we want now and to work towards something more desirable. It provides the fabricated-self with the patience and strength to follow through on choices to their conclusion. Perseverance and persistence are two of self-discipline's strengths.

Once activated, inner-potential can be used for the benefit of not only ourselves, but for the rest of humanity and the world. Diagram 7.1 shows what can be described as an energy bridge between the fabricated (physical) self and authentic (inner) self. If our consciousness is locked onto believing that the fabricated-self is what life is about, we are denying ourselves access to our full potential. In this case, the energy bridge that connects to the authentic-self is blocked. A major challenge in life is to change this false belief and to bring the fabricated-self back into the authentic-self in order for us to work with what I call our real-self. I define the real-self as the coming together of both the fabricated-self and the authentic-self. You may hear people talking about an individual being authentic. An 'authentic' individual is one who has managed to merge their fabricated-self with their authentic-self. How can you do that?

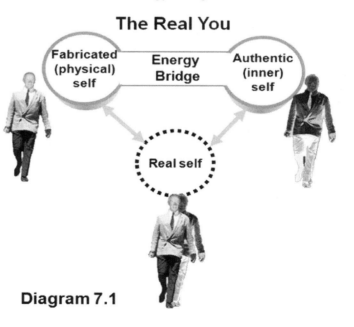

Diagram 7.1

Working with the concept of energy as the fifth dimension and what this means is a good start. In addition, we can also consider the following three-step process:

1. Relax by getting into a comfortable position, do some deep breathing and try some visualisation exercises (see chapter 4) to quieten the conscious mind and get rid of any busy chatter that may be circulating. Try to open a dialogue in your imagination with your authentic-self, which is basically you talking to your inner-self. It is probably best to do this in private!

2. Using your imagination, work through the concepts put forward towards the end of chapter 1 that describe the sub-atomic/quantum world. They are real and you are subject to these Universal Laws and dimensions. The idea is to help to remove any rigid boundaries that may have been put in place by false beliefs.

3. Change your thinking as you upgrade your belief system by working through step 2, above. Changing old false beliefs such as: I'm no good; I'm a failure; nothing ever works for me; I'm not lovable; money is hard to get; I need money to enjoy myself; I'm just a bunch of chemicals with no soul; everything in life is random; life is dog eat dog to survive, and so forth, enables you to see reality in a different light. You are actually re-framing how you are looking at your-self and life. It should contribute to enabling you to throw off the limitations that may have been holding you back from getting the best out of your life. Your perception of what is happening in life will change.

In saying 'you are the change', President Obama put fairly and squarely in each of our hands the challenge of changing not only ourselves but also of making a contribution to changing our country and ultimately the world. I use the word 'hands' here as a metaphor for our consciousness. It is within our consciousness that the secrets of how to use our infinite power lies. As always, having the right attitude, intent, integrity and compassion are important building blocks as you learn to release this power. The power that you release will not only have an energetic effect upon you, but also on everything and everyone, so use it wisely. An interesting Universal Law to keep in mind is that:

> 'the power you release in energy terms is returned to you tenfold'

So be careful how you use this power. Avoid negative power for it does untold damage to others and of course, to your-self.

Sorting out what Needs to Change

As I look back on my life, when I was thirty-four years of age, a door was opened in my unconscious mind during a Silva Mind Method course I attended in Washington DC. From that time onwards I have been involved in a continuous process of planting potential seeds of change in my consciousness (mainly my unconscious mind). Some of these seeds took a long time to grow, others not. The seeds are different parts of different Universal Laws. Understanding the various seeds that I elaborate on in the table below will strengthen the communication you have with your authentic-self and make life much more interesting and gratifying. As I started on my journey to raise my own awareness, I began without a clue about what I needed to change within myself.

My old false beliefs had unknowingly closed my mind to the realities of life. The false beliefs were like the weeds in a garden taking all the good nutrients from the soil and leaving only a small amount for the flowers to draw upon and grow. Nonetheless, planting the seed of what was a new concept to me, and the process that followed, opened doors within my consciousness that automatically raised my awareness causing a shift to a much higher level. From my viewpoint, looking at the process is like observing the growth of an acorn that has been planted and in the end will grow into a robust oak tree. Before growing into a proud, strong tree the acorn begins putting down some roots into the soil. Through these roots the acorn gets nourished and a tiny shoot pushes upwards until it breaks through the surface. The acorn's growth, however, can be affected by the density and type of weeds surrounding it. Removing those weeds allows it to grow in all its majesty. The acorn metaphorically represents the many concepts that have been described in the book. Anything that is preventing your inner growth can also be described as a weed that needs to be plucked out.

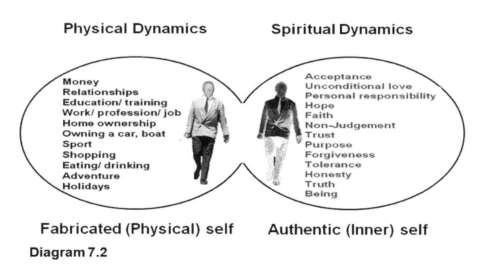

Diagram 7.2

Let us consider working for a moment with the two parts of our whole-self that we are already familiar with - the fabricated-self and authentic-self. From the perspective of our authentic-self we need to weed out any false beliefs. As false beliefs are weeded out, fresh seeds or truer concepts can be planted in their place. Such a weeding and planting process creates a transformation and shift within your awareness. When this has been done, there is potential to gain regular access to your authentic and real-self. In diagram 7.2 we can see the difference between the dynamics of the fabricated-self (physical) and the authentic-self (spiritual). An example of the physical dynamics of the fabricated-self is easily recognisable, but what about the spiritual dynamics of the authentic-self? To recap, the soul drives the authentic-self hence the spiritual dynamics. Education today is not geared to help us see the true picture. Rather, it is geared to the world of the fabricated (physical) self, the world of consumerism and celebrity culture.

Both the fabricated-self and the authentic-self need to be running together in parallel. The fabricated-self operates primarily in physical dimensions (the first paradigm – chapter 1) and the authentic-self in the sub-atomic world of energy (second paradigm – chapter 1). As indicated in diagram 7.1, the link between the fabricated-self and authentic-self is what I call a bridge of energy. If the bridge is blocked it needs to be cleared for both sides to communicate together. Clearing the blocks is essential if the challenges arising from the changes that are taking place in this 21st century are to be met. These changes are happening at a pace never before experienced.

My research has shown that due to the conditioning we have been subjected to, we live in a world which resembles smoke and mirrors. Perhaps the cleverest ruse is to deny us the understanding that, among other things, we actually incarnate in many lives to work through different life lessons. This is a requirement for our spirit to grow and it does this through each of its soul's different incarnations. My findings show that each soul is like a fragment of the spirit's energy structure (like a fragment of a hologram).

At birth, the different parts of our spiritual dynamics structure are usually in a balanced state. I say usually for there are souls who take on some extra challenges in terms of life experiences before birth while in the mother's womb. A soul may at times enter the foetus up to seven months before birth. It all depends on the life lessons to be learnt. An early entry into the foetus means that the soul requires some early conditioning before birth to ensure that it will encounter its life lessons soon after birth. For the majority of people however, the conditioning effect of life experiences after birth are what create an imbalance in their spiritual dynamics structure.

The quantum bio-magnetic field is programmed to ensure that we are confronted with a particular life lesson at an appropriate time. Conditioning (programming) after birth forms the core of the fabricated-self. As the fabricated-self distances itself from the authentic-self it begins to be strongly driven by ego and usually by powerful personalities/sub-personalities (diagram 7.1 and chapter 5). The purpose of this happening is to give each an opportunity to take over the conscious mind, at an appropriate time, to work through a situation/challenge. Now the challenge facing the soul is to bring the different parts of its spiritual dynamics back into balance within the conscious mind by working with the fabricated-self and authentic-self. The challenge for us, as we operate within our fabricated-self, is to recognise what weeding out of false beliefs has to be done to allow the fabricated-self to strengthen its connection with the authentic-self. Successful weeding means that we actually put ourselves onto a path where we can create a more desirable life story. Happiness is no longer an illusion but a tangible goal. That inner feeling of positive wellbeing, which we all have the potential to reclaim, returns to where it should be.

The table below shows some important examples of what I call seeds (part of spiritual dynamics) which can contribute to a particular state of mind (the left-hand column). These need to be planted (actually, replanted) in the conscious/unconscious minds. This will help in recognising the weeds to be plucked from the fabricated-self (old thinking, or false beliefs in the right-hand column that need to be removed). The middle column is the original thinking of the authentic-self which represents nurtured seeds that have been planted and are growing. Following this process creates a transformation within us, transmuting the weeds as they are plucked. This results in a greater understanding of what is going on during our life's journey.

Seeds (state of mind) To be replanted	Authentic-self: (new thinking) Nurtured seed	Fabricated-self: (old thinking) Weeds to be plucked
Love	Accepts love for what it is, uncomplicated, unconditional with no attachments	Sees love as conditional and needs to engage in attachment to feel safe.
Acceptance	Accepts life for what it is (one of many) and works systematically through the challenges (life lessons) as they occur.	Does not truly understand what life's challenges are about. Blames others for what is happening. *'Why me'* syndrome rules here.
Personal responsibility	Recognises what they are doing and what is happening in their life. Accepts full responsibility for what they are doing and knows that everything is as it should be.	Lacks commitment. Does not take full responsibility for their life and for what they are doing. Ruled by it is *'someone else's fault'* syndrome. Imbalance between male and female energies.

Hope	Knows that the difficult challenges are temporary and that the sunny uplands are just around the corner. Hope disengages ego.	Optimism which engages ego is in play. There is a feeling of abandonment when the going gets tough. Fear, worry and pessimism rule the day.
Faith	Unconditional belief reigns. Always has confidence that everything is as it should be.	Believes everything that happens is a random occurrence. Needs to control what is happening. Ego is the master here.
Non-judgement	Recognises times when it is acceptable to judge whether something might be life-threatening or in need of attention. Otherwise, does not judge anything.	Judges everyone and everything. Does not understand mirroring nor the effects of the bio-magnetic field. Blame is a driver here.
Trust	Recognises that the soul has signed up for different experiences and life lessons. Knows that the outcome of what has happened is as it should be.	Needs money and things to feel secure and for something to happen. Does not understand the concept of divine providence nor divine timing.
Purpose	Knows that there is a purpose behind everything that is happening. Understands that there is a path which provides an optimum exposure to meet life's challenges.	Is blinkered by setting goals and is constantly checking them to be successful. Is materially biased and money driven. Has little feel for real purpose. Believes life is a series of random events.

Forgiveness	Knows that forgiveness of self and others is part of a life's lesson. Realises the need to detach from person(s) concerned. Has an understanding of the soul's purpose and understands everything is as it should be.	Cannot forgive or has difficulty in forgiving as does not understand the real dynamics behind an incarnation in a physical body. Constantly judges and is angry. Does not realise that not forgiving causes a continuing energetic attachment with person concerned.
Tolerance	Understands what life is about and accepts what is happening knowing that it is meant to happen.	Does not understand what life is about, nor what is really happening.
Honesty	Listens to conscience and knows not to give in to temptation.	Deceives and cheats when necessary. Takes what it wants.
Truth	Understands there is no absolute truth.	Doesn't understand that there is no absolute truth
Being	Knows how to 'be'	Can never just 'be'

As the above seeds grow, so the contact between the fabricated-self and the authentic-self strengthens. In such a situation we are in a strong position to engage our full potential. Our ability to deal with the challenges confronting us and to recognise intuitively what needs to be done, will be enhanced.

Outer and Inner Potential

What is this outer and inner potential we all have? Is it your potential to make lots of money, to acquire material things and titles, or is it something else? Dividing your true potential into two parts clarifies these questions. The first part I call 'outer potential' and is associated with the fabricated-self as shown in diagram 7.2. The second part is 'inner potential'. This is what we are capable of doing through the authentic-self and is to do with personal development and soul growth. It is the real reason for us all being here. It is about planting those seeds again and doing the necessary weeding in the conscious/unconscious minds.

I have made the point that inner potential is associated with our ability to work through difficult and challenging situations/experiences (life lessons), and the way we actually handle them as they are attracted to us and vice versa. To engage in our true potential also means connecting with our passion(s) in life and with our creative-self. When our fabricated-self reaches maturity, it is possible to get a feel for its outer potential by monitoring how far we have got on in life in terms of job promotion, successful relationships, sports trophies, academic results, the number of titles we have been awarded, the house or apartment we have, the car we drive, and so forth. What a shock to the nervous system to discover that the outer potential dynamics has little to do with the real purpose of being here. It has, though, plenty to do with the illusion of life and how a lot of people would like it to be. This doesn't mean to say that we should not enjoy life to the full and enjoy ourselves as we journey!

Inner Power
The fabricated-self, through the ego, begins to get full benefit from the source of inner power, when it believes that we actually have a soul which never dies. Ego is unaware of this fact! When this happens the fabricated-self is able to communicate with the authentic-self more easily. Without this belief the fabricated-self has only a limited access to any inner power/energy because it has become blocked. We are not taught, in general, that we have what is really an inner spiritual energy, nor are we told about its power. The power is independent and superior to any physical limitations that we may have. To release this inner power requires us to be persistent and sincere in what we are trying to accomplish, and to walk with humility on the path that the soul creates for us. Most importantly, ego needs to be disengaged. As we find ways to disengage ego, more inner potential energy is released for us to meet particular needs demanded by any exposure to challenging experiences/situations. In today's 24/7 lifestyle, only a small amount of that store of spiritual energy is able to operate through us, because ego is locking our conscious mind within the world of the fabricated-self. Ego encourages us to try to get involved with only those things (activities, people, news media and so forth) that interest us (both positive and negative) and attempts to get us to bypass the things that do not interest us! There is, however, a universal spiritual truth which supports our inner potential that states:

'the soul will not create anything that we cannot handle'

At times, mostly unknown to us, we may try to go beyond our own spiritual capacity or potential, usually by taking on too much in the physical world. This is not a good idea, as it can result in a destructive result, from both an emotional and physical standpoint. In the physical world we are taught to over-reach ourselves, to keep pushing, and to aspire to go higher and higher. So why cannot we do the same spiritually?

The authentic-self through the soul works with what life is offering us. These offerings are created from the life lessons that our soul has actually attracted to us in the present moment (the 'now'). There is a need, once more, to distinguish between spiritual and physical life. In physical life we are conditioned to work through situations which have a beginning, middle and an end. On completion, we observe what we have done and will be satisfied or dissatisfied (an ego assessment).

Life tends not to be straightforward at times and we may try to bypass situations/experiences because we do not like them and are able to bypass them. In spiritual reality, life does not operate this way. If we attempt to bypass what we have attracted to us and are successful in doing so, a similar situation will be attracted to us in the future! The laws here are Universal Laws and are quite different as there is no escaping the opportunity to work through a life lesson. Any life lesson not successfully worked through at the time of death will have to be dealt with in a future incarnation.

Idiosyncrasies of a 'Being of Energy'
Just like trying to understand quantum mechanics, as we try to understand how human beings operate at an energy level, 'all is not as it seems'! What does this mean? Throughout the book I emphasise that as beings of energy we operate not only in the physical world but also in the sub-atomic world. Another attribute we have is that we emit photons of light (or particles of energy) from the physical body. Our photons, which are not visible to the normal eye, can affect the subtle energy bodies of those we come into contact with or think about from time to time - provided they are on the same energy wavelength as us, or we are projecting our thoughts to them! Remember that we are all connected and the photons can traverse space and time which are co-existent at the sub-atomic level. These photons can affect a program, or programs that are running in our energy field (the subtle energy bodies), causing a temporary change to the bio-magnetic attraction field. How does this work in real life?

An example of the photon effect could be where you have missed a transport connection and decided to walk across the road to buy a takeaway coffee. As you join the coffee queue you may not recognise anybody around you but a person in the queue next to you may be emitting a stream of photons with a calm emotional content that is on your wavelength and stimulates this affect in you. Most times, situations like this are not accidental and are being triggered by our inner-self or soul. A sudden urge not to ignore the telephone that is ringing, or to open the door, or to go on a trip, will all be triggered by the soul through the authentic-self. What is interesting here is that from a fabricated-self perspective in the physical world, this may be seen as wasted effort. I can assure you that it is not, for the fabricated-self through the ego can only understand a small part of what is actually happening to us.

We are all like biological tuning forks and can, at times be affected by those we come into contact with. We are affected by just being present with them! The amount of photon energy that we emit depends on how we handle the situation that we are in and the emotions that arise. By putting the best we have into a situation, we ensure that a high level of photons is radiated from a positive emotion. For the person who crossed the road to get a coffee, if the person next to them is very calm, then this is the emotion that will be picked up (unconsciously) provided the frequency of their fields is similar. Alternatively if they are angry (a powerful negative emotion) then this feeling will be picked up, adding to the receiver's agitation.

In Western physical reality, we are usually taught to be a fighter; to stand strong, stand tall, stand up for our rights, stand proud and fight! If we detect any resistance that is stopping us from achieving a goal, we should fight it and win. What we are not taught to recognise is that this is all ego driven, even when a serious illness is involved. I suggest that it is not the best way to go. Now what I am about to say may come as a shock to some of you because it certainly did to me! From the perspective of our authentic-self the opposite is usually true. That's because the resistance which you are experiencing is trying to tell you something. Your soul, through the quantum bio-magnetic field, never fails to bring to you the life lessons that it is important to acknowledge. From a spiritual perspective we all have a unique potential and our authentic-self will constantly drive us to meet this potential. What we need to recognise is that this potential may be different to that which is driving our fabricated-self in the physical world. If we fight something in the physical world we could be effectively ignoring a lesson that is being presented to us. And unknowingly we may be creating dark energy that supports and strengthens the situation.

Of course, this does not mean that we should just roll over when in a difficult situation. It is really a test to see how we handle a particular challenge. It takes more strength and courage to turn the other cheek at times than to stand up and fight. Bringing an experience into an acceptable balance between the parties involved including the authentic-self is what it is really about.

In the physical world, we can cunningly bypass potential blocks that may stop us achieving our goal. This is not possible in the environment of the authentic-self or soul. This may sound rather weak, or 'what a lot of wimps' you may be thinking. Not true, for the true strength that we take with us from life to life is how successful we are in meeting our spiritual goals and potential. It takes true courage to *'stay out of the dramas of life'*. This is a part of the purpose of being here. The real art is to recognise how to extricate our-self, if we are drawn into a drama. Being a president, or king, or queen, or chairman, or surgeon, or professor, or accountant, or banker, or clerk, or airline pilot, or sports person, or psychologist, or shop keeper, or plumber, or whatever, has little to do with what we take with us at the end of our life. These are character parts that are adopted to help in achieving life lessons by working through challenges as they arise! It is always a good idea to remember that an important Universal Law in the spiritual environment is:

'what goes around comes around'

Ego will deny this statement and tell you that what you are doing in terms of fighting is right, and your friends' egos will most probably applaud you on as you go about your business. And what goes around are dramas arising from disputes/arguments/debt/affairs/illnesses, and so forth.

Why Life can get Difficult - The Ego Trap!
Once again, most of us are unknowingly trained to work from the fabricated-self. Now the ego just loves both success and failure. Note that the words 'success' and 'failure' engage the ego. An important point to appreciate is that from a spiritual perspective there is really no failure, nor are there any losers. How many times do we hear that so and so is such a loser, or is a failure, purely and simply because they did not fit the metaphorical box that they were put in, where being successful is probably related to their profession, or business, or the titles they gain, or in material terms, or in monetary terms, and so on? In reality, from a spiritual perspective, there is no failure and certainly no loser, only a lost opportunity or a delay in working through a life lesson. That is because the soul works to ensure that we engage with our life lessons in spite of our ego. The form-based world is just a theatrical stage, nothing more. Our soul's growth is the reason for us being here.

The spiritual path that we follow in life may appear to be difficult at times, for we can be driven by thoughts of fairness and unfairness. Ego loves to take sides and make comparisons as we work through each of our life lessons in its diverse acts and supporting scenes. An important point to remember is that ego only sees what we see (and feel)! In comparison, our authentic-self has a much broader perspective on what is happening in our life because it operates in the multi-dimensional environment (time and space being co-existent) of the sub-atomic or quantum world. Recognising that there is nothing random about the life we are living can be difficult to accept. To increase our inner-feeling of positive wellbeing it is important that we understand why we are where we are. Summarising some key points about the spiritual side of life may clarify our awareness of what is going on in our lives. We can never:

- be born into the wrong family
- marry the wrong person (no matter how short the marriage is!)
- have circumstances and conditions in our life that are in any way contradictory to our spiritual purpose
- be denied what is spiritually on our path because of a situation/experience that we have forced to happen
- be denied an opportunity (in spiritual terms) until we have lived our allotted time or ended our own life.

Having read the above five bullet points, this does not mean that life has to be miserable or uninteresting. On the contrary, life is, as always, what we care to make of it. We create our own reality. To get the best out of life requires us to trust that life has a deeper purpose than just procreating, achieving success, fuelling the ego and buying things. It also requires us to work towards merging the fabricated-self with our authentic-self to enable us to hear the directions that our soul is trying to communicate. Listening to the authentic-self and trusting that the directions we receive are in our best interest is a major life lesson that we all face. Learning to trust is part of the spiritual dynamics test in life.

Do You Trust?

Have you the feeling that time is accelerating? From my own perspective, time began to accelerate really quickly from about 1994. Initially, this generated some concern with respect to finishing all that I felt I needed to do in life. In the scheme of things, as time is only energy, it is an illusion which our consciousness has been conditioned to accept. Accepting this concept can automatically enable an understanding within, that we actually have enough time to complete everything we need to do during our lifetime. Once you start measuring time, or assessing, or judging, or questioning if you have enough time, you automatically trigger anxiety, worry and fear. Living in the *now* means accepting there is a flow of time which we need not be concerned about. It also means accepting that we are able to complete the challenges before us within this time. That said, we absolutely need to trust that we have enough time to complete everything that we agreed to before incarnating! Any doubt that may arise means that we have heard the word trust but do not really 'get it'. In this case we need to go within and ask our-self:

'what is it that is causing me not to trust that I have enough time?'

It will most probably be a fear which the fabricated-self has raised in relation to not having enough time to do all the things we think we want to do in life. Trust is one of the big life lessons that we all have to deal with in society. It is one which is being sorely tested due to occurrences such as the scandals involving politicians, scientists, medical practitioners, priests, company bosses, celebrities, and so forth. It seems that those in whom we (our fabricated-self through the ego) have placed our trust and those who we have set up as role models are letting us down. The question that needs to be asked is:

'are all those people whom we trusted, and who we perceive as having let us down, just acting like mirrors reflecting back to us the lack of trust we have within ourselves?'

The answer to this question is 'yes'; they are simply mirroring back to us a lack of trust that we have about ourselves. Ask your-self the following questions; do you trust that you:

- are safe and secure?
- will have enough money throughout your life to meet your needs?
- will find the ideal partner?
- will remain in good health?
- will recover if you are ill?
- have attracted a relationship that will last ?

What sort of answers do you give to the above questions? It is important to take a step back and recognise that we are all living quantum bio-magnets. How we handle the experiences that are associated with the above questions has an influence on the answers.

As you read through this book, you may have had an outburst of anger when I first suggested that you are responsible for what happens to you. As I said earlier, it came as a shock to me when I discovered this. What! No one to blame or compare with, or accuse, or judge? Quelle horreur! However, the good news is, I also discovered that our amazing energy structure has an attraction factor responsible for us being attracted to or attracting to us the life lessons and challenges we face. Why is this good news? It is good news, because I also discovered that each of us has the ability to re-programme our energy field to affect what we attract to a degree. This can provide us with an opportunity to make some of the difficult life lessons we face easier to handle once we recognise what the lesson is about and what is actually going on. Trusting that what we are experiencing is part of a life lesson can reduce the emotional impact that may arise.

Some people seem to have so much, while others suffer great personal and material loss. Do you suffer from a lack of money, good relationships, job insecurity, being alone, or are being weighed down by anxieties about the future, or about understanding life, and so on? If you do, it is possible to reverse the cause of what you are feeling fearful about. Reversing the cause is enabled by bringing the cause of the fear to the surface in the conscious mind, working with it to bring it into balance and removing it. That itself can be a life lesson. Fears have a powerfully negative and unhelpful influence on our life story. To begin the quest to improve our life story, I suggest as a first step that we consider re-orientating our-self to live in the 'now'. There are great benefits to this, one of which is that it enhances your ability to manifest what you desire. For those who have a strong feeling of lack, whether consciously or unconsciously, gaining abundance can be a lifelong mission. Lack is synonymous with a lack of trust that your soul will deliver what you actually need, when you need it. There is a great secret here that I wish to bring to your attention. You already have the potential to be abundant and it is your fabricated-self and ego that is causing any feeling of lack, creating more lack and preventing your abundance from manifesting. I elaborate on this below.

Is Life Just?
The fabricated-self through the ego may feel hard done by because the body chosen in this lifetime came from a poor family, or a foreign country, or is the wrong colour, or is too fat, or too thin, or is a male, or is a female, or is living in what they perceive is the wrong country.. The fabricated-self wants celebrity physical characteristics, material things, titles, wealth and so forth. But all of this is really looking at life through the wrong end of a telescope.

Every step we take on life's path will either increase or diminish our energy – the light (photons) that we emit. As stated above, from a spiritual perspective, we are constantly emitting light photons (not in a visible spectrum). At times though, our spiritual light energy may require to be recharged so that we can deal with an approaching challenge/life lesson. This causes us, unknowingly, to be withdrawn from whatever we are participating in and to become inactive. How does this happen? It can happen by contracting an illness, or losing a job and not being able to find suitable employment, or being incapacitated due to an accident, and so forth. In such cases, nothing in life from the perspective of the fabricated-self seems to be going right. Other people may also see us as failures, as losers, or a sick person, or accident prone, or careless. When this happens, we may also be asking ourselves *'why me?'* What is not usually recognised here is that it is part of our spiritual purpose. It is not really the right time to be doing anything, because even the soul needs time to prepare itself to meet the new challenge which is just ahead. And the quantum bio-magnetic field needs a program update. The fabricated-self does not understand this rest period, nor does it want to!

As the soul prepares itself for the next challenge, the programming of the quantum bio-magnetic field will be updated and spiritual energy levels replenished. As we operate like biological tuning forks, we need to beat at a frequency that is in synchronicity with the new act/scene in our life play which is approaching. An interesting point to highlight is that the soul has to work with linear time in setting up the next act in our life's play. In addition, the soul is only given a part of its contract (the script for the act) at any time, through its host (the spirit). In spiritual life, our soul is like an apprentice and can only move ahead when it has passed its training assignments and is able to change the frequencies/programs of the bio-magnetic field to meet the next challenge. No one can do this for us, we have to do it for ourselves no matter how long it takes, or how dull, or dangerous, or tragic a situation we find ourselves in. There is no cutting corners or skipping lessons. It is all about taking *personal responsibility, acceptance, trusting and* taking the rough with the smooth. The rough times in life can sometimes be so overpowering of course that all we see is the tragedy of what is happening to us. Being in a state of grief can be one of the most difficult and tough experiences to come out of. There is little chance of understanding what is really happening while in a state of grief following the loss of a child or someone very close, the breakdown of a relationship or marriage, or losing your job, or home and money. In that grieving state, you begin to think that there is little chance, if any at all, of your coming to terms with the loss. Grief can be so overpowering that only time can heal together with an inner hope that life will become more bearable. In this state, an individual is locked within a virtual box that can only be opened, when the time is right, by them.

Dealing with a Loss – How can Life be Just?
Every one of us may have experienced a moment in life when we thought we had actually lost everything - perhaps employment, a family member, material gains, business, house, possessions, or a relationship. I certainly had one when I was well into my career. Looking back I recognise that I was most fortunate as I had excellent health. This was a gift which I did not fully appreciate at the time and which many of us take for granted. I had got out of Kuwait one month before Saddam Hussein invaded. Unfortunately, I was in the process of divorcing, which took over three years and stripped me of all the hard-earned capital that I had accumulated. My son, who remained with his mother, was most upset and I was faced with bills for his school fees, plus the need to pay the mortgage on my small house and so on. My home was very dear to me and I reached the decision that I must sell it to pay the bills. Added to all that, the housing market was at an all time low! In short, my fabricated-self world had collapsed, compounded into the bargain by having no job. My international professional background was strong but I just could not find an opening anywhere. What was I to do? I did not realise that this was one of those involuntary times, from the perspective of my authentic-self, that I unknowingly needed to recharge my energy fields and upgrade my quantum bio-magnetic field's programme so as to be able to work through new challenges which were approaching.

With so many disastrous events occurring at the same time I sat back in my chair one afternoon with an empty mind and just prayed. I prayed for forgiveness for anything I had done wrong against anyone, anyone I had caused to be unhappy during my life, including myself. I forgave myself for what had happened and I also forgave all those who might have also done something against me. That evening I slept well and in the morning I woke up no longer feeling stressed out of my mind. It was a touch of '*let go of everything and let God in*'.

This was a unique moment in my life but nonetheless one I would rather not repeat! Two days later, a close American friend and colleague with whom I had worked with in Kuwait, called to ask if my divorce had complete. Talk about synchronicity! I briefed him on what had happened and without a second's delay he asked how much I needed to get myself started in life again. No limit, just how much? Through his heartfelt generosity I paid my bills, kept my home, and finally got a new job, this time in Saudi Arabia, and was able to repay him.

During difficult times in life, I believe that the last thing we want to consider is the spiritual dynamics of what is happening. Yet it is in our best interest to consider doing so, as it can and does produce results. It produces results provided a channel is opened to our authentic-self. Listening to the authentic-self and recognising the synchronicity in life is the way to go. I was certainly in survival mode and was a perfect fit for the bottom of Abraham Maslow's basic external human needs (Chapter 6). Victim-consciousness, too, had set in!

So, is life just? Well that depends from which side we are looking at our-self. From a 'fabricated-self' perspective life is absolutely not just! But looking at life from the perspective of the 'authentic-self', the answer is purely and simply *yes*; life is just. Now accidents can happen (because of chaos energy), even on the spiritual side, so there can be some exceptions. I say 'can be' as only the individual concerned will know when they return to the world of spirit and no one else.

Looking at life from a spiritual perspective, it is important to recognise that in this environment, which is the environment we finally return to, the soul's quest for spiritual growth:

- takes no account of material, money or physical values
- does not acknowledge material/money success or failure
- acknowledges only that which is available in the present, moment by moment

So, how about the question 'should we take injustice lying down'? From a spiritual perspective, if you are being used in any way you will not carry the burden of these sins as they belong to the perpetrators. Worrying about them can only diminish your energetic state and reduce your capacity to deal with the situation. It is quite a challenge not to let a difficult situation/experience get you down when you are feeling low. If at all possible, hold up your head up high and keep repeating the following mantra to your-self:

'I have everything I need within me to deal with the situation I find myself in.'

Your authentic-self has whatever you need to see you through any difficult situation. In summary, it is important not to be frightened by life because:

'life is the servant of spirit'

Understanding the mechanics of the quantum bio-magnetic field provides an insight into how the field operates. It demonstrates for our consideration that everything around us can offer a clue to what we should be focusing on within your conscious mind. That's because it is more than likely reflecting (mirroring) a life lesson or lessons back to you in some shape or form. Sometimes what you are looking at may have very little to do with you. In this case, it is probably someone projecting their own stuff at you. The skill here is to be able to tell the difference.

So, to answer the question 'is life just', the true answer has to be 'yes'. But the true answer comes from a spiritual perspective. In our physical form the fabricated-self through both positive and negative ego uses *comparisons* when it is involved in a challenging life situation/experience. Two human/fabricated-self traits that we have all been well schooled in are making judgements and comparisons. This may be surprising once again, but a life lesson is not to make comparisons and judgements! By making comparisons and judgements life can never really be seen as just. There appears to be so much injustice, so much pain, so much anger, so much intolerance, so much lack of responsibility, so much poverty, so much illness and so forth. With this in mind how can life possibly be just? In summary, to understand why actually life *is* just we need to:

- merge our fabricated-self with the authentic-self.
- Increase our understanding of the true purpose for being here in a physical body.
- Increase our awareness by opening some doors within our consciousness to prise open that virtual box of thinking so as to cause a shift in our thinking. This will increase our understanding of why our life is as it is, and also of what is actually going on around us.

My own experience of losing what I believed was everything was lived through my fabricated-self. Had I known then about the existence of my authentic-self and its raison d'être, my emotional response would have been much kinder to myself. I would have reflected upon the event from a more balanced position. This would have programmed my quantum bio-magnetic field to attract a slightly less challenging outcome.

A wise friend once said to me many years ago, "John, you need to accept responsibility for living in the present (the 'NOW') – accept you are here to learn from what is happening to you and from what is happening around you. Try not to focus on the past or future for this is wasted energy as it only leads you down paths in life that are not in your best interest. Accept each day in your life as being the most important as it may be your last opportunity to do or say something to someone with a supportive intent which results in a positive outcome whatever the something is."

Slowly but surely, especially in recent years, I have recognised the wisdom behind these words. The wisdom I drew from them is that the things which:

- I was concerned (worried) about turned out to be the least important in my life
- I should have been concerned about but had not given sufficient thought to, turned out to be the most important.

In the above two statements, I used the word 'concerned' as the word 'worry' should be deleted from our consciousness! As pointed out in chapter 4, the word worry triggers the dangerous self-perpetuating Triad called worry, anxiety and fear which generates stress in great abundance! If you worry about an illness or an accident it keeps your consciousness locked onto a negative thought process, which just makes things worse. It also has the potential to attract more of the same. The problem/challenge I kept coming back to here was that I had not been given an understanding of the life processes that link the fabricated-self with the authentic-self, as well as what constitutes a life lesson. In such a situation, we are like a ship without a rudder. Unknowingly, we are not able to take advantage of the wind and tide as we drift towards what we believe to be our destination. How can we turn this unfortunate situation around? How can we create abundance in our lives and also live 'in the now' at the same time?

Abundance and Manifestation - Some Truths

A considerable amount of time can be spent worrying about abundance in whatever is missing from our lives. Three issues stand out that are worthy of our consideration. These issues are:

1. there is a need to differentiate between what the fabricated-self and authentic-self recognise as abundance and how they each go about achieving it.

2. becoming abundant in whatever we desire is affected by our intent, what we are focusing on, and expectations.

3. the timing of what is desired to manifest can make abundance seem elusive.

These three issues usually work together. Looking at the first issue, we can see that the fabricated-self (diagram 7.2. page 344) basically wants just about everything. The fabricated-self always has to have a process and techniques to try to manifest what it wants! I cannot emphasise the following statement enough, for it is the secret to being abundant on a continuous basis without effort:

'the authentic-self recognises its abundant nature and manifests its needs when required'

Moreover, the authentic-self does this continuously and usually within the unconscious mind. This does, however, require trust. The seed of what we desire is sown in the unconscious mind through our conscious thoughts; the authentic-self does the rest. The sooner we get into a regular communication with our authentic-self by merging the fabricated-self with the authentic-self, the quicker the manifestation of a need will take place. If we feel that what we desire is not manifesting, then I guarantee there is a high probability of a life lesson not being recognised and worked through, thus causing the delay; we have an energy block in place that needs to be cleared.

The second issue from above can be divided into three parts:

i. the first is to do with your intent. A strong intent anchors what you desire in your unconscious mind. If the intent is supported with a strong emotion, then this contributes powerfully to the manifestation process.

ii. the second part is with respect to what your mind is focusing on. Are you worrying about an experience which gave rise to a lack of something that occurred in the past, and/or are you worrying about not having what you desire in the future? To deal with this issue it is necessary to learn to live in the 'now' (the present). For us to have a balanced and happy life and also to attract what we desire, it is important to live in the now.

iii. the third part is where the fabricated-self always wants something now. It has no clue about divine timing and certainly has no trust in such a concept. If what we desire is for our higher good and there are no energy blocks then it will manifest at the right time.

Living in the now, the present, is the optimum state of mind to be in to ensure that a state of abundance is realised quickly - provided any blockages have been cleared. Abundance will then flow with ease.

Living in the Now (the Present)

Much has been written about living in the now, but there is a catch that can be easily missed. The catch is that it can take time for most people to work up to be in this position. Diagram 7.3 represents what is happening for someone who has been successful in developing the ability to live in the present moment. They no longer relate to what has happened in the past or what might be happening in the future. Journeying along life's path we are confronted with opportunities to make choices and decisions because of what is running in our quantum-magnetic field. The essence of what has been learnt (wisdom) from past choices/decisions made, plus the associated experiences, change this field, affecting the choice/decision to be made in the present. If a particular life lesson has not been learnt it will be repeated until it is

The power of living in the present

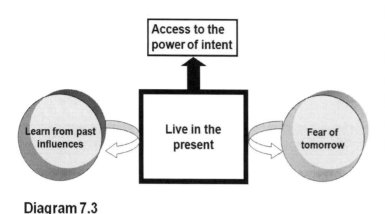

Diagram 7.3

recognised, worked with and cleared. To cut ourselves off from the learning derived from past decisions and choices at an early stage would be to put ourselves in a position where we keep making the same mistakes again and again. I use the following wise sage's statement a few times, that:

'history influences the present and affects the future'

Why is this statement important? A simple example could be that you might not get on well with your partner's parents and they insist on visiting you every Christmas and New Year and vice versa. You dutifully allow this to happen every year and have a miserable time. Until the life lessons arising from those involved are worked through and cleared each Christmas/New Year is guaranteed to be miserable. A key question to ask here is *'what is it that I need to learn from this experience for me to move on and not repeat it'?* The lesson could be as simple as setting boundaries to reduce interference from others.

Another example is if an individual loves blonds and this is their major criterion for deciding to enter into a relationship, but the relationships keep failing. I would suggest that they have cut themselves off from the wisdom that their past choices sought to impart to them. Even though blonds appear to be what they desire, something is obviously not working! They might try to justify their choice of partners with blond hair by arguing that their former relationships broke down for other reasons and refuse to consider that it might have to do with their insistence on blond partners. Unfortunately, they have trapped themselves in an ego-driven strategy and need to break out of it. The choice is theirs to make! They need to ask the same question as in the previous example. When they recognise what is going on and learn the lesson from it, their quantum bio-magnetic attraction field changes.

A natural instinct we all have, because of the conditioning we have been subjected to, is to identify difficult situations that arise in our work, home and social environments as problems. When a problem arises we take it apart to examine all its negative aspects. I can tell you that this approach is not in our best interest, because the conscious mind (and ego) loves spending time on negatives and in doing so is programming the unconscious mind with more of the same negative thinking. And what does that do? It programs the quantum bio-magnetic field attraction factor to bring to us – guess what - more of the same! To reverse this instinct the word 'problem' and how this word affects our consciousness needs to be understood and dealt with. How do we deal with it? Once again, quite simply, replace the word 'problem' with the word *challenge*. When our consciousness faces a challenge it automatically goes into solution mode. Negative thinking is all but eliminated as solutions are generated.

An issue that arises to stop us living in the now is that we can also worry about something that is to take place in the future. We may or may not have had a negative experience associated with what we are worrying about in the future. It doesn't really matter - there is some doubt about it which causes us to worry! Whatever it is, we think it may turn out to be bad, or we might not be at our best, or it might not happen, or someone we dislike may be there, or it may cost too much. Guess what that does? It creates exactly the same outcome as focusing on a negative experience from the past. It powers up the bio-magnetic field to attract the negative aspects of what you are focusing upon.

The conscious mind has four inputs that affect our ability to live in the now and also the level of abundance we can expect during our lifetime. These inputs are:

1. the thoughts that are running through our conscious mind on a daily basis. These thoughts are mainly affected by what we *see* and *hear* from all levels of the media. The thoughts are also affected by the conversations that we engage in about authority figures' views that we buy into, all of which contribute to the programming of the bio-magnetic energy field and attraction factor.

2. the programs/beliefs running continuously in the unconscious mind which contribute to the attraction energy field. The media is constantly planting scenes of lack, including poverty, that raise negative scenes with attached negative emotions within our conscious/unconscious mind. Together with negative thoughts related to poverty or 'lack' which are already in place, this almost supercharges the attraction field to attract more of the same. The same is true for other areas of abundance. Parents, relatives, siblings, teachers and authority figures can unknowingly plant thoughts about lack or poverty in us from an early age; it's all part of our conditioning.

3. the life lessons that the soul has agreed to work through. Some of these life lessons may be associated with having to deal with abundance or not having enough in comparison with other people. Such traces may have leaked through from a previous lifetime because of its powerful effect at that time. They can be removed by a regression therapist. We should not attempt to remove current lifetime life lessons as they are a fixed part of our life experience.

Part of the soul's growth challenge is to effectively plant messages or key words in the conscious mind when an opportunity arises to make a decision/choice. The unconscious mind can be said to be in competition with the conscious mind during the decision/choice making process. Competition can arise from:

4. the structure of our personality/sub-personalities with which we are born plus the masks we construct (the persona - chapter 5) as we journey through life.

To help us to live in the present and to create the abundance that we desire, there are eight points which we can consider and work through (diagram 7.4).

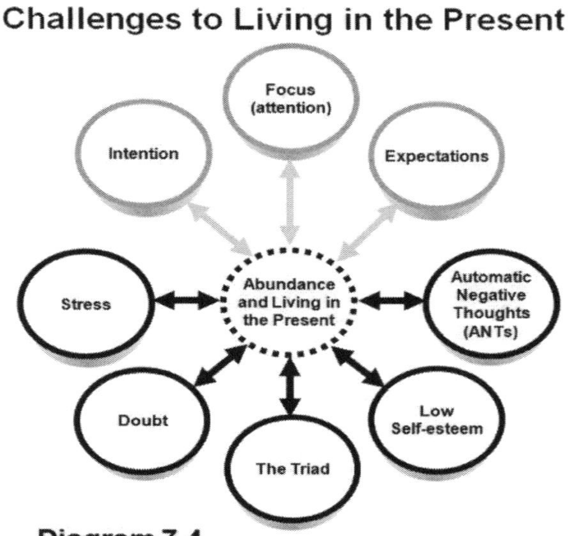

Challenges to Living in the Present

Diagram 7.4

These points form part of President Obama's:

'change that you have been looking for'

The above potential blocks have been covered in previous chapters but are so important for your success and wellbeing that I highlight some important aspects of them. The sections on creating abundance that follow represent a *life boat* we can use as we work towards merging our fabricated-self with the authentic-self. It will help in the manifestation of what we desire. A life lesson for us all is to learn to work out of the stress-free authentic-self. The lower five abundance blockers in diagram 7.4 are negative energy blockers. The upper three represent positive promoters.

Negative Abundance and Manifestation Blockers

Automatic Negative Thoughts (ANTs)

In chapter 4, I covered ANTs in some detail. Nevertheless, as they are a bad habit that stop us from living in the now and sabotage our attempts to manifest abundance, they deserve a few more comments. ANTs are one of our deadliest enemies; they sabotage success of all kinds. They can also lead to many psychological/emotional and physical illnesses (depression, post traumatic stress disorder, organ failure, tumours, and so on). ANTs initially go round and round and round the conscious mind. After a short time they become hardwired into the brain and become a major part of the filter process through which we view and experience life. People who have an ANT infestation wake up thinking about them; they think about them during the day; they think about them before going to bed and can even dream about them. Another challenge here is that the ANT can be locked onto something from the past, present, or future, or all three! These ANTs come in many shapes and sizes and can be negative thoughts about our-self, or about health, or family members, or friends and relations, or work, or work colleagues, or our ability to succeed, or our country, or some international event, or a house move, or a lack of money, and so forth. The list is endless!

Details of how to counter an ANT infestation are provided in Chapter 4. For us to have a fulfilling and happy life, it is advisable to get rid of those ANTs for they have the potential to make our life extremely unpleasant. ANTs keep the conscious/unconscious mind locked into producing a negative attraction energy field that prevents us from living in the present and greatly weakens the manifestation of abundance process. They also have a negative effect on our self-esteem.

Low Self-esteem

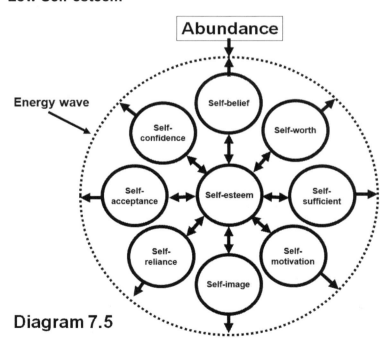

Diagram 7.5

After digesting the section on self-esteem in chapter 4, you may have already realised that it is a complex human attribute. Diagram 7.5 outlines the effects that a low self-esteem has on our personal attributes such as self-worth, self-motivation and so forth. When these are out of balance it affects our ability to create a regular flow of abundance whatever that abundance is about. The energy waves that are being sent out are via the quantum bio-magnetic field. Looking at the different attributes arising from self-esteem, when they are all in balance they will facilitate the natural flow of abundance. For most of us it is a lifetime's work to bring some of these attributes into balance. Is it any wonder that so many people are just not able to attract a regular flow of abundance? And yet most people are capable of improving a lack of abundance by bringing self-esteem into balance. I suggest how to change your self-esteem in chapter 4. For the three self-esteem attributes (self-worth, self-belief and self-confidence) at the top of the diagram, to be in balance, all the others have to be in balance too. If one or more of the other attributes gets out of balance it will negatively affect the top three attributes.

In turning around low self-esteem, we are dealing with transmuting negative (dark) energies that have caused an imbalance into positive and higher frequency (light) energies. The fabricated-self, encouraged by the ego, is easily led into situations that attract dark energies. The fabricated-self operates comfortably at a lower (or dark) energy frequency. In comparison the authentic-self operates comfortably with higher (or lighter) energy frequencies. This is part of our spiritual dynamics. These energies contribute to the mirroring process that is going on between ourselves and the world around us including the relationships we are in. Because self-esteem is negatively affected by false beliefs and ANTs, an associated off-shoot is the development of the stress-aggravating Triad: fear, worry and anxiety.

The Triad:
We should never underestimate the negative power of the Triad. Working through the Triad's various components will help to re-balance our energy and put us in a position to be able to boost our wellbeing and feelings of happiness. Moreover, this energy state will give our flow of abundance and health a boost.

Fear
We are all born holding different levels of fear built inside us. This is quite normal as the fears are there to keep us all alive. A fear can arise from an observable threat, or a threat that is perceived in the mind. An example here is someone telling us a disturbing story that we relate to in some way, or we see something that brings back a memory of a bad experience. When fear gets out of control it can paralyse our decision-making processes. In this case the fear can verge on paranoia. If this is the case, we need to explore within ourself what is causing the fear by going through the following two basic steps:

- o We can use regression therapy where the therapist can take us back to our birth and work forwards to find the cause of the fear.
- o Alternatively we can use self-hypnotherapy, but this time it is a bit like peeling an onion where you strip each layer off until you get at the root cause. A guide for doing this is given in Chapter 4. This approach is like having a conversation with our fear in our imagination. When we are in a relaxed state and our mind is clear of any chatter,

we can actually have a dialogue with our fear through our authentic-self. The fear is an emotion, which is energy, and this energy has a conscious awareness. Try asking your authentic-self if your fear has a message for you.

When we have found out why the fear is there, it is in our best interest to be rid of it. One way of removing the fear is to see it floating away in our imagination, perhaps attached to a balloon. It is important to fill the energy gap left by the departed fear with a positive emotion (some past pleasant experience). Try this fear removal approach and see what happens. Personally, when I am helping someone who is fearful, I prefer the approach of going back to when they were born and working forward until they locate the fear. As we are all a walking/talking quantum bio-magnet it is advisable to take action as quickly as possible. If we do not, there is a high probability that we will attract into our life something that the fear is trying to teach us. Such experiences will most probably be life lessons! One thing is for sure, if we are fearful it will certainly trigger worry.

Worry

Worry is an interesting state. It can lead to sweating, an increase in blood pressure, an increase in heart rate, even heart palpitations. Once, in conversation, my breath was taken away when I heard a friend say 'we all need some worry in our lives to make it more interesting'! But after much reflection and from a fabricated-self perspective, a little bit of worry does seem to add some contrast to our lives. And it can lead us to take precautions, if we perceive ourselves about to enter a risky situation. From an authentic-self perspective, worry is showing a lack of acceptance and trust with respect to what is happening to us. After all, we have attracted what is happening! There is an important lesson to learn here and that is not to worry. We should dismiss worry as soon as it enters our mind. Engaging in prolonged worry is not only a wasted expenditure of energy, it can drain us of energy very quickly. Worry is always very disempowering. A key statement here is:

'whether you worry or not, what is about to happen will happen'

Worry creates ANTs which program our quantum bio-magnet field to attract to us more of the same. An antidote to worry is to put a positive affirmation into our mind when a worry slips in. If we are worried about what is happening to a family member, for example a daughter called Mary, repeat ten times a simple affirmation such as:

'every day in every way Mary is better and better and better'

We can do this every time we worry about someone. We are an energy being and a walking transmitter/receiver of energy affecting what we are focusing on. When we worry about something we are transmitting negative energy into the energy field of the person or situation we are worrying about. If we are worrying about an individual, three outcomes could be anticipated:

1) the individual concerned will unconsciously pick up our energy transmission which can affect their performance.

2) the worrying can have a negative physiological and psychological impact on them and our-self. An inner feeling of positive wellbeing will be impaired.

3) the worrying will have a detrimental effect on the programming of the individual's and our own attraction energy field.

If we are worrying about a situation, then we are also contributing negatively to the energy around the situation and to a negative outcome, however minimally. Remember that everything is energy and we affect energetically what we focus upon. An excellent remedy to reduce your level of worry is to take up some form of *controlled visualisation* which is a relaxation technique similar to meditation. Engaging in such a relaxation process will help us tune out in our conscious mind any negative garbage that may be floating around.

We may not realise that if we are cooking a meal for the family and are filled with worry or negative thoughts, the food we prepare will be impregnated with negative energy. Can you imagine the effect of this? The food will have a negative effect on the digestive system and also deplete the energy of those who eat the food. What goes on within our consciousness always affects the energy balance within the body's cells. Prolonged negative thinking damages the cells, especially in the weakest parts of the body. Similarly, the energy structure of what we ingest has an effect on the body's cells. It may take five, ten, twenty or thirty years or more for the negative energies to affect the weakest parts of the body. But it will have an effect, sometimes life-threatening. Many people who worry a lot also suffer from being over anxious.

Anxiety
Anxiety is a really powerful emotion that has arisen from worry about a perceived or imaginary issue, or threat, or fear, that has arisen in someone's life. The issue could be related to finances, or a relationship, or health, or waiting for the results of something that is important, or being rejected by someone, and so forth. Like all emotions, anxiety transforms into different physical feelings within the body, which can take the form of high blood pressure, chest pains, heart palpitations, stomach aches, headaches, fatigue, nausea, sweating, trembling and so on. There are also psychological symptoms which include being irritable, feeling restless, feeling jumpy, feeling apprehensive, finding it difficult to concentrate, being constantly afraid, finding it difficult to calm the mind, and so on. Anxiety is a very potent state or condition and it is advisable to deal it with as quickly as possible. How

can you deal with anxiety attacks if they arise? There are two helpful approaches, the first through a breathing exercise (Chapter 2, page 86) and the second through a combination of breathing and visualisation (Chapter 4, Page 156). A common trigger for anxiety (and worry) is Doubt, which is hugely destructive on our energy systems. Doubt falls into a category that I call a Triad supporter.

Triad Supporters:

Doubt

A great stopper and destroyer of lives, doubt needs to be eradicated wherever we find it because it will cause chaos in our life! I cover doubt in detail in Chapter 4. Doubt begins as soon as we are born and its seeds are well and truly planted in us by the age of seven or so through false beliefs. Once planted, doubt proliferates throughout our lives. Once again, we have to thank authority figures for planting these seeds in us. These seeds also contribute to low self-esteem. Many seeds are really just thoughtless remarks such as 'you are a real mess; you are a failure; you cannot count for nuts; you are just useless at spelling; you cannot draw, you'll never be good at . . . ; you have lost your ability to analyse; money doesn't grow on trees, you'll never fit in', and so on. Such statements are usually made by those who should know better. Unfortunately it invariably never even enters the perpetrator's head to think about what they are saying and the impact their careless remarks are likely to have. These statements can be regarded as negative ego remarks. Similar remarks were most probably made to them as they were maturing. Doubt, especially in relation to the Self and our capacity to deal with situations, people or things, is therefore tantamount to self-inflicted emotional blackmail. In this context doubt is created from false beliefs that we have accepted as being true.

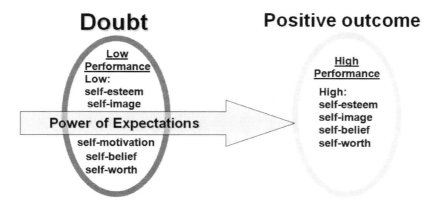

Diagram 7.6

Diagram 7.6 focuses on some of the effects of doubt and offers an antidote. By applying our very own built-in placebo, namely, the Power of Expectations, we have a natural antidote to doubt. Our placebo has the capacity to empower a positive outcome. A positive expectation can have the power to over-ride low self-esteem, or low self-worth, or a false self-belief. Failure is not really an option for us when we engage the Power of Expectations. Some aspects of doubt, of course, can be acceptable, as can certain aspects of fear. What are these aspects? They are straightforward and involve common sense. For instance, have I the ability to jump the width of that stream? Dare I jump out of this tree? The important thing is never to doubt our abilities but let common sense also prevail!

It is undeniable that the Triad, plus Doubt, can stop us from living in the present on a continuous basis; together they destroy the manifestation of what we want and are powerful inducers of stress. One thing is for sure in life, we all need to work on any stress as it arises and preferably before it begins.

Stress

I want to take you through the advantages to your wellbeing when you recognise the benefit of operating from the authentic-self in comparison with the stress-driven fabricated-self. Relaxation in today's 'always doing' society seems to be out of the reach of many. Technology has well and truly entered the workplace and the home and we can be on call or expected to work outside of the conventional eight-hour day. I hear from some of my close friends that a few of their colleagues boast of working 90 hours in a week! I am also aware that many people are working at two jobs just to be able to pay their bills. From a workaholic perspective, 'Quelle horreur' was my first reaction, having done it myself in the distant past.

One thing is for sure, in the past I was addicted to the buzz arising from the adrenaline rush caused by a high stress level, as I pushed myself to the limit.

Diagram 7.7

In diagram 7.7 the left-hand Stress Prone part of the diagram shows my understanding of what the fabricated-self and authentic-self are about. In this case both are separated by what I see as an impenetrable wall. There is very little, if any, communication between them. Our goal is to achieve a non-stress-prone state by working out of the authentic-self as much as possible. In a stress-prone state, the fabricated-self can go for gold (over-achieve, over-indulge, focus totally on work) without any interference or guidance from the authentic-self. How did this play out in my life? It all depended on the choices/decisions I made. And, needless to say, my choices/decisions were affected by the false beliefs (or programs) running in my unconscious mind. Some typical programs that I experienced were:

- **being fearful:** I was unemployed for some time and the fear of not finding a suitable opening induced me to take the first job that seemed suitable. The authentic-self knows the type of job that is suitable and also whether or not it is on the way, thanks to the quantum bio-magnetic field. As the authentic-self was not able to communicate its knowing through intuitive feedback to my fabricated-self, the fabricated-self was in panic mode. Unfortunately, the fabricated-self takes its cue from fear. Once this happens, worry and anxiety set in and any feelings of stress that are around begin to grow exponentially.

- **lack of trust:** taking the unemployed example again, the fabricated-self, when separated from the authentic-self, has no feeling for what employment is just right, or a partner who is just right, or a home that is just right, and so on. The authentic-self knows what the soul's plan is and will always attempt to communicate this to the fabricated-self. As the fabricated-self is in denial of how reality is created, life can become a battleground full of dramas. Doubt sets in and creates a lack of trust about how things are, and stressful feelings again begin to grow rapidly.

- **guilt:** the fabricated-self is addicted to judging, to making comparisons and blaming someone else for whatever is happening. This is one of ego's most favourite games. Guilt goes a lot deeper, though, and starts from what happens during childhood. Parents project their own guilt, usually unconsciously, onto their children. After all, they are only projecting what was downloaded onto them by those who knew better! Or did they know better? The answer here is that, starting with our ancestors, unless they individually questioned their attitudes and behaviour and made corrections, they more than likely passed on what was downloaded onto them to the next generation. The secret here is to think outside the virtual box of accepted thinking. In this 21st century, psychology cannot be regarded as being mainly for sick people but as a tool to explore what is happening within us. Without doing this, guilt can produce doubt which will subtly rule the roost and induce higher levels of stress at times. Guilt's original raison d'être was to bring our attention to situations where we were not taking 'personal responsibility' for what we were doing. Certain faiths or belief systems uses guilt as a powerful tool for control.

The fabricated-self tends to run on negative traits to do with fear, guilt, judgement, comparison, lack of forgiveness, lack of personal responsibility, and so forth. These are all part of the physical and emotional dynamics of the fabricated-self and they add to the level of stress that we may experience. Alternatively, the authentic-self works quietly behind the scenes with a set of spiritual dynamics as shown in diagram 7.2. The main task here is to integrate these spiritual dynamics into the life of the fabricated-self. In doing this, any existing stress level can be greatly reduced and be less of a burden.

When I hear about people putting extra long hours into their job, the comment *'get a life'* jumps out at me, for I too have been through a workaholic phase and realise that having a life which is *in balance* is the *'way to go'* (even though at times there is no alternative but to put in the extra hours just to pay the bills). During my workaholic periods I thought that I had a good life but it was really an illusion. I had little idea about what 'get a life' meant. I was living abroad like a prince, travelling first-class on business and staying in 5 star hotels. So what was missing? Understanding what life is really about is what was missing.

I did not realise that I was in denial of something and was unknowingly being very short-sighted. It has to be said that *'life is for living'*. A part of life, for most of us, is to work so that we can live a good life - not just to live for our work or just to pay the bills. The problem comes if we get caught up in a workaholic – addictive – atmosphere, feeling this is what we have to do if we are to get recognised and promoted. Such an approach to working life is a sure-fire way to promote stress, which is today's number one workplace killer. The trouble with this disease is that it creates three core problems amongst others: insomnia, addiction and depression.

Today, no matter where we turn: the media, television, films, sport, family, friends, leisure, and so on, we seem to be confronted with a drama-based environment steeped in stress or the potential for stress. This type of environment infiltrates our thinking patterns. We are encouraged to spend, spend, spend to get a good life. But do we really need to get the good life the way it is promoted to us, whatever the 'good life' may be? An important message to be aware of is, if this is happening to us, it is because we are letting it happen! It usually happens because strong ego-based forces, plus false beliefs, are running behind the scenes in the unconscious mind and affecting our behaviour. We have to take a step back, pause, take a deep breath and ask our-self:

'what is it that I really want out of life?'

There is a health warning here that we should be aware of. Make sure you are asking this question of our authentic-self because only our authentic-self knows what we need and what we should be doing. Our fabricated-self has infinite wants and will lead ua a merry (and exhausting) dance to obtain them. Your fabricated-self also wants to be involved in activities that boost the ego, especially dramas.

Emotions/feelings that result from a difficult experience become the foundation of many stress problems. This leads us back into considering the question: *'how do you feel?'* Such a question is lacking in our general education where the main focus is on gaining knowledge. We all have the power to say 'enough is enough' and to take corrective action (boundary setting). Any actions need to focus on our thought processes, attitudes and behaviour. They should also include getting into our emotions/feelings and developing an insight into and strengthening our emotional literacy.

Like most conditions, stress has a primary, secondary and tertiary state (see chapter 4). In the primary state we can get rid of some stress by exercising, having a good laugh, doing something we enjoy, playing sport, practising meditation, and so on. In the secondary state we may have allowed some ANTs to creep in and will probably require professional help to de-stress. Behind those ANTs may be some deep seated emotions and issues which have not been dealt with. It is best to stay off medication if we can, but this depends on the effect that high stress levels have on us. If we are in a tertiary stress state then we will need all the help and support we can get, both professional (therapist) and medical (including alternative).

To derive full benefit from living in the present, we need to make sure and deal with any stress that enters our life. I have argued that stress is an outcome of doubt, false beliefs, low self-esteem, ANTs, worry, anxiety, fear, and so forth. The causes of stress need to be recognised and dealt with as soon as possible as they affect the process of manifestation, living in the now and our physical and emotional health. An approach that you can use to help bring you back into a calm homeostatic state is covered in chapter 4. The most cost-effective method of all for de-stressing your-self is to learn to breathe properly. Using music and colours is also another low-cost approach to manage any stress that is caused by your daily activities.

Working through energy blocks that stop us living in the now and from being abundant in what we are meant to have, is such an important part of our life-challenge. We are in the arena of *life lessons*. When we are stressed it is an indication that something is not right. What is not right is that we have strayed off our natural life path and chosen a more challenging one - if we chose to recognise it. I mean that it is more challenging in terms of the intensity of the life lesson and its ultimate effect on our nervous system. Most writers prefer to focus on positive manifestation drivers that lead to creating abundance. But these will only work to a limited extent until what is stopping the manifestation is cleared. This is usually the result of negative energy blocks, and it is identifying and working through these energy blocks that ultimately leads to an increase in our feelings of inner positive wellbeing and happiness. It is 'the way to go'!

Drivers for Abundance and the Manifestation of Success

The Power of Intent

Much emphasis has been placed upon the fact that thinking not only has an effect on our physical and emotional self but also has an effect on other people, the planet and beyond. Does this sound far-fetched? Not if you understand that we are all beings of energy. Chapters 1 through 3 contain enough information for you to form your own opinion. The hidden advantages here are that as our consciousness accepts and connects with the concept of energy, we have an increased chance of accessing our creative-self and higher intelligence. Can you imagine that you actually have the ability to enter and understand the world of Leonardo de Vinci, the world of Shakespeare, the world of great artists, or scientists, or engineers, or chefs, or sports people, and so on? Even living in the present can become a regular occurrence as well as increasing the ability to enter the world of manifestation with greater ease.

Importantly, it is necessary to engage in a transformation that will lead to an inner change to enable us to meet future challenges with greater confidence and an understanding of what they are about. Part of this understanding is obtained from being aware of the fifth dimension and the Universal Laws of the sub-atomic world within which we all operate. Another part is by recognising how the power of our intentions affects the creation of what we desire. I define an intention as:

> *'a powerful thought in the conscious mind plus attendant emotion that supports the unconscious delivery of what we desire'*

When an intention of what is desired is set up, it passes immediately into the unconscious mind. Supporting the intention (the thought) with a strong positive emotion on what is desired supercharges the quantum bio-magnetic energy field and accelerates the manifestation process. We should keep in mind of course that if there are energy blocks (programs with an opposing outcome), this may not happen. The intention plus its supporting emotion will run continuously in the unconscious mind until the manifestation of what we desire is realised, even though the conscious mind is no longer focusing on what is desired.

When we are formulating what we desire in our imagination, it is important to supply sufficient detail to help the process of manifestation although we must not overcook it otherwise it can have a reverse effect on the outcome. Keeping it simple is the key. If any ANTs or doubt set in, this will deplete the energy field, thereby reducing the chance of success in achieving our desire, so getting rid of them both is essential. If our intention is ego-driven then this too can greatly reduce the chance of success. An important point to remember is that most things that are ego-driven are not usually for our higher good. If we are successful at manifesting what we want through a strong ego, it will most probably carry with it some interesting lessons to attempt to get us not to repeat the exercise in the future. So we should be aware of any after-effects (unfortunate situations) that arise! Perhaps the biggest secret of all, though, is to live in the present, using our imagination to see our-self already with what we want, and filled with a strong positive feeling of happiness. If we have no feeling of happiness or have a negative feeling, it is important to stop and question where our want is coming from. If the want is coming from the ego, we will need a complete rethink and a fresh start. In addition, remember that if we project our want into the future, our want will not be forthcoming because energetically it will be seen as a want, an 'not have', which produces a 'have not'!

We are our own agent of change and become all-powerful when we stay in the present with a positive intent, backed by a strong positive emotion in support of what we want or wish to do. How can we tell whether what we want to manifest is in our best interest? We can tell by the amount of resistance we experience as we practise the manifestation process. Look for the synchronicity (both positive and negative) in life to determine what the resistance is trying to tell us. It might be trying to get us to change direction, or it can be telling us that what we want is not right for us. The authentic-self is our greatest protector here. If we ask our authentic-self and listen to the guidance given, we will know whether or not what we have requested is for our highest good. Keep in mind that everything is energy. If the flow of energy is blocked then we need to go within and investigate the cause of the block.

The intent behind our thinking has never been more important than it is now. We are living through what is turning out to be a period of dramatic change. Not only does time appear to be accelerating, but it is also apparent that the whole fabric of our society is being shaken up. Life lessons are being brought to bear in a relentless manner. We are being faced with opportunities to correct past unacceptable attitudes, behaviour, actions and deeds within our lifetime and not some future one. The economics of how we do things is also being shaken up and not before time. Today's economics is well past its sell-by date! If we wish to find out the reason, it is necessary, once again, to raise our awareness to include the concept of the fifth dimension. This will enable us to think out of that limited virtual box. Once we recognise what is happening at a sub-atomic or quantum level, in comparison with the physical reality which we thought was the real thing, our consciousness will automatically begin to give us a different perspective on what is really happening. Our perception will change quite substantially.

Focus (attention)
In the West, we do not have a consciousness discipline that enables us to easily control all of our thoughts. Therefore, our focus can be weak. This may sound trivial, but it is a major problem that affects living in the present and the flow of abundance that we attract or not into

our lives. Our thoughts are usually in free flow mode, meaning they can flow out of the unconscious mind without thinking or sorting in the conscious mind. There can also be a tendency to focus on wants ('must have') and what is missing in our lives. If this is the case it means that we are coming from a position of lack. Yes, lack! I was completely unaware of this and also that I was programming it into my quantum bio-magnetic field. The end result when in a state of lack is that more of the same –want – lack - is attracted because of our focus on it. Once again it is important to remember that a want represents 'not having' which energetically attracts 'not having', and tons of it! Living in the present means seeing ourselves already with whatever it is that we desire, and feeling good about it. Why the feeling good? I emphasised above, when we feel good we generate a strong positive emotion which helps to speed up the manifestation process of what we focus upon. This positive emotion is also transmitted down to the cellular level of the body, which can give rise to an increase in feelings of wellbeing and happiness.

There are many workshops and seminars we can attend which are there to help us manifest what we want. Abundance is the name of the game and people are selling techniques and processes to help us achieve this end. What is not made clear is that generally these workshops are only working with the fabricated-self. It is so easy to prey on people's wants! A degree of honesty is required where presenters state up-front that their techniques have worked successfully for some people but not others.

If the abundance workshop is about manifesting money, an investigation into the spiritual dynamics of life shows that only a few individuals will be able to make millions or even billions in life; most will not. Those who make millions will have life lessons associated with this activity. It is important to note that most likely our life lessons include being financially comfortable and having all our needs met. It always depends on the lessons that we agreed to take on in this lifetime before we were born. It is also important to note that our authentic-self will always ensure we have what we need in life.

Expectations

As always, our expectations act as a placebo with respect to what we are thinking. The placebo effect is covered in detail in chapter 4. If you have any doubt about living in the now or about manifesting your desire, this will negate the placebo effect. It will automatically produce the opposite which is the nocebo effect. Both are guaranteed to work.

Creating a Flow of Abundance

From a fabricated-self's perspective, abundance involves being able to count what we have and what we want! Abundance is something which most of us desire and we often spend a considerable amount of time, money and effort in an attempt to find it, no matter what 'it' is.

Can we change our level of abundance in money, relationships, creative expression and so forth? Can we improve our health? To a degree we certainly can, but there is something which we simply must know. The first and most important point to make is that when we are able to communicate with and operate out of our authentic-self, abundance and manifestation will occur naturally without effort. Working from the fabricated-self, much effort is put into trying to be abundant, usually through attempting to manifest 'wants', most times with little success. Ego will constantly push your fabricated-self to try to get *everything* it wants. Ego does not trust, has no understanding of why it exists, and therefore, has no acceptance of the true nature of life. Ego uses judgement and comparison to get what it wants.

The different types of abundance we experience are usually interlinked. From the perspective of the fabricated-self, if we focus on one desired outcome, money for example, we might just be lucky enough to make a small increase in our monetary flow. I say 'might' in case we have not dealt with the block(s) that are holding us back from being truly abundant in this and other areas of life. I have made the point above that in the quest for abundance, if it is difficult and hard work to obtain, there is an energy block (a false belief, or issue/life lesson, and so forth) within. As the setback is being worked through it will clear the energy block, thereby enabling abundance energy to flow. If the flow of abundance is still unsatisfactory, then there are other blocks which need to be investigated and worked through. Most of what follows on 'abundance' is relevant for the fabricated-self, as the authentic-self automatically manifests what you need.

Bringing in Abundance

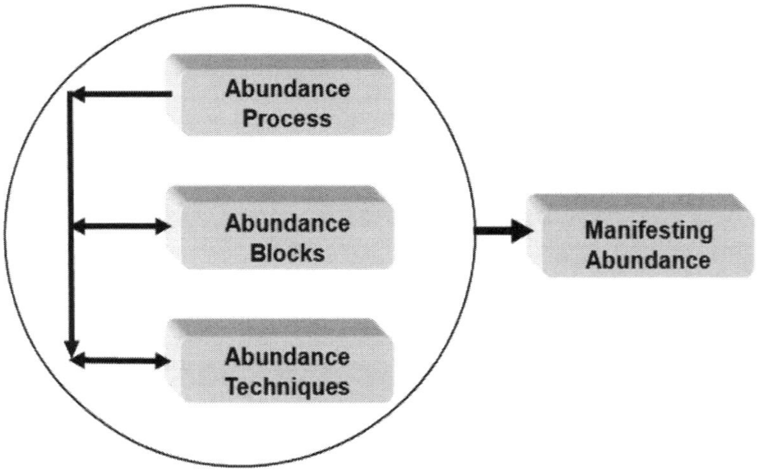

Diagram 7.8

The flow of abundance can be broken down into three separate stages, as shown in diagram 7.8. The actual techniques to attract abundance are straightforward and I describe them below. This book is designed to help you to get back into the flow of life, if you are not already there. Life in general should not be a continual struggle! If it is, the question *'why is my life such a struggle?'* needs to be asked. What is it that is blocking you from having what you want? I make some suggestions here to help in removing the cause of whatever is preventing your energy from flowing. This will contribute to an energy shift and transformation within to enable you to stay in the flow of life.

Abundance Flow Process

The fabricated-self prefers to work with the abundance and manifestation success drivers and does not want to work systematically through any blockages because of ego. Ego blocks out the authentic-self with great ease. Ego also loves the disappointment that can arise from an unsuccessful manifestation exercise because this provides ego with extra games to play and energy to feed off!

It can be difficult to grasp that we live in a Universe which offers infinite abundance, especially when we see people born into poor circumstances, or we are experiencing a difficult time ourselves. In such a situation, manifesting an abundance of what is desired can prove to be elusive. The elusiveness may stay until the energy blocks are located, worked with and cleared, so that the flow of abundance can take place.

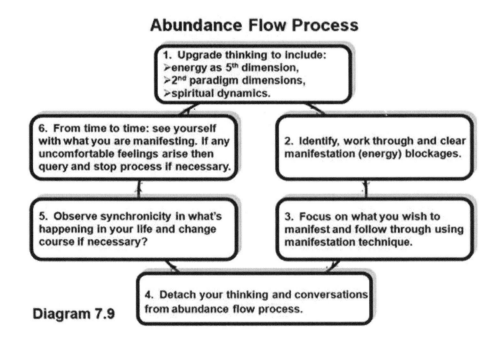

Diagram 7.9

Diagram 7.9 represents a six-step breakdown of the abundance flow process. The diagram is self-descriptive and each step is covered in detail below. As examples of where abundance might be desired/created, I present three types: good health; wealth; and relationships. There are, of course many more types of abundance such as an abundance of creativity, time, patience, positive outlook and so on.

To attract a balanced inward flow of abundance, the following six steps are recommended:

1. Work with your authentic-self's spiritual dynamics (Diagram 7.2); raise your awareness to think within the fifth dimension of energy and second dimensions paradigm. Work towards seeing everything in life as interconnected modules of energy, because you are transmuting one form of energy into another through the energy dynamics of the manifestation process.

2. At the time of writing this book, most countries have been going through a deep economic recession. This can play havoc with the abundance flow process as it can cause you to worry about money. Once you start worrying, you are programming this into your quantum bio-magnetic field. In such a state of mind an energy block will form which needs to be cleared. If you happen not to be worried, and nothing is happening with respect to creating the abundance that you want, you will still have an energy block. Go within to identify where the energy block is located and work to remove it. It is most probably a false belief.

3. This is where you bring in the manifestation technique described below. In creating abundance there is an overlap between the abundance flow process and the manifestation technique. During difficult economic times, there is an increase in the number of people turning their attention to focusing on manifesting an inward flow of money to balance the outward flow. And sometimes there is a desire to try to create a surplus. Like everything else on this planet, money is just another form of energy. Recognising this is an important step forward in creating an abundance of wealth which includes manifesting an amount of money that you desire. A health warning should be given here as manifesting money can appear to be deceptively easy. I say 'appear to be', as it all depends on the programs that are running within your quantum bio-magnetic field. If your manifesting approach is not working, go back to 2, above.

4. A key feature in the abundance flow process and manifestation technique is the importance of detaching your thinking and conversations from what you are trying to manifest, once you have followed the process through to 3, above. This is because you can unknowingly interfere with what you are trying to manifest through changes in mood (feelings). Other people you have spoken with may get jealous or resent what you are saying and this will interfere energetically with your abundance flow process and manifestation ability. Always remember that we are operating in the world of energy.

5. Once you have gone through the manifestation technique, it is important to stop focusing (thinking too much) on what you want, because your thinking can interfere with the process which is continuing in the world of energy. Instead, observe what is happening in your life and notice any synchronicity that occurs. By synchronicity, I

mean look for helpful or unhelpful signs with respect to your manifestation request, as you are going about your daily business. If the signs are unhelpful and nothing is happening, I would suggest that you reconsider your manifestation request. You may just need to change part of your request to something more suitable or drop it altogether. There will be a life lesson associated with this and it would be helpful for you to investigate what that lesson is.

6. If everything is going well and there are no negative signs with respect to your manifestation request, you can include this last step. Here, from time to time, see yourself with what you are manifesting and feel the benefits that you have gained for yourself and those around you. Sharing is an important feature of life. It is advisable not to follow this last step if there are any negative signs being brought to your attention. These signs are most probably trying to do you a favour and are suggesting that you rethink your manifesting request.

In summary, the abundance flow process provides us with an opportunity to:

- remove any energy blocks that are preventing us from manifesting what we want
- learn to live in the now
- find out whether or not we are on our life's path.

Keep in mind that even when we are on our life's path we may still encounter difficult challenges (life lessons). If we handle the challenges well, our emotional response should be positive and supportive. We can then move on to the next life lesson/challenge more quickly. If the challenge is difficult and we fight it rather than work through it, it is likely that it will remain with us until we stop fighting it. We should therefore ask our-self the question:

'what is it that I need to learn from the situation I find myself in?'

As we are working through the abundance flow process, the following manifestation technique should be used.

Abundance Manifestation Technique

The abundance manifestation technique is part of a 'life boat' that can support us while we are merging our fabricated-self with the authentic-self. Our fabricated-self needs such a technique to attempt to create the abundance we want. This is because the fabricated-self's perception of the world and how things operate is form-based, mechanistic and linear-time-biased. The authentic-self has no such constraints as it is operating in the world of energy. This is a good time to consider asking our-self the following question:

'why struggle when I can manifest with ease through my authentic self?'

And how do we do that? We work through our blocks and as we do so our fabricated-self will begin merging with our authentic-self. As we follow the abundance flow process above, unhelpful programs that are running within the unconscious mind, which interfere with the manifestation process, can be dealt with on a case by case basis. Diagram 7.10 shows a series of six steps, each being a part of the manifestation technique.

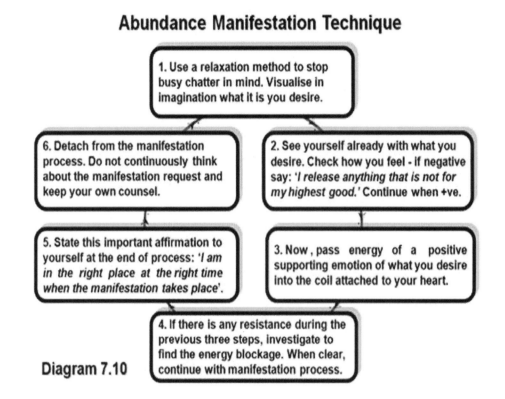

Diagram 7.10

Step 1.
To strengthen the manifestation process of what is desired, we can begin by using the relaxation method described in Chapter 4 as the conscious mind needs to be cleared of any busy chatter. Before you are able to clear your conscious mind with ease, you may have to remove some of the energy blocks that exist. In doing this you are creating an energy shift and transformation within the conscious and unconscious minds. What is this transformation? After you stop the chatter in your conscious mind, you will have the ability to control and clear your thoughts as well as to monitor what is actually running (the programs) within your unconscious mind. This will help you to monitor what is running in your unconscious mind by recognising what you say in conversation. Your remarks, at times, will give you an indication of what negative (and positive) programs are running. Such programs could be 'raising enough cash is difficult'; 'I never seem to find a loving, reliable girl/boy friend'; 'I'll never get promoted'; or 'just my bad luck'. All of these indicate an energy block that needs to be cleared. When you are in a relaxed state, see in your imagination what it is

you want to manifest. If you have a negative feeling while you are doing this, stop and investigate why. When you have a positive feeling you can move onto 2 below.

Step 2.

In your relaxed state of mind, visualise your-self with what you want in your imagination. Attach to the image that you have created a supporting positive emotion. Hold this in your mind for several minutes (no more than five) and then release the image and supporting emotion. Stop doing it earlier if it begins to feel uncomfortable. In this case, once again, see in your imagination the image of what you want. Monitor how you feel physically. Do you get an uplifting feeling or perhaps a tense negative feeling in your solar plexus or elsewhere in your body? If you have a negative or tense feeling then it is important to question why you are requesting what you wish to manifest. The negative feeling could indicate that it is an ego-driven request, or a request from the shadow side of a personality/sub-personality. There is a chance that in this state the request will manifest, but it will come with a health warning as the manifestation will not necessarily be for your higher good! You may not be aware of this, especially if the ego is driving your request. Behind such a request there could unknowingly be issues of poverty consciousness, envy, greed, jealousy and so forth. As you work through any abundance energy blocks, these types of issues may come to the surface and need to be dealt with. To protect your-self from what might turn out to be some unwelcome lessons, I would recommend that you use the following affirmation before making a manifestation request:

'I release anything that is not for my highest good.'

Using this affirmation can give you a degree of protection, if you make the statement sincerely. Follow, once again, how you feel. If you feel an inner positive response after stating the affirmation, move on to step 3. Otherwise investigate why.

Step 3.

There is a technique that you can use to strengthen your bio-magnetic field which is a major part of the manifestation process. If you are going through a difficult time in life, the following magnetic coil technique can help to expedite matters. When the conscious mind is still, see in your imagination a coil in front of you similar to the one shown in diagram 7.11. The coil is connected to the front and back of the heart. To put the coil into operation, see in your imagination the positive emotion of how you feel about your manifestation request passing through the coil like an electric current, from the front heart position all the way to the back heart connection. Carry on doing this for about five minutes. If you begin to

Diagram 7.11

feel uncomfortable before the end of this time period, then stop doing it. As you are going through this exercise, keep the image of what you desire to manifest in your imagination.

Step 4.

This step is really a check and balance on the manifestation process. If you have any negative feelings or you feel physically uncomfortable with what you are doing, it is time to stop. There will be an energy blockage indicating that what you are trying to manifest is not in your best interest. Work backwards to locate what the blockage is about. Is it a false belief? Is it trying to get you to change direction? Are you in contact with your authentic-self? If you are working solely from your fabricated-self, then there is a high probability that the request is ego-driven. Reconsider what it is you want and begin again. If your life is in desperate straits, the blockage could be stopping you in order to allow you to think again. In the most difficult type of situation such as selling your house, or a job change, or a partnership separation, and so forth, the blockage could be forcing you to make a difficult decision. It is your choice to make and a life lesson will be involved. Sometimes you might also experience a blockage that originates from positive ego. You feel ecstatic about what you want – no negative feeling here! Check out the reason why you want what you are trying to manifest. Is it to make you look good in comparison with others? Will it make you feel superior? and so on. If it does, then reconsider what you are trying to manifest. If it is a genuine feeling of compassion to help others (and your-self) without inflating your ego, then continue. If not, then re-think your manifestation request. Keeping your life in a balanced state is the name of the game.

Step 5.

When you have stopped visualising what you want and passing the energy current around the magnetic coil, say the following affirmation to your-self every now and then:

'I am in the right place at the right time when the manifestation takes place.'

This affirmation will strengthen the synchronicity of events that occur and ensure that you are where you should be. Look for supportive or non-supportive occurrences with respect to what you are manifesting. If nothing happens, go back to 2 above.

Step 6.

This last step is most important. It is absolutely essential that you detach your-self from the process of manifestation once you have completed steps 1 through 4. If you have not, or cannot, then you are coming from a position of lack and this means that you will attract more lack. You can practise seeing your-self with what you want just before you fall asleep or when you wake up for a few seconds, but no more. After you have done this, focus on something else and preferably something positive. Do not talk to anyone about what you desire for they may unconsciously be jealous, or envious, or non-supportive and their energies will affect the process negatively.

Now that you have an idea of the overall abundance process, you can apply it to the following three manifestation requests, or for whatever you desire. It is important to remember to clear any blockages that may be in place. Sometimes, you may be able to force a manifestation request through. But, as stated above, it will come with a penalty or health warning. Most certainly there will also be a life lesson attached to it.

Abundance in Health – is it Possible?
My medical friends assure me that we are either healthy or unhealthy. Using the term abundance implies the measurement of an amount and that does not really fit with the subject of health! However, this does not mean to say that you cannot change your state of health for the better. It all depends on your understanding of mind and body links, a subject that the medical fraternity has been slow to fully engage with. Now, what I write below may cause some discomfort until you strongly connect your fabricated-self with the authentic-self. There may be a gestation period before you actually accept what I have written below.

We all have many different types of life lessons to learn. Sometimes a particular life lesson can be related to a difficult health issue. *'This does not make sense* many of you may be thinking. You may also be thinking *no one in their right mind would take on a life with a serious health issue.* That is because we are not fully informed as to what our soul and life lessons are about. Today, with the energy changes that are affecting our planet, it is imperative to understand the purpose of our existence in a physical body. I am certainly curious about this, and I suspect that you are, too. A serious illness or accident can be, from a soul's perspective, associated with a life lesson which the soul has agreed to work through during the lifetime in its physical body. To understand what an illness or an accident is about it is important to ask:

'what is it that I have to learn from what is happening to me?'

This certainly turned my own life upside down. Moreover, I discovered from an energy perspective that to fight an illness through fear is to add to its condition, for fear generates negative energy which is detrimental to good health in that it damages the body's cells. The fabricated-self will always react through fear. Nonetheless, this does not mean that we are helpless! An important point to make is that if you have a serious illness or had an accident it is in your interest to ask your-self:

'what is it that I need to change in my life to prevent this happening again?'

A point to note is, because of the illness or accident there needs to be a change, for example, a shift in your thinking, or your lifestyle, or what you are doing, or in your relationships, or combinations of these. The message here is that changes need to be made so you can heal your-self and follow a new path in life.

As I said at the beginning of this section, you cannot count health! Most of us are born with good health but can unknowingly squander it as we journey along life's path. We can squander our health through a lack of exercise, poor diet, too much alcohol, drugs (medicinal and social) and through a lifetime of misguided thinking. Good health is something that is usually taken for granted until we are faced with a health crisis - an illness, an organ malfunction, a disease, or an accident. In general, a health crisis stops us in our tracks before we realise what an important gift good health is. I need to emphasise again that this may be one of the soul's life lessons. How we handle the crisis brings an opportunity for us to realise that we have the ability, to a substantial degree, to control how we feel physically and emotionally. The statement that it is *all in the mind* is appropriate here. In chapter 2 I made the point that the mind (both conscious and unconscious) drives the emotions and vice versa, all of which has an effect at the cellular level of the body. This means that the body's cells are aware of the emotions that we are experiencing. Another point is that the body's cells have genetic characteristics downloaded into them via both parents at conception as well as a set of our parents' false beliefs, amongst other characteristics! Why is this important?

It is important because after birth, negative emotional energy generated via ANTs, false beliefs, doubt, stress and so forth can all have a cumulative degenerative effect on the body's cells. This can eventually lead to a state of dis-ease, and dis-ease leads to tumours, organ malfunction and so forth. Moreover, the negative programs running in our field can also lead to us having an accident! The good news is that we all have a capacity to exercise control over our emotions and physical state of being. Positive emotions are like energy antibiotics and can have amazing healing properties. Positive expectations are another. What is it then that affects our ability to keep in good health? There are five key points to consider when a health issue or crisis arises that affects our health. The first three points relate to the state of dis-ease, or blocked energy:

1. Primary: early symptoms are detected of a physical and/or emotional problem that needs to be investigated and dealt with. As well as going through a standard medical protocol, an alternative/complementary approach could also be considered.

2. Secondary: a dis-ease (imbalance) has taken root and needs to be dealt with as early as possible. Medical aid is required and/or alternative/complementary approaches could also be considered.

3. Tertiary: this is a critical situation and combinations of surgery, pharmacological and other treatments will need to be applied. Once again, alternative or complementary approaches can also be included during the treatment period.

What I am about to say next may cause some discomfort, especially for those who may be in a tertiary state. Firstly, the medical approach is to deal principally with symptoms and not the causes of a life-threatening disease. To deal with causes it is necessary to understand the energy/spiritual dynamics of life and what is happening at a sub-atomic level. What are the spiritual dynamics of life? This leads to the fourth key point:

4. Understanding that you have a soul, and that the soul has a number of life lessons to grow through during its lifetime is important. It should heighten your awareness of the fact that there is a purpose to what is happening to you, as you journey along life's path. Some of the life lessons may not be pleasant, but are necessary for the soul's growth. The soul grows through situations and experiences that it attracts or is attracted to, all of which are associated with life lessons. It does this through the programming of the quantum bio-magnetic field. We are given an opportunity to make choices/decisions about what we do or say, or the attitude we project and behaviour we engage in. All of this plus the action we take and how we handle the situation indicates to the soul how much we have learnt, or not!

   Sometimes, the choices we make are limited, for example whether to have an operation or not. Taking myself as an example, I discovered, by accident (I had no symptoms), that I had an irregular heartbeat. My doctor recommended that I have a pacemaker fitted but I resisted until a full analysis was carried out because, like most people, I had a fear about having an operation. The surgeon and the team who carried out the operation were not only highly-skilled professionals but also first-class communicators and true artists at their profession. The artistic point is an essential ingredient for any top professional. For me, it was a good experience and one carried out by a team who cared. As it turned out, this was one of my life lessons which are associated with heart energy and some of that had become blocked. I am still investigating the cause and will work towards releasing the blocked energy. Another lesson was associated with learning to trust that the synchronicity of events which led up to the operation was confirming the need for it. My Chinese alternative medicine doctor noticed my irregular pulse first.

Identifying energy blockages that have caused a state of dis-ease is of utmost importance for our health. To do this, one way is to enter the unconscious mind and to go back to the time period when the energy blockage occurred. It is worth investigating a new breed of regression therapists who are capable of locating blockages and who also help the individual concerned to work through clearing them. They can also explore what the life lesson confronting the individual is about. Once an energy block which represents the cause of a particular physical state or dis-ease has been located, the next point to consider is that:

5. after removing the cause of the energy block, the dis-eased part of the body is still in place and has a life of its own. This means that the dis-eased physical part has still to be treated, until the affected body's cells are brought back into homeostasis (balance).

I usually take some flack when I boldly state during a workshop or one to one session that *we create our own reality* in life. This also includes the state of health that we create for ourselves. Just about everything that happens to us starts within the mind. I say just about because there can be external conditions that trigger a health problem such as polluted air, or polluted water, unsuitable foods and so forth. Some people are also born with a clinical condition which stays with them throughout their life, as it is a life lesson that the soul has agreed to grow through. This statement usually causes a lot of anger and much dis-belief in the West as we have been denied an understanding of what life and the soul are truly about.

If we are not feeling too good within our-self, or about our-self is there anything that we can do about it? There certainly is and the abundance flow process (diagram 7.9, page 377) can be used to help us work towards the best possible state of health. The following steps are suggested:

1. Reframe your attitude to what it takes to maintain good health. This means looking at what you are doing (and/or thinking) from a different direction to see what you need to do to create a more positive feeling. Start by recognising that your state of health is driven by your mind (consciousness) and that the thoughts and emotions you bring up on a regular basis contribute to how you feel physically and emotionally. If you have a clinical illness, see it as a challenge and work with it to determine what the life lesson is. It is good if you also begin to think about your-self as a 'being of energy' and follow through by understanding the different dimensions (second paradigm - chapter 1) that operate at that level. A major point here is that an upgrade of your awareness can put you in a position to transmute the negative energies that are affecting you. Changing your thinking to incorporate the world of energy puts you on a path where miracles (spontaneous remission) can be experienced.

2. Identify and work through any abundance blockages described above that you detect. As you are doing this, there are some steps that can be taken to improve your inner state of positive wellbeing which will lead to an improved health condition. These steps are all linked to what is running within your consciousness and are straightforward to implement. A good place to start is to try and keep your mind in a non-stressed state. Be careful about what you watch on television, news media and films. Be careful what you read in newspapers and magazines. The message here is

to stay out of anything that will cause a drama in your mind! Also, try to stay out of any family, or work, or social dramas. It is a human trait to focus on negative stories and adrenaline-producing material or situations. These all end up as programs running within the unconscious mind as well as in the quantum bio-magnetic field and can create havoc for you emotionally and, in time, physically.

3. When you are in a relaxed state in bed before you go to sleep and when you wake up in the morning, in your imagination see an image of your-self smiling and in perfect health. As you do this, bring in a warm positive emotion about an experience you have had. If you cannot recall such an experience, try to make one up. It is the positive emotion that is the power behind the visualisation exercise. Hold the image and emotion for about five minutes. It may dissipate earlier. If it does just let it go. Keep doing this exercise regularly.

In addition, bring something positive into your conscious mind before you go to sleep and when you first wake up in the morning, about what is going on in your life or has happened in the past. Try to accept that what is going on around you is mirroring something back to you as a lesson that is running in your unconscious mind. This can prove difficult at times as what is happening may not seem to make sense or you may think it is to do with someone else. Step back and isolate any negative experiences and their associated emotions as this is where ego and different elements of the persona will be joining in to feed off the energy. As you detach your-self from any isolated negative experience see if there is a message for you to learn from it. Once you have understood the message, release the negative experience; for example, attach it to a balloon and see it floating away into the distance. If you cannot pick up a message for your-self, then just release the experience, again with a balloon. Now, concentrate on a particular positive experience and bring in a supportive strong positive emotion to replace the departed experience. This experience is just a thought and an emotion. To help you in a situation where you are being bombarded with negative thoughts, state one of the following affirmations verbally or in your mind continuously until the negative thoughts stop. They *will* stop, because the conscious mind will get bored in time and give up. It is also a useful tool to get rid of ANTs. I suggest that you state a positive affirmation in your mind at least ten times before you go to sleep and as soon as you wake up in the morning. And I recommend that you consider using whichever is appropriate of the following affirmations:

Every day in every way I am feeling better and better and better.

Every day in every way I am in a calm and positive state of mind.

Every day in every way I am in a perfect state of health.

You can make up your own affirmation that takes into account a condition that you are being treated for such as:

Every day in every way I am growing a stronger and stronger immune system.

Every day in every way I am making a speedy recovery after my . . . (type of operation).

For those of you who are in good health I would suggest that you say an affirmation of thanks in recognition of your good fortune such as:

I am truly grateful for my excellent physical, mental, emotional and energetic good health.

It is important to recognise that *mind is the architect and builder* for not only your good health but also for how abundant you are in wealth, relationships and other areas of your life.

Abundance in Wealth

I have placed much emphasis on what blocks us from being abundant in our life and what we can do to help in manifesting our desires. You will have gathered that creating abundance involves changing your thinking to cause a shift not only in your conscious mind but also removing any false beliefs that are running in your unconscious mind. Finding the blocks that are preventing you from manifesting what you want is a must. If you are successfully working through the abundance blocks described above, there is a high probability that you are becoming more able to manifest, for example, money when you actually need it. Please remember, once again, that this section is designed to help you while you merge your fabricated-self with your authentic-self. This section should act, once again, like a life boat should you be journeying through stormy waters. A point worth keeping in mind is that most Western populations can be divided into three categories when it comes to creating an abundance of wealth. These categories represent those whose life lessons include:

- o making lots of money (a small number of people – a fraction of less than 1 percent)
- o being financially comfortable
- o facing a money shortage, experiencing a financial struggle and perhaps poverty (probably between 15 percent to 40 percent of the population in the West).

In difficult economic times action and results are required rather than listening to somebody pontificating about what to do. The action to be taken is into two stages. The first stage defines three universal rules that are part of the quest for the manifestation of abundance.

Stage 1

Rule 1: Recognise that you are a quantum bio-magnet and you are attracting what is running in your energy field. Investigate and remove the appropriate energy blocks.

Rule 2: If you focus on wanting a sum of money in the future or even in the present (the now) it will never happen. Crucially, this is because you want it and a 'want' generates a negative energy signature that has lack or scarcity attached to it. And lack begets lack. There is really *no* lack as the Universe is infinite in its supply of resources. To accelerate the manifestation process, see your-self in the present in your imagination feeling happy and with the actual amount of money that you would like. This will remove any doubt in your consciousness. If you feel you have some doubt, work to remove it, for it is probably caused by a false belief.

Rule 3: To maintain a flow of money, it is necessary to recognise that money is energy and that energy needs to flow to sustain it. See your-self in your imagination spending/investing the money that you have manifested on what you wanted it for. How do you feel when you are doing this? If you do not have a warm inner feeling then it is advisable to investigate why. Is the money you envisaged just to satisfy your ego? If it is, perhaps you need to rethink what you want. The purpose here is not to satisfy the ego, although there is a general tendency to do this. It is to satisfy the soul. If the negative feeling is because the money is to pay bills, reverse this thinking. Recognise that by paying your bills you are helping other people to keep their jobs and that they will be grateful. Reframe your thinking to a supportive thought and change the feeling to a positive one.

If the money that is manifested does not flow it becomes stagnant and can be lost. This means that if you just want money to give you a feeling of security by keeping it in the bank, there is little chance of the manifestation taking place. Many who accumulate money make their homes into fortresses to protect themselves and constantly worry about losing their money. The result of that is either they will experience their worst fears, or they are setting themselves up for a state which has the potential to manifest into an unwanted condition. Make the money circulate so that it works for you.

The fabricated-self needs large sums of money to feel secure and to constantly feed the ego with material things. The authentic-self does not and it manifests what is needed at the right time without prompting. The authentic-self knows that it can do this but the fabricated-self does not believe it can. Which self do you want to operate from? You may be thinking – 'well that is OK for someone like your-self but you do not have my problems and bills to pay!' I can assure you that most of us have our challenges and bills to pay. The word 'trust' comes to the fore here. The fabricated-self does not trust! Once you open a door to secure a strong communication with your authentic-self, you will be in a state where there will be an inner knowing which does not doubt and trusts in what is happening. As you work to get into this state, following the abundance flow process above can contribute to getting you there. If you are in difficult circumstances, practise the manifesting technique. Once again, I add a health warning and that is to be careful that you are not being run by your ego. Now that you are aware of what is happening in your consciousness when ego cuts in, it should be a lot easier to recognise and to make a correction.

Stage 2

Step 1:
Find a quiet spot to relax and make your-self comfortable. In your imagination see your-self as a cloud of coloured swirling energy suspended in an infinite cloud of energy. You have the ability to manifest what you want by transmuting part of the infinite cloud's energy into what you want. In this case it's money.

Step 2:
See in your imagination the sum of money that you want. How do you feel? If you feel negative or uncomfortable ask your-self why? It is important to identify the cause. Run through the energy blocks described in previous chapters to see if one or more resonate with you. Work through and clear the blocks. It is also advisable to state, before and after the manifestation request, the affirmation:

'I release anything that is not for my highest good.'

Be sensible with the amount that you request for if you have asked for millions and it is not in your soul contract, then nothing will happen. When you feel comfortable with the amount that you have requested, continue with step 3.

Step 3:
Bring into your imagination the coil image shown in diagram 7.11. Pass the positive emotion you are feeling into the coil allowing it to circulate from the front to the back. This will strengthen the bio-magnetic field attraction factor supporting your request for the amount of money you desire.

Step 4:
As the emotion energy is circulating around the coil, if it raises a negative or uncomfortable feeling it is advisable to investigate why. There is a block that needs to be cleared. Once again, investigate and clear the block.

Step 5:

It is important to go about your daily activities and take action where appropriate. As you do this it is good to state the following affirmation from time to time:

'I am in the right place at the right time when the manifestation takes place.'

Watch for any synchronicity happening in your life with respect to your manifestation request. You never know which direction your request will appear from.

Step 6:

This last step is extremely important and it is to *detach* your-self from the request. Do not think about the request on a regular basis. Certainly see your-self with what you have requested from time to time, for example when you are in bed, but only for a few seconds. It is best not discuss your request with anyone. All of this prevents any energetic interference with your request, including from your-self - a typical interference would be if you suddenly doubted that your request would be granted. One final point to bear in mind; everything has its own timing!

Abundance in Relationships

When I look back on my own relationships, I would have benefited greatly if I had had a broader understanding of what relationships are really about. Most of the information about relationships was just not available during my younger days. This is no fault of my parents or teachers as the subject has only recently entered education and the public domain for discussion. I use diagram 7.12 here and in Chapter 5 to indicate the different drivers

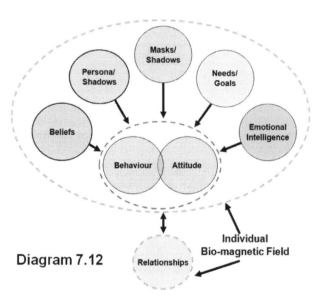

Diagram 7.12

(programs) that are running behind the scenes (in the unconscious mind). These drivers have an effect in any relationship we engage in. The three key relationship drivers are behaviour, attitude and the bio-magnetic field. The first two drivers are highly visible and the third is invisible. In life we can learn to disguise our behaviour and attitudes so we fit in, but we cannot disguise what is running in the bio-magnetic field.

I want to focus on five other drivers in addition to those shown in the above diagram, that contribute to understanding what is going on within a relationship. These drivers contribute a boost not only towards abundance in personal relationships but also in other areas of life (money, creativity, happiness, wellbeing, love and so forth). After elaborating on the five drivers, all of which are mutually inclusive, we will then go through the abundance process in the quest towards creating abundance in relationships. It might be helpful to revisit the relationship content of chapter 5 as an additional support in this quest. The first driver 'know your-self' stands out as the key to finding the path that will lead to the kind of relationships we want.

Driver 1: Know Your-self
First and foremost, as outlined in Chapter 5, the most important relationship in our life is the relationship we have with our-self. This includes the five upper elements in diagram 7.12 – beliefs, persona/shadows masks/shadows, needs/goals and emotional intelligence. How well do you think you know *your*-self? To make a start take two blank sheets of paper. On the left-hand sheet write any negative attributes you think you have and on the right-hand sheet write positive attributes. Ask family, friends and colleagues for their input. Try to be as honest as you can and keep your ego to a minimum! Take a step back from your-self and think of your behaviour and attitudes in different situations. What sort of moods and habits do you have? Do you suffer from short bursts of anger/temper and so forth? Include these on the appropriate page of your attributes. After reading Drivers 2 through 5 below take a step back in your imagination and have a good look at your beliefs –beliefs being defined here as '*what you accept as being true*' (nothing to do with religion). Self-esteem is important for your wellbeing and I repeat an approach below that you can use to measure your self-esteem. I suggest that you ask your-self some questions like:

- how much do I like or love myself? (self-worth)
- how confident am I? (self-belief and self-image)
- how self-motivated am I?
- what is my level of self-acceptance?
- how self-sufficient am I?

Think of a score from 0 to 10 where 10 is the highest and score your-self on each of the above questions. Any answer greater than 5 goes into positive attributes. Nevertheless, if the score is less than 8 then you have some work to do on your-self to find out what the false belief is that is causing the lower score. A score of 8 to 10 is good. Everything below 5 goes onto your negative attributes sheet, showing there is a need to increase the score to seven plus as this is a healthier state of emotional intelligence.

A considerable number of energy blocks arise from low self-esteem. Inner feelings of wellbeing and happiness are dependent on our level of self-esteem (diagram 7.13). If you follow the attributes/ scoring approach, it can act as a barometer to check the level of your own self-esteem. The more we think of our-self in a positive way on a daily basis the stronger the contribution we make to our self-esteem and the higher our feelings of wellbeing will be. We can use other people or material things to boost our morale and to increase these same feelings, but this will be only a temporary fix because this approach is ego driven.

Self-esteem and well-being are mutually dependent.

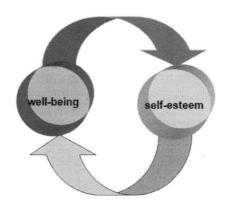

As we work with this Driver we may discover some surprises about our-self, both in positive and negative terms. Most people find more negatives than positives but if

Diagram 7.13

we did not have some negatives life could be quite dull and boring. Contrast is important for our growth in life and, indeed, ultimately for spiritual development. The negatives indicate where energy blocks may lie and should be seen as a gift. Such a gift provides us with an indication of what needs to be improved. A danger to be aware of is the influence that a strong positive or negative ego can play in our relationships. It can push us off our life's path and those around us may not be impressed because of our attitudes and behaviour. We always attract (see below) close relationships which will reflect back to us what is in our best interest to learn about our-self. We also mirror back to others what they need to learn about themselves (see driver 5). This is quite the opposite to what we would expect in a 'blame someone else society'. As we perfect this understanding, it has the potential to enable us to move on in life to better and better relationships.

Driver 2: Relationships - a Teaching Platform
Each person with whom we enter a relationship represents a teaching platform where we have the opportunity to find out more about our-self. As we take a closer look at our-self an opportunity is provided to create a life built around friends and a partner who are in tune with our positive needs.. This does not mean that our relationships will not encounter challenges! In helping people to change, I have heard from partners that they preferred their partner before the changes took place! This is because whereas they used to be predictable, now that they are running different programs in their energy field, they are not. They now have to re-adjust to their partner's new attitudes and behaviour or leave the relationship.

A soul's growth is mainly through the relationships we have with our family, friends, work colleagues and those with whom we come into contact with. Most certainly, relationships represent the soul's premier teaching platform. As I have emphasised, our attitudes and how we handle life's challenges is a major area of soul growth. For example, suppose you are at a ticket office or an airport check-in and the person opposite explodes over a trivial remark that you just made. How you handle your reply will be a growth challenge for your soul (as well as your fabricated-self). Similarly, an office colleague who suddenly explodes after a chance innocent remark can provide a unique opportunity . . . to, quite simply, stay out of any *drama* that may ensue! To pour oil over troubled waters and to be understanding with them is the 'way to go'. Why would you do that? You would do it because you do not know what has been happening in the individual's life. You also do not know what ANTs are running amok in their consciousness. You are being given a gift which is to see how constructively you *handle* the situation. If your ego jumps in and you react, then you will just be adding to the drama and nothing much will be achieved except satisfying each other's egos.

Driver 3: Relationship Harmoniser - Emotional Response

In all relationships, emotional intelligence (Chapter 6) and how we respond emotionally in different situations is an important key to happiness, and this includes, once again, the relationship we have with our-self. We all need to treat ourselves with respect and affection. If we do not do this for ourselves how on earth can we show the same to other people? Many people use hollow and inappropriate words that are not coming from their heart. The Heart energy centre is the centre of genuine emotions. When the heart centre (chapters 2 and 3) is activated, words have a warm and supportive emotion attached to them. If the words come from the Intellect (the head) they are usually hollow and lack any supporting warmth. They can also incorporate negative emotions generated by a negative ego or negative element of the persona. How many times have you heard a couple saying 'yes darling, no darling' in a heated conversation and the 'darlings' were certainly not coming from the heart!

Everybody has a continuous feedback relationship running between their unconscious and conscious minds, and vice versa. Such a relationship provides an opportunity to monitor any negative speech patterns such as the words and tone of voice we use and how we feel. It enables us to work on what is happening to us and to reverse any negativity. This negativity can be caused by some false beliefs/issues running within us that need our attention. Sometimes, there may be anger issues, or issues of low self-esteem, or issues related to impatience, or fear, and so on. Try not to criticise your-self as this can create an anger response within your-self or add to any anger that you may be feeling and expressing. Just as other people may take a criticism as a personal attack on themselves, you too will react emotionally to self-criticism. Ego loves this and will join in to create more of the same! Most of us are susceptible to reacting negatively to criticism, so we should not beat our-selves up if we make a negative comment or criticism either to our-self or others. That is, of course, provided you are not making a habit of it. If you are it would be as well to look into why you are doing this, for it is really about *your*-self and not about someone else.

Everybody has a degree of sensitivity and we trespass on it at our peril! In any relationship, that chance sarcastic remark backed up with a negative tone of voice, unfortunate body language and supported with an inner negative emotion can be devastating to those concerned. To be fair, much of the time in a particular situation the perpetrator is usually not aware of the caustic remark and is truly shocked later when the remark is brought to their attention. If this should happen to you, there is something important to consider: the perpetrator's mind was probably on other things and the caustic remark was the result of an accumulation of their negative emotions resulting from some previous situations in their life. You just happened to unknowingly hit a sensitive button and the perpetrator let the words flow out without thinking. In other words it most probably had nothing to do with you. The old maxim '*think before you speak*' is relevant here: not easy but worth remembering.

In such a situation bring what was said to you to the attention of the perpetrator. Point out how de-motivating such a statement *felt* and the impact it had on your feelings and most likely that of others present. The emphasis here must be on your *feelings* and not the content of what was said. If the perpetrator is in a bad mood it would be best to choose a time when they are not, otherwise you might just receive more of the same, with lots of drama! And what are we trying to do? S*tay out of the drama!*

As an example, my cousin Peter works for a large international consultancy firm. He was having a meeting with his three managers and the partner in charge of his division. Business is hard to find in a recession and they were looking at current client business, deployment of staff and business opportunities. Towards the end of the meeting the partner in a negative tone of voice commented that he wanted Peter to increase his client billing hours. Peter remarked that he would have to do fewer business development hours to do this. The partner's immediate response was 'you certainly haven't produced much business so I suggest you do something more useful'. This caustic remark devastated Peter's feelings, caused a loss of face in front of his managers and de-motivated all four of them. Each of them had put a lot of effort behind the scenes into their business development activities. They all felt deeply that they were not appreciated and that they belonged to a company that did not really care. The partner might have an intellect second to none and be good at sales, but his emotional literacy skills were appalling. A company is like a large quantum bio-magnet with an energy field that acts to attract or to repel business. Having a dynamic corporate culture is therefore essential to attracting a steady flow of business in both good and difficult times. It is also essential for the employees' level of motivation, productivity and inner feeling of positive wellbeing and happiness.

Driver 4: Being of Energy - Attractor Factor Field

How amazing to discover that you have either been attracted to or have attracted to you all the good things which happen in your life. Conversely, it is off-putting, to say the least, to acknowledge that we have also attracted all the difficult stuff! Nonetheless, there is a light at the end of the tunnel insofar as we have the ability to change the quantum bio-magnetic field to alter our life story for the better. Such a change does not mean that we will be able to by-pass difficult life lessons (nor should we), but it does mean that we will recognise what is going on and can deal more easily with any challenges confronting us in a more constructive manner. With practice we can all develop the ability to stay out of the dramas of life that may confront us. This is an essential skill to minimise our own and everybody else's stress level. When we are angry, not only will people see it in our body language, they will hear it in the tone of voice we use and they will sense it from our bio-magnetic field (diagram 7.14). As our conscious and unconscious minds contribute to our bio-magnetic field, an important point to consider is the effect on the cells of our body. Being happy nourishes them. Being unhappy, or miserable, or depressed, or negative, depletes the cells' energy causing an imbalance. There is a 'Catch 22' situation here for how we feel is an indication of our wellbeing. And wellbeing is the reflection of our bio-magnetic field which is affected by the programs running in the unconscious mind. To eliminate the 'Catch 22' situation requires us to ask the following question:

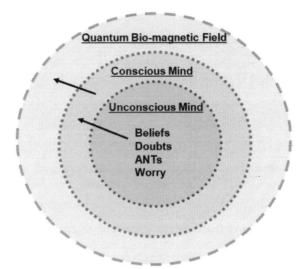

Diagram 7.14

'what is it that interferes with our capacity to change the quantum bio-magnetic energy field to our advantage?'

What interferes is basically the same type of energy blockages that stop us from living in the present and enjoying abundance. These blockages interfere with our ability to change our field. Diagram 7.14 shows four typical blockage creators, that run in the unconscious and conscious minds, namely: false beliefs, doubts, ANTs and worry. We are aware that these run within the unconscious mind around the clock and download in one way or another into the conscious mind when a particular situation, or event, or person triggers them. The thought (information plus supporting emotion/feeling) in the conscious mind is influenced by what is running in the unconscious mind. What can we do here to influence our quantum bio-magnetic field attraction properties to our advantage?

Using affirmations to re-script and reshape the unconscious mind can be enormously beneficial in the quest to change the quantum bio-magnetic field. Where we have to be careful is to make sure that we are not papering over a life lesson or issue that we are here to recognise and grow from. Each of our life lessons will have an information field and usually a strong emotion attached to it. Should an issue be re-scripted, that is - the information part is replaced with a different more positive story, or something we are in denial of is dealt with by using an affirmation - the emotion supporting the issue will still be in place as we have not dealt with it. As the main power lies in the emotion, it will continue running within the emotional subtle energy body and in the physical body making a contribution to our quantum bio-magnetic field. This attracts to us another situation which will give rise to the same type of emotion. This is part of the soul's mechanism to confront us with what we need to learn. The emotion has to be released for us to move on.

If we have not forgiven someone who has harmed us, using an affirmation alone to try to rectify the situation will not work. It will not work because we are in denial - not only have we not forgiven them but also we have not forgiven our-self. Yes, we actually have to forgive our-self as well! In this case, as a quantum bio-magnet we are part of an energy exchange that has been going on between us and the other person, which needs to be brought into balance. If we do not forgive the other person we leave an energy attachment with them. Worse yet, this can be carried forward into another lifetime! The other person involved will continue (unbeknown to themselves) to affect our energy field until we release them. Many times I hear people state that they cannot forgive someone, or a group of people, or the government and so forth. This is not a good idea for it will only attract more of the same into their lives (present and future) in one way or another until they have learnt to forgive.

What is important in the use of affirmations is to recognise when to use a general affirmation and when to use a specific one. The affirmation procedure in Chapter 4, page 193, is helpful here and we could consider using some of the following affirmations in a relationship situation on our own:

> *I am always releasing any relationship that is not for my higher good.*
>
> *I am always attracting to me relationships that are for my higher good.*
>
> *I am comfortable with the outcome of all my relationships.*
>
> *I am always learning something about myself from my relationships.*

A word of caution, at times some aspects of a relationship will represent the shadow side of our personality (chapter 5). This is to allow us to bring the negative aspects of our persona into balance, not to enhance them. We all have our shadows and part of our soul's growth is to allow us to work through them to bring them into balance when they get inflated.

Driver 5:   Mirroring: Recognising Ourselves in Others

When you are with someone, it is important to remember that you have attracted them into your space and vice versa. Besides engaging in social pleasantries, it might happen that one of us could hit the other's sensitive button. For example as a man, I am with a girlfriend who keeps asking me how I feel about the relationship. This could cause me to feel uncomfortable and leave me not knowing how to respond. She has, more than likely, unknowingly hit a sensitive button within my-self which is related to an issue (that I may or may not be aware of) about being open to discussing feelings in general conversation. There is a mirroring process at work here where she is reflecting back an issue that I need to deal with. The girlfriend (or some other person) is an actor on a stage who is acting out an issue whose script is running within my unconscious mind and which is being repeated back to me. As we are now aware (Chapter 2), we are all connected through our energy fields. Because the girlfriend's energy field is resonating at a frequency that matches mine, she is able to reflect back to me a particular issue. The best response would be, instead of getting aggravated and annoyed, to take a step back and look into my ability or lack of to express my feelings in meaningful terms. I could ask my-self '*is this a throw back to my parents*'? *Did they ever discus with me how they or I felt about something, or ask me about my feelings? How and where did I develop this lack of ease in talking about or expressing my feelings?*

Usually we express our feelings through the words and the tone of voice we use, but in this case it is a bit more. For every emotion we carry within ourselves, each one can manifest in a physical feeling within the human body. They can transform into a tense or a warm feeling in the stomach; a tingling sensation all over; an increase in our heart beat; an intense feeling somewhere in our body, or all over. What is required is for us to translate the feeling that we are experiencing into words. If we discover that we have no physical feelings at all, it means that we have a major energy block (frozen emotions) within us which we need to release. I am using a man/woman example here as men, in general, find it more difficult to express their feelings than women, who seem do it more naturally. The opposite is obviously also true.

A colleague of mine had a male client where abuse was a major issue that needed to be worked with. The man was physically abusive to his wife in private and the wife was verbally abusive to him when amongst friends. In meeting them both you would have thought he was the one having a difficult time. They were both mirroring their issue of abuse in each other. It turned out that abuse was one of his main life lessons. He did not realise this, although he had endured an abusive family relationship as a child. The man acted as a victim when his wife was verbally abusing him. She acted as the victim when he was physically abusing her.

This had gone on for some 20 years, with their children witnessing what was going on. Both of these people were in denial. The couple had no understanding of the basic psychology of what was happening between them and both had a low level of emotional intelligence. Nor had they an understanding of what the purpose of existence is about. They also did not recognise that what they were doing affected both themselves and their children. He thought therapy was for sick people, ridiculing in private those who sought professional help from a therapist in such matters - until he finally got the message that he needed some professional help himself. From an energy healing perspective, if they both deal with their abuse issue and bring it into balance they will also clear the issue which has been energetically transferred to their children. If they do not, their children may experience abuse or be abusers themselves during their lifetime. Sometimes this type of energetic transfer can skip a generation, but it will manifest itself in a later incarnation.

When someone is projecting at us, we might not feel anything at the time they are doing it. This means that it has nothing to do with us. If however we feel something strongly in the solar plexus (or elsewhere) then it is relevant to us. Sometimes we may pick up a bit of their negative energy when they are projecting but we will know intuitively whether or not it has to do with us.

Boost your Abundance in Relationships

In relationships, a health warning needs to be given. The warning is 'be careful what you ask for' as you may just get it. In other words, at times the life lessons that follow may not be to your liking! In summary, there are two stages, three rules and six steps to the abundance manifestation technique when applied to relationships:

Stage 1

Rule 1: Investigate and work to clear any abundance energy blocks that apply to your-self.

Rule 2: See in your imagination your-self living in the now (the present). Work towards anchoring your-self in the present. See your-self in your imagination already in happy circumstances with the individual with whom you wish to have a relationship.

Rule 3: Recognise that part of the relationship you have attracted to you, or vice versa, is teaching you something about your-self. If you fight with your partner, or colleague, or friend, or child you are really fighting your-self for they will be mirroring a life lesson back to you. Try to stay out of any drama!

If you blame other people for what is happening to you, or make a judgement about another person, or gossip about others, you will be operating from your fabricated-self. If you want to be popular, or centre stage, this is usually the ego taking over. As you are aware, ego is the fabricated-self's strongest ally. Now this does not mean to say that you should not be centre stage, or be very popular, or be a great leader. I simply mean that you need to determine which is driving you – the fabricated-self or the authentic-self? Knowing this will help in your relationships. As you work through stage 1 you can also begin working through stage 2.

Stage 2

Step 1: Find a quiet spot to relax and make your-self comfortable. In your imagination see your-self as a cloud of swirling coloured energy, like a gas cloud suspended in an infinite cloud of energy. You have the ability to manifest what you want by transmuting part of the infinite cloud's energy into what you desire. The person you desire to have a relationship with will be a part of this cloud.

Step 2: See in your imagination the relationship that you want being happy, progressive, supportive, strong, and so forth. How do you feel? If you feel negative or uncomfortable, ask your-self why? It is important to identify the cause. Run through the energy blocks described in this chapter to see if one or more resonate with you. Work through and clear the blocks. Before and after the manifestation request, it is also advisable to state the affirmation:

'I release anyone who is not for my highest good.'

Be sensible about the type of relationship that you request. Your soul knows who you should be associating with. If you pull in a relationship that is not for you it will not last long and picking up the pieces could prove emotionally challenging and expensive! When you feel comfortable with the type of relationship that you have requested, continue with step 3.

Step 3: Bring into your imagination the magnetising coil image shown in diagram 7.11 and the image of the person with whom you want a relationship. Pass the positive emotion that you are feeling into the coil, allowing it to circulate from the front of the heart to the back. This will strengthen the bio-magnetic field attractor factor supporting your request. Keep the image of who you want to have a relationship with in your imagination as you are circulating the energy.

Step 4: As the emotion energy is circulating around the coil, if it raises a negative or uncomfortable feeling then it is advisable to investigate why that is. Once again, investigate and clear the block.

Step 5: It is important to go about your daily activities and take action where appropriate. As you do this you can help your-self some more by stating the following affirmation from time to time:

'I am in the right place at the right time when the manifestation takes place.'

Step 6: The last step is very important and that is to detach your-self from the request. Do not think about the request on a regular basis. Certainly, see your-self with who you have requested in your imagination from time to time, perhaps when you are in bed, but only for a few seconds. Do not discuss your request with anyone. All of this prevents any interference with your request, including from your-self! A typical interference could be if you suddenly doubted that your request would be granted. One final point to keep in mind is that everything has its own timing! Working through the blocks that are preventing you from manifesting your abundance will not only result in your improving the potential to manifest your desire, over time, but will also put you on a path for you to write a better life story. The more blocks that you remove, the easier it will be to navigate your way through life.

Navigating Through Life

The 21st century requires a leap of faith for those who operate in what can be described as a typical reductionist scientific environment with its commensurate old ways of thinking. This reductionist way of seeing the world limits our capacity to understand what life is truly about. It limits an ability to think outside of our virtual box.

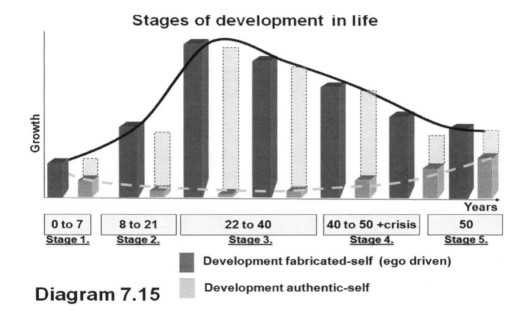

Diagram 7.15

In diagram 7.15 I have divided life into five distinct stages. The dark vertical column represents the development of the fabricated-self and the small medium-grey vertical column the development of the authentic-self. The dotted light-grey vertical column indicates ideally where the authentic-self should be in terms of growth - very much in line with the fabricated-self. The upper dark curve indicates the growth and decline of the fabricated-self's power and influence over time. I like to think of our planet earth as a university campus, or theatrical stage that enables us to grow through our life lessons. For those fully engaged in a life of continuous activity round the clock, the bottom light grey dashed curve shows the fall and rise of the potential of the authentic-self to communicate with the fabricated-self. During our formative years there is usually little chance of our authentic-self communicating with us. The lesson here is to recognise the importance of working with the authentic-self.

Stage 1: 0 to 7 years
In previous chapters I have emphasised that from birth to about 7 years of age is a critical period when conditioning of a child begins. The foundations of the child's belief system in relation to everything are being put into place. Emotions are a key factor in the way a child senses their life. Parents, grandparents, relatives, siblings and authority figures play a crucial role here. Their attitudes and behaviours contribute to the child's emotional framework. For most children a process begins where a separation is unknowingly enforced with the development of the fabricated-self over the authentic-self (diagram 7.15). The child's quantum bio-magnetic field is also being programmed to begin attracting different experiences into their life.

Stage 2: 8 to 21 years
Academic training begins and a child is greatly influenced by other authority figures such as teachers that enter their lives. New friends also affect their conditioning. For most children, by the time they reach adulthood, the fabricated-self has separated even further from the authentic-self (diagram 7.15). Their life story format is put in place. It is unfortunate that education focuses on the intellect and knowledge to the detriment of creative thinking, intuition (hunch capability) and intuitive intelligence. This unknowingly creates a substantial one-sidedness in the young adult's energy fields and it is in their best interest to redress the imbalance. There will be signposts along their path which will help them here, provided they recognise them.

Stage 3: 22 to 40 years
The young adult has left home and should be 100 percent responsible for their own life. They may engage in a career, marriage, raising a family, buying property and collecting stuff, or combinations of these. Ambition can take over, which reinforces the ego and powers the fabricated-self to run their life. Unless there is an activity or event such as an accident, illness, loss of employment, or a divorce, or the death of someone close, that stops the adult in their tracks and impels them to think about what is going on, the fabricated-self will most probably remain in control. During the early part of this time period, there is most probably a hunger for more knowledge. The top dark curve in diagram 7.15 indicates the quest to obtain more knowledge. The light grey dashed curve at the bottom of the diagram indicates the decline in the ability of the authentic-self to communicate with the fabricated-self through to the conscious mind. The individual's life story here is coloured by their quest to 'get on' in life. There is nothing wrong with this except that the fabricated-self can easily mislead the individual concerned by pushing them off their most beneficial path as they journey. With

positive energies induced by their authentic-self, there is a good chance that they will 'get it', make some changes in their thinking and life, and get back on course. Others will continue in the false belief that they know what is going on in their life. Somewhere along their path they may experience a situation, or situations that have arisen to purposely get them to rethink what they are doing, for example the breakup of a relationship, or being made redundant, or developing an illness. This can cause the individual concerned to begin to contemplate life by seeking to understand why things are as they are. They may start to wonder if there is actually a purpose behind it all . . .

Stage 4: 40 to 50 years (mid-life crisis)
Most people go through a period, usually in their forties, that can be described as a mid-life crisis although some can go through this experience at an earlier or later time. It all depends upon the life experiences we are subjected to - and of course we must remember we are the cause of our own experiences. Others involved in our experiences are just the actors on our stage who are helping us to work through our life lessons. At this stage in our life it is to our advantage to have begun to discover the true nature of life. It seems that in the West a considerable number are infected by what can be described as a round-the-clock, must-always-be-doing virus. There is little spare time to consider our mortality unless we ourselves, or someone close has had a serious illness, or accident, or died. It seems that it is necessary to experience a personal crisis before we seek to expand our awareness of life's purpose. Yet the earlier we 'get it' the quicker we can upgrade our belief system and our perception of what is happening to us. Unfortunately our comfort zone is like a magnet, a five star hotel, and anyone with common sense would certainly not wish to leave it. Or would they?

Stage 4: 50 years +
By the time we enter our fifties, if we have not yet experienced a mid-life crisis then it will hit us at some point. Sometimes the crisis will hit us strongly and if we are lucky, mildly. The change in our hormone levels can be a cause of some discomfort until our body readjusts. However, if we are in denial of a life lesson or lessons it will affect us energetically, a bit like building up a head of steam and being unable to vent off the surplus. An explosive situation! During this time period we generally begin to drop the masks that we took on board to help us on our journey. Or not, as the case may be. Our real self, that is our authentic-self, should begin to surface. This is helped by the experiences that we have gone through and the essence or wisdom that we have derived from them. Life can become less hectic and we may view our partners in a different light. Friendships have a closer and more significant meaning. Alternatively we can retreat further into our comfort zone. This is usually because of an unconscious fear of exploring life outside this zone. As we advance through our fifties there will be opportunities to 'get it' by consciously engaging in the spiritual dynamics of life.

Abundance Flow and Understanding your Life's Work

To be truly abundant, one must work constantly to ensure that the fabricated-self stays in the flow of life and that the ego is kept in check. Now, life is usually full of contrast which basically means that there are a lot of ups and downs. The cyclical nature of what is happening in your life may cause the fabricated-self to panic and to push you out of the flow. This is quite normal and the challenge here is to get back into the flow. Life situations/experiences can be pleasant, neutral or difficult. When a situation is difficult, the choices or decisions we make can contribute to getting us back into the flow. It is how we handle ourselves that determines this. If we handle what is happening in a way that is contrary to our spiritual purpose, we will create a new and perhaps more difficult path to follow. This path will have a more demanding flow. As we journey along this life path we will attract situations and experiences that will force us to look at what we have to learn until we 'get it'. Only then will we be able move back onto a more comfortable flow. In this flow, we are able to handle the most challenging situations and experiences with ease and quickly move on to the next.

Published surveys provide evidence that many people dislike their employment and large numbers even hate what they are doing. When you are happy, you are in the flow of life and will most probably be doing what gives you a good feeling. Certainly, it will involve something that you have a passion for. Nevertheless, in life *'all is not as it seems'* as we venture forward to make a living. To understand what this means there are some important points about life that we should consider.

- Life is cyclical, meaning that there are good times and difficult times, interesting work and boring work, rewards for hard work and no rewards, and so forth. Once again, life is very much about contrast, otherwise what a dull place our planet would be. Contrast is also about looking at what we are doing, or what is happening to us, in order that we might learn life's lessons and improve the choices and decisions we make. Finally, the contrasting experiences and situations in life can drive us to find out what our passion is and then to engage in it.

- We might gain experience through several jobs during our lifetime, each occupation providing a platform for us to engage in while working through our life lessons. I changed my profession six times from electronics, to physics to operational research, to international consulting to the United Nations and the World Bank, then to investment/merchant banking. I recognised when it was time to change because my authentic-self was pushing me to change. The stimulus to make the change was always my urge to engage in a new passion. Retraining for those various jobs was a challenge at times, but in the end I enjoyed that too. Some of my friends stayed in their profession their whole working life. Some even stayed with the same employer for their entire career. The latter is something about which many sit in judgement. Some employers, for example, see a great length of time in one job as showing a lack of drive and a fear of innovation. Ultimately, however, what happens to us depends on the type of life lessons we have agreed to work through. It can also depend on whether or not we find our passion. An important point to make here is that whether or not a job engages your passion, it represents a platform for you to work through your life lessons. Work for work's sake is still work, but working with a passion can mean an easier experience when you are dealing with your life lessons.

- We can also experience our passion through our hobbies and/or the activities we engage in outside working hours. When I was working overseas, a good number of my friends and I were having challenging times in life. This got me interested in the latest research in psychology (an odd passion!) that made sense to me. I developed a better understanding of myself and was also able to help some of my friends when they faced similar difficult situations. A few of my close friends had died of stress-related illnesses. I wanted to find an approach and develop some techniques that would enable me to help such people deal with the issues that were causing the stress. The more I was able to be of assistance to my friends the stronger my passion for psychology became. It is important to recognise that your life's work and passion is personal to you. I have a passion to raise people's awareness about life's journey, to help them on their way and to enable them to get to know their true self, their authentic-self.

- Experiencing our life's work by engaging in a passion is not always easy. It has a better chance of happening if we follow our feelings. What do I mean? How does it feel with respect to what you are working at now? Once you are engaged in your life's work you should find that it feels good and everything moves in a more natural flow. Life lessons that you experience may still bring you some extreme situations and/or experiences to deal with but these should be more easily worked through. If life is continually unpleasant at work, or in any other activity, then I would advise you to investigate within your-self why that might be so. It may be time to make a change. Alternatively, it may be that you need to look within your-self to determine whether or not you are stuck in a situation where you are working through a life lesson and are not 'getting it'. Observing what your attitude and behaviour is like is a good start here. Remember, your energy field is attracting to you and you to what is happening in your life.

- When we are attracted to our life's work, such factors as safety and comfort are not the real driving forces. This does not mean to say that they will not be included within your life's work. When I went to work in Kuwait, Iraq and Iran were in full conflict and

Kuwait could have been invaded. I sensed that I would be safe before moving to Kuwait and this feeling proved to be correct. My work there included my passion for being involved in different countries' development. I trusted that I was where I should be both in terms of location and circumstances. Security and comfort was not an issue, nor should it have been in this type of situation. I had many demanding challenges there which were more easily handled because I was engaged in my life's work. Only when the life lessons that I was there to work through and grow from were completed was I moved on. I was completely unaware of this. However, as synchronicity would have it, the good news is that I moved out one month before Saddam Hussein invaded Kuwait!

In my own case, as I travelled along my life's path, the different opportunities I attracted allowed me to change my profession. Each opportunity provided me with a new platform to engage in my life's work. Now here comes the tricky part. It was how I *handled* the situations I found myself in which was important. For each situation, unknown to me, represented a life lesson (or part of one). It was also about how my *attitude* and *behaviour* changed (hopefully for the better) and, most importantly, about the choices and decisions I made. If you are fortunate enough to be operating out of your authentic-self there is a good chance that it will reflect a passion. A doctor friend of mine chose to become an artist at age fifty. This reflected his true inner passion and authentic-self. All his previous experience in medicine was also a passion. It made a contribution to his life's work up to that point and was not in vain. This is because when he entered the medical profession his passion was to be of service. When this part of his journey was complete, he made a change to engage in another of his passions. In the last five years, I too have moved onto a path which represents one of my passions. And that is to raise not only my own awareness about the secrets of life, but also to share it with others. This is, of course, a part of my life's work.

I started my working life believing, like the rest of my friends, that the employment we engage in (the company, job title and salary) is what life is about. In this circumstance it is really what my fabricated-self wanted. I am now aware that there is much more to life than just satisfying my fabricated-self. Once I 'got it' by understanding why I am here in a physical body and what the purpose of being here is, my whole life began a gradual change for the better. Since my 'eureka moment' I have felt much, much happier. If you are in touch with your authentic-self, then you are more than likely able to make a change which fits, or is in keeping with your best interests. Being authentic is the name of the game, as it will enable you to more easily unlock your passions and to work with them.

As I look around I see many people locked onto old patterns of fear, challenging attitudes and behaviour, and not wishing to move out of their comfort zone. They are in denial of the changes that it would be very much in their interest to make. However, this is undoubtedly a part of their challenge in life. They will still continue to experience their life lessons but perhaps, at times, in less than pleasant circumstances. Why is this so? Many years ago one of my more advanced personal development teachers brought to my attention a Universal Law which states that:

> *'if you step back from a life lesson, then there is a good chance that it will return with ten times the energy it had before'*

This is to ensure that we finally 'get it'! The important point here is not the ten times but the fact that the attraction energy gets amplified to ensure that we meet and hopefully engage with the life lesson.

A recognised human condition is to hate change, especially if the change takes us out of our comfort zone. The only way most people will consider a change is when it is forced upon them! I had this happen to me when I left the World Bank. Once this happens the pain factor can increase and life becomes unpleasant. The same goes for entrenched attitudes, or releasing false beliefs which we initially accepted as being true, as well as an unquestioning acceptance of the 'status quo'. I feel slightly aghast when I see so many people putting so much effort and long hours into trying to make old forms and traditional approaches work. They have not realised that there may be new ways of doing what they are doing. Nor have they contemplated that perhaps they should consider doing something else. Once again, a great challenge for us all in life is to love what we are doing. If we do not, then it is time to consider a change.

To change what we dislike or hate at work, a change in our attitude is required to match the objective of loving what we are doing. This may sound odd, but that is because we have not been brought up to understand how the human energy structure functions. We are by now aware that the quantum bio-magnetic field attraction properties make sure that we are attracted to, or attract to us what is running in our field. What we dislike in life will represent a life lesson. Circumstances will present us with an opportunity to make a change in our attitude to what we hate. If we do not change, then the negative energies confronting us will get stronger. Now there is an interesting challenge!

A life lesson running in our bio-magnetic field will dissipate and not return after we have recognised what the life lesson is and have worked through it. That is unless there is a need to test us further to see if we have actually 'got it' one more time. A simple key to success is to turn your hate around to love. Yes, love what you hate. If you cannot do this then what you hate will have a detrimental effect on your progress along life's path and ultimately on your physical health. If you do not learn to do this, the hate or dislike experienced will keep repeating itself, just like a hamster on a wheel: until you 'get it'. Part of the process of abundance is to recognise the need to love what we're doing. If we cannot, and have checked that we are not being run by our ego, then it is time to make a change. If we are being run by our ego, or by some dominant sub-personality/personality, then we should attend to work on them to bring them into balance.

As emphasised in this chapter, learning to listen to our authentic-self is a principal key to attracting a natural and continuous flow of abundance. Continuing to work through life solely from the perspective of the fabricated-self can only enhance the dramas we experience and greatly reduce that inner feeling of positive wellbeing and happiness. An important feature of our inner guidance process is that it accesses information at a multi-dimensional level. The fabricated-self only has access to information at a less expansive physical level (numbers, information, knowledge, and so forth). It seems incredible that we are educated to believe that information/facts at the fabricated-self level are the source to use! It is essential that we use our levels of intellect/knowledge together with our multidimensional higher consciousness communication ability to achieve success and excellence in all our endeavours in today's world. This will enable us to stay in the flow of life and succeed. Successful people at the top of their game are doing this already (and always have done!).

To work towards creating a continuous flow of abundance we can consider adopting two more states of mind together with those suggested in the spiritual dynamics section discussed above. These states of mind come under the umbrella of *appreciation* and *gratitude*. A secret behind enhancing the flow of abundance is to be appreciative of our good fortune in the present and also to be thankful for our future good fortune. Being grateful for *everything* that happens to you seems to be a bit over the top. Many people say 'How can you make such a ridiculous statement?' Others may say 'You do not know the ghastly things that are happening to me in my life' This is effectively a *'cry for help'*. It helps therefore to acknowledge that, before incarnating, we have chosen to work through a number of life lessons, some of which may be unpleasant. Recognising the purpose behind them should answer this cry.

So many people do not show gratitude for the amounts of support they receive in life. The support could be from other people, or take the form of monetary and/or material gifts. In energy terms, not doing this can cause a blockage to a future inflow of support. Both appreciation and gratitude are important parts of the process of creating abundance in all its forms. Most importantly, an attitude of appreciation and gratitude has an amazing revitalising effect on the entire consciousness process and ultimately on our inner feeling of positive wellbeing and happiness. In such a state we are in a better position to write a more favourable life story.

Writing an Inspiring Life Story

It was during my late thirties that I began to recognise various repetitive patterns at work and play which had become a feature in my life. It dawned on me then that, contrary to popular thinking, life is not a series of random experiences. There were definite patterns that kept recurring in terms of my work scene, relationships and what I was involved in socially. Curious by nature, I began to look for the cause of these patterns and for ways that I could minimise any dramas (arguments/disputes/disagreements) that arose. There was a synchronicity occurring which was connected to some of the relationships and situations I found myself in. As I did not connect with the synchronicity, I have to confess that I was most probably in a state of denial. Later, I discovered that this was due to me unknowingly operating from my fabricated-self. Part of my challenge was to be less intensely focused through my fabricated-self. It took me many more years to break the habit. Only then did a picture gradually form in my mind which changed my perception of what life is about.

I could see from the picture in my imagination that the professional work I was involved in was simply a platform which attracted life lessons for me to work through as I journeyed. Moreover, my research had brought to my attention that it is the journey which is significant and not actually reaching a destination or achieving an outcome. This was most important for me, as I wanted to understand why I was experiencing, at times, unexpected extreme situations such as the death of some close colleagues and friends; or a sudden unexpected change of country residence and job; or being out in the forefront of my profession but not being able to control my direction, and so forth. Sometimes I was ill equipped (I needed to learn new disciplines and absorb more information) to handle the different projects I found myself involved in.

Moving step by step towards my career goals, I had either an empathetic or difficult boss, a high or low salary, lots of travel or very limited travel, interesting challenges, or just dull/boring experiences, and so forth. In my early days I only saw problems that needed to be solved instead of challenges that were crying out for creative solutions. It would have been so much easier if I had stayed in my comfort zone by remaining in my home country and in one profession! But this did not appeal to me. Fortunately I was blessed with recognising when my inner passion was on the wane. I also recognised when there was no way to re-ignite it (I did try!) and it was time to change. In fact, my whole system – spiritual, emotional, intellectual and physical, was shouting for me to change!

I am well schooled in the professional dogma of our time. By dogma here I mean 'an authoritative principle, belief, or statement of ideas or opinion, especially one considered to be absolutely true'. Fortunately, and in spite of this, I have always had an ability to take a step back and question what is going on in my life and why I am doing what I am doing.

Those who prefer not to change rarely question themselves by asking 'is what I am doing engaging my passion?' This is because the majority of us have been trained to do jobs, whether professional or manual, simply to fit market demands. The market place needs certain skills sets and we train ourselves through the education system to fill the appropriate slots as they become available. Seldom, if at all, does the subject of our passion come into our decision-making process when it comes to seeking employment.

The ego game, when seeking employment at the top end of the scale, invests in the type of jobs chosen and their titles, for example investment banker, lawyer, neuroscientist, teacher, accountant, engineer, IT professional, research chemist, physicist, and so forth. Salary is also important to the ego. If we are making lots of money and have lots of material things, then we are usually seen by our family, friends and colleagues as being very successful, as someone who has 'made it'. For my-self, all of this came crashing down when at a personal development workshop I was faced with the question "you are not your job, not your title, not your salary, not your house, car, boat, clothes, and so forth – who are you?" I was deafened by my own silence. *Yikes*, I thought – back to the drawing board to have another look at myself! That is when I began to systematically navigate back through my life's path and to mull over the extremes that I had encountered. Let me emphasise here that there is nothing wrong in having a materially good life. It is when excess is desired because of ego and greed that things get out of balance. Or when we spend too much time worrying about losing what we have!

I have always felt a strong inner negative emotion building up when my passion about the work I am involved in has played itself out. This is telling me that I should be moving on. Most times, such a situation occurred when I had just settled into my comfort zone. Any battles that were taking place in my mind, when I started to consider a change, were due to limitations in my thinking. Yes, that virtual box of thinking greatly influenced by my false beliefs was not really working in my favour. I was unaware of the benefits to be gained from integrating into my thinking the Universal Laws associated with the sub-atomic world and world of energy that we also inhabit. In this world we are all-powerful, especially when we learn how to program our quantum bio-magnetic field. The possibility of unravelling the secrets of life becomes a reality. Miracles become understandable and not some random event.

The path that leads to demystifying the enormous benefits derived from merging physical reality with sub-atomic reality into our lives is still a path less travelled. This troubled me to a degree and I set out to investigate why, especially, as our world is going through such extreme changes. We are surrounded by professions and establishment thinking that operate solely within their own dogmas and which do not take any account of the two worlds.

Their objective is to 'preserve the status quo'! Whole careers are successfully navigated and glittering prizes can be obtained without much or any thought of the two worlds and what it means. I see this as a honey trap! Physicist Max Planck made a revealing statement, which given my experience in the different professional environments I have been exposed to, makes good sense. He stated that:

> 'a scientific truth does not triumph by convincing its opponents and making them see the light, but rather because its opponents eventually die and a new generation grows up that is familiar with it'

The ego needs glittering prizes and once it obtains them the comfort zone can become so attractive that there is no apparent reason to leave it. An interesting point to consider is that each new generation has little or no problem dealing with the technological advances and new ideas which their parents may find difficult to understand and to operate with. However, this is not always a plus for the new generation. What is missing from the new generation is usually a great deal of the useful skills which their parents learnt. These skills can include how to grow things, make things, repair things and so forth. This needs to be recognised by young people themselves and by society as a whole, especially since the limitations of being solely involved with new technology can lead to unforeseen consequences. Our life and the lessons to be learned do not depend on technology. I suggest that technology is really an aid that we have been given by the Universe to provide us with more time to recognise and work through our life lessons and to have some fun! This point is not appreciated by most. Instead there is a tendency to be busy and constantly doing, around the clock! Are we increasingly on the hamster wheel?

The sooner we engage in the implementation of such practices as non-judgement, personal responsibility, non co-dependency, acceptance, tolerance, forgiveness and so forth, the better. This is crucial because it takes us back into the spiritual dynamics of life. Such a change in direction, if you take it, will have an amazing impact on your life. Happiness and that inner-feeling of positive wellbeing will be the rule rather than an exception. In this type of situation you will be able to write a much improved life story. The example you set to those around you can be infectious. Other people will then benefit from the changes you have made. Your fabricated-self will also have made a strong link with the authentic-self. You will sense where you should be going and what you should be doing with greater ease. For those who wish to take the ostrich approach to life and bury their head in the sand, life will be much more uncertain. The situations they experience, attracted by their quantum bio-magnetic field, will become more challenging until they 'get it'.

You will have realised by now that the process of writing a better life story is enhanced by thinking outside of that virtual box. I have emphasised in this book the reason so many seem to be unknowingly stuck in their virtual box of thinking. A considerable part of the reason is historic. Notwithstanding that, history also contains clues that can help us to open that virtual box lid! The ancient Greeks spent much of their time philosophising about why we are here in a physical body. Remember the message left by the ancient Greeks on the entrance to the temple of Apollo at Delphi, which translated into today's language is *'Know Your-self'*. This simple but subtle message proved to be of major significance to my-self because within these words lies a hidden secret in the quest to know *why we are here in a physical body*.

Today we are perhaps more fortunate than the ancient Greeks, as physicists have entered the sub-atomic world through quantum mechanics and particle physics. As a consequence, stepping into the world of energy has become more meaningful, as it presents us with a new platform to know ourselves more intimately. New dimensions are added to our personal development. Furthermore, it is worth repeating the following three points in the search to know your-self:

1. Communicating with the authentic-self can be a major challenge. It is a major challenge because the authentic-self is structured around the original persona (the face we show the world – chapter 5) at birth. We experience and work with different elements of the persona as we engage in our daily activities and life lessons. The objective here is to bring any extremes of the persona into balance. Any imbalance can make it difficult for the authentic-self to communicate with us. Ego, through the fabricated-self, is not necessarily our best friend when we attempt to do this.

    Accessing our natural creative abilities is achieved through contact with the authentic-self. In addition, our multi-dimensional communication capability (intuition/hunches) is also accessed through a channel to the authentic-self which is a link to higher levels of knowledge and an intuitive understanding that most have been denied access to because of a biased education and conditioning. It is an inescapable fact that as beings of energy we live in both a physical reality and the sub-atomic world. This partnership and the relationship between the two pieces is part of being citizens of the world. After all, we are all connected at a sub-atomic level, irrespective of our race or creed. We all come from the same source and that source is energy (the Force, or God source if you prefer).

2. I have emphasised in this chapter that a major challenge we face is to work with our authentic-self. As stated above, by the time a child reaches its teens most are being led mainly by their fabricated-self. Because the fabricated-self has infinite wants, a young adult tends to be led a merry dance by the ego as they travel along life's path. A major problem, which is slowly but surely being recognised, is that when the fabricated-self is in control it locks us into that limited virtual box of thinking. As

emphasised several times in the book, our task is to break out of this box if we are to meet the challenges of the 21st century with ease.

3. The concept of viewing the world as a theatrical stage on which each of us is the principal actor can provide a simple framework for us to understand what is going on in our lives. William Shakespeare (1564-1616) introduced this idea. Try seeing your-self in your imagination as being the principal actor in a number of different scenes which represent your life story. Each act with its associated scene and props represents an opportunity to work through a life lesson or lessons as you journey along your path. The scene is performed in your own personal theatre which is wherever you are located in the world. A most important point here is that you have the power to influence each scene. When you feel comfortable with this concept and with the notion of you as a 'being of energy', you will begin to be more at ease with the idea of life's journey taking place on your very own theatrical stage.

The soul operates behind the scenes as you work through your life lessons. The three main programmers of your bio-magnetic field are the soul, the authentic and fabricated-self. This means that the people, workplace, home, relationships, financial wellbeing and so forth that you have attracted, all support the life lessons that you find your-self, perhaps unknowingly, working through. As soon as you have passed the tests associated with a life lesson, you automatically move on. You may physically stay in one location (a town or village) where all the actors pass through your space (workplace, home) mirroring back to you what it is that you have to learn from. All the activities/events that you participate in will contain something, however small, that contributes to a life lesson. Alternatively, as in my case, you can spend your professional life working and living in different continents/countries and also travelling. It is important not to feel over sensitive or overwhelmed about mirroring here. As whether or not the concept of mirroring is recognised, we will still experience mirroring of an issue/life lesson.

Assimilating the above three points has the potential to empower you to write an inspiring life story. After all, this story is about you and no one else!

Importantly, the techniques and processes included in this book will empower you to boost: your relationships, flow of abundance of all kinds and your health and wellbeing. You are a powerful being of energy and the book provides you with knowledge about how to transmute the universal energies into what you desire. Practice makes perfection, so never give up, but continue working to clear any blocks. We all have them. The contents of this book have opened up a whole new world for me, and the concepts I have explored have increased my awareness to a level where I feel comfortable with where I am going in life. Everything that we are born to experience - our race, culture, religion, working life, social life, relationships, personal interests and so forth, I now recognise are platforms to help us and our soul to work through life lessons and challenges.

Ultimately, this book represents my truth. Your truth may be slightly different but that is all right because truth is not absolute, it is relative. There are universal truths and fundamental truths. We exercise choice and make decisions at times to ignore those truths, especially when they make the fabricated-self feel uncomfortable. In the end, each of us is the most important person in the Universe. We are like collections of individual sub-atomic particles connecting to the Force (our God source, chapter 1). Each particle has a conscious awareness and thinking capability. Individual particles provide the Force with a different and unique experience of life. To be whole means that the dark and light side of our soul and spirit must be in balance. Each soul's journey contributes to this balance. The dark side is not necessarily evil or wicked, it is simply the opposite of light. Enjoy your journey and write an inspiring story. Travel as a citizen of the world. Know your-self, let your life leadership shine so that you can take off and fly. It's Your Choice!

Epilogue

As a being of energy you really do have infinite potential. Applying the concepts behind the Universal Laws that support energy will bring you the life that you're meant to have, as you journey along life's path. Some of the 21st century concepts raised in the book have the potential to stretch your awareness about the meaning of the fabric of life. Accepting the concepts involves first assimilating and then accommodating them in the mind. This may take time but is quite normal. Adding the relevant content of the book as regards relationships, abundance, self-esteem and so on, to your already established action plans will prove its worth. For it will enhance your life in many different directions. Each of our lives is solely about our-self. This may sound somewhat selfish. It is certainly not, because each of us has life lessons and issues to discover. YOUR CHOICE will act as a guide here.

Drawing upon the 'all the world is a stage' as a model for life helped me to come to terms with many of the changes and challenging situations I've faced. You will experience different acts and scenes on your stage as you work through your own life's script, which includes your action plans. You have a chance to edit your script as you travel. There will be prosperous times, times of drama, happy times, stressful times. All of this creates contrast within your stage production, influencing your choices and the decisions that you make. It can also cause confusion, but this will be short-lived. Working with your authentic-self to connect the dots in your life as they relate to your experiences, will enhance your fulfilment and success.

Future Reality limited (www.yourfr.com) is a company that has been set up to offer support, through workshops and coaching, to help you to make the best choices/decisions to achieve what you desire. My weblog site www.jhleckie.com focuses on our energy attributes and offers a platform to raise any questions. A selection of e-Books will be posted, from time to time, to help with the journey. Connecting with your authentic-self is not the end of your story. It's the beginning of a new act. You will have more say about the stage props that you choose and the new life script that you write. You are the architect and creator of the reality that you experience. Choose well and prosper.

-

Bibliography

I recommend the following works which add more substance to this book. Each of the authors has contributed to my knowledge and inspiration to create a book that I hope will help the reader get to know their self more intimately and to see life with all its challenges from a balanced perspective. The book is designed to enable the reader to take back their power and to succeed in life.

A special thanks to Wikipedia which proved to be an excellent research tool, amongst others, and made my life easier during the writing of the book.

Book Name & Publisher	Author	ISBN
Ageless Body, Timeless Mind Random House (1993)	Deepak Chopra MD	184413044-4
Anatomy of the Spirit Bantam Books (1997)	Caroline Myss Ph.D	0-553-50527-0
Autogenic Training Souvenir Press Ltd (1990)	Dr Kai Kermani	0-285-63322-8
Biology of Belief Mountain of Love/ Elite Books (2005)	Bruce Lipton Ph.D	01550777701
Change your Brain Change your Life Piatkus (1988)	Dr Daniel G. Amen	978-0-7499-4191-8
Color Medicine Light Technology Publishing (1990)	Charles Klotsche	929385-27-6
Corporate Culture Penguin Books (1982)	Terrance Deal Allan Kennedy	0-14-009138-6
Creating Self Esteem Vermillion, Random House (1993)	Linda Field	0-0918-5734-1
Creative Visualisation New World Library (1995)	Shakti Gawain	1-880032-62-7

Cutting the Ties that Bind   Phyllis Krystal   0-87728-791-0
Samuel Weiser Inc (1999)

Destiny of Souls   Dr Michael Newton   1-56718-499-5
Llewellyn Publications (2002)

Eastern Body   Anodea Judith   978-1-58761-225-1
Western Mind
Celestial Arts (1996)

Emotional Clearing   John Ruskan   0-7126-7167-6
Random House (1993)

Emotional Intelligence   Daniel Goleman   0-7475-2830-6
Bloomsbury Publishing Plc (1996)

Hands of Light   Dr Barbara Ann Brennan   0-553-34539-7
A Bantam New Age Book (1988)

How to Befriend   John Monbourquettte   0-232-52430-0
your Shadow
Darton.Longman.Todd (2001)

Journey of Souls   Michael Newton Ph.d   1-56718-485-5
Llewellyn Publications (1996)

Life Alignment   Philippa Lubbock   978-1-906787-95-0
Heal your life and discover your soul's true purpose
Watkins

Light Emerging   Dr Barbara Ann Brennan   0-553-35456-6
A Bantam New Age Book (1993)

Miracles Through Pranic   Master Choa Kok Sui   971-0376-04-7
Healing
Institute for Inner Studies Publishing Foundation

Molecules of Emotion   Candace B. Pert Ph.D.   0-671-03397-2
Simon and Schuster UK Ltd (1997)

NLP in 21 Days   Harry Alder   0-7499-2030-0
Piatkus (1999)   Beryl Heather

Pranic Psychotherapy   Master Choa Kok Sui   971-91106-1-9
Institute for Inner Studies Publishing Foundation

Principles of Breathwork   Swami A Saraswati   0-7225-3830-8
Thorsons (1999)

Pygmalion in the   Robert Rosenthal Ph.D   978-190442406-2
Classroom   Lenore Jacobson
Crown House Publishing Limited (1992)

Q is for Quantum   John Gribbin   0-297-81752-3
Weidenfield and Nicholson (1998)

Quantum Healing   Deepak Chopra MD   0553173324
A Bantam New Age Book (1989)

Self-Healing   Louis Proto   0-7499-1844-6
Piatkus (1990)

Soul Psychology   Joshua D Stone Ph.D   9-0-345-42556-1
Ballantine Wellspring, Random House (1999)

Subtle Energy   Dr William Collinge   9-7225-3668-2
Thorsons (An Imprint of Harper Collins Publishers 1998)

Taking the Quantum Leap   Fred Alan Wolf   0-06-096310-7
Harper and Row, Publishers, New York (1989)

The Brain that Changes   Norman Doige   9-780141-038872
Itself
Penguin Books (2007)

The Causal Body   Arthur E. Powell   pre-1945
Theosophical Publishing House London Ltd

The Divine Matrix   Gregg Braden   978-1-4019-0573-6
Hay House, Inc (2007)

The Gift   Margaret Atwood   0-09-927322-5
Vintage (Random House 1999)

The Healing Power   Caroline Shreeve   0-7225-1456-5
Of Hypnotism   David Shreeve
Thorsons Publishing Group (1984)

The Hungry Spirit   Charles Handy   0-09-180168-0
Hutchinson London (1997)

The Power of Affirmations D. Armstrong Co Inc (1980)	Jerry Frankhauser	MSW0-9617006-1-0
The Power of Intention Hay House Inc (2004)	Dr Wayne W Dyer	1-4019-0216-2
The Power of Now Namaste Publishing (1997)	Eckhart Tolle	0-9682364-0-5
The Right Brain Manager Piatkus (1993)	Dr Harry Alder	0-7499-1899-3
The Tao of Physics Flamingo (an imprint from Harper Colins 1976)	Fritov Capra	0-00-654489-4
The Quantum Doctor Hampton Roads Publishing Company, Inc (2004)	Amit Goswami Ph.D	1-57174-417-7
The Turning Point Flamingo (1982)	Fritjov Capra	0 00 654017 1
Ultimate Journey Doubleday Publishers (1994)	Robert A. Monroe	0-385-47208-0
Who's Pulling your Strings? Thorsons Publishers Limited (1989)	Louis Protto	0-7225-1732-7
Why People Don't Heal and How They Can HarperPaperbacks (1998)	Caroline Myss Ph.D	0-553-50712-5
Your Sacred Self Harper Paperbacks (1995)	Dr Wayne W Dyer	0-06-109475-7

Appendix 1

List of Emotions

Abusive, affection, accepting, accommodating, agitated, aggressiveness, agreeable, affection, alarmed, alert, anxiety, amusement, analytical, anger, angst, annoyed, anticipation, anxious, apprehensive, apathy, arrogant, ashamed, authentic, aversion, awe, belligerent, bereft, betrayed, bewildered, bitter, bored, bullied, calmness, cautious, chaotic, close, comfortable, comfort, compassion, competence, competitive, complaining, complete, confident, content, contempt, confident, confused, constrained, controlling, courageous, cowardly, critical, cruel, curiosity, defeated, delightful, depressed, desire, desperate, destructive, determined, disappointment, discontent, disgust, distress, dominating, doubt, drained, eccentric, ecstatic, egotistical, elated, empowered, embarrassed, empathy, enjoyment, ennui, enthusiasm, envy, envious, erratic, excited, expectation, extroverted, euphoric, fear, friendship, forgiving, frightened, frustrated, generosity, glee, glad, gratitude, greed, grief, guilt, hate, happy, homesick, honour, hope, hopeless, horror, hostility, humbled, hurt, ignorant, impatient, inadequate, indignant, irritation, insecure, isolated, inspired, interest, intolerant, joyful, jealous, judged, lazy, likeable, lonely, lost, love, lust, mad, manipulative, melancholy, miserable, misunderstood, misjudged, mistrust, modest, moody, naïve, nervous, negative, obligation, obsessed, optimism, noble, nostalgic, pain, panic, paranoid, patience, passionate, passive, peaceful, perfectionist, phobia, pitiful, pleasure, possessive, powerful, procrastinating, proud, punishing, rage, reactionary, regret, repentance, repressed, remorse, resentful, responsible, ridiculous, righteous, resistant, ruthless, sadness, sadistic, satisfied, selfish, self-pity, shame, shyness, shock, shy, sorry, stable, stimulated, stubborn, submission, suffer, superior, surprised, suspense, sympathetic, terrified, tired, tolerant, troubled, trusting, unconcerned, understanding, unforgiving, unhappy, unresponsive, untrusting, vain, vengeance, victimised, violent, visionary, vulnerable, well-meaning, wise, withdrawn, wonder, worry, worthy, wrath, yearning, zest.

(source: Wikipedia)

Appendix 2

Organisations of Psychology & Therapy

The following can be used as an initial point of contact and they may be able to guide you to more specific therapies:

United States

American Psychoanalytic Association
309 East 49th Street
New York
New York 10017 (P 212 752 0450)
www.apsa.org

American Psychological Association
750 First Street NE
Washington DC 20002-4242 (P 202-336-5500)
www.apa.org

American Therapist Association
1111North Fairfax Street
Alexandria, VA 22314-1488 (P 703-683-6748)
www.apta.org

United Kingdom

The British Psychological Society
www.bps.org.uk

British Association of Psychotherapists
37 Mapesbury Road
London NW2 4HY
bap-psychotherapy.org

The Institute of Psychoanalysis
Byron House
112A Shirland Road
London W9 2EQ   (0207 563 5015)
www.psychoanalysis.org.uk

Specific therapies in their own right

Association for **Neuro-linguistic Programming**
100b Carysfort Road
London N16 9AP (0203 051 6740)
www.anlp.org

Gestalt Therapy
96-100 Clifton Street
London EC2A 4TP (0207 247 6051)
www.gestaltcentre.co.uk

Emotional Freedom Techniques
(for clearing emotional blockages)
www.emofree.com

The Hypnotherapy Association
www.thehypnotherapyassociation.co.uk

Printed by: Copytech (UK) Limited trading as Printondemand-worldwide, 9 Culley Court
Bakewell Road, Orton Southgate, Peterborough, PE2 6XD